Boston Ball

Rick Pitino, Jim Calhoun, Gary Williams, and
the Forgotten Cradle of Basketball Coaches

CLAYTON TRUTOR

University of Nebraska Press / Lincoln

The University of Nebraska Press is part of a land-grant institution with campuses and programs on the past, present, and future homelands of the Pawnee, Ponca, Otoe-Missouria, Omaha, Dakota, Lakota, Kaw, Cheyenne, and Arapaho Peoples, as well as those of the relocated Ho-Chunk, Sac and Fox, and Iowa Peoples.

Library of Congress Cataloging-in-Publication Data
Names: Trutor, Clayton, author.
Title: Boston ball: Rick Pitino, Jim Calhoun, Gary Williams, and the forgotten cradle of basketball coaches / Clayton Trutor.
Description: Lincoln: University of Nebraska Press, [2023] | Includes bibliographical references and index.
Identifiers: LCCN 2023004272
ISBN 9781496233356 (hardback)
ISBN 9781496237903 (epub)
ISBN 9781496237910 (pdf)
Subjects: LCSH: Pitino, Rick. | Calhoun, Jim, 1942– | Williams, Gary, 1945 March 4– | Boston University—Basketball—History. | Northeastern University (Boston, Mass.)—Basketball—History. | Boston College—Basketball—History. | Boston Celtics (Basketball team)—History. | Basketball—Massachusetts—Boston—History. | Basketball coaches—Massachusetts—Biography. | BISAC: SPORTS & RECREATION / Basketball | BIOGRAPHY & AUTOBIOGRAPHY / Sports
Classification: LCC GV884.P57 T78 2023 | DDC 796.32309744/61—dc23/eng/20230216
LC record available at https://lccn.loc.gov/2023004272

Set in Adobe Text Pro by A. Shahan.

For my mom, who taught me everything I know about sports

Contents

Illustrations

Acknowledgments

Like any book, this one is a collective enterprise. The efforts of John Rudolph at Dystel, Goderich, and Bourret; Rob Taylor and the folks at the University of Nebraska Press; the athletic departments at Boston College, Boston University, Northeastern University, Syracuse University, the University of Maryland, the University of St. Joseph, Siena College, and Canisius College; the libraries at Boston College, Boston University, and Northeastern University; and Mike Abelson, Dan Starr, John Maddock, Jim Overfield, Chuck Everson, Sonny Spera, Glen Field, Paul McDonough, Jay Twyman, Wally West, Ted Kelley, and Matt Gianatassio made this book possible.

I offer my sincerest thanks to all of them and to my family for a lifetime of love and support.

Finally, I'd like to express my reverence for the players and coaches from this exciting era of college basketball in Boston who have since died. Some of them died recently while others died many years ago. Think of this book as a living tribute to every one of them.

Boston Ball

Introduction

The Forgotten Cradle of Coaches

Pete Axthelm called it the "city game": the style of play that emerged on the asphalt courts, steamy gyms, and close-fitting fieldhouses of the Northeast corridor. It is an up-tempo and aggressive game, built around pressure defense. Fast-breaking offenses and drives to the rim. Slick ball handling and bravado. It is a game of speed, grit, guile, and skill. From Nat Holman's New York Original Celtics in the 1920s, to his City College championship team in 1950, to Philadelphia's Big 5 basketball schools, to Bob Cousy at Holy Cross and later with Red Auerbach's Boston Celtics, to Red Holzman's New York Knicks teams of the early 1970s, to the legendary street ballers at Harlem's Rucker Park—for close to a half-century, when people in the East thought of big-time basketball, they were thinking of the "city game," a term first popularized in Axthelm's account of Holzman's Knicks and the players he encountered at Rucker Park in the late 1960s and early 1970s. Recently Matthew Goodman reintroduced the term in his fantastic narrative history of City College's great teams of the late 1940s and early 1950s, *The City Game: Triumph, Scandal, and a Legendary Basketball Team.*[1]

At the very moment that Axthelm's book, *The City Game*, found a large audience among basketball fans, that very style of play was beginning to fade from the national landscape, in both the professional and college games. At the college level, risk-averse zone defenses and high-post offenses became the norm in many places as teams bided their time, searching for the best possible looks in the pre—shot clock era. The style of ball-control offense favored by Oklahoma A&M's (later Oklahoma State) Henry Iba had long been the norm in much of the country. By the early 1960s this deliberate, highly structured style of offense found its way into fieldhouses in every corner of the nation. In Atlantic Coast Conference (ACC) country, Dean

Smith's North Carolina Tarheels employed a purposeful ball-control offense that came to be known as the "shuffle." In the Midwest, Big Ten teams like Indiana, Michigan State, and Ohio State won with a brawny, more plodding style of play. Ball-control basketball proved to be an effective means of shutting down more running-and-gunning opponents, but it also wasn't terribly exciting. Teams holding the ball for several minutes each half threatened to kill off the sport's once rabid support in every corner of the country. Well into the 1970s, college and professional basketball seemed like ever smaller and more insular worlds. The sport was dominated by a handful of teams and lacking in the vigorous support that characterized it before a series of gambling-related scandals rocked basketball during the 1950s.

The reembrace of the big man during the 1960s and 1970s offered further proof that Henry Iba's ball-control basketball was winning the day. Iba's championship teams in the 1940s were built around ramming the ball inside to seven-foot pivot man Bob Kurland, one of several giants that dominated college basketball in the era. By the early 1970s, coaches had adjusted to rule changes meant to prevent seven-footers from completely controlling the game, inaugurating a new, more athletic era of big-man basketball. Even at UCLA, home of John Wooden's vaunted 2-2-1 press, the Bruins built around their enormous centers, parlaying the play of legendary big men like Kareem Abdul-Jabbar and Bill Walton into ten national championships. The path to college basketball success at the national level became a question of which schools could recruit the most talented centers, not which schools could build the best teams. Downstream in the National Basketball Association (NBA) and American Basketball Association (ABA), the likes of Jabbar, Walton, Bob Lanier, and Artis Gilmore followed in the footsteps of Wilt Chamberlain and Bill Russell in a big man dominated league.

Seemingly out of nowhere, a basketball revolution started in an unlikely place. A cluster of young coaches, toiling in relative obscurity in the same town (Boston) and at the same time (the late 1970s and 1980s), ignited a renaissance of the "city game." Working in the shadow of the Celtics, Red Sox, and Bruins, they unknowingly invented "Boston Ball," a simultaneously old and new path to the top of college basketball. A high school teacher in Dedham, Massachusetts, named Jim Calhoun quit his day job and took a pay cut to become the men's basketball coach at Northeastern University

(NU), a school that was transitioning to Division I. A cocksure, twenty-five-year-old from Long Island named Rick Pitino convinced Boston University (BU) to make him their head basketball coach. Pitino's boss, Syracuse coach Jim Boeheim, pleaded with his young assistant to wait for a better job to open, describing the BU position as the worst coaching job in the East. Coach Gary Williams left his position at American University in Washington DC, a school that played its home games at a National Guard armory, for Boston College (BC), where he had previously served under Tom Davis. Davis's BC Eagles teams excelled in the newly formed Big East Conference, but few outside the Chestnut Hill campus seemed to notice. The Eagles' footprint in Boston was strikingly small for such a successful program. Moreover, BC was still playing in the shadow of college basketball's biggest scandal in decades, the 1978–1979 points-shaving affair, which involved three of its players. When Williams took over as BC's head coach in 1982, the points-shaving scandal remained the primary thing that most people knew about the school's basketball program, as the federal trials of the players and mobsters involved in the case were ongoing.

The formidable challenges faced by all three coaches were overcome with a combination of hard work, craftiness, and attention to detail. Above all else, Calhoun, Pitino, and Williams were apostles of the "city game." Each one of them embraced the old-time religion of pressure defense, up-tempo offense, skillful ball handling, and board crashing in their coaching. They all played deep benches and built tight-knit teams. None of them had a Bob Kurland or a Bob Lanier in the middle they could dump the ball into for high-percentage shots. Instead, they created teams that played with passion, intensity, and intelligence. Their teams were always in peak physical condition, and, win or lose, the opposition was always in for a battle.

All three coaches transformed their teams in Boston into programs worthy of national recognition. In 1983 Rick Pitino brought BU back to the NCAA Tournament for the first time in a quarter century, guiding a team that had been crushed the previous autumn by the death of its captain and best player, Arturo Brown, who died of a heart attack during practice. Jim Calhoun led Northeastern to five league titles, five NCAA Tournament bids, and three upset victories in the NCAA Tournament in a six-year period during the early- to mid-1980s. Gary Williams took two undersized BC clubs that were perennially picked by the basketball experts near the bottom of the Big East to the Sweet Sixteen. On both occasions BC came within an errant shot of making it to the Elite Eight.

Collectively, Jim Calhoun, Rick Pitino, and Gary Williams played a profound role in the remaking of modern college basketball. The fast and physical play adopted by many of the best college teams of the late twentieth and early twenty-first centuries looked a lot like the basketball that Northeastern, BU, and BC played in the late 1970s and 1980s. A number of these great teams of the recent past were in fact coached by Calhoun, Pitino, or Williams. This trio won a total of six national championships and reached thirteen Final Fours between 1987 and 2011. All three coaches have been enshrined in the Naismith Memorial Basketball Hall of Fame in Springfield, Massachusetts. For close to a quarter century, their teams were almost continually in the conversation as contenders for the national championship. Each coach became a celebrity as college basketball and March Madness became a multi-billion-dollar industry.

Before Jim Calhoun turned the University of Connecticut (UConn) into a national power; before Pitino became the face of the Providence, Kentucky, and Louisville programs; and before Gary Williams brought Maryland its first national championship, all three coaches cut their teeth in front of modest crowds in the crumbling college gymnasiums of Boston during the 1970s and 1980s. *Boston Ball* is the story of a forgotten cradle of coaches. It details how three ambitious young coaches learned their trade in the shadow of the dynastic Celtics, professional basketball's most revered and successful franchise. Each coach crafted a distinct blueprint for building a winning program and did so through the collective efforts of his players, assistants, and athletic department staff.

Boston Ball fills a significant gap in the historical record of American sports. While the most high-profile tenures in each of the three coaches' careers are well known to basketball fans, few outside of the Boston basketball community seem to know much about the earlier periods in Calhoun's, Pitino's, or Williams's careers. Even locally, coverage of the three teams was limited in the print and broadcast media. The *Boston Globe* (referred to simply as "the *Globe*" in this book) at least wrote up accounts of most NU, BU, and BC games during this era. Many young journalists who went on to big things—including Jackie MacMullan and Lesley Visser—did a fine job covering local college basketball, but the paper's overall coverage of the teams seemed more like due diligence for the local sports scene than reporting on a genuinely mass attraction.

To one extent or another the coaches themselves have deemphasized this aspect of their respective careers in their official retellings. Pitino gives his five years at BU (1978–1983) a total of five pages in *Pitino: My Story*.[2] Williams spends four pages on his four years as BC's head coach (1982–1986) in his memoir, *Sweet Redemption*.[3] Jim Calhoun, who spent fourteen years at Northeastern (1972–1986), is the most verbose, covering his time as the Huskies' coach in two slim chapters.[4]

Boston Ball is more than a coming-of-age story for three coaches who went on to star on the national stage. For one thing, it is also the story of many other great coaches, some well known and others more obscure, who competed and coached alongside the three Hall of Fame coaches in this book. Three other coaches who figure prominently in *Boston Ball* belong in the Basketball Hall of Fame: Mike Jarvis, Tom Davis, and Kevin Mackey. Mike Jarvis, who twice coached BU to the NCAA Tournament after coaching at his alma maters, Northeastern and Cambridge Rindge and Latin, is an obvious omission from the Hall, having later revitalized flagging programs at George Washington and St. John's. Dr. Tom Davis, Gary Williams's mentor and the man who transformed BC into a power in the early years of the Big East, is one of the great tactical innovators in the history of college basketball. Kevin Mackey, Davis's and Williams's top recruiter and later the author of one of the great upsets in NCAA Tournament history, has made unique contributions to basketball at the high school, collegiate, and professional levels. The life's work of so many other fine coaches—including Jim O'Brien, Karl Fogel, Jack Leaman, Al Skinner, Dick "Duke" Dukeshire, Jim Bowman, Roy Sigler, Nick Macarchuk, and Pete Lonergan, as well as many other fine teachers of the game in the Big East and the Eastern Collegiate Athletic Conference (ECAC) North—is also discussed in this book. Without delving too much into the tactical nuts and bolts of the game, *Boston Ball* offers a window into the strategic diversity that characterized eastern college basketball in the 1970s and 1980s.

Boston Ball is also a story of recruiting: how coaches at lesser-known schools found the student-athletes that enabled them to compete for NCAA Tournament bids. Unable to lure the bluebloods that chose the brand name programs of the ACC, Big East, and Big Ten, Northeastern, BU, and BC each developed distinctive and consistently fruitful recruiting pipelines. Northeastern cultivated a "Pittsburgh Connection," a network that drew many talented if overlooked players from western Pennsylvania to the school on Huntington Avenue. The Huskies later developed significant pipelines to southeastern Massachusetts and to Baltimore/Washington DC, where they landed the greatest player in NU history, Reggie Lewis. Rick Pitino made extensive use of the network emanating from Howard Garfinkel's famed Five-Star Basketball Camp to sign players at BU. The young BU coach won many recruits in his old New York tri-state-area stomping grounds while finding a number of solid players in lightly recruited eastern Canada and northern New England. Despite its Big East affiliation, Boston College struggled to lure the most high-profile recruits in the Northeast to Chestnut Hill. Instead, BC proved incredibly creative under Tom Davis and Gary Williams at finding great players in less familiar places. The Eagles got a number of fine players out of the mid-Atlantic states, but BC's success in the first half of the 1980s is due in large part to the pipeline that the school's top recruiter, Kevin Mackey, built into Connecticut. Mackey convinced four future NBA players, none of whom was prized by the other Big East programs, to sign on at BC in the late 1970s and early 1980s. BC's "Connecticut Connection" served as the architecture for the school's two Big East regular season titles and four trips to the Sweet Sixteen in five years.

Boston Ball is set firmly in its namesake city but also in a very different time. This was Boston before the renaissance that remade the city into a destination for young people and immigrants from around the world. This was a post-industrial city, a shrinking city that was simultaneously showing its wear and scarred by urban renewal. Before its hospitals, tech sector, universities, home renovators, and endless construction projects became the primary drivers of an economic boom, Boston was much more a city of discrete spaces, and its colleges were one such enclave. For African American players considering a Boston-area school in the 1980s, the strife and violence of just a few years earlier during the city's busing crisis was not something of the past. Even after the most obvious signs of conflict diminished, Boston remained a place that seemed to run along several parallel tracks.

A sense of cultural divergence was certainly evident at the universities featured in this book. African American players who chose to play and study at Northeastern, BU, or BC found themselves on predominately white campuses on which they were a highly visible minority. For the sports teams that represented these universities, an inability to transcend their institutions played no small role in their limited bases of support. Boston's big-league teams were among the traditional cultural ties that bound people in the region together. Practically everyone I interviewed for this book used the exact phrase, "Boston is a pro sports town," to describe the place of college sports in "America's College Town." To be more precise, Boston is more a town with colleges than a conventional college town, where one institution is the social and economic focal point. No one university in Boston cultivates the kind of municipal unity one finds in Ann Arbor, Michigan, or Madison, Wisconsin, or Athens, Georgia.

Of the three schools, Boston College drew by far the largest and most consistent crowds to its basketball games, as its bandbox gym, the Roberts Center, was one of the most raucous venues in the Big East. Outside of the school's students and alumni, few others showed much interest in Eagles basketball. BC was a highly selective Jesuit institution nestled in Chestnut Hill. In many ways, BC felt more like its own orbit than a city school. In the case of archrivals Northeastern and BU, these were both historically large, private commuter schools that drew students from the surrounding towns and neighborhoods. It was much harder for these commuter schools, built along Huntington Avenue (Northeastern) and Commonwealth Avenue (BU), to develop large fan bases than it was for residential schools with a more permanent sense of campus life. As both institutions evolved into more selective and residential universities, they continued to struggle with cultivating strong identifications with their sports teams. Neither BU's nor Northeastern's teams benefitted from the affinities that come from representing a specific state, city, or religious group. All three schools had historically strong hockey programs, but in each instance they culled their support largely from alumni bases that had backed these teams for decades. Their fan bases were steady and rarely spectacular outside of the two weeks of Beanpot Hockey each year at the Boston Garden.

Boston Ball is also the story of a sport in transition. The adoption of the shot clock and the three-pointer happened gradually and then all of a sudden during the 1980s, forcing players and coaches to adapt quickly to the changing circumstances. The NCAA Tournament, too, changed significantly in this era. When Jim Calhoun took over at Northeastern in 1972, the NCAA Tournament had a twenty-five-team field. The National

Invitational Tournament (NIT) remained highly prestigious in the early 1970s and selected a sixteen-team field. The NCAA Tournament field grew considerably during the 1970s and 1980s before arriving in 1985 at the sixty-four-team bracket that still forms the core of the selection process. At the same time, the NIT declined considerably in prestige, even in its traditional bastion of support, the northeastern United States.

The creation of the modern system of conferences in eastern college basketball also figures prominently in this story. The amorphous ECAC imploded in 1979 with the formation of the Big East Conference, which coalesced around many of the ECAC's best basketball schools. BC earned a spot in the Big East after historic basketball power Holy Cross demurred. BU and Northeastern found themselves in a free-for-all as the remaining ECAC schools looked to form their own permanent leagues that retained the ECAC's automatic tournament bids. Both Boston schools ended up in the marriage of convenience known originally as the ECAC North before the league changed its name to the North Atlantic Conference (now known as America East). Instability reigned in the new league as membership and the configuration of the conference's playoffs changed frequently throughout the decade.

Most significantly, this is a story of teams—of the camaraderie, conflicts, triumphs, disappointments, and, sadly, tragedies experienced by the young men who spent the early years of their adulthoods playing and studying at these three fine universities. The backbone of this book is the more than ninety interviews I conducted with former players, coaches, team managers, journalists, and administrators from college athletic departments. I spoke with two of the three subjects of this book, Jim Calhoun and Gary Williams, both of whom were generous with their time and their recollections. I spoke with dozens of people associated with Northeastern, Boston University, and Boston College basketball during this era, as well as with many coaches, players, and administrators from opposing schools in the Big East and ECAC North. Collectively, their recollections provide tone and texture to this account of events often forty years old. More importantly, they offer a glimpse into the relationships that make up a team, the preparations they made to compete at the highest level, and the experience of playing highly competitive college basketball.

1

Pay Cut *(Calhoun)*

In September 1972, Jim Bowman received a letter from the Federal Bureau of Investigation (FBI). He'd been accepted to the FBI Academy, fulfilling a longtime dream of the Quincy, Massachusetts, native.[1] Two years earlier he'd received a similar letter, offering him an appointment to the federal law enforcement agency, but he turned it down. Bowman was twenty-seven at the time and an assistant basketball coach at his alma mater, Northeastern, where he'd been a stalwart on Dick Dukeshire's tough and physical basketball teams of the mid-1960s. Northeastern had been a power in the NCAA's "College Division" (now Division II) during the 1960s, earning six bids to the NCAA Tournament. Bowman took over as the coach of Northeastern's freshman team in 1969, a time of transition for the basketball program, which was in the multi-year process of moving up to Division I, then called the NCAA "University Division." In the fall of 1971 he became Northeastern's interim head basketball coach when Dukeshire took a season-long sabbatical, agreeing to coach the Greek national team as it attempted to qualify for the 1972 Summer Olympics.

The letter from the FBI arrived as Bowman neared his thirtieth birthday, the cutoff for enrollment in the Bureau. He had less than a week to decide whether to accept the FBI's offer or to continue on at Northeastern, where he may well have become the permanent head basketball coach. Dukeshire had returned from Greece, where he had contracted an undisclosed illness that prevented him from returning immediately to his job. While on the mend, Dukeshire put off his decision on coaching the upcoming season at Northeastern but eventually decided against it. When he was physically able, Dukeshire returned to Greece, where he again became coach of the national team.[2] Jim Bowman, too, decided against returning to Northeastern. He accepted the FBI's offer and served with distinction as a special agent for the next thirty years. "I was set on joining the FBI because I knew from my experience that to be a successful D-I [Division I] coach, your family makes a lot of sacrifices. Also, it was assumed that Duke was coming back. I had turned down the FBI in 1970 and knew I couldn't do it again," Jim Bowman recalled.[3]

Northeastern athletic director, Herb Gallagher, and his assistant Joe Zabilski, who had recently retired after nearly a quarter century as the school's football coach, had to find themselves a new head basketball coach less than a month before practice began on October 15. They asked around but found no takers among the incumbent college coaches they contacted. University of Pennsylvania assistant Rollie Massimino, New Hampshire's Gerry Friel, and Assumption's Joe O'Brien all apparently said no. Several area high school coaches with strong ties to Northeastern applied for the job, as did Northeastern assistant and basketball alum Mike Jarvis, the twenty-seven-year-old coach of the Huskies' freshman team. Gallagher and Zabilski instead went in a different direction, causing consternation and confusion within the Northeastern basketball family by hiring a little-known high school coach from Dedham to lead the program.

On October 2, 1972, Northeastern University announced that thirty-year-old Jim Calhoun would be its new head basketball coach, the school's third in less than one calendar year.[4] Calhoun accepted a pay cut to take the job. At Northeastern he would earn $13,800 a year. As a high school teacher and basketball coach in nearby Dedham, he'd made $14,600. Nevertheless, when Calhoun told his wife Pat that he thought he was going to get the job, he later wrote that "it sounded like I was saying, 'You know, I think Ed McMahon is going to pull up on the front lawn with the big check from Publishers Clearing House.'"[5]

"We were all in the dark. It was a little bit of a shocker. We didn't know much about him. [Calhoun] wasn't a whole lot older than us," freshman center Jim Connors remembered.[6] "They [Northeastern] never really interviewed anybody else. Herb Gallagher and Dukeshire sort of had a falling out," Paul Solberg said, making Calhoun the beneficiary of intrigue within the athletic department. Rather than hiring a Dukeshire disciple, Gallagher and Zabilski instead selected someone from outside the Husky basketball orbit. Solberg had been one of Dukeshire's most accomplished students. Twice the Northeastern point guard earned Little All-American honors while leading the Huskies to the District I College Division Championship in 1962 and 1963. He later served as an assistant coach for Dukeshire. Years earlier Solberg met Calhoun in Quincy's summer basketball league. The cocky Calhoun rubbed Solberg and his friends the wrong way, a feeling that remained when Calhoun got the Northeastern job.[7]

Calhoun would be one of the country's youngest head basketball coaches in the 1972–1973 season. Nevertheless, the thirty-year-old brought a wealth of basketball and life experience to the job. What came off as pugnaciousness and being stuck on himself to some was the product of hard-earned success bought with self-reliance and self-assurance.

James A. Calhoun Jr. was born on May 10, 1942, in Braintree, Massachusetts. His father and namesake Jim served in the Merchant Marines while his mother Kathleen raised their large family in East Braintree. Jim was one of six. He had two older sisters, two younger sisters, and a younger brother named Billy. In an already tight family the younger Jim was particularly tight with the older Jim, who shared his passion for athletics. The older Calhoun was a hard-throwing pitcher well into middle age. He often brought his son to Fenway Park or to see Weymouth High School football, a gridiron power on Boston's South Shore during the 1950s.[8]

While the younger Jim loved football and baseball, basketball proved to be his true passion. From seventh grade onward Calhoun worked closely with Fred Herget, who later became his high school basketball coach. Herget was also the head of the Parks and Recreation Department in Braintree, and Jim was his employee. "He [Herget] used to put all of us basketball players as the park directors. We had ten [parks] in Braintree. And he'd come to check if we were working but he also came to see how hard [we] were working on the game of basketball," Calhoun said.[9] Herget gave his players assignments to work on specific skills, conditioning, and strength while they minded the city's parks.

Solitary practice and self-discipline suited Calhoun's personality. He thrived under Herget's tutelage, becoming one of the state's top high school players. Braintree dominated the Bay State League and made frequent trips to the Garden to play in the Tech Tournament, then eastern Massachusetts' most prestigious postseason tournament. Calhoun later adopted many of the concepts he learned from Herget into his own coaching.

"He [Herget] always talked about 'what did you do today to improve your game?'" Calhoun said, citing basketball as one of the few sports where players can work on their game virtually every day of the year, practicing either inside or outside. He adopted this get-better-everyday approach in his own coaching, plying his players to work on their weaknesses every day of the off-season.[10] Beyond some ideas about pressure defense he had culled from a John Wooden book, Calhoun regards Herget and his own family as the primary influences on his coaching philosophy.[11]

A devastating family tragedy changed the course of fifteen-year-old Jim Calhoun's life. His father died of a heart attack at age fifty-three. A cruel neighbor informed the younger Calhoun of his father's demise while the teenager was playing in a Babe Ruth baseball game, yelling to him in center field that he should come on home because his dad had died. At that moment Jim Calhoun became the man of the house, responsible for his two younger sisters, who were soon to be entering high school, and his younger brother, who was still in elementary school. When not playing sports or doing schoolwork, Calhoun was earning a wage: separating metal at a shipyard, working in a candy factory, pumping gas, or jockeying a booth at a local fair. Following a decorated career as a high school basketball and football star, Calhoun turned down an athletic scholarship from Lowell State to meet his family responsibilities. His need to provide for his family became more dire when his mother began suffering from angina, a debilitating heart condition that forced her to spend long stretches of time in the hospital. For the next two years, Calhoun spent his days making gravestones, sandblasting for Settimelli Stonecutters in Quincy, while playing in several different basketball leagues at night.[12]

One night, the 6′5″ Calhoun rained in 40 points in a recreation league tournament in western Massachusetts. Bill Callahan, the head coach at American International College (AIC) in Springfield, happened to be at the game in nearby Holyoke and offered Calhoun a scholarship on the spot. He went so far as to secure the now twenty-year-old a job on the night shift at board game manufacturer Milton Bradley, enabling the young man to continue supporting his family. Calhoun wasn't sure what to do until he spoke with Herget, who'd maintained close ties with his former star, encouraging him to take advantage of the educational opportunities his athletic skills made available to him.

"He [Herget] checked in on me and said, 'You gotta get out of here. I talked to [your mother]; she's getting back on her feet. She's feeling much better. Your sister's out working. You need to get out of here before you get married or whatever the case may be. There's nothing wrong with getting married, but you have a lot more to offer,'" Calhoun said.[13] He accepted

Callahan's offer and went on to earn Little All-American and All—New England honors at AIC. The sweet-shooting Calhoun was the team's captain and leading scorer as a senior, shepherding the Yellow Jackets to a bid in the 1966 NCAA College Division Tournament, the first in school history.

After graduating with a sociology degree, Calhoun spent two more years in Springfield as a graduate then full-time assistant at AIC. Now married to his longtime love, Pat McDevitt, herself a Weymouth girl, Calhoun earned a draft deferment by remaining in graduate school, working on a master's degree in psychology while coaching. Later he earned a permanent deferment when Pat bore their first son, Jim. Seeking steadier employment, Calhoun took a teaching job in Old Lyme, Connecticut, and became the varsity basketball coach. He broke the school's thirty-game losing streak and transformed the team into winners over the course of two winters, earning conference coach of the year honors both times. Calhoun then moved on to Westport, Massachusetts, a town of just under ten thousand, lodged between the Rhode Island border and the city of Fall River. After teaching junior high and coaching the Westport varsity team to a 1-17 record, Calhoun returned home to the South Shore, taking another teaching/coaching job, this time at Dedham High School.[14]

Dedham was a sports town, just like Braintree, filled with tough, blue-collar Irish kids. But hockey, not basketball, had long been the local wintertime passion. Before Calhoun took over in Dedham, the Marauders had just one winning season in the previous twenty-five. They'd dropped thirty-seven straight to Calhoun's alma mater, Braintree. Dedham was also in the throes of a multi-season losing streak when Calhoun took over in 1970.[15]

"Dedham was my basketball laboratory. Dedham was where I could take my Fred Herget kick-in-the-butt 365 Day Formula for Basketball Success and lay it on an unsuspecting adolescent public," Calhoun wrote.[16] Calhoun had his charges playing in every off-season league imaginable. Like Herget, he became the town's playground director, set up a series of summer leagues, and got his players summer jobs, where he could drill them day after day on the game's fundamentals while checking in on their work at the playgrounds.

In year one, Dedham went 8-12. In year two, the Marauders exorcised every past indignity in the program's history over the course of one winter. Dedham defeated Braintree, won the Bay State League, completed an undefeated regular season, made it all the way to the state semifinals at the Boston Garden, and finished the year with a 21-1 mark.

Calhoun had just begun a new school year at Dedham when he learned of the Northeastern opening from Jerry Varnum, an NU alum who coached football at Dedham. Calhoun applied for the job on a whim and impressed in his interview with Gallagher and Zabilski. Former football coach Zabilski was particularly high on Calhoun. He convinced Gallagher that Calhoun was sufficiently familiar with college coaching from his time at AIC. Moreover, anyone who could turn Dedham into a winning basketball program surely had something going for him as a coach.[17]

Hopes were not high for the 1972–1973 Northeastern basketball team. Calhoun had less than two weeks before practice started to get a handle on his personnel. Even before the coaching intrigue, the prospects for the season seemed bleak. The Huskies' schedule consisted largely of University Division programs, and Northeastern's returning roster was undersized and lacking in experience and depth. The school offered just four basketball scholarships while many of its Division I opponents had as many as sixteen. The best players on the 1971–1972 team, Jim Moxley and Paul McDonough, had graduated. Senior guard Kevin Lecy quit the team after getting married. Another expected contributor, Peter Anderson, a schoolboy hot shot from Boston's Hyde Park neighborhood, transferred to Boston State.[18]

"Northeastern has a pretty good winning tradition, but people could never figure out how Dick Dukeshire did it with the talent. Now a guy with two years in Dedham has to come in and do the same job," the *Globe*'s Peter Gammons wrote.[19] Being underestimated was something that Calhoun and the Northeastern basketball program had in common. Relying largely on lightly recruited student-athletes from Boston and its immediate environs, Dukeshire built Northeastern into one of the country's most successful College Division programs, paving the way for its transition to the University Division in the late 1960s and early 1970s.

"Coach Dukeshire was one of the best coaches in all of New England. His preparation and attention to detail were unmatched. He ran incredibly organized practices and stressed fundamentals and discipline," recalled Glen Field, who played forward for Northeastern in the late 1960s.[20] In the first forty years of Northeastern basketball, the Huskies mounted just eleven winning seasons. Under Dukeshire, Northeastern posted eleven consecutive winning campaigns.

"I think he [Dukeshire] is the best coach that ever coached in New England," said Mike Jarvis, who played at Northeastern during the mid-1960s. "A lot of guys that played at Northeastern ended up going on to coach, mostly at the high school level. I remember him as a great teacher and a great person to build one's total stature, taking boys and turning them into men."[21] Jarvis counts himself among Dukeshire's coaching tree, having begun his storied career as a Dukeshire assistant immediately after his playing career.

Though Dukeshire was only in his mid-twenties when he became Northeastern's head coach in 1958, his players thought he was much older. Once Dukeshire built a culture of winning on Huntington Avenue, Northeastern's success as a basketball program, too, seemed like something that had always been.

"We constantly thought about the winning tradition. We were all very well aware of what came before us," Glen Field said.[22] Dukeshire found the perfect granite for the kind of team he wanted to mold in the blue-collar towns that surrounded Boston. Most of the young men he convinced to play their college basketball at Northeastern were commuters from eastern Massachusetts, like the vast majority of their classmates at the large and then low-priced private college. At the time, tuition was roughly $250 per semester, less daunting than at many other institutions in "America's college town." For the first-generation college students that made up almost the entirety of Northeastern's basketball roster, the school's pragmatic approach to education was also appealing. Then and now, Northeastern builds its undergraduate education around year-long co-operatives, known informally as "co-ops," experiential learning internships that give many of its students a foot in the door for their first jobs.[23]

Even if Dukeshire couldn't offer his players full scholarships (he often divided the offers into half-scholarships to accommodate more players), he could help them get an affordable college education close to home with clear job prospects at the end of the road. All the while, they could continue playing competitive basketball. "I was from Waltham. I come from a blue-collar background. I had seventy or eighty first cousins, and I was the first one to graduate from college," said Bill Stanton, who played at Northeastern in the early 1970s.[24] His experience was typical of the players who gravitated toward Northeastern.

For much of his tenure, Dukeshire had no assistants and did all the recruiting. He often went straight from practice to area high school games on the lookout for talent. Practices didn't start until 5:30 in the evening, enabling players to finish their co-ops for the day. Calhoun maintained this practice schedule, often running marathon sessions that lasted until 8:30 p.m. Additionally, Dukeshire coached freshman football in the fall and freshman baseball in the spring. Beginning in 1968, Dukeshire found himself increasingly in conflict with Gallagher (a self-professed hockey guy) and football coach Zibilski as he fought for a larger budget for his basketball program, which would be transitioning to Division I.[25]

Stylistically, Dukeshire's Northeastern teams played stout defense and ran a ball-control offense. His players were smart, hard-nosed, and committed to the team concept. The style made sense given NU's personnel, which was often undersized and less athletic than some of their opponents. Getting to the basket was a chore against NU's tough, physical teams. The Huskies rebounded well and were never afraid to tussle with the opposition. NU's teams played unselfishly and maximized the value of their possessions by rarely turning the ball over while working for high-percentage shots.[26] Northeastern was frequently one of the nation's top defensive teams and rarely surrendered more than 60 points in a game. At the same time, they rarely lit up the scoreboard to the same extent as more free-wheeling offenses.

"Great team defense and a controlled offense that took advantage of transition opportunities," is how Jim Bowman described Northeastern's traditional style of play. "We never played out of control, and our pace of play varied based on the strengths and weaknesses of opponents."[27]

Dukeshire was a master of technique. On the offensive end he taught his players to use the jab step before it even had a name, calling it instead the "rocker step." On the defensive end the Huskies frustrated opponents with a zone press, then an unusual tactic in college basketball.[28]

He taught toughness with toughness, preparing his players for the game with rough practices and rough talk.

"I was a quiet kid. Duke was pretty tough," Paul McDonough recalled.[29] In high school McDonough played for Huskies great John Malvey at Malden Catholic, one of several pipelines to Northeastern. Coach Malvey was easygoing. Playing for the intense Dukeshire was a major change to which McDonough eventually adjusted. Though undersized, the feisty McDonough was a significant contributor on the Northeastern teams of the early 1970s.

"Duke was very aggressive," Ed Minishak, who played a rough-and-tumble game even by Northeastern standards, said of his first college coach. "He was also my freshman baseball coach. I remember one time I pitched 12 innings and I threw pretty hard, and it was starting to go all over the place. He came out to the mound and said to me, 'I need someone out here with balls,'" before pulling Minishak from the game.[30]

"My brother and I are watching practice [at Northeastern], and they had to drag one guy off the floor because he went up for a rebound and somebody undercut him and he busted his arm," Bill Stanton, then a high school player in Waltham, said of the first Dukeshire-era practice he saw in person. "They had to literally carry him off to the side. He didn't go to the hospital. He just sat there and tried to watch. I remember saying to my brother, 'These fuckers play some defense.' We saw them beat the crap out of each other, and I said this was the place that I want to play."[31]

Throughout the 1960s the Huskies received strong support at Cabot Gym, their on-campus home floor that seated around three thousand. Though modest by the standards of major college basketball, the support Northeastern received from students, alums, and community members was impressive considering that the commuter school had no dormitories from which to draw students and extremely limited parking in the densely populated surrounding neighborhoods. Moreover, Northeastern athletics got far less press coverage than more established athletics programs at Harvard and Boston College, making the Huskies' fan support far more dependent on word of mouth. People attending Northeastern basketball games had to make the conscious choice to build their evenings around coming to campus.

By the early 1970s attendance started to wane at Northeastern basketball games. NU's teams continued to post winning records, but the transition period to the NCAA University Division kept the Huskies out of contention for the postseason as they were not yet qualified to compete for a bid to the NCAA Tournament. The competition NU was facing also made it more difficult to maintain their success on the floor and in the stands. "Without a conference and with a schedule half of which still consisted of College

Division teams, there was really no chance of participating in postseason play. We had a very successful '68–69 season, but the excitement and anticipation of a tournament invite was missing," Glen Field remembered.[32]

The challenges Northeastern faced as it transitioned to Division I became particularly evident during Jim Bowman's season as interim head coach in 1971–1972. NU lost its first four games by a total of 7 points, including losses to regional powers UMass, Boston College, and a nationally ranked Harvard team at the Boston Garden. Northeastern turned things around and fought its way to a 12-9 record, significantly worse than its 17-4 campaign of the previous year but itself a striking achievement. Bowman's team played its toughest schedule yet and had just one returning starter. Thankfully, that starter was forward Jim Moxley, who combined Dick Dukeshire toughness with an athleticism that was rare among Northeastern basketball players of the era. He was an elite scorer and rebounder and just the guy you'd want on your side in a fight. "He [Moxley] was our team leader. That was the baddest white boy that I ever saw. He'd run through a wall, or if a fight broke out, he's the one you wanted to get near. He led by example. If I was in the bunkers, I'd want him next to me," guard Joe "The Show" Delgardo said of his teammate and captain in 1971–1972.[33]

Led by Moxley, Bowman took a back-to-basics approach in 1971–1972. He favored a more conservative offensive game plan than Dukeshire, typically relying on a stack offense to generate competitive shots. Instead of zone presses Bowman went with a man-to-man built around physically imposing your will on the opposition. "Oh, was he tough," John Boutin, then a junior forward, said of Bowman. "I think I still have skinned knees and skinned elbows because he just loved you to take a charge, loved you to dive on loose balls. He wanted there to be a lot of contact under the basket when you're fighting for rebounds. He taught me how to become a man. He was tough as nails and made you tough as nails."[34]

"I loved playing for Jim," Paul McDonough said. "Our temperaments are very similar. He was demanding, but I always knew where I stood with Jim."[35]

Though just an interim coach, Bowman received several nominations for New England Coach of the Year in 1971–1972 for finding a way to post a winning record under such adverse conditions.

Calhoun's situation entering the 1972–1973 season would be even more dire. Northeastern would be playing just as difficult a schedule while fielding a team that was nearly as inexperienced as its predecessor. On top of this, the new head coach would have almost no time to discern what talent he had in place. The Huskies had a cadre of returning forwards that included John Barros, Rick Brault, John Haviland, Sam Jordan, and John Boutin, none of whom was taller than 6′6″. Each one was a rugged rebounder in the Dukeshire model, but collectively they offered little in the way of offensive firepower. Northeastern's top returning scorer, guard Mark Jellison, had averaged just over 11 points per game. Sophomores Jim Connors (6′7″) and Bill Stanton (6′10″), both of whom had excelled on NU's freshman team the previous year, gave Northeastern more size, but the degree to which they would contribute on offense remained unclear.

Starting in the 1972–1973 school year, freshmen could play on varsity for the first time in decades. The newly hired Calhoun threw cold water on the idea that he'd be playing his freshmen or changing things up tactically from the way Dukeshire or Bowman ran the team. "I certainly wouldn't hesitate to use current freshmen if they could help, but then Jim told me that it isn't too good an incoming crop. My basic philosophy is like Duke's—defense, ball control," Calhoun said.[36]

One freshman who stood out from the crop was John Clark, a 6′0″ guard from Pittsburgh. Despite having been selected for the Dapper Dan Roundball Classic all-star game, the first national showcase of its kind, Clark received surprisingly little notice from major college programs. It was a Northeastern basketball alum in Pittsburgh, Dr. Richard Mullins, who brought Clark to the attention of the Huskies' coaching staff. Mullins was the director of Carnegie Mellon University's Upward Bound program and a mentor to the academically minded Clark.

"Richard [Mullins] contacted Northeastern, and at the time Coach Bowman and Dukeshire were there. My recruitment began with Richard making a phone call in the spring of '72 and Bowman saying, 'Yeah, bring him up; let's see him.' Then I visited Northeastern, and my good friend Joey Delgardo showed me the campus and took me around the city to the different spots. That was a good experience. And Coach Bowman said he'd offer me a full scholarship to attend the school," Clark recalled.[37] The recruitment of Clark to Northeastern by way of Dr. Mullins came to be known as the school's "Pittsburgh Connection," a pipeline of talent that brought several of the most celebrated players in program history to Boston.

"I recruited John Clark. I took him to the Temptations concert and he had a ball, and I convinced him to go to Northeastern. Jim Calhoun ended up starting him his freshman year. That boy was good. I have to admit he was better than me," Joe Delgardo conceded.[38] Once practice began, everyone saw the remarkable talent that had joined their team. Quiet and cerebral, Clark combined speed and athleticism like nobody else that had ever donned a Huskies uniform. He could also shoot the lights out of any gym. Calhoun valued his deft passing skills and made him his point guard. "John Clark was one of the most intriguing personalities I ever had, not only because he was a really good player who kept things in balance, but because he was also a great student," Calhoun said.[39]

"A real quiet, almost shy type of individual," is how John Boutin described his friend Clark. "I think a lot of it had to do with [the fact that] there weren't a lot of Black players on the team and that it was the first year that freshmen were allowed to play varsity ball. He was the only freshman on that team."[40]

Not everyone was as welcoming as Boutin. Clark was one of the few African American players on the roster and one of the few players from outside the Boston area. He was the only freshman on the varsity, a freshman who started ahead of upper classmen, and a young man who played a much different brand of basketball than the rough-and-tumble style adopted by many of his teammates.

"It was awful," John Clark said of his first-year practices at Northeastern. "I broke my jaw. I broke my hand. Asshole fell on my ankle. Had to have surgery on my ankle. All my injuries happened at practice. Fights would break out where guys would hit me or do something to me, and of course you've got to hit them."[41]

Calhoun, as a rookie coach, didn't intervene. "He [Calhoun] didn't do anything," Clark said. "Either he was so focused on his own stuff, or he didn't pay attention to it. I remember when my jaw was broken; there was a loud pop in the gym. It was Saturday morning practice. This unnamed asshole ran by me and he elbowed me right in my face. I didn't have the ball. The play wasn't there. And he struck me, and it broke my jaw. I immediately grabbed my head, and everybody stopped and looked at me. And coach said, 'Let's go. Let's keep playing.'"[42]

Clark believes his poor treatment by some teammates was primarily racially motivated, placing it in the context of the city's racial tensions, which culminated in the Boston busing crisis of the mid-1970s. From a wide lens, this makes sense. Much of the racial animus in and around Boston during the 1970s pitted the white working class (from which Northeastern drew most of its basketball players) against African Americans. At the same time, though, exceedingly physical practices were the norm not only of the Dukeshire era, but also of the early years of Calhoun's tenure. Jim Connors, for example, was a newcomer to the varsity as a sophomore who ended up starting ahead of upperclassmen, and he was also an out-of-stater. He too squared off with teammates during practice but not to the same extent as Clark. The drills Calhoun ran also contributed to the physicality of practice. Either way, the rough treatment faced by newcomers to the Northeastern basketball program could be seen, at best, as a rite of passage and, at worst, as a form of on-court hazing, particularly odious in the case of Clark because of the racial overtones.

"The boxout drills were pretty physical. You could do anything but punch or kick a guy. It was very aggressive," Ed Minishak said.[43] Minishak remembers that several players left the program because they couldn't handle the physicality of practice. In the boxout drill, players had to secure three straight rebounds before they could leave the station. Newcomers to the program were always the targets and often had agonizingly long stays under the rim.[44]

While Calhoun was figuring out the character of his new team, one area where he needn't worry was on the basketball fundamentals of his veterans. At the same time, Calhoun placed a new emphasis in practice on conditioning, anticipating the more up-tempo style of play that would slowly but surely become part of Northeastern's repertoire. "Dukeshire and Bowman had made us so fundamentally sound," John Boutin said. "We could set a pick and make sure that we made the move that enabled us to get off. We knew how to box out. Because we weren't a big team. We weren't a Boston College. We had to work our tails off to be able to compete because we hadn't had the opportunity to recruit as a Division I team for very long."[45]

Calhoun expressed enthusiasm to *Northeastern News*, the campus newspaper, about what he'd seen in practice. He noted what a great all-around player team captain Mark Jellison was, stating that "[the] only thing we don't ask him to do is collect tickets at the door." He also indicated that the speed John Clark brought to the backcourt would enable the Huskies to break out of their ball-control offense more often than in previous years. Defensively, Calhoun planned to rely on man-to-man with occasional shifts to zone.[46]

The mad scramble of an off-season came to an end on Tuesday, December 5. The Huskies opened the 1972–1973 campaign by traveling across town to play rival Boston University at Case Gym. Ron Mitchell's BU team was a club on the rise, boasting a significantly longer and more athletic roster than Northeastern's. Two future NBA players, center James Garvin and junior forward Ken Boyd, along with leading scorer Kenny Walker, gave the Terriers one of the most dynamic lineups in New England. Garvin, Boyd, and company outgunned Northeastern in an 87–74 triumph. NU led by as much as 11 points early in the second half before BU's trio of stars took over, scoring 47 of the team's 59 second-half points. BU often got second or third chances on the offensive end, enabling them to win by double digits in a game where they were outshot 57 percent to 43.[47]

"At the end of the game, I got into a tussle with one of [BU's] players, and it turned into a brawl," Ed Minishak recalled. "We were down, so we had to foul someone. I ran up to foul this kid, and he took off. I stuck my leg out trying to get a charge. I must have gotten him in the thigh. When the game's over, we are shaking hands, and, to quote Jim [Calhoun], 'Instead of shaking hands, they started throwing rights.'"[48] The postgame fisticuffs were far from the last time Northeastern and BU would get into it before, during, or after a game. It was also far from the last time that Northeastern found themselves in a fight that season. "We had a lot of fights. We had a fight with Tufts, we had a fight with St. Anslem's, we had one with LIU, and I think Minishak started every one of them," Bill Stanton said.[49] Beyond a willingness to mix it up with their foes, this Northeastern team soon showed an ability to shut down the opposition at the defensive end while opening it up on offense.

On December 9, Calhoun earned his first collegiate win as Northeastern pummeled St. Michael's College of Vermont, 83–66, thanks in large part to newcomers John Clark, who led the way with 20 points, and Jim Connors, who went for a 19-point, 12-rebound double-double. After dropping a 70–68 decision to Army, Northeastern reeled off five wins in their next six games. In these contests Calhoun's teams played conservatively, relying on the approach that the veterans of the Dukeshire era had learned from the previous coaching staff. NU topped 70 points just once while holding their opponents' offenses in check. "Initially we played more controlled, slower basketball, which I always did not like," Jim Connors said. "He [Calhoun] was afraid to rock the boat too much because [Northeastern] had always been kind of a control, tempo team that always relied on their defense."[50] Connors proved himself to be Calhoun's most effective low post player, averaging nearly a double-double for the season.

Northeastern, now 6-3, got the chance to avenge its opening night loss to BU in the opening round of the Beanpot Basketball Tournament, held at the Boston Garden. While the Beanpot Hockey Tournament had been a highlight of the city's winter sports calendar since the early 1950s, Beanpot basketball had been a little-attended afterthought. However, the two-week tournament was still a big deal to the teams competing in it, particularly BU and Northeastern, who had long enjoyed a heated rivalry.

Northeastern looked like a completely different team in the January 8 rematch, outrunning and outrebounding a BU team that looked like NU's superior in both measures back in December. Unfortunately, the wildly entertaining game was played before a sparse Garden crowd of just over 1,100.

Clark commandeered Northeastern's offense, creating open looks for the likes of Mark Jellison (29 points) and Ed Minishak, who exploded for 20 points off the bench. Northeastern, too, outmuscled a bigger BU team, winning the battle of the boards. BU's big three of Boyd, Garvin, and Walker each scored at least 20 points, but it wasn't enough to stop a relentless Northeastern team. A Clark layup in the game's final minute sealed BU's fate in the 97–87 Huskies victory. "The first game I played at NU was against BU, and the lights were too bright and I couldn't see. I couldn't catch the ball. It felt like I was living through a nightmare. The second time we played those guys, I had gotten my legs underneath me, and I burned them. I remember feeling vindicated in my own mind. You saw the worst of me, and now here's the best of me," John Clark said.[51]

"What is a player like you doing at a place like Northeastern?" an unnamed reporter asked Clark after the Beanpot win. "Who cares?" Calhoun yelled in response across the winning locker room.[52] NU kept the momentum going by beating Springfield and pulling off a major upset in a scheduled game against Harvard, their opponent three nights later in the Beanpot finals. The Crimson avenged their 73–69 loss at Cabot by obliterating the Huskies 103–65 on the Garden's parquet floor. Harvard was led by future NBA draft picks Floyd Lewis and James Brown, who went on to a decades-long career as a football commentator on CBS and Fox. "We had them [Harvard] on the regular schedule on Friday night in our own gym. We were playing them again on Monday in the Garden in the Beanpot. We just out-toughed them Friday night, made their life miserable," Bill Stanton said. "We go to the Garden to play them a couple nights later, and they kicked the shit out of us. The only consolation for me was getting to play as a sophomore on the Garden floor in junk time."[53]

As January faded into February, Northeastern just kept winning, defeating nine of its next ten opponents, often in convincing fashion. The Huskies won five of the games by at least 15 points. "We've gotten rid of the old Northeastern image," Calhoun said in late January 1973.[54] Offensively the Huskies played much more up-tempo than in previous years and presented multiple looks, allowing guards Jellison and Clark to dribble penetrate, distribute, and display their talents as jump shooters. In the low post, Brault and Connors banged it out with the competition and made steady offensive contributions. All four of them averaged in double figures for the season.[55]

While John Clark earned Calhoun's praise as the "best freshman in New England," it was Mark Jellison who made the most striking transformation among the returning players under Calhoun.[56] Jellison went from being a solid if unremarkable player in his first two varsity seasons to one of New England's top scorers as a senior, averaging just under 19 points per game. The sharpshooting guard would be selected in the eighth round of the 1973 NBA Draft by the Baltimore Bullets.

Northeastern's newfound offensive output did nothing to the team's traditional prowess on the boards. The Huskies averaged 10 more rebounds per game than their opponents thanks to the physical play of Rick Brault, Jim Connors, John Barros, Sam Jordan, and John Haviland in the low post. Clark and Jellison, too, proved to be adept rebounders from the point and shooting guard positions.

Then and now, Calhoun credited his success in his first year to the talent and basketball culture that Dukeshire and Bowman had already put in place.[57] "Calhoun came in and had to live with what he had, and he did very well with them, but it was different," John Boutin said. "He was far more offense-oriented and allowed for shots to be taken by individuals that the previous regime did not necessarily allow. Some of our shooters really got off on that. They really enjoyed that—guys like Mark Jellison, Ricky Brault, and John Clark."[58] Entering the final two weeks of the 1972–1973 regular season, Northeastern boasted an 18-5 record, earning them a ranking as high as number two in the UPI's New England College Basketball Poll.

Despite having one of New England's best University Division programs in the winter of 1972–1973, Northeastern was on the outside looking in at postseason tournaments—namely, the more eastern and independent-oriented NIT.[59] Concerns by NIT organizers about Northeastern's ability to draw fans to the Madison Square Garden—based tournament almost certainly hurt its chances at earning a bid. Against Harvard and Assumption, Northeastern had drawn standing-room-only crowds to Cabot, but many of the team's early contests had been sparsely attended. Overall average attendance at Northeastern games that season hovered around 1,800. "Early on in the season, we did not have a lot of support. At the Cabot Cage, we'd probably get 400 people that would show up for a game," John Boutin said. "We really thought we were going to get a shot at an NIT bid. But as it turned out, Calhoun, because it was his first year, he really didn't have the political clout and the networking capabilities to be able to swing it. And because we didn't draw that well, the NIT was always looking for teams that would sell tickets."[60] Losing back-to-back games to Farleigh Dickinson and UMass in late February likely sealed Northeastern's postseason fate.

In the end, Fairfield and UMass represented New England in the sixteen-team NIT. Final Four—bound Providence College (PC) earned New England's bid in the twenty-five-team NCAA Tournament. While Providence and UMass had reputations that preceded them, a case could be made that the Huskies rather than the Fairfield Stags should have earned an NIT bid. Fairfield certainly had no better a recent reputation at the Division I level. The Stags had lost more games than they had won in each of the four previous seasons. Fairfield ended up with a weaker overall record. The Stags' primary advantage appears to have been their proximity to New York City, which made them a better potential draw at Madison Square Garden.[61]

In the Huskies' final game of the season, Mark Jellison buried a twenty-five-footer with one second remaining to give Northeastern a 78–76 win over Long Island University, pushing the upstart Division I independent to a 19-7 overall record.[62] "We proved we can hold our own against the best," Calhoun said of the team's accomplishments that winter, regardless of the NIT snub.[63] From day one as Northeastern's coach, Calhoun displayed an aggressive assuredness in himself and his program. From a young age, he'd been forced to rely on himself and things were no different for him when he got to Northeastern. He was an outsider on Huntington Avenue. He was initially regarded as underqualified by some in the Northeastern basketball orbit. He was coaching a team that was expected to struggle as it transitioned to Division I. All he did was go out and finish number three in New England behind Providence and UMass.

Despite the straight-out-of-the-starting-gate success Northeastern basketball enjoyed under Calhoun, the coming years were a time of transition for the program. As their young coach learned to ply his trade at the Division I level, the Huskies would play against an upgraded slate of opponents that changed from year to year as an independent.. The team would also struggle over its on-court identity as Calhoun and his assistants worked to build recruiting pipelines beyond Boston and its immediate environs.

2

You Come Highly Recommended *(Pitino)*

Roy Sigler announced his resignation as Boston University's men's basketball coach in February 1978, several weeks before the conclusion of the Terriers' 1977–1978 season. At the time of Sigler's proclamation, the Terriers owned a 7–14 record on the year. Athletic director (AD) John Simpson prompted the resignation, letting his veteran coach know that his aspirations for Terrier basketball were more in line with the success of the BU hockey program, which won its third national championship of the decade later that spring. Simpson himself was responding to a mandate for institutional excellence pushed by BU president John Silber. Ambitious, erudite, and confrontational, Silber oversaw the transformation of Boston University into a nationally recognized institution of higher learning over the last quarter of the twentieth century. Simpson played no small part in helping Silber bring his vision to life.

A BU alum and a former Marine, the energetic Simpson took over as AD in 1975, hell-bent on remaking the school's lackluster athletic department into something more than a collection of also-rans who shared facilities with the school's nationally recognized hockey program. In 1977 Simpson hired highly regarded Dartmouth assistant Rick Taylor to rebuild BU's once vaunted football program. Taylor soon turned the Terriers into a Yankee Conference power and a mainstay of the Division I-AA football playoffs. The new AD transformed several brand-new BU women's athletics programs into out-of-the-box winners, including its rowing, field hockey, and track programs, the track team coached by two-time Boston Marathon winner and 1984 gold medalist Joan Benoit.[1]

But John Simpson's hopes for his hoops program were pretty far-fetched when one considered the state of Terrier basketball in 1978. BU posted four consecutive losing seasons under Sigler, including a 10–15 mark in his last year. Unlike BU football, Terrier basketball had no golden age to conjure in its delusions of grandeur. A 1959 trip to the Elite Eight was the single anomalous moment of March Madness in school history. While BU hockey played to standing-room-only crowds at four-thousand-seat Walter Brown Arena, BU basketball played to friends and family at Case Gym. Case was the size of a high school gym and located two floors up from Walter Brown in the same athletic complex. The gym came to be known as "the Roof" because of its location upstairs from the main arena.

Just four years earlier Sigler had taken on the BU basketball job in part because it made him a full-time employee of the university rather than the part-timer he'd been for much of the previous decade. Before accepting BU's men's basketball job, Sigler served as BU's men's soccer coach, leading the team to a 48-47-11 mark between 1966 and 1973. In the winter months, he coached the BU freshman basketball club. At the time, soccer was his true passion. During his college career, Sigler played soccer in the fall, basketball in the winter, and golf in the spring at Maryland's Frostburg State. Soccer had been by far Sigler's best sport. In 1961 he'd been named an All-American defender. Following his departure from BU, Sigler returned not to soccer but to his native Maryland, where he sold insurance and eventually became a beloved color man for Mount Saint Mary's basketball.[2] "Great coach and great guy. He [Sigler] was very engaging when he recruited me. I had good years for him. We had some talented teams my first two years, but whatever the reason may be, it didn't work, and the athletic department decided to make a change," Glenn Consor said.[3] Consor played point guard for two seasons under Sigler, running a Terriers' half-court offense that generated 74 points per game in 1977–1978.

Former BU assistant coach Ed Leibowitz described Sigler as a "wonderful human being. Roy was a good bench coach and a very well-organized practice coach, and he was a tremendous believer in the student athlete. We didn't have guys that weren't academically capable of doing the work."[4]

"We were so close," Leibowitz said. "If we could have gotten a couple more guys and had a little more time, we could have gotten it done."[5] In fact the talent level on the Terriers' roster had improved significantly over the course of Sigler's time as head coach. Thanks in large part to Leibowitz, who had served as Sigler's lead recruiter, BU landed several players who would prove to be top-notch Division I basketball players, including three that were selected in the NBA Draft.[6]

Hailing from the Flushing section of Queens, Glenn Consor was a classic New York City point guard. At Bayside High, he displayed the toughness, ball-handling, and distribution skills that made him a coveted recruit. Consor chose BU over the likes of Florida, Richmond, Florida State (FSU), Arizona State, and several Ivy League schools. "I loved Boston and everything about the school. Both the academics that BU was offering me and that I was going to start as a freshman. I didn't want to sit," Consor said.[7]

Joining Consor in the backcourt was Tom Channel, a 6'3" guard from Portland, Oregon, who had played several years of minor league baseball in the Minnesota Twins organization. "I signed Thomas Channel twice," Ed Leibowitz recalled. "I signed him once when I was an assistant at Nevada. He was playing at Mt. Hood Community College [Oregon], and I saw him there. I signed him, and he never showed up in Reno because he gave baseball another year."[8] In the meantime, Leibowitz moved on to BU and convinced Sigler to give Channel a try. "An amazing athlete. He [Channel] was the prototypical NBA guard. Strong like Joe Dumars. Could jump and could shoot," Consor said.[9] Older than his teammates by several years, Channel was a cool, laid-back character who also happened to be movie star handsome.

Wally West came to BU after a season of junior college basketball in Kansas. The 6'9" center was ready for a return to city life.

"Wally West I got because of the old Boston Shootout," Leibowitz said.[10] The Boston Shootout was an annual tournament and showcase of some of the country's best high school players. Beginning in 1972, BU hosted the event every June at Case. Before AAU Tournaments dominated college recruiting, the Boston Shootout pitted city and regional all-star teams from across the country against one another over the course of a three-day weekend. The likes of Adrian Dantley, Patrick Ewing, and Bernard King showed off their respective games at the Boston Shootout, which later moved to the Boston Garden before closing up shop in its original form in 1999.

"I was one of these guys that was there from eight o'clock in the morning until ten o'clock at night, meeting every coach I could meet," Leibowitz said. "And I met the coach of Pratt Community College [Kansas], and we went to T. Anthony's and had pizza. We became friends and he got me Wally."[11]

"When I got to college, I was just raw. A street player from Chicago," West said. Over the next few years West would build on that ingrained physicality to become a versatile presence in the low post.[12]

Leibowitz convinced 6'6" Desmond Martin to join West in BU's front court after seeing Martin play for a team representing Brooklyn at the 1977 Shootout. "We had a nice time while we were there. We didn't win all of our games, but Leibowitz saw me play and they needed some big men, so he recruited me," Martin said.[13]

The most consequential player Sigler and Leibowitz brought into BU was Steve Wright, a 6'9" forward from Montgomery County, Maryland. Wright was slight and quiet by nature, but he was also the best shooter anyone at BU had ever seen. "Steve was a very funny guy, but he was also kind of introverted," Glenn Consor said. "I was coming from New York with a New York attitude. Our personalities—they were like Frick and Frack. I was a little more outspoken—or acting like a New Yorker. He was more timid and shy. I remember that in my freshman year we just connected on the court really well, with backdoor plays, and we knew each other's moves. We lived together, and we were best friends."[14] Wright was the team's MVP as a sophomore, averaging nearly 12 points and 7 rebounds per game in Sigler's last season at the helm.

Despite the confluence of young talent on BU's basketball roster, Sigler had not turned things around sufficiently by the winter of 1978 to hang onto his job. Nevertheless, his players regarded him as a man worthy of great respect. Sigler's higher-ups at BU clearly held him in esteem too. At Sigler's final home game, a come-from-behind overtime win over Vermont, the athletic department honored him with a plaque thanking him for his decade of service to Boston University.[15]

John Simpson spent March 1978 searching for his new basketball coach. He cast his net around the region and came up empty. Holy Cross assistant Jim Dougher said no. Army assistant Pete Gaudet said maybe. UMass head basketball coach Jack Leaman, the star of BU's legendary 1959 tournament team, gave his alma mater a hard no. But he offered Simpson a suggestion. Leaman encouraged the harried BU AD to call up his former point guard, who was making a name for himself as an assistant at Syracuse.[16]

Richard Andrew Pitino, aged twenty-five, qualified as a basketball lifer by the time John Simpson first heard his name. Born in Manhattan in September 1952, Rick was the third son of Rosario (Sal) and Charlotte

Pitino. Sal was a building inspector, and Charlotte worked at Bellevue Hospital. Both of Rick's parents commuted into the city from their home in Cambria Heights, Queens, the old stomping grounds of New York City's first legendary point guard, Bob Cousy. By the time Rick was school aged, he spent a considerable amount of time by himself, just playing basketball. The family moved out to Bayville on Long Island's North Shore before Rick finished grammar school. The teenaged Pitino attended St. Dominic High in Oyster Bay and became one of Long Island's top high school basketball players. A point guard who could shoot the lights out of any gym, Pitino's combination of talent and tenacity made him a coveted recruit. Before settling on his college selection, Pitino visited seventeen interested schools.[17]

During high school, Pitino started attending Howard Garfinkel's Five-Star Basketball Camp. Garfinkel was a basketball junkie originally from the Bronx who ran a scouting service called High School Basketball Illustrated, which informed coaches around the country about prospects from the New York metropolitan area. Pitino attended the second-ever Five-Star Camp in the summer of 1967. At the time it was a gathering of roughly 150 prep players and a handful of coaches in Honesdale, a small town in northeast Pennsylvania's coal country. Unlike other sports summer camps, which focused primarily on giving players the opportunity to play and coaches the opportunity to see potential recruits in the flesh, Five-Star was explicitly a teaching camp. Garfinkel and his like-minded compatriots—which by that time included Hubie Brown (then a high school coach in New Jersey), Bobby Knight (then coaching at Army), and Chuck Daly (then serving as an assistant at Duke)—built the camp experience around a series of stations where players worked on improving the particulars of their game: dribbling, bounce passes, footwork, one-on-one moves. Five-Star instructors broke the game down into its component parts and taught campers to play basketball with a cerebral physicality.[18] "We'd sit on the cement and listen to them [Garfinkel and Hubie Brown]. It was riveting. Their passion, their fundamentals, the way they taught, the way they motivated was incredible," Pitino said in his Basketball Hall of Fame induction speech, paying tribute to two of his most significant mentors.[19]

This fundamentals-first, building-from-the-ground-up approach influenced not only the young Pitino, who became arguably Garfinkel's most famous disciple, but also several generations of players and coaches. Over the next four decades future coaching legends like Pitino, John Calipari, and Billy Donovan, as well as future NBA greats like Michael Jordan, LeBron James, and Patrick Ewing, learned to ply their trade at Five-Star. Invites to the camp, which later relocated to the campus of Robert Morris University (located conveniently next to the Pittsburgh airport), became a veritable golden ticket for high school players. It gave them the opportunity not only to learn from the best, but also to play against the best. "The Five-Star Family" and its accompanying network became basketball's most esteemed pipeline.[20]

The influence of Garfinkel and Five-Star on Pitino was evident almost immediately. As a teenager, Pitino displayed the kind of on-court awareness that earned him the "coach on the floor" moniker from every coach who ever had him on his roster. The marathon practices and focus on the teaching of minute details, which became Pitino's trademark, emerged from the Long Islander's experiences at Five-Star.

The reputation Pitino won at summer camp and on the courts of Nassau County got the attention of Jack Leaman's UMass program. The Redmen (rechristened "Minutemen" in 1972) were running roughshod over the Yankee Conference, winning at least a share of the league title in 1968, 1969, and 1970. Long Island was well-trod recruiting turf for UMass. In 1969–1970, a 6'6" sophomore from East Meadow, New York led Massachusetts to yet another Yankee Conference title and a bid in the NIT. Julius Erving was no ordinary college star. "Dr. J," as he was already known, had become one of just five players in NCAA history to average more than 20 points and 20 rebounds per game for the season. Though prohibited from dunking at the time by NCAA rules, Erving's acrobatic play brought an unprecedented degree of dynamism and artistry to the game above the rim. Standing-room-only crowds jammed into UMass's dingy Curry Hicks Cage to see college basketball's most heralded player east of Westwood.

In the fall of 1970, Leaman added two more Long Island blue chippers to his roster: Pitino and Al Skinner, a tough and athletic 6'3" shooting guard from Malverne High. Freshman year, the pair drove up to Amherst together in Pitino's car.[21] Skinner and Pitino played on the freshman team that winter and faced off against the dazzling Erving only in practice. Erving was even more of a man among boys as a junior, leading UMass to a 23-4 mark and another trip to the NIT in what proved to be his final college season. The ABA granted Erving a hardship exemption, allowing him to sign on with the Virginia Squires.

When sophomores Pitino and Skinner joined the varsity squad in the fall of 1971, their fortunes skewed in different directions. Skinner started immediately at shooting guard and became one of the team's best players. As a sophomore, Skinner finished second in scoring and led the team in rebounds despite standing only 6'3". In all three years of his varsity career, Skinner earned All—Yankee Conference honors. Pitino, on the other hand, sat mostly on the bench. He entered fall practice with all of the bravado and bluster he displayed in later years as a head coach, telling anyone who would listen that he was going to be the starting point guard. Leaman stayed with his incumbent point guard, senior Mike Pagliara, instead. Pitino declared war on Pagliara in practice, continually upping the ante until the two got into a fistfight during a January 1972 intersquad scrimmage. Pagliara broke his finger in the fight, and Leaman suspended Pitino for the rest of the season.

Pitino spent almost the entire calendar year of 1972 in Leaman's doghouse, eventually earning his way back into the coach's good graces. A more mature Pitino, now a junior, took over as UMass's starting point guard. Unlike in his high school days, Pitino's job was not to score. He was the distributor and shepherd of Jack Leaman's ball-control offense. Pitino rarely shot the ball, and the team still won. With Pitino setting the table, 21-7 UMass returned to the top of the Yankee Conference in 1972–1973 after a mediocre 1971–1972 campaign. The now Minutemen returned to the NIT, where they advanced to the quarterfinals. In his senior year Pitino captained a UMass team that again won the Yankee Conference and scored another trip to the NIT. At the time of his graduation, Pitino held the school's career record for assists.[22] "Jack [Leaman] had a certain style of play that you had to conform to, and it proved to be very successful. You had to be tough defensively. On offense, you've got to be willing to control the ball," Skinner said. "The way he [Pitino] wanted to play and the way he was asked to play were two different things. He didn't have the freedom that maybe he would have liked to have had. I think we all conformed to do what was best for the team."[23]

After college, Skinner spent the next six seasons in the ABA and NBA. As a member of the ABA's New York Nets, Skinner started alongside college teammate Julius Erving on the 1976 ABA champions. While Skinner had been a late-round pick of the Boston Celtics, Pitino had gone undrafted. Instead of pursuing offers to play overseas, Pitino got right into coaching. He accepted a graduate assistant position at the University of Hawaii, working for a twenty-eight-year-old head coach named Bruce O'Neil. Pitino impressed both as a recruiter and a teacher of the game at Hawaii. He plied his contacts at Five-Star, where he became a counselor, and in the tri-state area to build a recruiting pipeline from New York to Honolulu. Pleased with the results, O'Neil made Pitino a full-time assistant for the Rainbow Warriors, but O'Neil's tenure proved short lived. O'Neil got caught up in a series of recruiting scandals and was fired late in the losing 1975–1976 season. Pitino took over as interim coach down the stretch and posted a 2-4 mark. Hawaii ended up on probation as a result of the charges, which included accusations that Pitino provided three players with free airline tickets from New York to Hawaii, a charge he vehemently denied.[24]

Pitino returned to New York that spring on the lookout for a job. After a few anxious weeks he received a phone call from Syracuse's brand-new head coach, Jim Boeheim. The call from a Five-Star brethren came the night before Pitino's wedding. After years together, Pitino would be marrying his high school sweetheart, Joanne Minardi. Boeheim and Pitino agreed to meet up the next day, April 3, 1976, in the lobby of the Americana Hotel in Midtown Manhattan between the ceremony and the reception.[25] When Boeheim arrived, he called up to Pitino in his hotel room and told the groom he needed twenty minutes of his time. Four hours later Pitino had the job, had postponed his honeymoon, and told his wife they were headed for Syracuse. The new Syracuse assistant immediately hit the recruiting trail with Boeheim. In the first week, the pair signed two future All—Big East performers: forward Louis Orr and center Roosevelt Bouie.[26]

For the next two seasons, Boeheim, Pitino, and Boeheim's old Syracuse classmate Bernie Fine formed what was almost certainly the best young coaching staff in the country. The Orangemen won a school record twenty-six games in 1976–1977, finished sixth in the final AP Poll, and reached the Sweet Sixteen. They followed it up with a twenty-two-win season and another trip to the NCAA Tournament. In addition to being Boeheim's advance man in recruiting, Pitino oversaw the institution of a lockdown man-to-man defense at Syracuse to complement the Orangemen's free-wheeling offense. Syracuse was already well known for its impenetrable

2–3 zone, but during Pitino's tenure feisty guards like Hal Cohen, Ross Kindel, Larry Kelly, and Jim Williams frequently flexed to a man-to-man that confronted the opposition directly.

"I did it for the experience," Rick Pitino later told the *Globe*'s Michael Madden. "I went to BU so I could go through the ropes of being interviewed." Boeheim discouraged him from even considering the BU job, which the Syracuse coach regarded as one of the worst in the East. Go take the interview, Boeheim advised Pitino, but wait for a better job to open before taking the leap. Boeheim didn't have to tell Pitino about BU. He'd seen it firsthand as a player at UMass. "I remember playing against BU and seeing 50 people in the stands and recalling how nobody seemed to care about the sport," he told Madden.[27]

"You come highly recommended by a coach who was a great player for us here named Jack Leaman," John Simpson told Pitino in their first phone conversation in March 1978.[28] The AD had failed to lure a current Division I coach to Comm Ave. Thus his focus had shifted to Division I assistants like Pitino with strong backgrounds in recruiting rather than a Division II coach unfamiliar with such pitched battles for players. Simpson's desire to build up the Terrier basketball program and Pitino's superlative skills as a salesman served the young coach well the afternoon of their first face-to-face meeting. The interview turned rapidly into a negotiation. Simpson agreed to offer BU basketball fifteen full scholarships, the maximum allowable under NCAA rules. Previously, Sigler had worked with six scholarships.[29] Simpson offered Pitino a $20,000 recruiting budget, which was hardly the stuff of big-time programs but was significant within the context of New England college basketball. It was also three times as much as the previous coaching staff had received annually. The initially skeptical Pitino was suddenly ready to move his family to Massachusetts.[30]

Pitino's salary was slotted at $17,500 per year—certainly more than Sigler had made as head coach but certainly less than Pitino made as an assistant in central New York. The young coach would be able to make more money in the summertime by hosting a basketball camp—a perk that was becoming ever more common in the college coaching ranks. Simpson even threw in a car, a Renault Le Car. It was hardly the most comfortable vehicle for the 6-foot-tall Pitino, but this "windup toy," as he later described the subcompact, was a lot better than Roy Sigler's complimentary car, which didn't exist.[31]

A four-line story in the sports section of the March 31, 1978, *Globe* revealed that Boston University would name twenty-five-year-old Rick Pitino its head basketball coach at an 11 a.m. press conference at the Case Center. In two of the first three stories in the BU student newspaper, the writers misspelled his name as "Petino."[32]

Simpson made it clear at the introductory press conference that he was making an investment in BU basketball with the hiring of Pitino. Sigler had functioned on a shoestring budget, similar to other unheralded New England college programs. Pitino would work with a beefed-up budget, though by any measure not an especially beefy one. And he would be expected to win.

The cocksure attitude that became Pitino's signature was on full display at the press conference. "I hope we can rival the hockey program here," Pitino announced less than a week after Jack Parker's BU Terriers defeated archrival BC to win the NCAA championship.[33] Parker's first championship team featured four future members of the 1980 "Miracle on Ice" U.S. Olympic team, including Team USA's two best known players, team captain Mike Eruzione and goaltender Jim Craig. "We intend to build the program to the point where we can play Boston College, Holy Cross, and Providence," Pitino explained, citing New England's top three college programs at the time. "We'll be very well disciplined as a team. I can tell you that. I intend to motivate players too," Pitino stated at the presser, foreshadowing the rigors that returning players and incoming recruits would face in the fall.[34]

While some in the Boston basketball orbit found Pitino's bravado refreshing, he irritated the hell out of others. "He was very cocky and very arrogant," longtime WCVB sports anchor Mike Lynch said. "His claim to fame was that he'd played on the same team with Dr. J at UMass. Well, Rick Pitino can't do any of the physical things that Dr. J can. That was the marketing point, the selling point for the people over at BU to come see him."[35]

Pitino hired Bill Burke, who had just guided Nazareth High School in Brooklyn to a New York City championship, and former BU basketball great Kevin Thomas as his assistant coaches. He brought in recent University of Maine standout Bobby Warner as his graduate assistant. He chose not to retain Ed Leibowitz, who had followed Simpson's instructions and continued to pound the pavement for recruits even after Sigler's resignation. Considering his success in recruiting with just six available scholarships and essentially no budget, Leibowitz held out hope that he'd find a place on Pitino's staff.[36] "He [Pitino] interviewed me for less than half an hour and let me know I wouldn't be retained. I had known him superficially in New York/New Jersey, but I wasn't his friend or one of his guys. I wasn't a Five-Star/Howard Garfinkel guy," Ed Leibowitz said.[37] Leibowitz later transformed Massachusetts Bay Community College into a nationally ranked junior college program.

"I don't think it is going to be difficult to recruit players to Boston University," Pitino said at his introductory press conference.[38] The statement came straight out of the make-your-success-seem-effortless playbook and was itself a pitch to potential recruits. The confidence Pitino showed in the direction of his basketball program proved a great enticement to interested players. Pitino planned to pursue players he'd recruited to Syracuse but who had not yet committed to the school. In a clear demonstration of his recruiting prowess, Pitino delivered almost immediately on his promise to sign top-notch players at BU.

Three plum recruits, all of whom Pitino had recruited for Syracuse, signed on as the new coach's first recruiting class. Johnnie Ray Wall, a hyper-athletic 6'3" guard who had been named Albany, New York's prep "Player of the Decade"; Gene Jones, a heavily recruited 6'3" guard from Virginia Beach who had impressed at the previous summer's Five-Star Camp; and John Teague, a 6'4" forward from Anderson, Indiana, who had dominated at the 1978 Boston Shootout, went from potential Orangemen to brand-new BU Terriers.

"[Johnnie Ray Wall] was probably one of the best athletes I've ever seen," his classmate John Teague said. "He could jump out of the gym, he was fast as lightning, had great ball handling skills, and was a decent shooter. He was probably the fastest player on the team."[39] Wall had been a multi-sport superstar at Albany High School. He was said to possess a thirty-eight-inch vertical and had received as many Division I football offers as basketball ones. Following his college basketball career, he even received a tryout with the New England Patriots.[40]

Pitino spotted John Teague at the 1978 Boston Shootout. He was playing for an all-star team from Indiana coached by former Boston Celtic Bill Dinwiddie. Teague had signed a letter of intent to play at Butler University, but Dinwiddie convinced his young star that he could still talk to the Boston University coach. Teague powered his way onto the all-tournament team and threw down enough spectacular dunks in competition to earn second place in the slam dunk contest, despite not participating in the event because he was too sore after the games to compete.

Teague flew home from the Shootout, still interested in BU but uncertain of his future.[41] "When I got home, there was an assistant coach [Burke] from Boston University that was literally waiting on my doorstep," Teague said. "The assistant coach stayed there for like two or three days and wined and dined me and my family and talked to my parents about me attending Boston University. He left, and two days later another assistant coach [Thomas] showed up. And he talked to my family for another day or two. And then he left, and Pitino showed up the following week."[42] After receiving all of this attention, Teague spoke with his father about his future. His father said it was his son's decision, but it was obvious which school was more interested. BU had spent weeks doing everything imaginable to sign him, while Butler's head coach had yet to come for a visit, despite living just forty miles away. Teague succumb to Pitino's full court press and changed his commitment to BU.[43]

Gene Jones, who possessed a deadly jump shot, said, "Rick started recruiting me at Syracuse. He and Coach Boeheim had come to my house. I was signed, sealed, delivered going to Syracuse. Then Howard Garfinkel called and said Rick was going to Boston and I should give it a look."[44]

Jones visited BU at the same time as Cincinnati high school standout Jay Twyman. The pair had become friends at Five-Star. When they parted ways after an enjoyable visit, both players thought they were headed to BU. Jones ended up deciding on Boston while Twyman accepted an offer from Frank McGuire's powerhouse South Carolina program. Before changing his commitment, Jones made a call to central New York. "I talked to Coach Boeheim, and he gave me the OK," Jones recalled.[45]

Heading into the fall of 1978, Rick Pitino had the building blocks for a bright future—a robust recruiting class and a handful of strong returning players. The big question was whether the young coach could mold these young men into a winning team.

3

Once Again, Not That Much Is Expected of the Eagles *(Williams)*

Toward the tail end of *Goodfellas*, Henry Hill (played by Ray Liotta) and his associates shoot the breeze as they prepare to whack Morrie the wig dealer (real name Martin Krugman, played by Chuck Low). Morrie, who moonlights as a bookmaker, has worn out his welcome with Hill's crew. He's been pressing too hard for his cut from the Lufthansa heist. He also owes the crew a considerable amount of money.

"Did you hear about the points we were shaving up in Boston?" Morrie says as he sits down in the front seat of a freezing Cadillac on a cold winter's night with Tommy Desimone (played by Joe Pesci), seated behind him. Before Morrie can tease out the details of a plot involving three Boston College basketball players, two small-time bookie brothers in Pittsburgh, a friend of theirs who knows a guy in New York, Hill, and, eventually, the lion's share of the Lucchese crime family, a screwdriver is impaled through the back of Morrie's head by Pesci's character.

The yarn that Morrie was starting to spin began in the summer of 1978. Rocco Perla, a small-time hustler in Pittsburgh, renewed his acquaintance with a high school classmate named Rick Kuhn. Kuhn was a senior forward on the Boston College men's basketball team who played sparingly. Rocco and his brother Tony convinced Kuhn that they could all make a lot of money if they manipulated the scores of BC's basketball games that season. If BC won close when they were heavily favored or lost big when they were an underdog, the Perlas could place sure bets on the games and pay off the players who helped them out. Kuhn allegedly brought teammates Jim Sweeney (BC's starting point guard) and Ernie Cobb (the Eagles' leading scorer) in on the scheme.

In the meantime the Perla brothers tried to maximize their windfall by calling on a real-deal gangster friend of theirs named Paul Mazzei.

Mazzei was a Pittsburgh-based drug dealer with connections to the New York mob—namely, Henry Hill, whom he had befriended during a stint in federal prison. Hill turned the small-time hustle into an operation with the full backing of the Lucchese crime family. Lucchese boss Paul Vario charged Hill and Jimmy "the Gent" Burke (played by Robert DeNiro in *Goodfellas*) with organizing the scheme. Hill and his crew placed bets on select BC basketball games with bookmakers across the country so as not to raise suspicion by making large wagers on seemingly nondescript college games. In November 1978 Hill traveled to Boston to meet with the Perlas, Mazzei, Kuhn, and Sweeney. Together they coordinated the payments to the players and figured out which games on BC's schedule to manipulate.

According to federal prosecutors, nine games were affected by the point-shaving scheme. Depending on whom you ask, the parties involved made either a few hundred, a few thousand, or a few hundred thousand dollars as a result. The degree to which the plot affected BC's overall performance that winter also remains a matter of dispute.

Whatever the impact, Boston College was a much-improved team in 1978–1979. The Eagles went 21-9, their best team in five years. BC's season ended in a game not affected by the scheme—a 91–74 shellacking at the hands of UConn in the ECAC playoffs, then the only route for New England teams to the NCAA Tournament. Ernie Cobb averaged 21.3 points per game that season, earned All-East honors, and finished his career as BC's third-leading all-time scorer. Jim Sweeney led the team in assists in 1978–1979 and finished his college career in 1980 as the school's third-leading assist man. Rick Kuhn played less than ten minutes per game as a senior and averaged just 3.5 points.

By November 1980, the events of the winter of 1978–1979 all seemed in the past. Kuhn, Sweeney, and Cobb had graduated and gone their separate ways. Boston College was preparing for a season that culminated in the team's first Big East regular season title and a trip to the Sweet Sixteen. Few outside the circle of men involved in the plot were even privy to what had happened two winters earlier.

That was the case until Hill was arrested in late 1980 on charges of drug trafficking and criminal conspiracy for his role in the $6 million Lufthansa heist in December 1978, then the largest robbery in U.S. history. Fearing that his former associates had a contract on his life, Hill turned state's evidence and told federal investigators about a number of crimes, including the point-shaving plot at Boston College, leading to the indictments of Mazzei, Burke, Kuhn, the Perla brothers, and eventually Cobb (the only person charged in the case who was acquitted). Sweeney testified against the accused. For the next three years, the trials of those involved in the plan were national news stories. In Boston, the point-shaving trials provided local newspapers with years' worth of front-page fodder. The stories of Kuhn, Sweeney, and Cobb received far more coverage than BC basketball ever did locally for its on-court successes or failures.

In the shadow of the point-shaving scandal, the game's biggest in three decades, Dr. Tom Davis was building Boston College up into a legitimate basketball power. Quietly. Despite its deserved reputation as "America's College Town," Boston is not a college sports town in the way that Ann Arbor, Michigan, or Columbus, Ohio, or Tuscaloosa, Alabama, is. In more conventional college towns, big-time amateur athletics are the only game around. Boston is a big city with big-city amenities, including its beloved professional sports teams. The Bruins, Celtics, and Red Sox all have massive, fervent fan bases that have followed the teams closely for generations through the city's ever-pugnacious print and broadcast media. At the time of the point-shaving scandal, the now ever-present Patriots were a rinky-dink, underfunded operation playing at an erector-set stadium down in Foxboro. But they still got exponentially more coverage than even the best local college teams.

In Boston, college sports programs enjoy a niche following that consists primarily of their students and alumni. This was particularly true of college basketball. No matter how good the local teams were, their success paled in comparison to that of the Celtics, who were in the process during the early 1980s of renewing their multi-decade professional basketball dynasty. "Unfortunately, the Boston College job was not a destination," WCVB's Mike Lynch said. "It was a launching pad. [If] you stay here in Boston, you're competing against the Celtics and every other professional team. It has been a place where you prove you can compete at the highest level."[1]

Destination or not, the Boston College job was a great opportunity for thirty-nine-year-old Tom Davis. Davis took over in Chestnut Hill in 1977, replacing Bob Zuffalato, whose BC clubs had struggled to 9-17 and 8-18 finishes the two previous seasons. Davis had grown up in Wisconsin and played college ball at tiny Wisconsin-Platteville. He spent most of the 1960s as a high school history teacher and basketball coach in Milledgeville, Illinois, and later in Portage, Wisconsin. Davis had won big in high school, adopting a pressing-style defense and up-tempo offense that made use of the depth on his rosters at Portage. Davis parlayed his intellect and acumen as a basketball coach into a graduate assistant position at the University of Maryland under Frank Fellows while working on a doctorate in history.

During his tenure at Maryland, Davis befriended Gary Williams, who had been a cerebral and tough starting point guard for the Terps under Fellows's predecessor, Bud Millikan. Millikan retired after the 1966–1967 season, Williams's senior year. Like Davis, Williams took a graduate assistant position under Fellows. Neither Davis nor Williams was long for College Park. Davis snagged an assistant's job at American University. Williams returned home to Camden County, New Jersey, taking a job teaching social studies and coaching basketball at Woodrow Wilson High School in the city of Camden.

The twenty-four-year-old Williams had grown up just east of Camden in Collingswood, a blue-collar borough just outside the hard-scrabble city best known as the home of Campbell's Soup. Williams had been a self-described latchkey kid. His mother left the family while he was in middle school, and his father worked as a check sorter at the Federal Reserve Bank in nearby Philadelphia. By the time he was in high school, Williams had made a second home for himself at the local high school gymnasium and adopted his head coach, John Smith, as a surrogate father. Williams became one of New Jersey's most heralded high school guards of the early 1960s, earning scholarship offers from several collegiate programs in the Mid-Atlantic states. Williams had his heart set on the University of Pennsylvania, one of Philadelphia's Big 5 basketball powers, but he didn't have the grades to get into the Ivy League school. So he settled on Bud Millikan and Maryland, which proved to be an excellent fit for the tenacious young guard.

"You couldn't play for Bud Millikan unless you were willing to play hard on the defensive end of the court. In practice, we would practice two and a half hours on defense and ten minutes on offense," Williams wrote.[2] While Bud Millikan's Maryland teams played conservatively on offense, walking the ball up the court and getting into a series of sets, Williams favored an offensive approach that was being developed by his friend Tom Davis. The "flex" or "zone" offense pioneered by Davis and Williams was built around the continuous motion of all five players, perpetually cutting and screening. The system creates numerous opportunities for shooters to get open looks while simultaneously wearing down opposing defenders, especially when it is combined with the pressure defense and frequent substitutions favored by both Davis and Williams.

While Davis was working at American alongside another youthful coach, Tom Young, who later brought teams at Rutgers and Old Dominion to the NCAA Tournament, Williams was rapidly earning a reputation as one of New Jersey's best prep coaches. Williams's Woodrow Wilson Tigers teams were not only laden with talent—five players on his club played Division I basketball—but his Tigers' teams were also remade in his image. They adopted the defense-first style that Bud Millikan had ingrained in a generation's worth of Maryland basketball players, including Williams, who proved to be his finest disciple.[3]

After years of playing second fiddle to crosstown rival, Camden High, Woodrow Wilson High basketball became a genuine phenomenon in the state of New Jersey during the winter of 1969–1970. Williams's aggressive, pressing teams wiped the floor with their competition, including Camden High. In a city still reeling from a September 2, 1969, riot that left a fifteen-year-old girl and a Camden police officer dead, the success of the Tigers was a source of civic unity. Williams's team included Black, white, and Hispanic starters, reflecting the demographics of the diverse industrial city. Equally diverse crowds, which numbered in the thousands, watched the black-and-orange-clad Tigers plow through twenty-six consecutive opponents on their way to the state title game against East Orange.[4]

More than ten thousand fans packed Convention Hall in Atlantic City for the state title game. Woodrow Wilson won the game going away, earning its first state title since 1949. A year later Williams left New Jersey for a chance to coach in the college ranks. His old friend Tom Davis had accepted the head coaching position at Lafayette College, a small, private school in northeastern Pennsylvania. Davis needed an assistant, and Williams shared his commitment to the pressing, running, and trapping style of basketball the pair had worked out at Maryland.

"I was very fortunate that Tom got me into college coaching," Gary Williams recalled. "I was a high school coach in New Jersey. I always thought that that's what I was going to be. When Tom got the Lafayette job, he called me up and said he really wanted me to be his assistant.

But there was a catch to it."[5] Lafayette's soccer coach had just resigned. The money earmarked in the athletics budget to hire Davis an assistant had just become the budget to hire a new soccer coach. Davis said that the assistant's job was Williams's for the taking if he would also agree to coach soccer, a sport that Williams had never played. Williams turned Davis down. Initially.

"Do you really think you have another way into college coaching?" Davis asked Williams.[6] The Woodrow Wilson coach had few connections within the college ranks. After some more prodding, Williams took the job. He packed up his young family and headed to Easton, Pennsylvania, accepting $2,000 a year less for the position than he had earned as a high school teacher in New Jersey.

"Believe me, the hardest thing I've ever done in coaching is the first day I walked out onto the field at soccer practice. I was twenty-five, and my seniors were like twenty-two, twenty-three," Williams remembers. "And I knew nothing. I knew basketball drills. I knew how to get into shape. I just leveled with the players and said, 'You guys've gotta help me.' And they were great. Because back then there were no scholarships for soccer either. These guys played because they loved to play and we were okay."[7] For the next five years Williams coached men's soccer at Lafayette, posting a career record of 27-37-13.

While Lafayette soccer verged on respectability under Williams, Lafayette Leopards basketball thrived under Davis and his soccer-coaching assistant. In six seasons at Lafayette (1971–1977), Davis's teams won nearly three-quarters of their games, never finished worse than second in their conference, and earned two bids to the NIT. Playing against teams with much more heralded recruits—including Temple, Delaware, St. Joseph's, and LaSalle—Lafayette outhustled, outran, and outsmarted its opposition year in and year out in the East Coast Conference.

The laconic Davis and firebrand Williams formed a superb team both on and off the court. In public they had a good cop—bad cop dynamic while in private they were co-conspirators in the creation of a new approach to the game, one that seemed simultaneously contemporary and old-fashioned. They found a way for smaller, seemingly less talented teams to frustrate larger, stronger, more heralded teams into submission.

Future University of Vermont (UVM) basketball coach Tom Brennan spent a significant amount of time with Davis and Williams during their years at Lafayette. Brennan, a former standout at the University of Georgia, lived in Easton at the time and often refereed the Leopards' intersquad scrimmages. "I used to go to the games, and it was funny because they'd both [Davis and Williams] be up, coaching, and that was when assistant coaches sat. They used to bump into each other five, six times every ten minutes, calling to somebody or coaching somebody up," Brennan said. Brennan remembered them both as "great guys" and said that even then, Gary was "every bit as intense as he appears to be, sweating right through his suits."[8]

In 1977 Davis accepted an offer to become the head coach at Boston College and brought Williams with him. The pair hit the ground running in their rebuild of the school's moribund basketball program. As Davis and Williams attempted to recruit talented players to Chestnut Hill and put their up-tempo system in place, they also worked to win over the school's alumni, who remembered a time in the not-too-distant past when the Eagles were a power in the east. "When Tom Davis was there and Gary was his assistant, those guys were good at making contact with me as a former player," former BC star Jim O'Brien remembers. "They actually gave me a complimentary membership to their cage club. They were very gracious to me."[9] As a sophomore, O'Brien starred at point guard for a Bob Cousy—coached Eagles team that reached the finals of the NIT. By the end of his run at Chestnut Hill, O'Brien held the school's assists record and had scored nearly 1,300 points. He was named New England Player of the Year as a senior and spent four seasons in the ABA. Following a brief stint as a paper salesman, O'Brien got back into basketball, serving as an assistant for Dom Perno at UConn, one of New England's top college programs in the late 1970s and early 1980s.

"Tom Davis was a very personable guy. A great recruiter. The type of guy that was tough for a mom and dad to say 'no' to," Mike Lynch said.[10] While Davis presented well to moms and dads, the none-too-secret key to Boston College's excellent recruiting in the late 1970s and early 1980s was another one of his assistant coaches, Kevin Mackey. The former coach of Don Bosco Prep in Boston's South End, Mackey was not only one of the most successful prep coaches in Boston history. He was also a known commodity in inner-city high school gyms, at city summer league games, and on urban blacktops across the Northeast. Mackey had developed a strong rapport with coaches, players, and families in many poor and predominately African American neighborhoods. It was Mackey who persuaded many inner-city kids to even consider playing ball at Boston College, a school whose demographics were largely white and affluent. Mackey recalls: "Tom said to me—he was very honest—'Kevin, I do the coaching, and I need someone to get me the players.' I said Tom, 'I'll be happy to do it.' And so we're off to the races."[11]

While Williams assisted Davis with the Xs and Os as he had at Lafayette, Mackey convinced a number of highly talented, if not heavily recruited, players to come to Chestnut Hill.

"When I began recruiting, the big high school programs told me, 'You look at my third, fourth, and fifth players.' And I said, 'Well, what's wrong with your first and second player?'" Mackey said.[12] Coaches told him that BC was a hockey and football school. Mackey persisted. He pitched young men on the quality education they'd receive at Boston College and the school's fantastic location. When BC joined the new Big East basketball conference, it gave Mackey another tool in recruiting players, particularly those who had been overlooked by other major programs and who wanted to compete at the highest level.

In the late 1970s and early 1980s Mackey pounded the pavement all along the Northeast corridor in search of elite if often overlooked talent. He provided Davis with a roster capable of competing for championships in what emerged as college basketball's best conference for the duration of the next decade. He signed a speedy and cerebral guard from Boston's English High School named Dwan Chandler; a rugged forward from New Hampshire named Rich Shrigley; a versatile, athletic forward from Elizabeth, New Jersey, named Burnett Adams; a tenacious bulldog of a defender from the Bronx named Terrence Talley; Stu Primus, a chiseled and high-flying guard from Lynn, Massachusetts' Classical High School who was just as heavily recruited by BC's football team as its basketball program; and a 6'9" deadeye shooter originally from England named Martin Clark.

The aforementioned players in and of themselves could have cemented Kevin Mackey's reputation as a fantastic recruiter. But his prowess was made most evident by the haul of players he got out of the Nutmeg State. Four Mackey recruits from Connecticut went on to star for the Eagles in the early 1980s, forming the core of the BC clubs that excelled every March over the next half-decade. All four players from this "Connecticut Connection" also went on to suit up in the NBA. Two of them came out of rough-and-tumble Bridgeport, Connecticut. The first member of Mackey's Bridgeport tandem was a chiseled 6'8" power forward out of Bassick High named John Garris, who transferred from Michigan after sitting on the bench for two seasons. The other was John Bagley, a 6'0" guard from Warren Harding High who combined toughness, athleticism, and on-court smarts. Mackey also brought in Jay Murphy, a sweet-shooting 6'11" southpaw from Meriden, Connecticut, whom other top programs thought was too slight for the big time. The most intriguing of Mackey's signings was a 5'10" guard from Hartford named Michael Adams, who had excelled as a boxer in his youth. Adams had been one of Connecticut's top prep players but scared away scouts with his lack of stature and unorthodox shooting style. Mackey convinced Davis to take a chance on him, and it soon paid off handsomely.

"A lot of kids related well with him [Mackey]. He knew what a city kid needed to be nurtured into a young man," Stu Primus said.[13] Given Boston College's stringent entrance requirements, this haul of talent constituted an embarrassment of riches. Every coach before or since Davis at BC has complained of the difficulty of getting potential recruits admitted to the Jesuit school. Nevertheless, talent on its own does not win basketball games. It took the efforts of Davis and his top assistant, Williams, to turn this cadre of talent into a winning team.

"Tom [Davis] was brilliant. A detail guy, very thorough in his preparations. Thorough in his practice planning. He was really a pioneer in terms of the things he did on the basketball court," Paul Brazeau said.[14] Brazeau worked for the BC basketball program as an undergraduate under Tom Davis and later became an assistant coach at his alma mater under Gary Williams and Jim O'Brien. "Technically I probably learned as much basketball being coached by Tom Davis as I did from any coach that I had throughout my career," Jay Murphy said.[15]

"Tom [Davis] was a genius, strategy-wise. He was way ahead of everybody. He worked very, very hard at it, and he was a great teacher," Kevin Mackey said. "And Tom was a lot tougher than people realized in practice and in private. He's a wonderful guy. He was great to me. But he was no pushover, and the kids knew that. And they responded to him. And the style of play, with the pressure, and the reverse action continuity on offense, the full court pressure defensively, the substitutions. No one else had that formula."[16]

"He [Davis] was a tough-minded coach. Very knowledgeable of the game. Very fair, and he knew his stuff," Michael Adams said.[17]

Tom Davis's success as a teacher of basketball at Boston College was bolstered in large part by his longtime assistant, Gary Williams, who was a similarly gifted practitioner of the game. What Mackey was to recruiting, Williams was to installing the system that had succeeded so spectacularly at Lafayette. Gary Williams put his charges through the ropes, physically and mentally, teaching them a high-pressure defensive system that consisted largely of pressing and trapping opponents before they reached half-court. Before BC even started basketball camp, the coaching staff assigned players a grueling fall running program that had them ready to sprint up and down the court at similarly intense practices, which then made game days seem like days off by comparison.

"I was always the type of coach that liked to play up-tempo. Press quite a bit. Look to run when you get a rebound," Williams recalls.[18] On the offensive end, Williams and Davis put in place the "zone offense," which enabled BC's speedy and sturdy guards to dribble penetrate opposing defenses, create open shots for the Eagles' post players, and wear down opposing defenses with the considerable amount of energy it took to contain such an attack. "Gary [Williams] was a fun guy, a personable guy, an excited guy. Very intense, much as he was as a head coach," Brazeau said of Williams as an assistant.[19]

The virtues of the system, the players, and the culture that Davis, Williams, and Mackey put in place at Boston College soon showed up on the court. In their first year at Chestnut Hill, the Eagles nearly doubled their win total to fifteen. Basketball insiders also took note of the exciting, aggressive new style of play BC adopted that season. Boston College averaged nearly 83 points per game in Davis's first year, nearly 10 more than the previous season. This inaugurated an era of BC basketball that included some of the country's highest scoring teams, year in and year out. After the 1977–1978 season, Williams returned to the DC metro area, accepting the head coaching position at American University, his mentor's old stomping grounds. Davis and company kept building at BC, winning twenty-one games in the infamous 1978–1979 season.

In 1979, Boston College became a charter member of the Big East Conference. It surprised much of the basketball cognoscenti that the fledgling basketball-centric league would take a flier on a program that had only recently shown its muster on the court. Those in the know said BC only got a spot in the Big East because it gave the league easy access to the Boston Garden, thus achieving conference commissioner Dave Gavitt's stated goal of playing the league's games in the Northeast's largest and most prestigious arenas.

In 1979–1980, most of the eastern basketball press picked the Eagles last in the new league. Instead they finished fifth out of nine teams and played in the NIT, their first postseason appearance in six seasons. The four teams that finished ahead of the Eagles all made the NCAA Tournament. The next year, 1980–1981, the Eagles were again picked for the bottom of the Big East. After news of the point-shaving scandal broke, fans on the road sprayed Barbasol on the BC team and threw disposable razors at them when they came on and off the floor. Nevertheless, BC won the Big East regular season championship, earned a bid to the NCAA Tournament, and made it to the Sweet Sixteen. In 1981–1982, they returned to the NCAA Tournament and fought their way to the Final Eight. Every success they had further ingrained an "overachievers" label that print and broadcast journalists across the country had inscribed on Tom Davis and the Boston College basketball team.

"They were always an underdog team that was underestimated a little bit," Paul Brazeau said. "They were good players that took a lot of pride. They practiced hard. They were a good group of guys."[20] Despite all their success, it was tough for this team to get much attention, even in the Boston press, aside from the ongoing coverage of Rick Kuhn's federal trial. "The problem is," Gary Williams said of his time in Boston, "there's so much going on, you're never going to be the whole show."[21] Williams felt that sportswriters treated BC basketball fairly during his time in the city, but the team, despite its Big East pedigree, was always an afterthought when compared to Boston's professional clubs.

The idea that Dr. Tom Davis consistently coached up his band of under-achievers into a fearsome force come March rubbed some of his players the wrong way.

"The one thing about Davis is he always told people, 'Well, we don't have a lot of talent' and all that nonsense. And told us to keep expectations down. But basically it was self-serving for him. We won two Big East [regular season] championships. We made it to the Final Eight. You don't do that with so-so talent," Burnett Adams said.[22] Adams said that he was one of several players on BC's roster during the early 1980s who would have been better served playing elsewhere. He, for one, did not flourish as he thought he should have in a system he came to regard as rigid and unconducive to his development as a player. Adams went on to star overseas after his career at BC, where he was a part-time player valued primarily for his defensive and shot-blocking abilities. "[Davis] turned a lot of great athletes into robots. Instead of a more fluid type of offense, he ran a more controlled offense. Bounce pass. Bounce pass. I don't think he took advantage of the athletes that were there," Adams said.[23]

Tom Davis is certainly guilty of promoting the bounce pass, which he regarded as safer than chest passes when working the ball into the low post. But his success at BC speaks for itself, notwithstanding criticism of the coach's embrace of the "underachiever" label. That success, though, did not necessarily breed warmth between Davis and a number of his players. While "Dr. Tom" maintained cordial relationships with the press, some of his players regarded him as frosty and distant. Others looked more favorably on Davis's reserved demeanor.

"There was no personality. We found out by accident that [Davis] lived maybe a half mile up Comm[onwealth] Ave. from Boston College. There was no real connection with him other than Xs and Os," Stu Primus said.[24]

"He insisted on the 'Dr. Tom' title. Davis was pretty stand-offish," recalls Mike Rofles, who covered the Eagles for *The Heights*, BC's student-run newspaper.[25]

"He was a very private guy," said Matt Gianatassio, who served as a manager for the BC basketball team and had a very different view of Davis. "Kept a lot to himself. He was definitely a businesslike guy. I got along very well with him."[26] On several occasions, Gianatassio babysat for Davis's son, Keno, who went on to his own successful head coaching career at Drake, Providence, and Central Michigan.

"Tom Davis was a typical head coach," in Jay Murphy's estimation. "He was business but let you relax a little bit when the time was right."[27]

While Tom Davis rebuilt BC into an eastern power, Williams was creating a mid-Atlantic power at American University, a school that played its home games at an armory in Arlington, Virginia, built during the Cleveland administration.[28] Playing in the same East Coast Conference he'd coached in at Lafayette, Williams brought the pressure defense, fast-breaking offense, and mid-Atlantic recruiting connections he'd cultivated over the previous decade to American. Results came quickly. In 1980–1981, Williams's third season on the job, American won the East Coast Conference's regular season championship and earned a bid to the NIT. In 1981–1982, the American University Eagles won another twenty-one games and returned to the NIT. In the aftermath of the season, Duquesne, Seton Hall, and UNC-Charlotte all offered Williams their head coaching jobs.[29]

While Williams fielded offers from programs up and down the East Coast, Boston College made its deepest run yet into March. An eighth-seeded BC team had ousted San Francisco, DePaul, and Kansas State en route to the Midwest Regional Final against Clyde Drexler, Hakeem Olajuwon, and a high-flying, fast-breaking Houston Cougars team that was soon to be immortalized as "Phi Slama Jama."

"I don't think they really knew anything about us," Burnett Adams said of the favored San Francisco Dons team that BC played in the opening round. San Francisco featured a 7-foot force named Wallace Bryant and guard Quinton Dailey, who was one of the country's leading scorers. The Chicago Bulls made Dailey a lottery pick in the June 1982 draft. "We were a much more well-rounded team than they were. We were much deeper than they were. It wasn't a shock when we beat them," Adams said.[30] BC's pressing defense frustrated the Dons all evening. While Dailey got his 28 points, Bryant was held to just 10. Previously little-known freshman guard Michael Adams proved especially disruptive as the Dons tried to navigate BC's traps and press. While John Bagley, BC's top scorer and on-court leader, had foul trouble all evening, his teammates picked up the slack offensively, shooting better than 60 percent from the field. The Eagles outlasted the Dons, 70–66.

It was a shock to almost everyone not associated with the BC basketball program that the Eagles knocked off DePaul, the number-one seed in the Midwest region and the number-two-ranked team in the country. Ray Meyer's DePaul Blue Demons hadn't lost since December. All-American 6'9″ power forward Terry Cummings had been all but unstoppable that winter. Averaging nearly 22 points per game (ppg) and 12 rebounds, Cummings was a genuinely immovable force in the low post. Once again, Boston College, regarded by the basketball commentariat as too small to compete with Cummings and his crew, benefitted from being underestimated.

"I later found out through a friend that they [DePaul] didn't even have a scouting report on us," Burnett Adams said. "I was told that they had a footnote on Bagley. I don't think they took us seriously. They had no idea who Michael Adams was. My friend there said they just had a few scribbled notes. They didn't even prepare for us."[31] Bagley—who Ray Meyer later said he'd never seen score a basket on film—led BC with 25 points, while the comparably anonymous Adams added 21. While few Eagles fans made their way to Dallas's Reunion Arena for the game, Boston College quickly won over the roughly thirteen thousand in attendance with its aggressive style of play. Garris, Shrigley, Murphy, and Burnett Adams held Cummings in check, keeping him to 20 points, while much of the Blue Demons' starting five languished in foul trouble. By the time BC forced its twentieth turnover of the game with its patented press, the Eagles had the game well in hand. Boston College won, 82–75.

Against Kansas State, Michael Adams came off the bench and made his presence further known to a national audience. While the Wildcats focused on Bagley, Adams took over the game, scoring 11 of his game-high 20 points in the second half and sealing the 69–65 win with a late game steal. Tom Davis and the Eagles found themselves one win at St. Louis's Checkerdome away from a trip to the Final Four. "We saw cameras but didn't realize we were being watched across the country and perhaps across the world. I think a lot of us didn't understand the significance of it, and I think that was a good thing because there was no real pressure. There were no real nerves because we were seeing ourselves and not understanding the moment," Stu Primus said.[32]

On March 21, 1982, eighth-seeded Boston College played sixth-seeded Houston for a trip to the Final Four. The battle between the upstart teams was a full-on fast break for most of the game. Bagley led the charge for BC, dropping in 26 points in a full forty minutes of action. In the end, Houston outgunned BC, 99–92, in a game that many observers regarded as the most exciting of the 1982 tournament. BC's undoing that afternoon was a reserve freshman guard named Reid Gettys. When Boston College got into foul trouble, Houston coach Guy Lewis inserted Gettys, an unparalleled foul shooter, into the lineup. Gettys finished off the Eagles by hitting 10 consecutive free throws late in the game.

In defeat, Davis was none too happy with Bruce Pearl, his senior student manager. Pearl, who went on to coach UW-Milwaukee, Tennessee, and Auburn to the NCAA Tournament, had displayed enough basketball smarts during his time at BC to take on the role of scouting the Eagles' upcoming opponents.

"I remember getting back on a chartered plane, and Tom Davis was standing at the door. We were like, 'Uh oh. Oh shit. What's going on?' And we heard this argument. Bruce Pearl had given us the scouting report on Reid Gettys. Tom Davis went up to him and said, 'You've got to walk home from this plane after that scouting report,'" Stu Primus said. Primus said the flight home was made even more unpleasant by the huge storm they got caught up in, which caused the plane to make substantial dips on several occasions.[33]

On March 29, the *Globe*'s Lesley Visser broke the story that Tom Davis had been offered the vacant head coaching job at Stanford, a change of scenery that the forty-three-year-old coach was strongly considering. Stanford, which was coming off a 7-20 season, offered to pay Davis a reported $150,000 annually, nearly twice what he was making in Boston. Davis apparently relished the idea of rebuilding yet another program. The University of Wisconsin, the flagship university in Davis's home state, was also apparently seeking out his services as head basketball coach.[34]

According to Visser and several subsequent accounts, the continuing fallout from the point-shaving scandal remained a significant source of distress in Davis's life, even though Davis, the vast majority of players in his program, and the BC athletic department had nothing to do with the scheme. Davis had apparently nearly resigned his post in early 1981 after *Sports Illustrated* published a cover story entitled "Anatomy of a Scandal," authored by Henry Hill with the assistance of Douglas Looney, which gave the mobsters' blow-by-blow account of the plot.[35]

On April 1, Stanford announced that Tom Davis would be its new basketball coach. Davis never explained in detail his decision-making process other than to say that he thought that he and his family needed a change. BC athletic director Bill Flynn spoke in a similarly cagey fashion, declaring that it wasn't any one reason that led to Davis's departure. "I think he was also unhappy during the scandal," Flynn admitted. "How much [his departure] had to do with that, I don't know."[36] According to Flynn, he and Davis had discussed the possibility of Davis's leaving Boston College just two months earlier, not long after a federal judge imposed a draconian ten-year prison sentence on Rick Kuhn for his role in the point-shaving scheme. Distraught over the sentence, Davis just wanted to distance himself from the whole story. But he didn't show it in public, remaining a steady presence on the BC sideline as his team made an unprecedented run in the NCAA Tournament. Davis never came close to reaching the heights at Stanford that he had in Boston, posting three losing seasons in four years before taking the job at Iowa and returning to his native Midwest.

"It shocked us all that Tom Davis, after going to the Final Eight, leaves Boston College to go to Stanford. I mean, that's what college coaches do. They go get paid and go to a different place, but he had a whole team coming back," Michael Adams recalled.[37] Davis, who played a deep bench, would have had five of the players he referred to as his "starting seven" back for the 1982–1983 season—that is, if John Bagley decided to return for his senior year instead of entering the NBA Draft, where basketball experts regarded him as a surefire first-round pick.[38]

Rumored candidates for the BC job included Williams, Mackey, UConn assistant Jim O'Brien, Bob Dukiet of St. Peter's, and Lou Campinelli of James Madison. O'Brien, Dukiet, and Campinelli were all BC alums. Flynn said it was imperative that BC hire a coach promptly with national signing day for recruits rapidly approaching on April 14. The players rallied around Mackey, who had recruited and worked closely with all of them. Junior John Bagley, sophomore forward Martin Clark, and freshman guard Michael Adams made a presentation to the search committee on behalf of Mackey, citing both their comfort with the coach and their preference for a coach who would keep Davis's aggressive, pressing style of play in place.[39]

The desire of BC's veteran players to maintain the running style of basketball favored by Davis was an asset to the candidacy of Williams. The thirty-six-year-old Williams had certainly put into practice what he learned under Davis. He had turned his American University team into a near-replica of the teams he'd coached at Lafayette and Boston College. Williams later asserted that his willingness to play a deeper bench and substitute more frequently was the primary difference between his tactical approach and that of Davis, though Davis often went ten-deep on his bench in competitive games.[40]

The American coach emerged quickly as a favorite for the job. He demonstrated his commitment to the BC job by turning down an offer from Duquesne that he had nearly accepted.

"I didn't know who Gary Williams was," Stu Primus said. Williams had left for American before any of the returning players matriculated at Boston College. "I was approached by Bill Flynn, and he asked me who I thought should be the next coach, and I said Kevin Mackey. Kevin Mackey pushed me more than anybody to understand what I needed to be. A lot of kids may have a parent or a teacher or an ex-coach that can help them through tough situations. I got those life skills from Kevin Mackey," Primus said.[41]

"I was an assistant at UConn when the BC job opened. I didn't really apply for it, but I got a call from Bill Flynn, asking me to come up and talk about the job," Jim O'Brien said.[42] The BC alum was thrilled for the opportunity to interview for the position, but Flynn quickly dampened his hopes.

"But don't get the wrong impression," Flynn told O'Brien. "You're not getting this job. You have to go and become a head coach someplace and get some experience. And if it ever opens again, then you could be considered a viable candidate."[43] As much as anything, Flynn wanted O'Brien to get the lay of the land—to meet boosters, trustees, and what Marquette coach Al McGuire referred to as the "memos and pipes," the administrators and faculty members who held sway on campus. Several weeks later, O'Brien got the head coaching job at St. Bonaventure, a long-esteemed program in rural western New York that was struggling in the new Eastern Eight, a league that eventually evolved into the Atlantic-10. Several years later, O'Brien would get another crack at the Boston College job.

On April 5, Bill Flynn called a press conference to announce the hiring of Gary Williams as Boston College's new head coach. Williams, who typically kept it close to the vest at press conferences, said that he had not been looking to leave American. The opportunity to coach a respected basketball program in a city his family loved, along with the challenge of coaching in the newly prestigious Big East, persuaded him to take the job. Williams, reportedly doubled his salary to $75,000 per season—significantly less than most coaches made in the Big East and half of what Davis would be earning at Stanford.[44]

The rapid turnaround in hiring Williams and the continuity he brought to the program helped BC retain a strong recruiting class that featured physical, athletic forward Roger McCready from New York City; Russ Doherty, a 6'7" power forward from Wayland, Massachusetts who had been the state's top prep player the previous winter; and Dominic Pressley, a speedy guard whom Williams recruited out of his DC-area pipeline. Further ensuring the continuity in the BC program was the retention of Kevin Mackey, who turned down an offer from Davis to follow him to Stanford.[45] "There was a lot of continuity, with Gary [Williams] having coached with Tom [Davis]. Much of the pressing defenses and zone offenses. A lot of things were similar in terms of the philosophy and style of play. Much of the nomenclature was the same, how they numbered the players. What they called their offenses and defenses was a carryover," Paul Brazeau recalled.[46]

One source of continuity in the BC basketball program that remained in question for much of the spring of '82 was the team's top player, rising senior guard John Bagley. Bagley was considering seeking out a hardship waiver for entry into that June's NBA Draft. Draft experts said Bagley was a definite first rounder. "John was a baller. He could penetrate and score. You couldn't guard him on the dribble. His strength was unbelievable," Paul Brazeau said.[47] The 6'0" guard had been the Big East Player of the Year as a sophomore in 1981, averaging 20.4 points per game. As a junior, he again earned All-Big East honors and topped 21 points per game. In tournament play, Bagley had been one of the driving forces behind BC's runs to the Final Eight and Sweet Sixteen in consecutive years. "John was easy to get along with. Don't know that I've ever seen him really get mad," Jay Murphy said.[48]

Bagley discussed his future with Williams and announced in late April that he was returning to school for his senior year. Two weeks later, Bagley changed his mind and declared for the draft, with Williams's blessing. Cleveland picked Bagley twelfth in the first round, and he went on to a productive eleven-year NBA career. "Larry Bird told me, 'The best passing guard I ever played with and that Kevin McHale ever played with is John Bagley,'" Kevin Mackey said.[49] Bird befriended Mackey during their shared time in Boston and later hired Mackey as a scout for the Indiana Pacers.

Despite the loss of Bagley, BC looked to a have a solid team returning that fall—maybe not a Final Eight team but a club that could compete in the ever more treacherous Big East. Bagley's partner in the backcourt, speedy point guard Michael Adams, would be returning, as would a cluster of productive big men: Jay Murphy, Burnett Adams, John Garris, and Martin Clark. The hyper-athletic tandem of Stu Primus and Terrence Talley was likely to get more minutes in 1982–1983, while the additions of an athletically gifted forward like McCready and a similarly spry guard like Pressley would further help BC replace other key departures from the '81–82 club—namely, power forward Rich Shrigley and shooting guard Dwan Chandler.

Nevertheless, all major sports media outlets picked the Eagles to finish in the bottom third of the nine-team Big East in 1982–1983. Some publications picked BC last. The hometown *Boston Globe* figured the Eagles for seventh. Yet the *Globe* conceded in its college basketball preview that "once again, not that much is expected from the Eagles and, once again, BC will surprise," making the Eagles' 1982–1983 edition a typical Tom Davis—Gary Williams team.[50]

4

Getting over a Hump *(Calhoun)*

On Saturday, February 5, 1977, the western half of New York state was still cleaning up from its most treacherous blizzard in recorded history. Winds of close to seventy miles per hour turned a ten-inch snowstorm into several feet's worth on sidewalks and roadways at the end of January and beginning of February. Cities from Buffalo to Rochester and all the way to Syracuse in central New York declared states of emergency in a storm that cost nearly two dozen lives in the region. That didn't stop a shambolic, standing-room-only crowd from filling Syracuse University's 9,500-seat Manley Field House to watch the Orangemen annihilate an utterly overmatched Northeastern Huskies team, 110–70.

"They had ten thousand people packed in there, and they killed us. Holy shit. The arena is packed. And everything was by bus back in the day. And we saw all the snow. We thought the game might be cancelled," recalls Paul Porter, who played at Northeastern in the late 1970s.[1] "The Manley Zoo," Syracuse's student section, had responded to the introduction of Northeastern's starting five with their typical retorts: Who's he? Who cares? So what? Big deal! Eat shit![2] And the retorts only got harsher from there as Syracuse's lineup of track stars in basketball shorts ran past the Huskies for forty minutes. Despite an evening's worth of pummeling at the hands of Marty Byrnes, Roosevelt Bouie, and Louis Orr, Jim Calhoun didn't slink back to the locker room without giving Syracuse coach Jim Boeheim a piece of his mind.

"[Calhoun] and Boeheim were cursing each other out at the end of the game because they [Syracuse] were running up the score," Porter said. "And Calhoun said to [Boeheim], 'I'll never forget this.' And [considering] all the battles he had with Boeheim years later, he was right. He never did."[3] Calhoun, like the young men who chose to don the red and black in this era, remained defiant in the face of a noteworthy set of obstacles.

The lumps that Jim Calhoun's Northeastern Huskies took that night at Manley Field House offer a snapshot of the struggles the NU program faced as it fought its way over the hump in Division I. After a surprising 1972–1973 campaign, Northeastern hovered around the .500 mark for the rest of the decade, never in serious contention for a bid to the NCAA Tournament or the NIT. The 1973–1974 Huskies earned a respectable 14-11 mark before the Calhoun-coached club embarked on a five-year stretch in which the team never finished more than two games over or two games under .500. Part of the reason was the more difficult schedule Northeastern began playing when it shed most games against New England College Division opponents in favor of Division I adversaries. The likes of Penn, Holy Cross, and Syracuse now dotted Northeastern's schedule more frequently than did St. Anslem, Tufts, and St. Michael's. Part of the reason was that Northeastern was a Division I independent, lacking a regular slate of opponents to prepare for, year in and year out. Calhoun, too, was learning to ply his trade at the college level, figuring out the right style of play for his program and finding the players to make it all work at the Division I level. Gradually Calhoun gained the resources to build up his team, first securing six scholarships from the athletic department, then eight, before finally getting the full retinue of scholarships to help the Huskies compete with their peers in eastern college basketball.

"We weren't in a league back then, so it was like, 'Who are you playing now?'" Jim Connors said. "Our schedule was in flux all three years as we added better teams and dropped some of the poorer ones. I do think you lose a bit of identity when there isn't a conference or standings."[4] Calhoun was clearly frustrated by the dynamics that slowed his program's development but maintained a public face of optimism about the Huskies' future. The growing pains Northeastern basketball faced in the 1970s were certainly not unique among Boston-area schools. Harvard, BC, and BU all struggled to one extent or another during the decade, trailing the likes of Holy Cross, Providence, UMass, UConn, Rhode Island, and Fairfield in the pecking order of New England basketball.

"He [Calhoun] had a disadvantage in recruiting because he didn't have a big budget as the program transitioned from Division II to Division I," said Dave Caligaris, who starred for Northeastern in the mid-to-late 1970s. "It wasn't in a league. It was an independent, so you have scheduling issues, budget issues."[5] Fan support also dried up at Cabot during the 1970s. The raucous houses of the 1960s were a distant memory by the mid-1970s, when game attendees consisted largely of friends and family.[6] The same old challenges Northeastern basketball faced as a commuter school playing in a congested city neighborhood with limited parking were exaggerated by the team's mediocrity during the decade. Plus Northeastern started charging students a dollar to attend games beginning in the 1973–1974 season, a further discouragement for those on the fence about attending.

Lacking a conference, Northeastern basketball sought out sources of program identity where it could find them. One major source, Beanpot Basketball, disappeared during the 1970s, first moving to on-campus venues for 1974 before disappearing altogether after the 1976 tournament. Despite Northeastern's lack of recent success in the tournament, Calhoun was one of the most vocal proponents of the event, which he regarded as a showcase for college basketball in the region. Well into the 1980s, Calhoun advocated for the revival of the tournament but found no takers among the other Boston area schools. Nevertheless, Northeastern basketball hung tough and held its own in this era of transition, which included many low-key successes of its own. Moreover, Calhoun and his compatriots were sowing the seeds for the program's development into not only a regional power, but also a nationally recognized dynamo of basketball excellence.

The Northeastern program suffered a significant loss after the 1972–1973 season when assistant coach Mike Jarvis left to become an assistant for recently retired Celtics great Thomas "Satch" Sanders, who had accepted the head coaching job at Harvard. Jarvis, who had been a well-respected reserve on Dukeshire's teams of the mid-1960s, became one of Dukeshire's assistants right out of college while teaching physical education in the Cambridge public school system. Jarvis was a superb liaison between players and coaches, as well as a great teacher of basketball fundamentals, particularly the defensive side of the game. Jarvis served for a time as the coach of Northeastern's freshman team and played a significant role in the transition of the program from the Dukeshire-Bowman era to the Calhoun era.

"I was a non-starter, and my role in practice as a player was more [as] the guy who prepared the first team for the game. I spent most of my time on defense, most of my time just trying to get guys to play harder and to get better, so I was partly already coaching," Jarvis said.[7]

Despite being passed over for the Northeastern job, Jarvis made no outward sign of his displeasure with the decision to hire Calhoun. He simply continued his work, molding the student athletes in the Husky basketball program. It was the pull of a unique opportunity, not a sense of being pushed away, that convinced Jarvis to take the position at Harvard. "[Harvard] was in the same city that I grew up in, and I was able to work out an arrangement with the superintendent of schools where I was able to schedule all of my classes in the morning. Basically I was through teaching by noontime, and I was able to go over to Harvard, just walk through the Harvard Yard into the building that we were housed in. To have the opportunity to coach at the collegiate level and work with one of my heroes, that was just incredible," Jarvis said.[8]

The historical significance of Sanders, an African American, coaching in the Ivy League was also clearly not lost on Jarvis, who knew all too well about the limited head coaching opportunities for African Americans at the college level. Following in the footsteps of John McClendon at Cleveland State University (CSU) and Will Robinson at Illinois State, Sanders was one of the first Black head coaches in major college basketball. In a different era, Jarvis, though only twenty-seven at the time, may well have been hired as Northeastern's head coach given the same set of circumstances. His combined nine years of experience in a highly successful program as a coach and a player would have offered stability to a team that had just gone through an extremely destabilizing series of events.

"I thought the world of him [Jarvis]," Jim Connors said of his freshman coach.[9]

"Jarvis saw effort and how you played. He saw when you were down and needed a kick in the ass. He saw when you were down and needed a pat on the back. I would run through a wall for him," Bill Stanton remembered.[10]

"Jarvis has a strong love of the game. Mike pays great attention to detail," Joe Delgardo said. "His practices were his preparation for the game. By the time you got to the game, he didn't have to do a whole lot of coaching. Because we knew what the hell he wanted us to do."[11]

Any tension between Jarvis and Calhoun was not evident to the players, several of whom cited how well the pair worked together. Depending on who was asked, Calhoun or his predecessor, Jim Bowman, was the good cop to Jarvis's bad cop, or vice versa. "Both Calhoun and Jarvis were good X and O guys. They took plays and developed them in relation to the players. If you ran a double screen, [Jarvis] knew who to have come off the pick. He knew who could take the outside shot or take it to the hoop," Delgardo said.[12]

As a Black coach on a team with relatively few Black players, Jarvis apparently made a point of keeping tabs on the lives of Northeastern's African American players away from the court. While Jarvis unquestionably wanted to keep players on the straight and narrow as students and athletes, the approach proved a mild annoyance to some players. "He had a strong influence on us off and on the court. We wouldn't get in trouble because Coach Jarvis knew what was going on in the hood. He'd say, 'Joe, I heard you were over at so-and-so's the other day.' I'd say, 'You sound like my mother, coach,'" Joe Delgardo said.[13]

"I think he felt he should help me keep my nose clean. It seemed like my freshman year he would get on my case because I would hang out with too many thugs or too many druggies or something. Whoever I was hanging out with, he thought they weren't the right group of people," John Clark said.[14]

Despite the loss of Jarvis, as well as four seniors who were part of Calhoun's regular rotation, Northeastern found a way to have another winning season in 1973–1974. In year two of the Calhoun era, John Clark only got better, willing the Huskies to victories on several occasions while helping them hang tough against superior opposition. At the same time, NU retained its toughness in the transition, as holdovers from the Dukeshire era, including John Barros, John Boutin, and Ed Minishak, made significant contributions to Calhoun's 1973–1974 team.

"It was a great group of guys. We all had the same purpose, and that was to bring the team a win. And we worked hard as hell," said John Boutin, who played significant minutes as a senior and often started. "I worked my ass off for four years to make sure I didn't give them any reason to cut me. Senior year, finally, I got the opportunity to shine with Calhoun."[15] "We use bump-and-run tactics. I say our kids are exceptionally aggressive," Calhoun said in January 1974, citing team captain John Barros as the personification of this style of play and a player who deserved more recognition for his efforts.[16]

As more of the Dukeshire-era players graduated, John Clark became the on-court leader of the Huskies. During his junior year, 1974–1975, Clark became Northeastern's all-time leader in assists and scoring, remaining diligent and low key in the process. "He [Clark] doesn't want the spotlight. He's about the most reluctant star I've ever seen. We stopped the game to call attention to the record and he pushed everyone away," Calhoun said on the night that Clark broke John Malvey's all-time scoring record.[17] Clark piloted the Huskies to several significant upsets during his playing career, including an opening night stunner on December 1, 1974, over a Fairfield club that had made consecutive trips to the NIT. The win was a milestone for Calhoun. "Beating that team [Fairfield], that had been ranked, that had been in the NIT, whipping them in our gym, that's one of [Calhoun's] first big wins," Bill Stanton recalled.[18] Clark led the way with 18 points, a dozen assists, and several key steals. Stanton, too, provided NU with a major spark that evening, diving after several loose balls and scrapping with the Stags in the low post.[19]

Despite his low-key personality, Clark was a leader both in games and in practice, mentoring many of the team's younger players, including Dave Caligaris. "I played one-on-one with John as a freshman and a sophomore after one out of every two practices. And he would kill me. He had a control about his game and his personality. I learned a lot from him," Caligaris said.[20]

In the meantime, Clark garnered numerous honors off the court for his academic success as an accounting and business administration major while completing a co-operative with the U.S. Department of Transportation. Clark was an eighth-round selection of the Boston Celtics in 1976. He later earned an MBA from the University of Chicago before starting his own professional services firm back home in Pittsburgh.

For a time, a divide between incumbent players who favored NU's traditional ball-control style and newcomers to the program who favored a more up-tempo approach was evident on the roster. One of the most significant challenges Calhoun faced during the era was maintaining a steady course in the stylistic evolution of Northeastern basketball.

"We didn't have the athleticism to play full court," Dave Caligaris said. "In those days, you didn't see man-to-man all over the court like you see nowadays. We had zone presses; we had zones. When Calhoun started to move the tempo up in later years, he would do much more 2-2-1–type pressing."[21] "I think as much as anything coach [Calhoun] had blowback [from fans] on too many Black players being in the game. I think he probably had blowback on the speed of the game as well. Me and Billy Rosary and Steve Ramos. Ramos was the fastest dude I've ever seen between the foul lines. Coach and I had a lot of conversations about the game and strategy—that we should have been playing a faster-paced game, as well as applying pressure full court with the guards we had on the team," John Clark said.[22]

"The problem is that if you had a skilled kid who was an athlete, we weren't going to get him," Calhoun said of his teams in the 1970s. "And if you had a skilled kid who wasn't an athlete, we might get him. But that would make us a slow, plodding team, which isn't the way I wanted us to play basketball. I wanted to get up and down. I wanted to have pace. Pressure, running, full court. That type of thing. Trying to get as many possessions as we could. And it made us, eventually, into a really good team."[23] As Calhoun recruited more athletes and installed a more up-tempo style, he began expanding his bench, often playing ten or eleven players rather than the seven- or eight-man rotations he used earlier in his time at Northeastern.

During the Huskies' period of mediocrity in the mid-1970s, Calhoun consistently brought in talent that contributed to the evolution of Northeastern basketball. In the fall of 1973, Calhoun brought in Steve Ramos, a speedy small forward from New Bedford, Massachusetts, the first of several excellent players that Northeastern lured from the city. The addition of Ramos to Northeastern's lineup aided in the shift toward a more up-tempo style of play under Calhoun. Ramos started for the vast majority of his four years as a Husky and twice finished second on the team in scoring. "He [Ramos] could run the floor like nobody I've seen. He could bolt on a fast break. Especially my senior year, when I was a captain, I encouraged Calhoun to let us run it and press. We had some pretty good guys that could get up and down the floor at that point," Jim Connors said.[24]

Connors himself contributed to the Calhoun-era youth movement. He was one of the Huskies' most athletic big men, enjoying a highly productive career on Huntington Avenue. For many years, he held NU's single-season and career field goal percentage records.[25]

Also joining the fold in fall 1973 was the second member of the "Pittsburgh Connection," Keith Motley. A big, physical 6'8" center, Motley exuded the old-school toughness that had long been the signature of Northeastern basketball, but he did it with a more robust frame than his often-undersized predecessors. Anyone who thought they could mess with Motley in practice or in a game soon learned that he was not nearly as charitable as his friend John Clark. "We're playing and somebody does something funky to him [Motley] in the game, he turns around and he hits them and punches them and kicks them in the belly. And then he goes back to the game," John Clark remembered. Clark, instead, tried to get his retribution within the context of playing, either through physical retribution or, in the case of the player who broke his jaw, withholding the ball from him in games. Motley's method was more effective, Clark concedes.[26] "Keith was big. And strong. And a great leader. He wasn't a jumper, but he was the enforcer. He was the big knock-you-around-if-you-come-in-the-lane guy," Paul Porter said.[27]

As important as his on-court contributions were the leadership skills that Motley brought with him to Boston. He proved to be a bridge among his teammates, between players and coaches, as well as to the broader university community and beyond. Following his playing career at Northeastern, Motley became a Calhoun assistant, proving to be a talented teacher of the game, a mentor to many young players, and a persuasive recruiter. At the same time Motley coached at Northeastern, he was pursuing a career in higher education administration, which culminated with his long tenure as the chancellor of umass-Boston.

"One of my dearest friends in the world, John Clark, was also an incredible basketball player at Northeastern," Motley said. "We grew up together. We were like brothers. He was going to Northeastern, and he told Jim Calhoun that there was this guy in Pittsburgh, Pennsylvania he needed to go see. Coach Calhoun and Coach Jarvis came down. Coach Jarvis, quite frankly, was one of the few African American coaches at the time who came into my house for a visit."[28] Though recruited by Jarvis, Motley would be joining the nu program just as the coach was leaving. In a certain sense, Motley would go on to serve in a similar capacity to Jarvis in the program—as a highly respected African American player on a majority white team who became a team leader before becoming one of the team's coaches. From day one, Motley regarded himself as a stakeholder in the development of Northeastern basketball under Jim Calhoun.

"Coach Calhoun was a young pioneering coach who was helping North-eastern move into Division I at the time," Motley said. "It was something I could buy into. I liked building things. It was an opportunity for me to not only come to a city that had an academic focus, but also to help build an athletic program like we were able to do at Northeastern," he added, emphasizing that what Calhoun was building was an extension of Northeastern's already impressive legacy in the NCAA's College Division.[29]

"He [Motley] had a lot of just natural charisma. Keith was the most influential leader in my whole time there. Even after Keith graduated, he stayed involved as an assistant coach. He had your back at any time, in part because he was a big, strong guy, but also because he got along with everybody," Dave Caligaris said.[30] Simultaneously an agent for social change and for reconciliation among the people he encountered, Motley was a leader in Northeastern's African American Institute and benefitted from Calhoun's consistent support for his endeavors. Amid Boston's racial turbulence of the 1970s, the Northeastern basketball program was a space where a genuine give-and-take of cultural preferences and ideas took place. When Calhoun came to Northeastern, he told his players that they were going to project a clean-cut image, and he required them to trim their long hair or facial hair. The day after this announcement four Black players, led by upperclassman Sam Jordan, came to his office and explained the cultural meaning they invested in their afros. Calhoun relented, promising to judge players' appearances individually, based on their neatness, rather than making a blanket statement about their respective coiffuring.[31]

The subject came up again during Keith Motley's tenure on the Northeastern basketball team, as several players came to practice wearing braids to make sure their afros were neat at game time. Unfamiliar with the custom, Calhoun kicked them out of practice for the then outlandish hairstyle. The next time they came to practice, Motley and his teammates explained the situation to Calhoun, who thus adapted.[32] "Coach went out of his way to make sure those challenges were minimized," Motley said, referring not only to hair, but also to the way that Calhoun navigated the potential fault lines on the team's roster.[33] The young coach fostered a culture of common cause on his team despite the competing desires of players for game time, their cultural differences, and their preferences for differing styles of play.

"There were times when he [Calhoun] would receive nasty letters for playing five Black players," Motley recalled, "but then there were times when the Black students would protest because he wasn't playing all five Black players. I remember one time vividly that coach's sons were there for the game, like they always were, and the students were protesting.

They were saying mean and nasty things, and I didn't want his sons to hear that so I went to the stands and told them to chill."[34] Motley, the president of Northeastern's Black fraternity, went into the stands and told them to remove anti-Calhoun banners and quit it with the vulgarity. They abided. Calhoun was genuinely appreciative of the gesture. "There was a lot of peer pressure going on at that time, and it took some guts from him [Motley] to side with the white coach," Calhoun later said.[35]

This incident took place during the 1975–1976 season, a time of unprecedented racial tension in the city. The city's busing crisis was still in the news, and it involved students who lived very close to the Northeastern campus. Boston public schools were still receiving bomb threats from opponents of busing. The assertion of racial meaning into events as seemingly insignificant as which players took to the floor in a basketball game was par for the course in mid-1970s Boston. Calhoun, who had little experience coaching African American players when he took the job at Northeastern, proved to be a steadfast supporter of Black student athletes. John Clark credited Calhoun's success in large part to his willingness to listen to his players, treat them as individuals, and adapt to changing circumstances.[36] "Quite frankly, I would not even be involved in basketball with anyone except Jim. He took a strong stand for the black athletes at the U at a time when it was not such a well-thought of idea," Motley said years later.[37]

While Northeastern was building up its recruiting pipelines outside the Boston area, a pair of superb talents from close to home came to Huntington Avenue. The first was Holliston's Dave Caligaris, a gunner who broke John Clark's career scoring record. Caligaris still holds the school's season record for points per game, averaging nearly 25 a contest in his senior year, 1977–1978. The son of a Northeastern economics professor, Caligaris got tuition remission, saving Calhoun a precious scholarship. Until late in his senior year of high school, Caligaris received little notice from recruiters, having played at a Class D program.[38]

"Dave Caligaris was the best shooter I'd ever seen," Paul Porter said of his left-handed teammate.[39] From any range Caligaris was deadly. He almost never missed a free throw either. The forward displayed particular accuracy from long range before the NCAA adopted the three-point shot, an addition to the game that would have surely increased his scoring numbers even further. Having Caligaris in the game at small forward gave Northeastern something that resembled a three-guard look, enhancing the speed and versatility of the Huskies' lineup and enabling them to play at a more rapid pace and with more spacing.[40] "Sometimes I was better from way out than I was close," Caligaris said of his shooting.[41]

Caligaris got better every season. As a freshman, he averaged just 5 points per game. As a senior, he averaged nearly five times as many, earning him District I All-American honors. Teammates cited his unmatched work ethic in practice and preparation for games. "I would pick something between every season and work on it pretty religiously—strength training, offensive skills, ball handling, athleticism. I actually improved my vertical jump by eight inches. I used this machine called 'The Leaper,'" Caligaris said, referring to the infamous piece of '70's workout equipment that caused many basketball players to develop back problems, most notably future number one overall NBA Draft pick Kent Benson.[42]

Following his collegiate career, Caligaris played professionally in Greece after being cut by the Detroit Pistons, who selected him in the fifth round. In addition to his on-court skills, Caligaris earned a slew of academic honors as an accounting major. Twice he was named an Academic All-American, and he received a nomination for a Rhodes Scholarship. Caligaris later earned an MBA at Harvard. "I used to tell him that for a rich kid with those high SATs, you don't mind hitting people. He was a physical player, a tough, tough kid," Calhoun said.[43]

Northeastern brought in its next great playmaker in the fall of 1976 as a walk-on. Dorchester's Bill Loughnane, whom Calhoun came across playing travel basketball, soon earned a scholarship and became a fixture in the NU attack.[44] Loughnane took over at point guard for John Clark and held down the position for the next four years. Though he offered little of Clark's scoring prowess, Loughnane was an outstanding playmaker and a vigorous defender. His playmaking ability enabled many of the excellent athletes and scorers who soon joined the program to exercise their talents. As a senior, Loughnane surpassed John Clark as Northeastern's all-time assist leader.

"Bill was incredibly intense. I know why he is a great coach," Dave Caligaris said, referring to Loughnane's subsequent career as one of the winningest high school coaches in Massachusetts prep history. "He just understood the game and saw the floor. His face would get so red when he got mad at a call or something. Calhoun had to calm him down a little bit. Off the court he had a laid-back personality."[45]

"I was a faster point guard who tried to make other people better. I had terrific guys playing alongside me. Calhoun let us know what our jobs were, and I knew that my job was to get the ball to them," Loughnane said.[46]

While Northeastern's roster and style of play evolved over the course of the 1970s, so did Calhoun's approach to practice, which became increasingly focused on conditioning and drills that suited the team's new tempo on the hardwood.

"First, you got there on time. He [Calhoun] ran guys. He was in their face. It was very regimented. These were hard-charging practices where the guys got competitive with one another," team manager Scott Cohen recalled.[47]

"Pre [NCAA practice] rules, it was three hours, minimum. When they started having rules, then he had to structure practice. He always structured it, but he based it on a lot of things. He was an old-school coach originally, but he aged well. Back in the day if somebody missed a layup, everybody's running twenty laps and doing twenty suicides. His concern was physical basketball. If you didn't box out, if you allowed somebody to chump you on the court, he was offended by that. Then he started getting the kind of athletes that could be physical, run, and jump." Keith Motley said.[48]

Over time, Calhoun adopted and soon emphasized weaving and two-on-two drills in practice to build up the functional wind of the players on his team.[49] He also ran them. Constantly. "If we were not playing well, you were going to hear it, and the next day you could expect to feel it. It got to a point in some ways where you got numb to it. Even then he [Calhoun] was a really hard-working guy. He just had to get over a hump. Once you get over the hump, you get better players, a better budget, and can recruit from a larger radius," Dave Caligaris said.[50]

Year by year, Northeastern was accruing talent and making use of its now full retinue of scholarships to build up its Division I basketball program. The tipping point for NU's rise to Division I prominence came with the class that matriculated in the fall of 1977.

In May 1977 Northeastern announced the signing of a large, agile forward from Brockton High School named Chip Rucker. Calhoun had spotted the 6'7" leaper at the Boston Shootout the previous summer. Since Rucker's father worked at BU, the school's basketball program put little effort into recruiting him, figuring he would take his father's tuition remission and simply show up to play on Commonwealth Avenue.[51] Rucker, who clicked immediately with Northeastern's coaching staff, had other ideas. Long and energetic, Rucker was an adept rebounder, particularly on the offensive end. He proved to be the first in a new generation's worth of athletic big men to star for the Huskies.[52] The gregarious Rucker also possessed an infectious enthusiasm, making him a team leader from the moment he arrived at Cabot. "He [Rucker] could jump to the moon. Rebounded his rear end off. And he was fun to play with," Bill Loughnane said.[53] "Chip was a character," Jim Calhoun said. "He could rebound the heck out of the ball. Thank God we got him because he really helped us. At 6′7″, he was long, and he could match up with a 6′10″ guy because he could leap so well and was quick to the ball."[54]

Joining Rucker on Huntington Avenue that fall was the latest in Northeastern's "Pittsburgh Connection," a 6′1″ guard from Braddock, Pennsylvania, named Donald "Pete" Harris. Calhoun first spotted Harris at the Dapper Dan All-Star Game and, with the help of Keith Motley, pursued him vigorously, convincing the highly sought-after guard to pick NU over offers from Big Eight and Southeastern Conference (SEC) programs.[55]

"You should have seen the way he [Calhoun] talked to my father, my mother, and even my grandmother," Harris said of his recruitment. "He explained that they shouldn't feel alienated by me going away, that he wasn't going to make me forget where I had come from." The coach tried to sell players on the school's academics—namely, its unique co-op program, as well as the charms of Boston itself. He also focused on developing a rapport with the player's family, which, in the case of Pete Harris, clearly worked.[56]

Harris played with great intensity and spent lots of time outside practice working on the particulars of his game. Blessed with strength and speed, he simultaneously had an attention to detail that made him into an elite player. "Pete was a really quiet, understated guy. But he was legit as a freshman," Dave Caligaris remembers. "He was talented in an efficient way, which is rare for a freshman. He came in right away and made a significant contribution to the program. Pete was tough—outside shooting, taking it to the basket. You knew he was special."[57]

Like John Clark before him, Harris earned the moniker of "quiet leader" from his teammates, but just like in the case of Clark, that quietness did not indicate a lack of toughness. More than once Harris responded to an elbow or a blow from an opponent with a strike of his own that inevitably made the aggressor wish that he hadn't messed with the kid from Braddock, PA.

The building through recruiting continued in 1978 as the Huskies added three more significant talents: Perry Moss, a 6'2" guard from western Massachusetts; Dave Leitao, a 6'7" power forward from Northeastern's pipeline in New Bedford; and 6'6" forward Eric Jefferson, another Braddock, Pennsylvania native from the "Pittsburgh Connection." Each of the new recruits added a different dimension to the roster. While Moss would join Harris as another explosive performer in the Huskies' backcourt, Leitao would be a physical, athletic board crasher. Though roughly the same size as Leitao, Jefferson brought a smoothness to his game, being both a strong shooter and an excellent passer.[58]

For those outside the program, the first glimmer that something new was afoot with Northeastern basketball came early in the 1978–1979 season as the Huskies' young core of Moss, Leitao, Jefferson, Harris, and Rucker, along with junior Bill Loughnane, raced to a 6-2 start, the school's best in eight years. Playing the up-tempo style of basketball that was becoming Northeastern's signature, this team scored a series of upsets, including road wins over Maine and Army. Eventually this early incarnation of the big, bad Huskies of the 1980s came down to earth, struggling as the schedule toughened up, and finishing the year at 13-13. But with this cadre of young talent and a newly athletic style of play, Northeastern approached the 1980s as a program on the rise. The Huskies would soon find themselves in a brand-new conference and playing in a new but nearly ancient venue. Amid these changing circumstances, Northeastern would become one of the foremost basketball dynasties of the 1980s.

5

Great Kids *(Pitino)*

"Practices under Sig [Sigler] and Leibowitz were very calm and mild and orderly and short. Under Rick [Pitino], they were marathons," Desmond Martin said. As a sophomore, Martin lost twenty pounds playing for his new coach.[1]

"Sometimes I was too tired after practice to go eat," Glen Bressner said.[2]

"We were running about five miles a day, and that's just on the track, not counting all the suicides," Wally West remembered.[3]

"We had a ten-minute drill where we're on the third floor of Case, and if you got kicked out of practice for throwing a bad pass or doing something that we considered silly, then you had ten minutes to run down three flights of stairs, go to your locker, put on your sweats, run out to the track, run a mile, come back in, put your sweats back in your locker, get back up the three flights of stairs, and get back to practice. If you didn't make it, you had to do it again," John Teague said.[4] Typically, the "ten-minute drill" was done in the cold and snow of a Boston winter.

"Anyone tell you about the brick drills?" Glen Bressner asked. "Two building bricks taped with white athletic tape. And at the end of practice, you would be required to do these brick drills to exhaust the number of mistakes you made during practice. You got assigned a brick drill for every bad pass you made or if you had a turnover. There was a tally of bricks behind your name on the ledger. At the end of practice you had to remove all those bricks behind your name. What it meant was that you had to do defensive slides from one end of the baseline to the other. And you had to do twenty of those rotations in a minute with bricks in your hands for each brick. And this was after three hours of practice," Bressner, a veteran of many post-practice bricks, reminisced.[5]

"And then we had a drill we hated called '170 in 4,' where we had to hit 170 layups in four minutes as a team. And you had people that would stand there and pass you the ball as you went up and down the court, and you had four minutes to do that," John Teague recalled.[6]

"Practice six to eight in the morning. Then individual instruction, full court, ball-handling drills, conditioning drills, shooting drills for an hour and a half between your class schedule. Then three to six at night with full-on stations and garbage cans you threw up into, then dinner and study hall from seven till nine. It was brutal. The NCAA put in the rule limiting the number of hours you could practice per week because of Pitino's practices. That's why they call it the 'Pitino Rule,'" Jay Twyman said.[7]

"We were in the gym before class started. We were in the gym during our breaks. And then we had practice at four. And the practices were incredibly disciplined, and it was tough to get through. But he taught us how to win," Glenn Consor said.[8]

"Pitino knew what he was doing. He made sure that those were memorable days for us in a weird way. He took me to the edge. Pitino made me sharp in everything I did. By the time I left BU, I could dribble like guards," Wally West said.[9]

"I can honestly say that I became the best player that I could have possibly been under him. I wish I would have had him for four years," Glenn Consor said.[10]

"With no restrictions of time beyond getting to class and hitting the books, a coach could improve players' skills just by working closely with them," Pitino wrote of his time at Boston University before the "20-hour rule" came into place.[11]

On October 15, 1978, at 12:01 a.m., Rick Pitino held his first official practice at Boston University, adopting the ritual of "midnight madness" that Maryland's Lefty Driesell had started earlier in the decade. Before his team broke a sweat, the BU athletic department hosted BU alums and supporters for a cocktail party. In front of the assemblage, Pitino introduced his team, talked about the exciting slate of opponents BU would be bringing to Boston in the coming years, and put his team through a vigorous forty-five-minute workout.[12] The physical exertion Pitino expected out of his players would not wane for the next six months. At the time Pitino was the youngest coach in the country. What he lacked in experience, he made up for with energy, work ethic, and knowledge of the game. What he lacked in gravitas, he made up for with his natural gifts as a teacher and a psychologist. Most important, he had a clear vision of what he wanted BU basketball to look like in the 1978–1979 season.

Pitino taught basketball in a hands-on fashion. He set up stations just like those at Five-Star to teach the nuances of the game. The "Boy Coach," as he was known around the BU athletic department, frequently challenged his charges to one-on-one or two-on-two games before, during, and after practices. Full-court scrimmages that resembled track meets were an everyday occurrence. Pitino, just two or three years older than many of his players, participated in many full-court scrimmages and competed with the same intensity as he coached. On occasion he nearly came to blows with some of his own players over a shove, an elbow, or a hard foul during one of these uniformly physical affairs. Combine all of this with a conditioning regimen that would have made even Soviet hockey coach Anatoly Tarasov wince and you had a basketball team that was primed to attack the opposition.

"The fitness level and hard work fed directly into Rick Pitino's playing style, which was to press and run for forty minutes," said Tom Masters, who played on Pitino's first BU team. "He didn't show up at BU and formulate any strategy based on the personnel available to him. He was going to mold the players he inherited to the style he wanted to play."[13]

"When Pitino came, things immediately changed," Wally West said. "He brought a culture to the program that we were going to be big time. Pitino came in with that modern style—we were pressing, we were running."[14]

Much of the molding that took place during the morning and evening practices and individual instructional sessions in fall 1978 focused on the installation of Pitino's preferred running and pressing style of basketball and the preparation of his new charges to play in this system. "Defense. I've always prided myself on the way my teams have played it over the years—an infamous and intense full-court press. I like to think of it as a relentless, focused assault on our opponents, one that involves precision positioning and maximum conditioning, and, one that, ideally leads to offense," Pitino wrote on page one of his memoir, *Pitino: My Story*.[15]

"Roy [Sigler] did not press at all," Desmond Martin said. "Normally when you're down a few points late in the game, you press. Rick pressed the entire game. Ninety-four feet, the entire game, there was pressure on the ball. Half-court traps, three-quarter traps, full-court traps. We loved it because everybody was in shape. And at that time nobody could really deal with the traps."[16]

"Constant motion, backdoor cuts, and disciplined teamwork" is how BU forward Steve Priscella described Pitino's system—one in which an attacking defense flowed into an attacking offense.[17] Pitino encouraged shooters to take advantage of the open looks that this perpetual movement on the offensive end created. Rather than relying on the patterned offense taught by Jack Leaman, his mentor at UMass, Pitino favored the more freewheeling offensive approach he learned from Jim Boeheim at Syracuse. Pitino referred to BU as the "home of the fast break" in several interviews that season. He drummed into his team, their opponents, and the media the idea that BU would continually be on the attack.

"We're playing a new type of game this year. Every time we get the ball, whether it be a steal, a rebound, or anything, it's run," Steve Wright said in a piece for the BU *Daily Free Press* about how well suited the junior forward was for Pitino's system.[18]

"I think our biggest guy may have been Wally West at 6'9"," John Teague said. "We were a bunch of small guys, 6'5" and 6'6". We got out, and our motto was to push the ball. We played good defense because we were smaller, hitting the glass, and we had to move our feet a lot. So that's where all the brick drills and all this running came in. He [Pitino] felt that if you were in better shape than your opponents, then they would wear down in the second half."[19]

Pitino believed a basketball game to be a siege, a conflict of competing collective wills. Like any reasonable leader digging in for a siege, Pitino believed the best way to win was to bring the most manpower to bear. In that spirit he played one of the deepest benches in college basketball. Throughout his tenure at BU as many as ten, eleven, or twelve players registered significant minutes in most games, forcing even the team's top players to subjugate their vanities to the coach's team concept.

Though certainly on the small side, BU's 1978–1979 rotation had considerable depth. Junior center Wally West was joined at forward by Steve Wright and John Teague. In reserve, the Terriers featured forwards Desmond Martin, Darryl Floyd, and Tom Masters. Initially, 6'6" sophomore forward Ken Fiola looked to figure in the rotation, but a serious knee injury brought his season to an early end. Team captain Tom Channel and junior point guard Glenn Consor started in the backcourt, while Gene

Jones and Johnnie Ray Wall were an explosive duo in reserve. Among BU's standard ten-man rotation, only Channel was a senior.

The 1978–1979 season was BU's last as an independent team playing for a bid to the ECAC's New England championships. The Terriers faced a tough schedule that included New England powers Holy Cross, Rhode Island, and Connecticut, as well as hometown rivalry games with emerging programs from Northeastern and Boston College. The slate would only get harder in subsequent years, as Pitino worked diligently to schedule daunting road contests for his team. This approach would help make his Terriers battle-tested by the time they faced league opponents.

College basketball writers around New England acknowledged the talent on BU's roster in their 1978–1979 previews but emphasized the steep hill Pitino had to climb to win or foster much interest at the milquetoast basketball school.[20] The *Globe* complimented Pitino on the new attitude he brought to BU basketball. The paper praised John Simpson for his new investment in the program. Pitino's assertion, though, that the Terriers' Tom Channel "[would] be the best guard in New England when the season [was] over" was a little much for the *Globe*'s sports staff, which had seen enough of Holy Cross's Ronnie Perry and BC's Ernie Cobb to think otherwise.[21] The BU *Daily Free Press* gave its optimistic estimation of the team's chances that winter, both on the court and in the stands: "Rick Petino [*sic*] will lead his team to a refreshing .500 or better season, and the fans will turn out to support the cagers," the unnamed editorialist wrote.[22]

The small BU basketball family knew that something different was afoot on Babcock Street, site of the Case Center. Basketball writers around New England had an inkling of this as well. Whether or not the basketball team, even if it had a fantastic season, would get anyone else at BU to notice was a different question. Not only did the basketball Terriers have to compete for attention with the defending national champion hockey team that played downstairs from them. They also had to compete with the city of Boston itself, one of the primary reasons that students chose to attend BU in the first place. Unlike a state university or a school with a strong religious affiliation, BU lacked the obvious geographic or cultural ties that bound its student body to the idea of supporting representatives of the institution. This became particularly pronounced as BU evolved in the 1970s from a largely commuter campus into a school that drew applicants from across the Northeast. Moreover, students interested in sports other than college hockey were a mere twenty-minute trolley ride away from the Boston Garden. When the weather got better, Fenway Park was a five-minute walk from the east end of the BU campus. "With the exception of parents, friends, alumni and visiting fans, Terrier teams usually play before small and uninspiring crowds," Gary Cohen of the *BU Daily Free Press* wrote in January 1979, bemoaning the lack of student support for the school's athletic programs. In Cohen's estimation, this included BU's championship hockey team, which drew the majority of its support from alumni and community members in the hockey-mad market of Boston.[23]

"Everyone has said that the students at Boston University are apathetic towards athletics, but they've never done anything about it. I don't believe in apathy, and I'm out to prove that within two years we'll pack Case Center and hopefully get a new facility in the future," Rick Pitino said of the challenge of winning his new university over to basketball.[24] Pitino and his players stood on street corners along Commonwealth Avenue, handing out flyers to undergraduates like a garage band, encouraging people to come see them play.

"We've hit every dorm on campus and we're still not done. Now we're going to floor meetings. We're hitting every floor in Warren Towers," Pitino told a reporter from the *BU Daily Free Press*.[25] Working closely with new athletic department promotion man Bo Ruggerio, Pitino created a courtside "BU Pound" at Terriers basketball games. The young coach envisioned "the Pound" as his home court advantage—a rowdy student section similar to what he'd seen at Syracuse's Manley Field House. The "Manley Zoo" played a decisive role in many Syracuse basketball games, consistently disrupting and intimidating opponents in the years before the central New York school opened the Carrier Dome in 1980.

For three dollars, students got a red and white "Pound" T-shirt and season-long admission to a roped-off section behind the opposing team's bench at Case. In early November, Pitino told the *Daily Free Press* that over two hundred students had signed up. If that was true, then the "Pound" suffered from significant absenteeism. At most of BU's sixteen home dates that winter, a fifty-person "Pound" counted as a good showing. A "Fastbreak Club" for alumni and BU parents fared slightly better. At each home game, several "Pound" and "Fastbreak Club" members selected from the stands got a crack at a half-court shot for a chance to win a stereo, a television, or a trip to Florida. The historical record remains silent on whether anyone hit a half-court shot or collected any of these prizes.[26]

A student didn't have to pony up three dollars in "Pound" dues to attend basketball games. BU students got free admission to the games with an ID. The athletic department tried many other inducements to lure undergraduates to Case. Students in attendance at the February 14 game against Wagner were invited to a postgame "beer party." Case Gym public address announcer Jeff Schleger tried to rile up game attendees with NBA arena-style introductions and pronouncements similar to Andy Jick at the Boston Garden or Dave Zinkoff at Philadelphia's Spectrum. Promotion man Bo Ruggerio planned to lure students to a game against George Washington that happened to be on Washington's birthday by handing out two hundred free cherry pies. Unfortunately, Ruggerio left the pies in his car the night before the game, and they froze solid. Ruggerio tried to thaw them out in the athletic department's sauna, but the pies collapsed and turned into a sickly sweet and smelly mess that lingered for weeks.[27]

Boston University's first look at a Rick Pitino–coached team in competition came against Carleton University. In front of a typically tiny exhibition-game crowd, the Terriers easily disposed of the elite Canadian university in a glorified scrimmage. Point guard Glenn Consor lit up the scoreboard that evening, much to Pitino's dismay. Just like Jack Leaman had earmarked Pitino to be UMass's on-court quarterback, Pitino expected Consor to fulfill the same role. "Glenn had a career high," Wally West recalled. "After the game Pitino came in the locker room and said to him, 'You're selfish.' He made him go run five miles. We followed our boy outside and cheered him on."[28]

Just a few weeks into the Pitino era, a sense of comradeship forged in a set of shared, intense experiences was already evident on the BU basketball team. It remains so to this day among the men that played for him at Boston University. Consor, who rapidly developed into just the kind of player Pitino wanted as his point guard, embraced this sensibility as thoroughly as anyone on the team. "He [Glenn] was a guy that thought the game. He was like a little Pitino. He was a true leader and a true point guard," John Teague said.[29]

On the Tuesday after Thanksgiving 1978, 855 people watched the regular season debut of Rick Pitino's Boston University basketball team. The visitors at Case that evening were the St. Peter's College Peacocks from the ECAC Metro.[30] "Man, did you guys start running? Guys, do you stop pressing?" Desmond Martin said was the reaction of St. Peter's and all the teams that faced the Terriers early in the 1978–1979 season. "They didn't expect it because the year before everybody said BU was a doormat. But when the guys came back in shape, ready to press, willing to press, it was a complete turnaround."[31]

BU came out ready to attack that evening, harassing St. Peter's ball handlers and threatening every Peacock pass from the outset. The press facilitated BU's fast-breaking offense. Leading the charge for the Terriers was captain Tom Channel, who scored a game-high 22 points. Fourteen of them came in a nine-minute stretch early in the second half, when BU built its lead up to 11 points. Some costly turnovers late in the game helped St. Peter's fight its way back into contention. A clutch defensive rebound with three seconds remaining by Wally West, who posted an 18-point, 10-rebound double-double, helped BU hang on for a 75–71 win. The postgame quotes from three players in the *Daily Free Press* demonstrated the team's new consensus of confidence. All three told the student reporter that they never doubted the game's eventual outcome but were concerned by the inattention to detail the team had shown in the game's final stretches. Just six weeks after Pitino had held his first practice as BU coach, his team was talking about the game just like he did.[32] "Rick said, 'We're going to win this year. We're not going to be somebody's doormat.' He put a winning attitude into our heads. And we worked hard. The day of the game was a day off from being tortured, from being yelled at. And we reveled in that," Desmond Martin said.[33]

BU faced a much stiffer opponent in the second game of the season. A University of Maine team coming off a 17–8 campaign traveled to Case the following Saturday. BU jumped all over Maine in the early going, holding a seven-point lead midway through the first half. Sloppy shooting and signs of fatigue from the Terriers' fast-breaking, board-crashing, and full-court press first line helped Maine hang in the game. While Pitino threw an assortment of packages and personnel at the Black Bears, veteran Maine coach Skip Chappelle kept it simple and steady. At the half BU led by just three. "He [Chappelle] was a laid-back guy. He was a really good coach, and he kept it real simple. We had a simple offense and a simple defense," said Jeff Holmes, who played for Pitino at BU before transferring to Maine. "At BU I was on the scout team, and it was tough. With Skip we had two or three things we worked on with each opponent."[34]

In the second half, Chappelle relied on his superstar to carry the load. Junior forward Rufus Harris, 6'4", who went on to be drafted by the Boston Celtics, took control of the game. He shot 9 of 13 in the second half, scoring 20 of his 28 points after the break. Maine headed back north on I-95 in possession of a 72–63 win.[35]

BU didn't have time to agonize over the defeat, nor did Pitino have much time to inflict agony on his players. On Tuesday night, the Terriers headed across the state to play Pitino's alma mater on its home floor and face off with his old college coach. Roughly twenty-five hundred people turned up at Curry Hicks Cage to see Jack Leaman's 1-1 UMass Minutemen take on his apt pupil's 1-1 Terriers. This was not the same kind of UMass team on which Pitino had played four years earlier, nor was it the same shambolic atmosphere he had witnessed at the Cage as an undergraduate. After dominating the Yankee Conference for close to a decade, UMass found itself in the middle of the pack in the "Eastern Eight," the new basketball conference it had joined the previous season. Conference foes like Villanova, Pitt, and Rutgers proved to be well ahead of the Minutemen in the league's early years. The half-full fieldhouse that greeted Pitino and BU at UMass demonstrated the waning of interest on campus already in the early stretches of the 1978–1979 season. It got much worse over the winter. UMass went winless in the "Eastern Eight" and won just five games all season. The Minutemen drew crowds that would not have been out of place at Case. Leaman would be out of a job at season's end.

BU rammed the ball inside against an overmatched UMass front line, inducing the Minutemen into a staggering 34 fouls. The Terriers turned those fouls into 34 points from the free-throw line. Boston University led by 10 at the half and never faced a serious challenge down the stretch. The 72–63 win improved BU's record to 2-1 as it prepared for another weekday commute. This time the Terriers' charter bus was headed for Worcester and a showdown with perennial New England heavyweight Holy Cross.

The Crusaders were unquestionably New England's most successful college basketball program—the only team in the region to have won both the NCAA and NIT Tournaments. While based in Worcester, Holy Cross played far more often at the Boston Garden than any of the city's college programs, and it played to larger crowds. Celtics legends Bob Cousy and Tommy Heinsohn had both learned to ply their trade at the Jesuit school. Under the leadership of head coach George Blaney, the Crusaders posted four consecutive twenty-win seasons entering the 1978–1979 campaign while earning two trips to the NIT and one to the NCAA Tournament.

The 1978–1979 edition of Holy Cross basketball featured a rugged frontcourt that included forward Dave Mulguin, center John O'Connor, and Garry Witts, a sharpshooting 6'7" forward who later played for the Washington Bullets. The centerpiece of Holy Cross's attack was in its backcourt: 6'2" shooting guard Ronnie Perry, who was New England's best college basketball player of his era. The son of Holy Cross athletic director Ron S. Perry, the younger Perry was a star on the basketball court and the baseball diamond, just like his father. At West Roxbury's Catholic Memorial, Perry became the leading scorer in the history of Massachusetts high school basketball and was simultaneously the state's top high school baseball prospect. Already a local legend by the time he enrolled at Holy Cross, Perry averaged 23 points per game as a freshman in 1976–1977, the most of any freshman in the country. He was selected ECAC Rookie of the Year and named a second-team All-American. Despite being the focus of every defensive strategy the Crusaders faced, Perry continued to light up the scoreboard and average more than 20 points per game in subsequent seasons.

BU's approach to Perry was no different than anyone else's. Consor, Jones, Teague, Wall, and Channel smothered Perry into a woeful 3-for-10 first half from the floor. Nevertheless, Holy Cross's robust front court kicked in enough to keep the hometown team out in front 35–30 at the half.

Holy Cross held on tight to its lead throughout the second half as wave after wave of BU lettermen barraged the Crusaders on both ends of the floor. Freshman John Teague particularly stood out in the contest, battling his way to 14 points and 8 rebounds. Boston University cut its deficit to a single point on twelve different occasions that evening. BU's chances faded when Channel, who scored 12 points, fouled out late in the contest. Perry went 6 for 6 from the line down the stretch, helping Holy Cross secure a 72–65 win. The *Globe*'s Lesley Visser complimented BU's "inexperienced and wonderfully precocious team" for its performance against one of New England's perennial powerhouses. George Blaney congratulated BU as well, saying that his team was able to hold on for a win only by "kickin' and a fightin.'"[36] "Ron Perry is a great player, but Tom Channel is the best prospect in this area," Pitino said after the game, still building up his senior shooting guard while needling the Holy Cross All-American.[37]

BU then traveled to Storrs, Connecticut, for their third game in six days against a traditional New England power. A bigger, stronger UConn team pummeled BU in the first half and led 49–28 at the intermission. BU made it interesting for a time in the second half by turning the game into a running and gunning affair. Steve Wright finished with an eye-popping 42 points in the 92–84 defeat. Wright pumped in points from the wing, the low post, and the high post with equal accuracy that evening. His dominating performance was all the more impressive since he matched up that evening against Cornelius "Corny" Thompson, the 6'8" freshman juggernaut who would go on to be named New England Player of the Year. Wright and a cadre of defenders held Thompson to a mere 10 points.[38] The break for final exams came mercifully after BU's next outing, a 67–65 stinker of a home loss to unheralded Adelphi that dropped the Terriers record to 2-4.

The confidence that BU showed for much of the fall semester returned with the players after the break. Immediately, they proved themselves capable of living up to their early-season promise. On December 23, BU went on the road and upset Fairfield, a team that had played in the NIT the previous year. The Terriers' 84–76 overtime win was buoyed by commanding offensive performances by Steve Wright (28 points) and Tom Channel (26 points), both of whom were by then on the radar of anyone who paid attention to eastern college basketball. After knocking off Fairfield, BU topped Farleigh Dickinson and Stonehill before heading over to Huntington Avenue for the first of its matchups with rival Northeastern. At the time, the BU-Northeastern rivalry had cooled off from the 1960s and early 1970s, when both programs were either competitive or at least competing for the now dormant Beanpot Basketball title. Nevertheless, the January 9, 1978, contest between a 5-4 BU team and a Northeastern team that was once again hovering around .500 was a rivalry rooted in personal experiences. "We knew them. They knew us. They came to our school looking for girls. We went to their school looking for girls at parties," Desmond Martin said.[39]

"We used to get into it on the playgrounds with Northeastern guys. It was a war then. Some of them lived over in the Fens. The BC guys and us got along well. There was just something about us and Northeastern," Gene Jones said of the rivalry, which would soon reignite into one of the hottest in the East.[40]

The embers of animosity were flaring up not only among the players, but the coaches, too, were developing their own tense relationship. "I used to go running around the Charles River and sometimes Jim [Calhoun] would be jogging the other way. I saw him and he saw me but we'd both put our heads down and run right by each other," Pitino wrote.[41]

Just 1,631 people turned up at Northeastern's Cabot Gym for the first matchup of the Pitino-Calhoun rivalry. While the crowds were not nearly as intense as they would be in subsequent games, this closely contested matchup foreshadowed the reemergence of the crosstown rivalry. BU prevailed, 61–60, in a physical, sloppy game, with BU's leading scorers, Steve Wright (19 points) and Tom Channel (20 points), pumping in the final 6 points of the game. Just after the final buzzer sounded, Northeastern freshman sensation Perry Moss drained a half-court shot that was waived off by officials.[42]

Riding a four-game winning streak, BU seemed like a legitimate threat to make the ECAC playoffs. Their next home contest, a rematch against Connecticut would surely show how well Pitino's rapidly improving Terriers could compete against New England's best. Promotion man Bo Ruggerio tried to create a big-game atmosphere at Case that evening. He convinced nearby Abingdon High School's pep band, Salem High School's cheerleaders, and a local baton twirling team to perform on BU's behalf at the game. The regulars among the roughly one thousand fans in attendance that night were not used to such pomp and circumstance at Case—the trappings of a typical high school basketball game.[43]

With Red Auerbach in attendance, BU played with a tenacity and grit that was frequently shown by the teams Auerbach coached, hanging in there against the bigger and stronger Connecticut Huskies. BU's all-out assault proved more effective at home, as the Terriers harassed and confused UConn into a series of first-half turnovers. Pitino kept shifting between his full-court press and a 2–3 zone, emulating a strategy Davidson had used successfully earlier that season against the Huskies. BU's poor shooting kept the game close, as the Terriers led just 25–20 after twenty minutes, despite completely controlling the pace of play. Second-half foul trouble, the perennial bane of Rick Pitino's Commonwealth Avenue existence, stymied

BU's efforts to close the game out. When Wally West fouled out with more than five minutes remaining, Corny Thompson, who led UConn with 21 points, took control, enabling UConn to fight its way into a 54–54 tie at the end of regulation and eventually escape with a 63–62 overtime win.[44]

The 6-5 Terriers moved on from their close call against Connecticut by pummeling UVM, 92–65, at Case. The Vermont win served as prelude to BU's rematch with Northeastern. Freshman standout John Teague came into the rivalry game a little worse for wear after breaking his nose against the Catamounts. Early on, BU looked in fine fettle against Northeastern. The 932 fans in attendance saw the "home of the fast break" going full force in the first half, as the Terriers built a 12-point halftime lead through their aggressive play on both ends of the floor. Point guard Glenn Consor, typically the team's distributor, took advantage of Northeastern's focus on Tom Channel and ripped off 17 points on 8 of 9 shooting. The Huskies were not ones to back down, though, particularly in a rivalry game. Pete Harris came out of the locker room and led the Huskies back into contention, matching BU's second-half shooting slump with a 20-point eruption that put Northeastern in position to make a late-game run. Instead, Steve Wright and Tom Channel combined to put the clampdown on Northeastern, combining for 15 points in the game's final five minutes. BU's 80–73 win completed their second consecutive season sweep over Northeastern. The two intense January 1979 games between Pitino's BU and Calhoun's Northeastern teams offered a taste of things to come in the reignited rivalry.[45]

BU then reeled off wins against Vermont, New Hampshire, and Brandeis to increase its winning streak to five. Michael Madden profiled Pitino and the upstart BU basketball team for the Sunday, January 21, 1979 *Globe*. The article on the "Boy Coach" introduced sports fans across New England to the raving young genius on Comm Ave and contributed to the mythology that already surrounded him. "Pitino is a hustling street type from Long Island, his voice nasal with a New York accent and his style pushy with the city's arrogance," Madden wrote.[46] The *Globe* columnist described the triple sessions that had become the norm at BU—on weekdays, on weekends, and even on Thanksgiving. The coach augmented the character Madden sketched in his profile by offering up several eye-opening quotes. "They'd [BU] been losing here for so long, and losing badly, that I expected to find some losing characters, some bad actors, but I found out these were great kids here," Pitino said, describing players who were almost all fewer than five years younger than he. Pitino even went into the psychological games he played with his players, specifically with the team's leading scorer, Steve Wright. "I told Wright that he'd either be a great player or I'd cut him. I told him to get off the fence or I didn't want anything to do with him."[47]

Clearly this approach worked. For the season, reigning team MVP Wright improved his scoring from 11.7 points per game as a sophomore under Sigler to 20.8 per game as a junior under Pitino. Wright had played every single second of BU's first twelve games and would average better than thirty-seven minutes per game for the entire season.

BU, now 11-5, tumbled twice at the end of January to top-notch opponents. A larger, more athletic, NIT-bound Old Dominion team stomped the Terriers at the Norfolk Scope, 90–72. BU followed that up with a loss to Maine in Orono.

A third straight loss looked imminent in the early going against Siena on February 6. Instead, BU raced back from a 15-point deficit to score a 72–66 home win. The victory set up a showdown between the now 12-7 Terriers and the Rhode Island Rams, who were widely regarded as New England's best team. BU would be entering the game short-handed, as Tom Channel had severely bruised his right knee in the win over Siena. Channel suffered the injury Tuesday night, and it remained unclear until minutes before the Thursday night tipoff whether the BU captain would suit up against the Rams. Channel told his coach he wasn't sure how he would do it, but he would play against Rhode Island (URI).[48]

Injury or not, this genuinely consequential game drew far more interest on campus and in the region than any of the Terriers' previous games that winter. The enticing matchup drew enough interest to sell out all 2,500 available tickets in advance. Rhode Island's devoted fan base scooped up many of the seats. Nevertheless, this sudden run on tickets was BU's first sellout in years.

The most anticipated BU basketball game in twenty years began poorly. Rhode Island jumped out to a 6–0 lead, thanks to a pair of BU turnovers. Both were self-inflicted wounds by the Terriers, who attempted to turn the game into a horserace from the opening tip. Pitino called timeout just 1:19 into the game. When the players returned to the floor, they went right back into their full-court sprint. The erratic look of BU's early attack looked ever more deliberate as BU gunned its way to the lead, 17–16, with eleven minutes remaining in the first half. The 2,500 people that cramped into Case got a show. On defense, it was BU's full-court surveillance that caused all the turnovers. On offense, BU displayed its freewheeling, shoot-if-you're-open strategy to the fullest that evening, allowing Wally West (16 points) and Steve Wright (18 points) to take advantage of the looks the Rams left for them. No one took greater advantage of the atmosphere and tempo of the game than Tom Channel, who ravaged URI for 35 points. Knee injury and all, Channel scored 24 of those points in the second half. URI star and future New York Knicks first-round pick Sly Williams had just the opposite kind of night, scoring 19 points in the first half before succumbing to the Terriers' smothering defense. BU led for most of the game and held as much as an 11-point advantage before URI tied it at 64 with just over three minutes left. BU responded in kind, holding Williams in check in the game's final stretches. A 15-footer from Channel with 2:41 remaining gave BU a 66–64 advantage that it never relinquished. Final score: *Boston University 75 Rhode Island 69.*[49]

"Sly Williams and I got into it, and I literally ended up in the stands chasing this guy," John Teague recalled. "I remember Coach Pitino telling him, 'Our kids are fighters, and if you think he's scared of you, he's not. You just made a tremendous mistake because you just woke up the lion.' And then we get back to the locker room, and he says, 'Are you crazy? He could have killed you!'"[50]

The win was the most significant of Pitino's brief tenure at Boston University. It was BU's first over Rhode Island in six years. It further demonstrated that BU could play with anyone in the region, including the club that was widely recognized as New England's best. The victory improved BU's record to 13-7 while dropping Rhode Island's to 16-5.

Everyone loves a winner, and in the aftermath of the URI win, the *Daily Free Press* ran a piece extolling the job Pitino had done with the basketball program. Several students who were regulars in the "BU Pound" talked about how Pitino had remade them into basketball fans. BU players Glenn Consor and Steve Wright gave testimonials to the effort and intelligence their coach put into his job. Athletic director John Simpson even got into the act. "Rick Pitino took a program in the doldrums and made it exciting. He made it exciting because he's a quality teacher and he has the ability to motivate the guys," he said.[51]

After playing to a full house against Rhode Island, BU roughed up an overmatched Richmond team, 85–69, in front of roughly 250 people at Case.[52] Two nights later, Wagner came into Case and left with a 73–72 win. The Seahawks, who were coached by P. J. Carlesimo and went on to win twenty-one games and earn a bid to the NIT, played in a similarly aggressive and high-flying style as BU. Pitino and Carlesimo would later become reacquainted as rivals in the Big East.

Clearly the Terriers got over the Wagner loss quickly. They pasted a season-high 124 points on UNH on Saturday afternoon and followed it up with a Washington's Birthday win over George Washington. Gene Jones played decisive minutes off the bench against George Washington, scoring 14 points, including the first two buckets of the second half. The freshman guard demonstrated the depth of BU's bench as he filled in for an ill Tom Channel, who played limited minutes that evening.

The win over George Washington moved BU's mark to 16-8, putting them in position to play its way into the four-team ECAC tournament in the first weekend of March in Providence. The Terriers' next-to-last regular season game was a trip up Commonwealth Avenue to face Tom Davis's 20-7 Boston College Eagles, who were also enjoying a rapid turnaround. This de facto ECAC play-in game pitted longtime rivals against one another in a matchup of suddenly similar teams. BC's slashing and cutting zone offense and pressing defenses closely resembled BU's style of play.

In front of a raucous, standing-room-only Roberts Center crowd, Tom Davis's BC team outpressed, outran, and outshot Boston University. BU hung around in the first half, just a couple baskets behind the Eagles. While Steve Wright, who drew the majority of BC's focus, started slowly, Tom Channel scored 17 of his 29 points to keep the Terriers in contention. Boston College blew the game wide open in the second half, shooting an astounding 69 percent in the game's final twenty minutes. BC turned eight steals directly into buckets, more than accounting for the margin of victory in the 99–84 Eagles win.[53] "Boston College completely outplayed us. They deserve to represent New England in the ECACs," Pitino said in defeat.[54] The loss knocked BU out of contention for the ECAC Playoffs. BC joined UConn, URI, and Holy Cross the following weekend at the Providence Civic Center for the final edition of the New England playoffs. Eventual champ UConn pummeled BC in the semifinals.

BU took its frustrations out on Assumption in their finale, a 117–79 clobbering at Case. 1,152 fans watched Tom Channel close out his college career in style with a game-high 25 points. All thirteen Terriers scored in a game that Boston University had well in hand well before the halftime break. The win put BU's final record at 17-9, the most wins by a Terriers team since their trip to the Elite Eight twenty seasons earlier. "I was very worried that there would be a letdown after the loss to BC and not making it to the ECACs but these guys went out and did the job like they have all season long," Pitino said. "I'm very proud of them."[55] The end of the 1978–1979 season was no time for rest. Pitino had players in the weight room the next afternoon prepping for the 1979–1980 season.[56]

Postseason plaudits proved modest for BU basketball despite their tremendous season. A March 2 *Globe* postmortem on the 1978–1979 ECAC regular season congratulated BU on its fine year, despite its being left out of the New England tournament. The Terriers "played good if erratic basketball," and the New England Coach of the Year was "obviously" Pitino, the *Globe* intoned.[57] The region's sports writing fraternity thought otherwise. Pitino finished a distant second in New England Coach of the Year balloting, behind Connecticut's Dom Perno. Tom Channel earned second-team All-New England honors. He was selected in the third round of the NBA Draft by the San Diego Clippers, who cut him in training camp that September.

Less than two weeks after BU finished its 1978–1979 campaign, Pitino signed a four-year extension, an unprecedented move for an athletic department that kept most coaches on year-to-year contracts.[58] Pitino took little time to celebrate the extension, spending significant stretches of the spring in search of more players.

"Recruiting is much more nerve-wracking than playing tough games on the road. This time of year, you have no idea if you're number 1 on a kid's list or number 3," Pitino told *Newsday*'s Don Markus for a feature story that spring about the life of college basketball coaches on the recruiting trail.[59] Pitino and assistant Bill Burke came close to signing superstar shooting guard Stewart Granger out of Burke's old Brooklyn stomping grounds, Nazareth Regional High School. Burke had coached Nazareth to a Class AA New York State championship in 1977 before heading to BU. Granger had led the 1979 team to another state championship and was one of the city's most coveted recruits that season. Instead, Granger signed on at Villanova and became a featured player in Rollie Massimino's backcourt.

Despite losing out on Granger, Pitino signed one of the celebrated recruit's teammates, 6'5" forward Arturo Brown. Brown was born in Panama and began playing basketball only in eighth grade. Nevertheless, the athletic and diligent Brown transformed himself into a two-time All-City performer. Though smaller than a lot of the low-post players he faced in New York, Brown earned a reputation as a dogged rebounder with a great touch as a scorer. Though not as heavily recruited as Granger, Brown turned down offers from Providence, St. Joseph's, and Virginia to be a building block on Rick Pitino's BU team.[60]

Pitino drew his first drips from a new honey hole in northern New England that spring. He signed a 6'9" forward from Sherman Hills, Maine, named Mike Bouchard, as well as a fast and fiery 5'11" point guard out of South Portland named Brett Brown.[61] Brown combined lightning speed with the equally fast sense of on-court awareness of a coach's son. Brett's father, Bob, was his high school coach and had built his boy into an intuitive scorer, defender, and distributor. The Browns led South Portland to an undefeated state championship run in March 1979. "Recruiting Brett turned out to be a two for one deal. When recruiting Brett, I became very friendly with his father, Bob. I liked Brett as a player but I loved the intensity of the practices Bob ran. A few years later, I hired Bob as an assistant with BU," Pitino wrote.[62]

A total of six players signed on to become Boston University Terriers. Only the "Brown Brothers," as Arturo and Brett came to be known, made it past their first season on Rick Pitino's team. Both became part of the foundation for BU basketball's future.

6

Pack the Bags. We're Off to Albuquerque *(Williams)*

"The best basketball in the city of Boston was in the Roberts Center in September," Jay Murphy said.[1] Murphy was the first of more than two dozen people to tell me this. For much of the 1980s, this was certainly the case.

Weeks before Gary Williams held his first official practice as Boston College's head coach, his players were having it out on their home floor with the city's best professional and collegiate players. Before the NBA began its training camps in late September and before the NCAA let coaches hold their first formal practices on October 15, BC's well-worn gym was the not-so-secret center of the basketball universe.

Every September several Boston Celtics made the Roberts Center their informal home court as they got into playing shape. Roberts regulars during the 1980s included Kevin McHale, Cedric Maxwell, Danny Ainge, Bill Walton, Scott Wedman, and M. L. Carr. Larry Bird, Dennis Johnson, and Robert Parish all made appearances at Roberts but less frequently than their other teammates. Joining the Celtics in these informal games was the entirety of the BC basketball roster, as well as a smattering of stars from BU and Northeastern, including Gary Plummer, Tony Simms, Mark Halsel, and, later, Reggie Lewis.

"You want to talk about some pretty high-level pickup games," Jay Murphy said of the annual rite of passage for BC basketball players. During the 1982 iteration of this Roberts Center tradition, Murphy worked closely with Celtics legend Dave Cowens, who was attempting a comeback.[2] Joining Cowens in the gym that September and attempting his own comeback was Marvin "Bad News" Barnes, the former Providence College All-American and ABA standout who was at least as well known for his transgressions off the court as his prowess on it. Chris Ford, who had just retired from the NBA, played in the pickup games that September before becoming a volunteer assistant coach for the '82–'83 Eagles.

"There'd be like six or seven or eight guys that would show up at a time," Russ Doherty, who was then an incoming freshman, recalled. "We'd be playing three Celtics and two BC guys against two Celtics and three BC guys. And for the most part, the Celtics played pretty hard."[3] "If you don't win, you don't stay on the floor, so there were some pretty competitive games there," Jay Murphy remembered.[4] "It was great having the Celtics come up. That helped our confidence. It was great to see Michael Adams and Danny Ainge fighting it out on the floor, battling for the last point," said Steven Benton, who played for the Eagles from 1985 to 1989.[5] Among the Celtics, Ainge stood out as a character. "My mental image of Roberts in September is Danny Ainge playing basketball in flip-flops," BU basketball manager Mike Rosen remembers.[6] Rosen, a consummate basketball junkie, drove his friends Gary Plummer and Tony Simms up Commonwealth Avenue to play in the pickup games and stuck around to watch.

Stu Primus recalls playing full court, one-on-one against Ainge on several occasions. "Stu, if you miss a shot, I win," Ainge would tell Primus before they played. And Ainge would be right. He would never miss.[7]

Just as much of a character on the BC side of things that September was center John Garris. "It was early September, and we'd just got back on the court," said Gary Williams, who watched the pickup games from the stands, "and here comes John Garris on his bike. Parks it in Roberts Center. John jumps right into a game, and if you didn't know the guys, you couldn't tell who the Celtics were. Garris looked as good as anyone on the court that particular day. I called him over and said, 'John, you must have really been working.' He said, 'Coach, I've got to be honest. This is like the first time I've played since May.'"[8]

As talented as he was laid back, Garris was liked by all but was something of an enigma to the coaching staff. "He was 6'9", had great reflexes as a defensive player," Gary Williams said of Garris, whose athleticism, shooting prowess, and strength in the low post proved to be a major asset for BC in the upcoming season. "You weren't afraid to throw him the ball anywhere on the court. If he would have loved the game, he could have been one of the better players in the NBA."[9]

While the September pickup games could be as intense as Garris was relaxed, the competition at Roberts created an atmosphere of collegiality among the players in attendance. "I'm so glad I had that experience, that I got to hang out with McHale and Danny [Ainge] and Dennis Johnson. I could always tell my friends and kids that I played with some of the greatest basketball players of all-time," said Troy Bowers, who joined the Eagles in the 1983–1984 season.[10] The relationships that developed between BC players and members of the Celtics led to many friendships. Not infrequently BC players were guests of the Celtics at the Boston Garden and were invited to postgame dinners.

Just because his players trained with the Celtics didn't mean that basketball writers in the East thought Gary Williams's team stood much of a chance at repeating its recent performances. Prognosticators for all the major newspapers in the Northeast projected the Tom Davis-less, John Bagley-less Boston College Eagles no better than fifth for the 1982–1983 season.[11] The Big East coaches' preseason poll also slated BC at fifth. No one on the BC roster made the preseason all-conference first or second team.

Previews of the Eagles noted their experienced frontcourt with veterans Martin Clark, Jay Murphy, Burnett Adams, and John Garris holding down the fort. The departures of Dwan Chandler and, especially, John Bagley from the backcourt made both guard positions a major question mark. With Bagley and Chandler, BC had two guards who frequently drove to the basket and created open looks for Murphy and Clark. The extent to which BC's new backcourt could execute this remained to be seen. While Michael Adams had played well down the stretch for BC, the 5'10" point guard's upside remained unclear to many observers. At the other guard spot, newcomer Dom Pressley and sophomores Stu Primus and Terrence Talley looked to contribute, but "After Mike Adams, there's no one with any experience," Gary Williams conceded about his backcourt.[12]

Williams told the *Globe*'s Michael Madden that he intended to press for forty minutes and substitute frequently, essentially an exaggeration of the system that he had helped Davis put in place at BC several years earlier. "I think you'll see that BC will be more emotional than it was last season. If guys make a good play, I want them to enjoy it," Williams said. He reiterated that his team would run more than Davis's team and not just in transition. BC's roster was laden with speed. He planned to use it to the team's advantage.[13]

Williams had prepared his team for this style of play in the preseason, putting the players through the same kind of conditioning drills and severe practices as his predecessor Davis had done. Endless 40- and 100-yard sprints on the football field plus frequent five-mile runs in the six weeks before the season prepared the players for the rigors of Gary Williams's running offense and full-court press.

"Everyone on that team was extremely competitive," Russ Doherty said. "Everyone on that team worked their asses off in practice. And you didn't really have a choice about that."[14] "Nobody there had an ego. Everybody wanted to win," Stu Primus said.[15] In Williams, they had a coach who was just as intense as they were in getting ready for the season. Williams, on occasion, punted a basketball into the stands at Roberts to get his point across. "Gary was a fiery guy. A lot of passion and energy," Jay Murphy said. "With Gary you felt like some guys would run through the wall for him. You loved playing for him."[16]

"We always talked about how we weren't going to allow the other team to dictate the way we played. It was up to them to match up against us. Part of that was just to give your team confidence. I think that gave us an advantage," Gary Williams said.[17]

"With Gary Williams, it was a lot more full-court press," Stu Primus remembered. "It was an up-and-down style. Great tempo. We played 94–50."[18] For veterans, the learning curve of Gary Williams's system proved minimal, as he used much of the same terminology as Davis. "It was the same numbers. If a play ended in 0, it was man-to-man. If it ended with a 5, it was zone. In full court, the first number was 5. If it was three-quarter, it was 4. If it was 10, you played half-court man-to-man. If it was 50, you played full court man-to-man. If it was 55, it was full-court press zone. The terminology was easy," Jay Murphy said.[19]

"When we ran our offense, there were like seven cutters before you took a shot—that's a guard-to-guard pass where the extended person would cut through the lane. That wears the hell out of them, and they don't know what the hell we're doing. And then we'd go three cutters and a shot. It was an ingenious system. They had to play a zone against us. It was designed to wear people down," Stu Primus said.[20]

Boston College hit the ground running, putting into practice all the team had worked on in the leadup to its non-conference slate. They opened the 1982–1983 season with a trio of home contests against profoundly overmatched regional opponents. The Eagles disposed of St. Michael's, Stonehill, and the University of New Hampshire with great ease, winning each game by at least 32 points, scoring at least 90 in all three with Williams's fast-breaking offense, and getting everyone on the roster plenty of minutes. Easy wins or not, the crowds at Roberts got their first look at Gary Williams's approach to in-game coaching. They saw a head man very different from the crouching stoic who had preceded him. Williams could be seen stomping up and down the sidelines and sweating up a storm soon after tip-off in games like these, which BC had well in hand well before halftime.

BC's first real test came on December 6 at Matthews Arena as the Eagles faced Jim Calhoun and Northeastern University, the two-time defending ECAC North champions who had advanced to the second round of the 1981 and 1982 NCAA Tournaments. The previous March, the Huskies had nearly knocked off Big East power Villanova to advance to the Sweet Sixteen. Nevertheless, Tom Davis's BC clubs had bested the Huskies in all four of their meetings, typically in convincing fashion. Despite losing a cluster of standouts from their 1981–1982 team, Northeastern returned a fast and physical team, led by its frontcourt of Mark Halsel and Roland Braswell.

Northeastern and BC raced up and down the court throughout the first half, pressing, trapping, and fast breaking the game into a 26–26 tie at the eight-minute mark. Eventually, Northeastern, too, fell prey to BC's press. Dom Pressley broke the 26–26 tie by picking off a Phil Robinson pass and bringing it home for a layup. Pressley's interception kicked off a 13–2 BC run that put the Eagles in control for good. The pace of play remained fast and furious in the second half, but frequent harassment from Burnett Adams, Garris, and Murphy kept Braswell in check for the rest of the game. BC won, 92–79.

After a two-week hiatus for final exams, BC returned to action on December 21, taking on a Fairfield program that had fallen on hard times. Martin Clark, Jay Murphy, and Michael Adams all pumped in at least 20 points in the 99–79 win before a half-empty Roberts Center. Less than four miles away Tom Davis and his 5–0 Stanford club beat Harvard, 81–77, on the former BC coach's first trip back to Boston. Stanford wasn't in town long enough for Davis to meet up with anyone from BC besides the recently graduated Rich Shrigley, who sat in on a Stanford practice.[21]

Western Kentucky awaited Williams and company after the Christmas break. In a tightly officiated game, to say the least, the Hilltoppers upset BC in the opening game of the Cotton States Classic at Atlanta's Omni

Coliseum. Boston College outscored Western Kentucky by 18 points from the field, but Western Kentucky took 43 foul shots to BC's 11. The Hilltoppers hit enough of them to hang on for a 74–68 win. BC looked sluggish the following night but still found a way to eke out a win against Columbia in the consolation round, its last game of the year.

As 1982 turned into 1983, Boston College entered conference play, averaging more than 95 points per game, shooting 57 percent from the floor, and boasting an 8-1 record. BC led the nation in almost every major offensive category. This was a more aggressive team—one that relied less on the zone offense and more on a fast-breaking style that was all Gary Williams's own. "I just like to be aggressive. I think that's the key thing. It's hard to separate the offense and defense. If we're aggressive defensively, it seems like we play better offensively," Williams wrote of the style of play he brought back to Chestnut Hill with him.[22]

Still, this Boston College club that had made it to the Final Eight the previous season found itself on the outside looking in at the AP Top 20. It was more than just the old "overachievers" label keeping them outside of the rankings. BC's early schedule had been soft. With the exceptions of Northeastern and Western Kentucky, BC played most of its non-conference games against small New England colleges.

Boston College opened league play on January 4, 1983, at the Meadowlands in East Rutherford, New Jersey against virtually the same Villanova Wildcats team that had beaten them three times the previous season. Rollie Massimino's club had ended BC's run in the 1982 Big East Tournament in the semifinals. Nova later joined the Eagles in the Final Eight, falling to eventual national champion North Carolina in the East Regional. Big, nasty, and well-coached, Villanova's 1982–1983 team featured a starting five that all played in the NBA: burly center John Pinone; explosive guards Stewart Granger and Dwayne McClain; versatile power forward Ed Pinckney; and freshman Harold Pressley, a 6'7" dynamo recruited out of BC's backyard in Uncasville, Connecticut. Making matters worse for their opponents, this cadre of basketball talent was being coached by one of the sport's great tacticians.

"Rollie Massimino was a mastermind. If you gave him more than a day or two to prepare, we usually didn't lose," said Chuck Everson, a reserve center on the '82–'83 Nova team. "Mostly we were a slow-down, patient team. Fast break when we had to. Very good defensively. We played multiple defenses. In one possession we might change the defense two or three times. That became tricky for other teams to play against because they didn't know if we were in a man-to-man or zone or what we were in."[23]

Villanova had been in the preseason top five but faltered early on the road against Kentucky and dropped a Big 5 rivalry game at the Palestra to Penn. The Wildcats entered 1983 with the number 14 spot in the AP poll. The Saturday night showdown at the Meadowlands was one of the most interesting opening weekend games on the 1983 Big East schedule, not only because it took place at such a prominent venue, but also because the contest would serve as a measuring stick for two programs whose performance against non-conference opponents made it unclear just where they stood within the powerful league. It proved to be one of BC's most frustrating games of the season.

Villanova, led by big man John Pinone, took control of the blocks from the game's outset. Pinone scored a game-high 24 points, 16 of which came from the line. Villanova led 33–27 at the half and extended its advantage to 9 points early in the second. Persistent in its press, BC started to wear down its brawnier opponent, cutting the lead to five midway through the second half. John Garris, whom Pinone held to just 2 points in the first half, got hot in the second and ended up with 20 for the game. Michael Adams, too, picked his spots, penetrating the Wildcats' defense and scoring 21 points.[24]

As BC battled its way back into the game, the roughhousing under the basket got more intense. Burnett Adams and Pinone got into it after Pinone lingered in the BC forward's face after blocking a shot, leading to pushing and shoving between the teams. Moments later Harold Pressley got a receipt from Jay Murphy for an evening's worth of poking and prodding. Murphy planted his elbow firmly in Pressley's chin, leading to a technical foul on Murphy, Murphy's ejection from the game, and some self-described embellishment on Pressley's part. In Pressley's stead, Pinone hit both foul shots, and Villanova never looked back. The Wildcats won by a 79–72 margin.[25]

BC rebounded from the Villanova loss with a pair of blowout wins at the Roberts Center. The Eagles pummeled rookie coach P. J. Carlesimo's rebuilding Seton Hall Pirates in conference play and did a similar number on Rhode Island. The convincing victories served as tune-ups for Williams's team as they prepared for their next clash with a Big East titan.

Next on the slate were the third-ranked and undefeated St. John's Redmen. As usual, Lou Carnesecca's team played a disciplined, man-to-man defense that was overseen by his assistant, Al Lobalbo, one of the most respected minds in basketball. The Johnnies' half-court offense was just as renowned for its discipline. No team in the country had a better reputation for their shot selection than St. John's. "Coach Carnesecca instilled in us the importance of finding the best shot we could each possession. He was a very nurturing, fatherly coach with an open-door policy. Very accessible. Taught us accountability toward one another," Johnnies forward Ron Stewart said of his legendary former coach.[26]

St. John's had finished third in the Big East in 1981–1982 and reached the second round of the NCAA Tournament. The Johnnies returned every major contributor for 1982–1983, and it showed. They opened the season by upsetting North Carolina at the Springfield Civic Center and had recently defeated Georgetown at Madison Square Garden [MSG].

The Redmen boasted arguably the best shooter in the country in 6′6″ sophomore forward Chris Mullin, a hometown hero whose place in New York City basketball lore was already well established. Joining Mullin on the wings were a pair of agile scorers in David Russell and Billy Goodwin, while 7′0″ sophomore Bill Wennington trolled the middle.

After morning shootaround, the BC players spent the afternoon in their dorms, watching North Carolina upset second-ranked Virginia. Earlier in the week, number one Memphis State had fallen to Virginia Tech. Suddenly, BC's game that evening was a shot at the presumed number one team in the country, come Monday morning's release of the AP poll. But on a snowy Saturday night, Boston College upset St. John's before a standing-room-only crowd at Roberts. Despite the treacherous conditions on the Bay State's roadways, a similarly treacherous crowd greeted the visitors from Queens.[27] "Excuse my French, but the Roberts Center was a bitch. Yellowish lighting and the student body was literally hanging over the railing on the top level. And BC was good," Ron Stewart recalled.[28]

BC blitzed St. John's early, racing to a 10–2 lead on the strength of a pair of buckets each by Murphy and Garris. Murphy proved to be a mismatch for the Johnnies' big men all evening, scoring 19 points on just 10 shots. "Jay Murphy was a problem: 6′11″, with the ability to shoot from distance, and also pretty crafty with the ball," said Ron Stewart, who was frequently tasked that evening with guarding Murphy.[29]

BC led by as many as 11 points in the first half, with Michael Adams leading the way for the Eagles on both ends of the floor. BC's barrage of full-court and three-quarter presses forced St. John's into a dozen first-half turnovers. Adams turned several steals into easy fast break buckets for the Eagles, including a thunderous first-half alley-oop to Garris. On the evening, Adams scored a then career-high 27 points, earned five assists, and made eight steals. Never before had Adams demonstrated his mastery of the pressure basketball that Tom Davis and, now, Gary Williams had put in place at Boston College in as dramatic a fashion as he did that evening.

Despite the intensity of BC's attack, St. John's eventually fought its way back into the game. BC led by just 1, 36–35, at the half. It was Chris Mullin's 10-for-13 shooting and 22 points that helped the Redmen hang tough. A Mullin jumper early in the second half gave the visitors their only lead of the game. Eventually, Billy Goodwin kicked in for 12 on the offensive end, and Bill Wennington made his presence known in the post on defense.

With just 2:53 remaining, the Eagles led 57–54. At this point, Michael Adams took control of the game, hitting six straight foul shots down the stretch and finding Jay Murphy for an easy layup over the course of the next ninety seconds. With BC leading by 8 and just 1:25 on the clock, Adams stole the ball at midcourt and raced in for a layup. Johnnies guard Keith Williams goaltended the ball, giving BC a 66–56 lead and effectively ending the game. The fans at Roberts Center counted down to zero to punctuate what was arguably the Eagles' biggest regular season win in recent memory. It was also BC's first win against an elite opponent that season, proving that the Eagles' 11-2 record was the product of something other than a soft non-conference slate.[30] "They [St. John's] probably thought they could come in and walk all over us. I think we'll get some national respect now too," Michael Adams said after the win.[31]

Despite the win and their 11-2 record, BC remained unranked in the following Monday's AP Top 20 poll. The Eagles did no favors to their case for a spot in the poll that Monday night. They hosted thirteenth-ranked Syracuse and got absolutely clobbered. The previous season, Boston College beat Syracuse on three occasions. This time, Syracuse won, 102–85, the first time an opponent had reached triple figures on BC in five years. Syracuse was the only team in the Big East that ran like BC, and on this particular evening the Orangemen proved themselves to be the true thoroughbreds in the conference. "We liked to get out and run—getting the ball off the rim and getting out and running, trying to get easy buckets," Syracuse point guard Gene Waldron said of the Orangemen's style.[32] "We were not the most patient on offense. You got the ball, you were looking to take the shot," his teammate Sonny Spera said.[33]

Defensively, Syracuse was no slouch either. While most clubs in the East favored man-to-man, head coach Jim Boeheim and assistant Bernie Fine had crafted a 2–3 zone that was among the country's most impenetrable defenses. "That zone was very effective against a lot of teams. A lot of guys weren't shooting the great jump shots the way they do now," Waldron said.[34]

Despite boasting a roster that included such outstanding shooters as Jay Murphy, Michael Adams, and Martin Clark, BC sank very little against Syracuse's zone that evening. BC shot just 37 percent from the field to Syracuse's 63 percent.

Syracuse's efforts on both ends of the floor were fueled in part by the annoyance the Orangemen felt with the crowd at Roberts that evening. During player introductions the BC student section pelted the Orangemen with oranges. Gary Williams got on the PA system and asked them to stop, but the occasional orange continued to rain down from the balcony on Syracuse for the rest of the evening. Syracuse senior shooting guard Erich Santifier contributed 30 points toward the cause while his classmate, small forward Tony Bruin, added 29.[35]

Boeheim kept his starters in well after the game was out of hand. Never one to suffer in silence, Boeheim bemoaned the crowd at Roberts, calling it "an unfair place to play" and saying he left his starters in because "I didn't want to take a chance. The only way to control the crowd at BC is to score."[36]

BC bounced back with a road win at Connecticut and a 68–63 victory over Pitt at the Roberts Center. The wins improved BC's record to 13-3 overall and 4-2 in the league as it prepared for a road trip to the Capital Centre in Landover, Maryland, to face the Georgetown Hoyas. John Thompson's Hoyas had been an eastern power since the mid-1970s, but the 1981–1982 campaign was when the program became a nationally recognized basketball phenomenon.

That season, a freshman that Thompson had recruited out of Cambridge Rindge and Latin School became the most talked about college basketball player in the country. Patrick Ewing was a 7'0" defensive force, the strongest, most athletic big man anyone had ever seen coming out of high school. He went to high school less than six miles from Chestnut Hill and had grown up less than ten miles from the BC campus. At age twelve, Ewing had immigrated from Jamaica to Cambridge, Massachusetts. It didn't take long for people to realize that this young man had a unique talent for basketball.

"When I was a high school coach at Don Bosco, I was working at the Boston College summer camp between Patrick's eighth- and ninth-grade year. Patrick Ewing was on my team," Kevin Mackey said. "I had heard of Patrick, but I hadn't seen him play. He was obviously bigger and stronger than all the kids in his age group. And then when we started to play, he was head and shoulders ahead of them—defensively aggressive, rebounding wise, and he was developing offensively. He was in a class by himself. We won every game and the camp championship. I worked very, very hard to get him to come with me to Don Bosco."[37]

Instead, Ewing attended school at another Boston-area basketball power, the recently merged Cambridge Rindge and Latin School. Formerly two separate high schools, Rindge Tech and Cambridge High and Latin School, the new two-thousand-student school opened in 1977. The following year "Rindge," as the school came to be known, made Mike Jarvis its head basketball coach. Jarvis had played on Rindge Tech's 1962 state championship team before suiting up for Duke Dukeshire's teams at Northeastern University. He later served as an assistant basketball coach at Northeastern and Harvard while teaching physical education at Rindge Tech. Jarvis first met Patrick Ewing when he was in junior high school, helping to instruct him in the fundamentals of basketball. The pair has had a special bond ever since. "The thing about Patrick was that he was special because of the person that he was and because of the way that he had been raised by his mom and his dad. It was all about working hard and trying to do the best you can and getting back up after you get knocked down. Patrick was one of the easiest players to ever coach because he was one of the hardest-working players I ever coached," Jarvis said.[38]

The combination of Jarvis and Ewing at Rindge, along with an accomplished supporting cast that included future UConn star and George Washington coach Karl Hobbs, became one of the most successful in high school basketball history. Rindge won three consecutive state titles (1979–1981) and went 77-1 during that stretch. For much of this multi-year championship run, Ewing was the most coveted prep player in the country. The Ewing family relied on Coach Jarvis to oversee their son's recruitment, enabling the family to retain as normal a life as possible while finding the college that provided the best fit for the young basketball star.

"We put together a plan and a timetable and basically asked everybody to respect it. We told all the college coaches that if they didn't, they would be eliminated from the recruiting process," Jarvis said. "In those days, a coach could call every day or come over every day. There weren't as many rules the coaches had to abide by, so we had to set up a system with rules they had to abide by."[39] By the start of Ewing's senior year the list was whittled down to six schools, which included both BC and BU. In the end, the choice came down to UCLA and Georgetown, with Patrick choosing to become a Hoya. The school was close enough to home for the family-oriented Ewing but was far enough away to help him avoid some of the smothering local attention he would have received had he stayed in Boston. Ewing's mother also preferred that her son play for a Black coach if given the opportunity.[40]

Even though Ewing chose not to attend BC, the perception that he was strongly considering Chestnut Hill helped the school in recruiting, Kevin Mackey asserts. "We got a tip that he was going to go to Georgetown, but they were going to have three finalists and they weren't going to make the announcement till after the season. I said, 'Tom [Davis], if we have Patrick as a finalist for Boston College, I'll be able to get two or three other very good kids easily because they think Patrick will be coming to Boston College.' And we did."[41]

Patrick Ewing's arrival at Georgetown enhanced not only the Hoyas' performance on the court, but also the program's national profile. Since taking over at Georgetown in 1972, John Thompson had transformed the Hoyas first into a regional power and then into one of the most prominent programs in the new Big East Conference. Entering the 1981–1982 season, Georgetown had four consecutive twenty-win seasons, earned three consecutive bids to the NCAA Tournament, won the inaugural Big East Tournament in 1980, and reached the East Regional final that same year.

Georgetown reached new heights in Ewing's freshman year, winning thirty games, blowing out the competition en route to another Big East title, and battling its way to the national championship game. A jumper from the corner by North Carolina's own freshman phenom, Michael

Jordan, in the waning seconds of the title game was all that kept the Hoyas from cutting down the nets at the Louisiana Superdome. While the "Hoya Destroyas," as they came to be known, marauded through the season, nationally televised games on CBS and ESPN made Ewing, the looming presence just under the rim; the equally imposing and far more brooding John Thompson; and Georgetown's nearly all-Black basketball team a striking presence before both live and television audiences. Georgetown was simultaneously beloved and reviled. Nearly everything Thompson's team did during this era was seen by large segments of the public and press through the prism of race.

Just as he had been by opposing fans in suburban Boston, Ewing, as well as his teammates, was subjected to frequent abuse from opposing fans that was steeped in no small part in racial animus. At the same time, sportswriters and basketball commentators fed the flames by regularly accusing Georgetown of "ruining basketball" with its physical play. Without question, the ire that Georgetown drew from opposing fans was to a great extent a product of the team's aggressive defensive style, which, sometimes fairly and sometimes unfairly, earned the Hoyas the reputation of playing dirty. "If you were playing Georgetown, you were getting bumped like a pinball machine," Syracuse point guard Sonny Spera recalled. Probably no team got into it more frequently with the Hoyas or with more ferocity than Syracuse, who became the Hoyas' arch-rival over the course of the 1980s. Spera continues: "The way that they played the game and pushed the rules on certain things, I thought it was a travesty. But they did it effectively. Physical, in your face, pressure D. We are going to maul and hammer you, and if you have the ball and you're not protected, we're going to run through you to get it."[42]

"I think the beauty and the brilliance of what John Thompson did is he had a tremendous amount of talent there. and sometimes when a team is full of talent, they don't play quite as hard. but his teams were just tenacious on defense," BC guard Ted Kelley recalled.[43]

During the 1981–1982 season, BC split its games with Georgetown, falling 67–51 at the Capital Centre and winning a wild 80–71 contest at the Roberts Center. "In Patrick Ewing's freshman year, when Georgetown came to town, we played the game in Roberts Center. The capacity said 4,400, but there had to be 5,000 or 5,500 people in there. It was just a mass of humanity. I remember having to call security because people were opening the windows in the men's room and people were climbing in. You couldn't get a ticket. The place was just insane," BC manager Matt Gianatassio remembered.[44]

The crowd was on Ewing's case all evening, frequently returning to a chant of "Ewing Can't Read," a reference to his allegedly subpar SAT scores and apparent need for tutoring and remedial reading courses. Rick Pitino had made a similar assertion to the *Boston Globe* during the later stages of Ewing's recruitment, stating, "I would say we would have had the greatest difficulty in getting him accepted. He was never accepted at Boston University."[45] Regardless, such assertions were, at best, a bad look on the part of both the BC student section and BU's head coach.

Georgetown's poor performance at Roberts and the unwelcoming atmosphere that greeted the team encouraged John Thompson to push Big East commissioner Dave Gavitt to move the 1983 game at Boston College to the Garden. "Thompson went to Gavitt and said, 'Hey Dave, this is supposed to be a big-time league. What are we doing playing in this bowling alley for? We should be playing in the Boston Garden in front of 13,000-plus people,'" Kevin Mackey said.[46] All 14,451 tickets to the March 2 BC-Georgetown game sold out within three days of going on sale.[47]

Well before BC and Georgetown tangled in March at the Garden, they met in late January at the Capital Centre, another one of the loudest (and also largest) venues in the Big East. This 1982–1983 Georgetown team was still loaded with talent but clearly missed the three seniors who had started on the previous year's club, especially point guard Eric "Sleepy" Floyd, who had been the team's on-floor leader. In addition to Ewing, the '82–'83 Hoyas boasted a rugged, athletic frontcourt with fellow youngsters Bill Martin and David Wingate. They had a similarly youthful and talented backcourt featuring Michael Jackson, Anthony Jones, Horace Broadnax, and Fred Brown.

Despite the Hoyas' youth, the AP ranked Georgetown number two in its preseason poll. They had not quite lived up to expectations. They had dropped four games already, three of them to teams ranked in the top ten. The other loss came against a roster full of Gary Williams—recruited and -coached players at American University. In the leadup to the Georgetown game, Williams consulted with Eddie Tapscott, his successor at American University, about how his team had pulled off a 62–61 upset of the Hoyas earlier in the season using Williams's own pressure defense.[48]

BC's press frustrated Georgetown throughout the first half. The continual harassment of Ewing kept the Cambridge native in check all evening. BC's defensive cadre held him to just 9 points. The Eagles led by as many as 10, but Georgetown's defense clamped down in the latter stages of the first half, giving BC just a 3-point advantage at the break.

Early in the second half, Georgetown took the lead, relying on the speed of its backcourt to dribble penetrate and manufacture points. Hoya big man Ralph Dalton broke a 41–41 tie with 16:21 remaining, drawing a foul from Burnett Adams while cramming in a tight layup from the low post. Officials teed up Gary Williams, who protested the call with unusual vigor even for his expressive self. Williams later complained to reporters that Thompson had avoided a technical during the game despite cajoling the officials just as mercilessly as he had that evening.

Dalton hit his technical foul shot, giving the Hoyas a 3-point lead they would soon expand. Georgetown led by as many as 7, but BC chipped into the Hoyas' advantage and had the game tied at 67 with 2:37 remaining. Clutch shooting by Jay Murphy, who scored a game-high 26 points, helped keep the Eagles in the contest. The last few minutes of the game consisted of competing slow-down offenses. BC took possession with the game still tied at 67 with 1:05 remaining. Gary Williams instructed Michael Adams and the offense to hold the ball until he called timeout with fourteen seconds left. Off the timeout, Martin Clark inbounded the ball to Adams, who drove straight to the lane. Georgetown's Gene Smith slapped the ball away from Adams. Hoya forward David Wingate scooped up the ball and raced down the floor. He laid in the winning basket as time expired.[49]

While the defeat stung, BC had shown once again that it could hang tight with the heavyweights of the conference. Besides, BC had a return date with Georgetown in a few weeks at the Garden.

Boston College rebounded from the Georgetown loss with a weeknight road win over Providence before a return date at home with Villanova. At the time, Villanova was ranked eleventh and sat in second place in the Big East standings, behind St. John's, with a 6-1 mark. Pinckney, Pinone, and company faced a much different BC club than the one they had man-handled in the Meadowlands a few weeks earlier.

This time, Williams upped BC's athleticism on the floor by increasing Stu Primus's and Terrence Talley's time. The pair logged more than twenty minutes each and set the tone for the Eagles' aggressive approach to the game, helping BC win the turnover battle, 17–7. BC went toe-to-toe with a bigger Villanova team on the boards, meeting the Wildcats' physicality with plenty of roughhousing of their own. A particularly churlish home crowd at a sold-out Roberts Center no doubt contributed to the Eagles' 37–31 advantage on the boards. At the half, Nova led, 35–32, but three straight jumpers by Jay Murphy early in the second helped BC tie the game at 44. The teams traded makes and misses for much of the second half until Michael Adams whizzed a bounce pass to Dom Pressley that he laid in to give the Eagles a 54–52 advantage with 7:42 remaining. Boston College never trailed again, winning 76–70. The victory moved BC firmly into the top half of the Big East, improving their overall record to 15-4 while giving them a 6-3 mark in league play, good enough for third place.[50] Subsequent wins over Seton Hall and Holy Cross set BC up for a Tuesday night Alumni Hall matchup with sixth-ranked St. John's. Since faltering at the Roberts Center, the Redmen had won eight out of nine, a run that included wins over Villanova, Syracuse, and Georgetown.

"The Roberts Center was a very, very tough place to play with that sponge-like, rubber floor," Chuck Everson recalls. "Harold Pressley's freshman year, him being a New England kid and going to a Pennsylvania school, the crowd rode the heck out of him. Every time he touched the ball, the chants were, 'Harold, Harold.' It was deafening, and it definitely got to him," Everson said of the fans, who no doubt also recalled Pressley's run-in with Jay Murphy several weeks earlier.[51]

The Eagles earned a spot in the AP Top 20 poll for the first time that season, just before the St. John's game. This was in fact the first time that Boston College had been nationally ranked since Bob Cousy was still coaching on Chestnut Hill in 1969. Peter Gammons of the *Globe* wondered in his February 14 column if voters took to heart the "underachievers" label that many in and around the BC basketball program embraced so giddily. Did the idea that BC was a team of coached-up underachievers feed into the lack of respect they received from national pollsters?[52]

Whatever the reason, eighteenth-ranked Boston College once again made it clear that they belonged in any discussion of college basketball's best teams in their matchup with St. John's. BC went into one of the most hostile environments in college basketball and absolutely annihilated the Redmen, 92–75. St. John's led early in the second half, 48–47, before BC went on an 11–0 run and owned the rest of the evening. Jay Murphy cut the Johnnies to pieces from the wing and in the post, scoring a career-high 30 points and adding 11 rebounds. Stu Primus provided a further spark to BC, coming off the bench and scoring 13 points while harassing Chris Mullin and David Russell all evening. Mullin fouled out of the game with five minutes remaining, largely due to the efforts of Primus, who drew St. John's leading man into a couple of clumsy fouls.[53]

An awful Saturday night in Syracuse's Carrier Dome tempered the triumph of the previous Tuesday night in Queens. The Orangemen took BC back to the woodshed for an even worse beating than the Eagles received in their earlier encounter. The nearly thirty-one thousand fans in attendance at the central New York football stadium were even more raucous than usual, compelling an Orange team that dominated from stem to stern. Syracuse played faster, quicker, and more physically than a BC team that was known for all of those things. Silky smooth guard Erich Santifer netted 22 while his backcourt mate Gene Waldron dropped in 21. Syracuse led by as much as 20 in the first half and ended up winning by a 108–88 margin.

"The dome is cavernous. It's a tough atmosphere, especially if you don't play there all the time and you're coming from a bandbox like the Roberts Center, where the walls are right behind the backboard," Russ Doherty recalled.[54] "It's [The Carrier Dome's] so big. Your depth perception is a bit off with your shooting. And you're looking for an orange rim in a sea of orange shirts," Chuck Everson said of the torments of playing at Syracuse.[55] Two nights later, BC looked just as bad against UConn at the Huskies' ancient on-campus fieldhouse. Boston College turned the ball over thirty-three times and appeared sluggish throughout, falling 86–80. BC returned to form against Pitt, winning by a lopsided 70–52 margin.

With two games remaining in their 1983 Big East schedule, BC found themselves in third place in the league standings. At 10-4 in the league and 20-5 overall, the Eagles were a game and a half back of first place Villanova, a half game back of number two St. John's, and a half game ahead of sixteenth-ranked Georgetown, whom they hosted on a Wednesday night before a sold-out bipartisan crowd at the Boston Garden.

"We [BC] couldn't control the sale of tickets, and Big John [Thompson] knew that all of Cambridge would be coming over to see Patrick [Ewing] play in the Boston Garden," Kevin Mackey said.[56]

"The place was kind of split between people who wanted you to beat him [Ewing] because he was from Boston and didn't go there [to BC], and there were always the Ewing fans. Plus, Georgetown was obviously very popular. You'd see tons of Georgetown jackets and hats at the games," Matt Gianatassio remembered.[57]

The Hoyas fell behind early, succumbing frequently to the virulent press to which BC's eleven-man rotation subjected them. BC led, 47–41, at the half, but Georgetown rallied in the second and took the lead late into the game. Leg cramps forced Michael Adams to miss significant stretches in the second half, allowing his Georgetown counterpart, Michael Jackson, to take advantage of his absence. In all, the Georgetown guard scored a game-high 26 points.

With less than two minutes remaining, Georgetown led, 80–74, when Patrick Ewing fouled out of the game. As Ewing sat on the bench, BC mounted a comeback, penetrating the Hoyas' defense in ways that would have been unthinkable had the Georgetown center been anchoring his team's 2–3 zone. At the end of regulation, BC and Georgetown were tied at 82.

"It became a different game when Ewing fouled out," Jay Murphy said.[58] Overtime consisted largely of the two teams holding the ball, looking for the decisive moment to put one in. For Boston College, that came with just over two minutes remaining, when Michael Adams hit a 15-foot shot to give BC an 86–85 advantage. Georgetown went back to holding the ball, waiting for its own decisive moment down the stretch. With four seconds remaining, Georgetown's Michael Jackson attempted a 17-footer for the win that caught the rim. John Garris grabbed the rebound, got fouled, and added one more point to the Eagles' margin of victory.[59]

BC ventured home from North Station with an 87–85 overtime victory over their frequent nemesis, finding themselves in an enviable position as the regular season approached its final weekend. The victory also marked college basketball's raucous return to the Boston Garden, where it had once been a frequent attraction, especially in the 1940s and 1950s heyday of Holy Cross basketball.

Everything just fell into place for the Eagles in the aftermath of the Georgetown win. Villanova eked out a win over St. John's, then fell to Syracuse at the Carrier Dome. Georgetown recovered quickly from its loss to BC at the Garden and put it to a suddenly mortal Villanova team. Boston College, a team that had been picked by almost all of the basketball smarts for the bottom half of the Big East standings, would get a chance on Senior Day to secure a share of the conference's regular season title. All that stood in the way of a 12-4 final record in the Big East were the Providence Friars. BC's southern New England neighbors hadn't had a winning season since Big East commissioner Dave Gavitt trolled the Friars' sideline, but Providence always proved a tougher adversary than its record indicated. In the previous BC-PC matchup, the Friars hung tough thanks to the offensive prowess of shooting guard Ron Jackson and the low-post presence of sinewy forward Otis Thorpe.

Boston College blitzed the Friars from the opening minute, taking a commanding 26–8 lead less than ten minutes into the game. Providence made a couple of runs, but the game never got closer than 8 points. At the end of the evening, BC cut down the nets to celebrate its second Big East regular-season crown in three years. Adding to the evening's excitement was the news that BC had earned the number one seed in the upcoming Big East Tournament by winning the tiebreakers over co-champions Villanova and St. John's. The Eagles had won three of their four games against the Wildcats and Johnnies.

Top seeded and fourteenth-ranked Boston College faced Seton Hall at Madison Square Garden in the quarterfinals. Eighth-seeded Seton Hall had disposed of Providence in the previous day's play-in game. By the time the Eagles and Pirates tipped off a little after 9 p.m., the inaugural Big East Tournament at MSG was a sensation, a convergence of cable television, best-in-the-nation college basketball, and shambolic support from crowds that extended from the Garden floor to the building's concave ceiling. For students and alumni from the member schools, as well as basketball heads from the tri-state area, Madison Square Garden in early March became a place of pilgrimage. And it felt like that already after the day's quarterfinals matchups, all of which were gut-wrenching battles. Syracuse had outlasted Georgetown in the 4–5 game, while Villanova escaped a near catastrophe against UConn. Tournament host St. John's pushed past Pitt in front of a crowd that sounded a lot like their typical home dates at the Garden. An unprecedented five teams that played at MSG that day reached the forty-eight-team NCAA Tournament field.

The perennial underdogs from Boston College found themselves in an unfamiliar position as the heavy favorite in their first-round matchup with Seton Hall. They found themselves in a similarly unfamiliar and unfavorable position at halftime, trailing by 10 to a Pirates team that won six games all season.

"I tried not to get too emotional in the locker room," Williams said of his halftime speech.[60] Whatever he said worked. BC went on an unfathomable 41–9 run in the second half. Senior John Garris led the charge with 23 points and 8 rebounds. Final score: *Boston College 79 Seton Hall 56*. Next on the agenda was Syracuse, who had pummeled the Eagles in both previous meetings that season. Syracuse had plenty of reasons not to take lightly a BC team that surmounted a double-digit deficit in the 1982 Big East Tournament to defeat the Orangemen in the quarterfinals.

It wouldn't be the pressing defense and attacking offense that Tom Davis had employed in the 1982 BC-Syracuse Big East Tournament game that turned the tide in the 1983 edition. Williams took a different tack, dropping the full-court press altogether for just one night. The idea started with one of his veterans, Jay Murphy, who suggested that trying to press once again against Syracuse, who had excelled in transition during their two prior meetings, was the basketball equivalent of walking into a left hook. The nearly twenty thousand fans in attendance that evening saw the typically aggressive Eagles drop back into a zone defense, keeping Syracuse from getting all the good looks they did in their earlier matchups.[61]

"We lost aggressiveness on our outside shots. We tried to force it in too much," Jim Boeheim said of Syracuse's performance that evening.[62] The Orangemen had also lost one of their top scorers in Tony Bruin, who mustered just seven minutes of action on a sprained ankle. This enabled BC to key in on the typically dynamic Erich Santifer, who scored just 9 points.

BC kept Syracuse in the game with poor shooting. The Eagles hit just 38 percent of their shots from the floor and led by a single point, 35–34, at the half. Syracuse big man Leo Rautins posted a team-high 23 points to the 11 by his BC counterpart John Garris, who fouled out with nearly five minutes remaining. On the offensive end it was Jay Murphy and Michael Adams who won the game for Boston College. Murphy found the angles around the perimeter and in the post to net 23 points. After a shaky first half, Adams turned it on coming out of the locker room, scoring 20 of his 25 points in the second half. Together, the pair scored BC's first 23 points of the second half. Down the stretch, a flailing Syracuse team spent the final minutes of the game fouling BC, but the Eagles were just too good at the line (14 of 16) to submit. BC won, 80–74.[63] "In my time at BC, Michael [Adams] took a backseat to no one," Ted Kelley said. "Michael's ability, his confidence, his tenacity, his feel for the game, his skill level, his feel for the ball. He could handle the ball like it was attached to his hand. He could get to the hoop and make unorthodox plays."[64]

Every BC basketball fan, whether old line or newly minted, was suddenly in search of tickets for Saturday night's final. "When it went to MSG in '83, that's when it [the Big East Tournament] really took off," Matt Gianatassio said. "They [BC] kept advancing on and on. People coming down on the train, people driving down on the bus. People looking for tickets. I remember getting a call from Congressman Ed Markey looking for tickets, and there were none to be had."[65]

In the final, St. John's outlasted Boston College, 85–77, getting revenge in front of a strongly St. John's crowd for the two blemishes the Eagles had made on their record earlier in the season. The Johnnies led by 6 at the half and maintained a similar cushion the rest of the night. Tournament MVP Chris Mullin, who led the Redmen with 23 points, seemed to sink a timely basket every time BC threatened to make a run. Despite playing in front of what was essentially a St. John's home crowd, Gary Williams was strikingly magnanimous after the game, complimenting the host venue for its fine service to the conference and congratulating the newly crowned champs from St. John's.

"That hurt. I thought we were good enough to beat them [St. John's], but it was a very tough atmosphere to play in. But it was a great experience and a great environment to play in, to give you confidence going into the NCAA Tournament," Gary Williams recalled.[66]

"Maybe we wanted to win too bad, to share with everybody the feelings we have for each other," Michael Adams told reporters after the game.[67] Nevertheless, Garris and Murphy earned All-Tournament honors for BC, and the Eagles proved once again that their success was no fluke. A national audience that numbered in the millions had also seen Boston College's performance that weekend, thanks to coverage on the USA network and NBC. NBC's Marv Albert and Bucky Waters sang the praises of BC's hard pressing attack, especially Michael Adams, whom Waters referred to on numerous occasions as a "waterbug," a descriptor that has been used to describe Adams's tenacious style ever since. But the loss still stung.

The NCAA Tournament committee slotted Boston College fourth in the West Region, which was to be played in Corvallis, Oregon, home of Oregon State University and little else. The Eagles drew the Princeton Tigers in their first tournament game. To earn a shot at Boston College, Princeton had employed its uniquely methodical and motion-heavy slow-down offense to perfection in preliminary round games against North Carolina A&T and Oklahoma State. The tournament-tested Tigers rode an eleven-game winning streak into their game in Corvallis with the eleventh-ranked Eagles.

Boston College's second-round contest against Princeton made the case for the shot clock about as well as any basketball game that has ever been played. The legendary Pete Carill's Tigers club succeeded more at frustrating the Eagles than outscoring the fast-breaking team from the Big East. After winning the opening tip, Princeton's starting five passed the ball around fourteen times before taking their first shot. This presaged the game's final thirty-nine minutes, in which the Ivy League champions relied on dozens of back-door cuts and picks to play keep-away from the Eagles. Rarely did Carill's club even sniff at the basket for the first forty seconds of a possession. Initially the Tigers manufactured enough open looks to hold a 10–7 advantage at the twelve-minute mark.

Once Princeton's shooting went cold, the Tigers' chances of advancing dwindled. BC held a 24–23 advantage at the half, thanks largely to Jay Murphy's 12 points on 6-for-7 shooting. Murphy led Boston College in scoring (17 points) and rebounds (10) for the evening. The Eagles' defense ramped up considerably in the second half as well. Michael Adams and Dominic Pressley started to pursue Princeton's ball handlers much more aggressively than they had earlier in the game. BC ended up holding Princeton to just 5 of 22 shooting in the game's final twenty minutes. In a game Gary Williams called a "bore," BC beat Princeton, 51–42, and earned its third straight trip to the Sweet Sixteen.[68]

Awaiting the Eagles at the regional in Ogden, Utah, was top-seeded University of Virginia (UVA). Ranked fourth in the country, the Virginia Cavaliers were probably the most high-profile team in the tournament field because of their senior center, the most high-profile player in college basketball. Ralph Sampson, the Cavs' 7'4" center, was in the midst of the third consecutive season that ended with him being named the Naismith College Player of the Year, a feat that only Bill Walton had previously achieved. Despite the remarkable success that Sampson enjoyed during his collegiate career, his Virginia team had yet to win a national title. During Sampson's senior campaign practically every sportswriter in the country had commented on this being his last shot to win a title. Few players in the history of college basketball have been the subject of as much focus and scrutiny as Ralph Sampson was during the home stretch of his collegiate career.

Sampson was far from the only asset on Terry Holland's Virginia club. Its backcourt combined speedy point guard Ricky Stokes and Othell Wilson, who was a fantastic jumpshooter and one of the most physically robust guards in the country. In Rick Carlisle, the University of Maine transfer, UVA had a legitimate gunner on the wing. At the public practices, the spectators at Weber State's Dee Events Center and the assembled media had no interest in Virginia or Boston College. Their focus was on Sampson, who received standing ovations for every movement of his body and got almost every question at the presser. Sampson, who was peevish even at his best moments, seemed thoroughly checked out of the proceedings and admitted to little else—other than knowing next to nothing about his upcoming opponent. Like many of the players in Ogden, Sampson seemed to be affected by the elevation in the Rocky Mountains, which sat 4,500 feet above sea level. He spent much of the press conference breathing into a paper bag to treat his hyperventilation.[69]

Conversely, Boston College knew all about Virginia. John Garris had plenty to say about how he planned to play against Sampson. "One thing I know is I've got to take it right at him. You pull up and he'll swat the ball away; you've got to go right into his face," Garris said. He went on to tell reporters of his dream finale to the upcoming Sweet Sixteen matchup. "I'd like to take the ball at midcourt and all five of their guys be back there on point and let Ralph be the last guy back there, trying to block me. Then I'd go right over Ralph and slam it," he said.[70]

Well before the game's final stretches, Garris, Murphy, Burnett Adams, and the rest of the BC frontcourt were taking it to Sampson, harassing him mercilessly under the hoop. While Sampson had found his way to 15 points in the first half, he picked up his fourth foul just twenty-three seconds into the second. The game had been a hard-charging one from the outset, one that favored BC's style of play. Boston College guards Michael Adams, Stu Primus, and Dom Pressley had harassed UVA's backcourt of

Othell Wilson and Ricky Stokes into several turnovers while the Eagles' frontcourt—namely, Garris and Murphy—found plenty of opportunities to score.[71]

"I'll tell you what I was thinking when he [Sampson] got his fourth foul. Final Four. Final Four. Pack the bags. We're off to Albuquerque now," Burnett Adams told the *Globe*'s Michael Madden after the game.[72] Virginia soon proved itself a team capable of dealing with adversity, or, quite possibly, it was a highly talented team that played more fluidly when it wasn't expected to build everything around Sampson.

Without the services of Sampson, Virginia got incredibly hot, peeling off a 15–1 run that was aided and abetted by BC's atrocious shooting. The Eagles, strangely, slowed the pace of play and seemed more hesitant to push the ball into the low post with the absence of Sampson. Garris did not score for an eight-minute stretch in Sampson's absence. Virginia's rebounding improved as well. Sampson's replacement, Kenton Edelin, and power forward Craig Robinson grabbed a combined 24 rebounds that evening for Virginia. A 3-point Eagles' lead turned into an 11-point deficit. BC had started to fight its way back when Sampson finally returned to a 70–64 Virginia lead. Sampson and company extended the lead to as much as 14 before BC responded with its own ferocious comeback in the game's final minutes, going on a 20–9 run to close out the game.[73]

With just under a minute remaining, UVA held an 89–83 advantage. Virginia was able to withstand BC's final assault thanks in large part to Carlisle, who scored 6 of his team-high 23 points from the line in the final minute. Virginia held on for a 95–92 victory, advancing to the West Regional Final, where it fell against Jim Valvano's Cinderella NC State team that went on to win the national title.

Boston College had won a school-record twenty-five games in 1982–1983. Gary Williams lost out to Lou Carnesecca for Big East Coach of the Year but finished third in voting for AP National Coach of the Year, behind Houston's Guy Lewis and Washington State's George Raveling. Williams had also been named the All—New England Coach of the Year. Adams, Murphy, and Garris all garnered second team All—Big East honors and first team All—New England honors. Garris was named New England Player of the Year.

As the BC basketball team accepted a slew of postseason honors, one of the most beloved figures in the program decided to leave Chestnut Hill and take advantage of a new opportunity. On March 28, Kevin Mackey accepted the head coaching position at Cleveland State University, a member of the Mid-Continent Conference that had struggled to an 8-20 record the previous season.

"I wanted to be a head coach. I wanted to have my own program," Kevin Mackey said. "Mike Tranghese, who was the assistant then to Dave Gavitt, approached me and said, 'Kevin, Dave said its time for the top Big East assistants to become head coaches.'"[74] Gavitt made a call on Mackey's behalf to the athletic director at Cleveland State, singing his praises. "When I went out to Cleveland State for a visit, the athletic director picked me up at the airport, and the first thing he said to me was, 'I can't believe it. Dave Gavitt called me. I talked to Dave Gavitt.' I said, 'Oh, my Lord; I've got this thing. I better be careful what I say.'"[75]

The loss of Mackey was a genuine blow to the BC basketball program. The school lost not only its top recruiter, but also a coach who had built such a strong rapport with so many of the players. In no time, Mackey built Cleveland State up in his image, filling his roster with tough, talented, inner-city kids who proved very quickly that they could compete with anyone in America.

While Kevin Mackey was building up Cleveland State's program, Boston College faced a new set of challenges that came with the national reputation they'd earned and re-earned over several winters.

7

Northwestern *(Calhoun)*

Jim Calhoun's Northeastern basketball program ventured from the 1970s into the 1980s in a new conference and with a new home court.

For the 1979–1980 season, Northeastern would be joining the ECAC North, a creature that emerged from the cosmological shakeup the Big East's formation wrought upon college basketball. Connecticut, Boston College, and Providence departed the old ECAC New England, an amorphous regional entity that came into the view of eastern basketball fans every late February or early March. A four-team tournament pitting New England's best Division I programs competed annually for an automatic bid to the NCAAs. The remnants of the four traditional, loosely aligned ECACs—New England, Upstate, Metro, and South—all faced defections to the new Big East. Suddenly their members were in a mad dash to form new leagues that hung on to the ECAC's standing tournament bids. The ECAC North combined private New England Division I programs BU, Northeastern, and Holy Cross (which turned down an offer from the Big East); the three flagship public universities of northern New England; and Rhode Island, as well as Canisius, Niagara, and Colgate from the old ECAC Upstate. Rather than playing a traditional round-robin conference schedule, the ten teams would compete for eight bids to an ECAC North tournament based on their records. Eventually, this would change as the ECAC North evolved from a temporary alliance into a permanent league. All told, it amounted to a confusing, ever-evolving situation in the early years of the new conference.[1]

Nevertheless, Calhoun, like most coaches in the new league, expressed optimism that the configuration would give his team a clear identity, a clear path to the postseason, and a definitive shot at competing for an NCAA Tournament bid. Rhode Island and Holy Cross, the new league's most prominent programs, expressed the strongest reservations about the future of this marriage of convenience and seemed most likely to look elsewhere for greener pastures.[2]

Canisius and Niagara, two of Buffalo's "Little Three" traditional Catholic basketball powers, were happy in the short term just to join a league with an automatic tournament bid. St. Bonaventure, the third of Buffalo's "Little Three," had been invited to join the Eastern Eight, the forerunner of the more prestigious Atlantic-10, because it had the largest on-campus gymnasium of the three institutions.

At the same time, Canisius and Niagara found themselves completely divorced from the context in which they'd cemented their reputations. The Buffalo schools sat at one pole, and the Boston schools sat at the other. "We were left out hanging, not being able to get in that conference [Eastern Eight]," Canisius coach Nick Macarchuk said of not only Canisius's exclusion from the more competitive Eastern Eight, but also Niagara's. Macarchuk credits Canisius's esteemed athletic director, Dan Starr, and his successor, John Maddock, with finding the Golden Griffins a home in the ECAC North, keeping the school out of the increasingly perilous ranks of the independents.[3]

"It made for some strange bedfellows," said Donn Esmonde, who covered college basketball for the *Buffalo News* in the 1980s. "Canisius and Niagara have played each other since the early 1900s. But neither had much prior contact with, say, Maine or New Hampshire before being tossed into the same boat."[4]

Just weeks after the announcement of the ECAC North, Northeastern University made another decision that would have a profound impact on the future of its basketball program. In October 1979, Northeastern purchased the Boston Arena from the Metropolitan District Commission, the state of Massachusetts's parks department. Located steps from the heart of Northeastern's campus, the St. Botolph Street arena opened in 1910 near the intersection of Huntington and Massachusetts Avenues. For nearly fifty years, the five-thousand-seat arena had served as the home of Northeastern hockey. It would soon replace Cabot as the home of Northeastern basketball. Still in use today, the arena is the country's oldest active venue for college hockey and for college basketball.[5]

Describing the Boston Arena as "historic" would be a gross understatement. It served as the original home of the Boston Bruins and hosted the Boston Celtics' first game. Celtics owner Walter Brown first laid down his soon-to-be-famous parquet floor at the Boston Arena, not the more well-known Boston Garden. Over the years, the arena hosted Beanpot Hockey, speeches by Presidents Theodore Roosevelt and John F. Kennedy, and decades' worth of prize fights and professional wrestling. Virtually all the city's college hockey programs called the building home at one point or another. The likes of Joe Louis and Jack Dempsey fought there while rock n' roll pioneer Alan Freed was arrested there for allegedly inciting a riot at a 1958 concert.[6]

By the late 1970s, Boston Arena looked all of its nearly sixty years of age. Northeastern purchased the building for $250,000 and soon began making extensive renovations. Originally, the school called the building "Northeastern Arena" but in 1982 renamed it Matthews Arena in honor of George J. Matthews, the NU alum who had played a decisive role in raising the money to revamp the building. By the time of its rechristening, Matthews Arena had a new roof, entirely new seats, new lighting, and new bathrooms. Visitors to Matthews were now greeted by an ornate façade at the arena's entrance that had been plastered over during the 1930s. Once spectators entered the building, they walked into a lobby that seemed right out of an early twentieth-century movie house.[7] Thanks to the efforts of many in the Northeastern community, Matthews became one of the showpieces of college athletics and a brick-and-mortar ambassador for the university itself. The revitalization of the old Boston Arena and Northeastern University basketball were simultaneous and often overlapping renaissances taking place in the same space during the 1980s.

Though initially skeptical, Calhoun eventually embraced the new venue. "Cabot was intimate. It was a tough, tough place to play," the coach said. "I liked it eventually at Matthews because it quote-unquote 'looked big time.' Matthews had the feel of an arena. And they did great work on it. At first it was a little cold with the ice under it," Calhoun said, much like BU's Walter Brown Arena.[8] Eventually, Cabot became Northeastern's practice space, and Matthews became the Huskies' game-day home.

Jim Calhoun also made an important addition to his coaching staff for the 1979–1980 season when he hired Karl Fogel, who had spent the three previous seasons as the head coach at Division III Curry College in nearby Milton, Massachusetts. Fogel took over for highly respected assistant Nels Nelson, who left college coaching for a better paying position at General Electric. Fogel earned respect quickly in the Northeastern program. He had few peers as a basketball tactician and played a profound role in the evolution of the Huskies' style of play in the 1980s. He also proved a tremendous asset as a recruiter. "Karl Fogel doesn't get as much credit as he deserves for the success of Northeastern basketball," Keith Motley said. "Karl has a pretty passionate personality, so some of the guys had a problem with that. However, Karl had a great basketball mind. And I buffered him with the players."[9]

Northeastern returned a highly experienced team in 1979–1980. Senior captain Bill Loughnane and his classmate Bob Schoening, a rugged center, were far from the only veterans on the club. Junior guard Pete Harris had been the number three scoring sophomore in the country while Chip Rucker, also a junior, was a problem in the low post. Sophomore Perry Moss was on the verge of becoming an explosive scorer, while second year-man Eric Jefferson was arguably the team's most versatile and polished player. Incoming freshman Charlie Heineck, a bruising 6'9" center from Reading, Mass., gave the Huskies plenty of depth in the frontcourt.

The region's basketball press figured them middle of the pack. The *Rochester Democrat and Chronicle* picked them sixth, while the *Boston Globe* slated Northeastern fifth.[10] In spite of its middling forecast, the *Globe* predicted big things soon for Northeastern. "[NU] seems determined to erase the Division 2 image that still seems to linger along Huntington Ave with the winos and the uprooted trolley tracks," intoned the unnamed author of the *Globe*'s 1979–1980 college basketball preview.[11]

The Huskies went 4–3 in the 1979 portion of their schedule. They won a season-opening tournament at Brown in which Pete Harris took MVP honors, scoring 41 points over two nights. Next on the agenda was a trip to Tuscaloosa, where Northeastern more than held its own against Alabama, a team that finished third in the SEC and made it to the second round of the NIT. The Huskies led by 1 at the half and trailed by just 4 with 9:55 remaining. The Tide's athleticism eventually overwhelmed Northeastern, and the home team won by an 88–73 margin. NU looked less competitive at Georgetown a week later, falling by 20 to a team that had reached the Final Eight.

Northeastern opened many eyes early in the season by going on the road and pounding Pete Carill's eventual Ivy League co-champions, Princeton, 74–52. NU roughed up the Tigers, forcing ball-control Princeton out of its game and overwhelming them on the boards. The Princeton win was emblematic of the kind of basketball that earned the Huskies newfound respect from their regional peers. Northeastern impressed on the boards, winning decisively in this aspect of the game in each of its wins. Rucker, Schoening, and Heineck had become a wrecking crew in the low post. NU finished the season in the top ten nationally in rebounding margin. The play of Northeastern's backcourt did even more to turn heads. Pete Harris was again averaging more than 20 points per game, while Moss and Loughnane split time at the other guard spot. Moss averaged nearly 12 points per game that season, while Loughnane again led the team in assists.

What seemed on the verge of taking hold early in the season came to fruition in the first few weeks of the 1980s. After hanging tough against a hellacious early slate of opponents, the Huskies obliterated a half-dozen regional foes, improving their record to 10-3 by late January.

When asked what made his 1979–1980 team so much better than its predecessor, Calhoun had a clear answer. "The difference is we've matured. We're poised, and we have flexibility. And it helps to have Pete Harris for the late minutes when the game gets tough," Calhoun said.[12]

"We got more athletic. We were definitely quicker and faster," Bill Loughnane said. "Whenever we took the court that year, we thought we were going to win. I think we thought we were good enough to beat anybody."[13] "We'd become a tight group, Pete [Harris], Perry [Moss], Eric Jefferson, and me," Chip Rucker recalled. "Joining the ECAC allowed people to see how good we had become."[14] Rucker had one of the most dominant performances of his career during the six-game winning streak. He posted a 26-point, 11-rebound double-double at Maine, helping the Huskies overcome an excellent Black Bears team led by Rufus Harris and the always hostile crowd in Orono. NU's 86–75 win at Memorial Gym was just Maine's second home loss in the previous forty-four home dates.

After falling on the road to Drexel, a now 10-4 NU team commenced with another winning streak, which included league wins over New Hampshire and Maine. The Huskies were proving adept at winning with a variety of approaches to the game. Northeastern could run past less athletic teams like UNH. Against Siena, NU sat back in a 1-2-2 zone and forced the Indians (now Saints) into a series of mistakes. A come-from-behind 74–71 win at home against P. J. Carlesimo's stampeding Wagner team was the Huskies' fifth consecutive win. Against Wagner, Calhoun employed a tenacious press that wore down Carlesimo's Seahawks. Cool as ever, Pete Harris finished off a 21-point night by sinking a pair of free throws with nine seconds remaining to seal the win. The game against Wagner, a NIT team from the previous year, offered visible proof that basketball was again an attraction on Huntington Avenue. The game drew the first full house at Cabot in recent memory.[15]

"When I got there, we [Northeastern] were drawing two hundred people to the gym, but by the time I left, we were like rock stars on the campus," Chip Rucker recalls.[16] While Rucker was a rock star in his own right, there was no bigger attraction on the Northeastern basketball team that the backcourt tandem of Pete Harris and Perry Moss. No opponent could put the clamp down on both of them. One of them was bound to have a big night every time Northeastern took the floor.

Against Long Island University (LIU), Harris and Moss combined for eight consecutive fast break points in the game's first three minutes for another large Cabot crowd. Harris finished with 24 and Moss, 15, in a 67–48 blowout win. The victory was NU's sixth in a row and twelfth in its last thirteen games. The now 16-4 Huskies were primed for their annual matchup with Rick Pitino's 16-3 BU Terriers, who were every bit as good as their suddenly unstoppable rivals. In the final minutes of the LIU game, fans at Cabot started chanting, "Bring on BU," a request that would be granted two nights later.[17]

The Huskies headed across town for the most consequential NU-BU matchup in years. "This is a city series that the city can finally take seriously," the *Globe's* Michael Madden wrote the morning of the game.[18] A standing-room-only crowd of 2,800, which included plenty of NU fans, greeted them at Case. The crowd that evening was treated to one of the genuine classics of the shared Calhoun-Pitino era as Pete Harris nearly single-handedly fought off BU's stem-to-stern press. Harris went for 30 and NU won out on the boards, but the continuous defensive assault by the Terriers forced the Huskies into 23 turnovers. BU pulled away late for an 85–78 victory, marking the Terriers' fifth consecutive win in the series and seventh out of the last eight.[19]

Players on both teams recognized that the rivalry was reheating every time they took the floor against one another. "You knew you were going to have a packed house. You knew there was going to be animosity from the last player on the bench to the head coaches. We wanted to be the top dog in the city," Bill Loughnane said.[20]

"They were really intense games," recalled BU point guard Glenn Consor, Loughnane's counterpart. "We always played well against Northeastern. In fact, through the years, I would see Calhoun, and he's an amazing guy. He would remember everything. He'd put his hand around me and say, 'I remember the 12 assists you got against us.' He'd remember detailed stuff."[21]

The loss pushed the Huskies a game and a half behind BU in the conference standings. It also turned the seemingly invincible Huskies suddenly mortal. Northeastern scored hard-fought road wins over New Hampshire and Massachusetts before dropping a clunker to St. Francis of Brooklyn. Ankle injuries suffered by both Pete Harris and Chip Rucker in the St. Francis game contributed to the loss.

A bruised-up Northeastern team returned to Cabot for a matchup with Army. Coached by Mike Krzyzewski, the Knights were well below .500 but always put up a serious fight. NU had beaten Army, 61–60, the previous winter on a 30-footer at the buzzer by Perry Moss. No such heroics were needed in their February 1980 matchup, but the game was, once again, a barn burner. Army hung in there against Northeastern, minimizing NU's blitz with a tight man-to-man defense and a ball-control offense. Moss again sealed the deal against Army, sinking both ends of a one-and-one with fifteen seconds remaining in NU's 61–57 victory. In defeat, Krzyzewski hailed Harris and Moss as the best guards they'd played all year.[22]

Northeastern concluded the regular season at home against Boston College. Every seat at Cabot was sold in advance of tip-off for the first time in years. Not only was 19-6 Northeastern having a fantastic year, 17-7 Boston College was having another strong campaign under Tom Davis, holding its own in the inaugural season of the Big East. The Eagles would end up losing by a bucket in the second round of the NIT to Ralph Sampson and Virginia, the tournament's eventual champion. If BU was the hated rival that had NU's number in recent years, BC was the nemesis who played at a slightly higher level, recruited slightly better players, and always found a way to beat the Huskies. BC had topped Northeastern in sixteen consecutive meetings, dating back to 1964. Under Davis, BC had adopted a ferocious press and the relentlessly slashing zone offense that became the Eagles' trademarks. Davis featured at least ten players in his attack in 1979–1980, and eight of them averaged at least 5 points per game.

BC's ruthless attack quickly got the best of Northeastern that night. The Eagles led by 9 at the half and were never seriously threatened in the game's final twenty minutes. The 76–67 final score was closer than the game played. Pete Harris missed the game's last eight minutes after fouling out, and BC had led by as much as 16. "I got the strange sensation that we were just as happy to be merely playing Boston College before three thousand fans as opposed to beating Boston College," a clearly annoyed Calhoun said of his team's unemotional performance.[23] BC would continue to frustrate Northeastern in the coming seasons.

Northeastern's sluggish performance in the regular season finale was followed up by an even more uninspired one in the ECAC North playoffs. Skip Chapelle's Maine Black Bears came down to Cabot and beat Northeastern convincingly, 66–52. Maine's blowout win was even more puzzling considering that the Black Bears' top player, ECAC North Co-Player of the Year Rufus Harris, missed long stretches of the game in foul trouble. The Huskies simply shot poorly, got into foul trouble, and did not dominate on the boards in their usual fashion. "After the BU game, it seemed like we lost our killer instinct," Pete Harris said. "Seemed like our whole season was built around beating them."[24]

Northeastern finished its best season as a full-fledged Division I program at 19-8. The Huskies won as many games as Calhoun's first team but did so within the context of a league and against a much more difficult schedule. The emergence of Northeastern as a contender in a conference with an automatic entry into the NCAA Tournament was the result of a slow but sure evolution of the Huskies' style of play and personnel under Calhoun.

"All of a sudden, he [Calhoun] realized that he had athletes that could press all over the court, even if they were 6′7″ or 6′8″," Keith Motley said.[25] In the coming years, Northeastern stockpiled big, athletic threes and fours. Chip Rucker and Dave Leitao were the first in a long line of uncompromising rebounders that could run up and down the floor with anyone. Northeastern's frontcourt in the early 1980s anticipated the style of play adopted at the professional level later in the decade by the Detroit Pistons. Think of Rucker and Leitao as proto—John Salleys, Dennis Rodmans, and Rick Mahorns.

"Our style of play was basically the same all the years I was there," Karl Fogel said. "We prided ourselves on being a tough team. We were always a great rebounding team. We stressed up-tempo, changed defenses, and relied on our guards to exploit matchups to score."[26] NU's hard-line frontcourt play was matched by the simultaneous slashing and precision of its now elite backcourt. With the departure of Holy Cross great Ronnie Perry after the 1979–1980 season, Harris and Moss were arguably the league's best returning guards.

Rick Pitino once said he would have traded two recruiting classes to get Pete Harris, and it's easy to understand why. Harris broke Northeastern's all-time scoring record as a senior and became just the fifth player in New England history to score 2,000 career points. In a *Globe* profile of Harris, ECAC North coaches showered him with praise. Maine's Skip Chapelle called him a coach on the floor, while Holy Cross's George Blaney attested to his toughness and durability.[27] "I remember him as someone that the whole team looked up to," team manager Scott Cohen recalled. Teammates honored Harris by voting him captain of the 1980–1981 squad.[28]

Perry Moss shared minutes with Bill Loughnane during his sophomore year but had by then clearly emerged as a major scoring threat, averaging close to 12 points per game. Moss's athleticism was evident from the day he stepped on campus, but his tremendous work ethic helped him develop his nascent skills as a shooter and ball handler. Lightly recruited relative to some of his teammates at prep power Wilbraham and Monson Academy, Moss accepted Northeastern's offer not because it was his first-choice school but because it was his best opportunity to play at the Division I level. "A lot of kids come in and tell me they want to be a great player," Calhoun said in a 1982 profile of Moss. "Perry came in and asked, 'What do I have to do to be a good player?' When he learned that, he came back and said, 'What do I have to do to be great?'"[29]

Moss came from a family of dedicated athletes. His father, Peter Sr., had been a boxer in the Navy. His brother, Peter Jr., had been an All-Ivy League basketball player at Brown. His basketball-playing sister, Paula, had been New England Women's Player of the Year at Tufts. His mother was the dean of women at Amherst College. Before taking up basketball, Perry had been an accomplished martial artist and brought that analytical, physical discipline to the court. At home or on the road, Moss ran the bleachers daily to keep up his wind.[30] "Perry Moss was a beast. The best athlete I've ever seen, pound for pound," Paul Porter said. Moss was particularly renowned for his jumping prowess. During his time in the NBA, Moss apparently beat out 76ers teammates Julius Erving and Charles Barkley in an informal contest measuring their respective verticals.[31] "He [Moss] was one of those guys that didn't weight train but could do two thousand pushups. A strong guy and a character. Smart as heck," Calhoun said of Moss, who proved to be as clutch as anyone that ever donned the red and black.[32]

Northeastern entered the 1980–1981 season as a favorite in the ECAC North, returning all its major contributors with the exceptions of Loughnane and Schoening. The one caveat to Northeastern's projected success was its unfavorable schedule, which included eighteen road games to just nine at home. Six of those road contests would be played during in-season tournaments, which had become a regular feature of NU's scheduling.

Further bolstering NU's chances in 1980–1981 were the top-notch recruits that Calhoun and company added to the already stacked roster. Sinewy 6'1" guard Phil Robinson from Jersey City gave the Huskies greater depth in the backcourt, while NU added a pair of impressive big men in Roland Braswell, a 6'8" forward from Brooklyn's Bishop Loughlin, and 6'6" Mark Halsel, the latest pull from the Pittsburgh well.

While Robinson and Braswell made significant contributions throughout their careers, the signing of Halsel was a genuine coup for Northeastern. Halsel had been the city of Pittsburgh's leading prep scorer the previous winter at Schenley High. Originally, he signed a letter of intent to play at Robert Morris, but the Colonials withdrew their offer after Halsel suffered a knee injury during his senior year. Halsel had grown up tough on Pittsburgh's down-at-the-heels Polish Hill. His first basketball hoop was a chitlins bucket his older sister Deborah cut the bottom out of and cleaned out for him. The nine-year-old boy spent many afternoons shooting a nerf ball through that bucket. Deborah later got him a real basketball hoop. When Mark was eleven, his sister died of a brain hemorrhage. Halsel persevered through the grief and grew into one of the best basketball players in the city's history.[33] "Mark was the toughest player we ever had. He was great going to the basket and a great dunker. Talented offensive rebounder. Impossible to box out," Karl Fogel said.[34]

Easygoing and always laughing off the court, Halsel was all business between the lines, diving for loose balls and doggedly fighting for every rebound. Though not a great leaper, Halsel had the strength and tenacity to assert his will in the low post. "If you were in a game and you had to rebound against him, he'd win, and if he didn't, you wouldn't be standing," Calhoun said.[35] No player symbolized the "big, bad Huskies," as they came to be known in basketball circles, as thoroughly as Mark Halsel.

Northeastern opened the 1980–1981 season the way that Mike Tyson would answer the opening bell of a title bout later in the decade. The Huskies not only defeated their opponents. They came out attacking them, often breaking their will well in advance of halftime. The largely local opposition NU faced before Christmas tried successfully at times to slow them down, rope-a-doping their way to competitive games by holding the ball in the pre-shot-clock era. Nothing they could throw at Calhoun's team stopped them. The Huskies went home for Christmas an undefeated team and the talk of New England college basketball.

The *Globe*'s Lesley Visser profiled Calhoun, coach of the 6-0 Huskies, in mid-December. Visser sets the scene by describing Calhoun asking a group of eight young men playing pickup basketball at Cabot to come back later so that the undefeated Huskies could hold their 5:30 p.m. practice. The piece described the long-term transition of Northeastern basketball from a Division II program into a Division I program on the verge of something big. "Perhaps no school in the country is blessed with so dedicated a coach who receives such little recognition," Visser wrote.[36]

Visser also gave a sense of the people behind the names that had filled Northeastern's box scores for the past few seasons. She wrote of colorful Chip Rucker, smooth Eric Jefferson, and Dave Leitao, the team's glue guy. Pete Harris, the quietest guy on the team, got the most notice, having recently broken Northeastern's all-time scoring record. Harris described Calhoun as a coach that players could go to with their problems and a leader who cultivated a sense of comradery in the locker room. "The great thing about playing here is that everybody is nice, polite. The kids on campus open doors for each other and say 'thank you.' On the team, we all get along. It wasn't like that when I was growing up," Harris said, comparing his life at Northeastern to his upbringing in Braddock, Pennsylvania.[37]

Northeastern celebrated Boxing Day in Portland, Maine, crushing the Black Bears, 70–50, at the Civic Center in the first round of the Best Holiday Classic. The victory offered a semblance of revenge for the season-ending loss Maine inflicted on them the previous spring. NU took a once-fervent crowd of 3,600 out of the game quickly. Northeastern held the hot-shooting Black Bears to less than 40 percent from the floor and pilloried them on the boards, outrebounding Maine by 20. Maine had no answer for either Moss (18 points) or Harris (22 points).[38] The next night against UNC-Charlotte, foul trouble, which became the bane of Calhoun's existence, put the Huskies in a hole from which they never recovered. Moss and Harris each spent much of the second half on the bench with three fouls, and the 49ers won the tournament title, 75–62.[39]

In the New Year's Fairfield Boys Club Tournament, NU topped Towson State in overtime before beating the hometown Stags at the foul line. The Huskies hit more than 90 percent of their free throws against Fairfield, including five straight down the stretch to seal a 79–69 win. The Huskies' third and final regular season tournament didn't go nearly so well. Northeastern had a terrible weekend at the Florida Southern Festival in Lakeland, Florida, losing both games in the four-team tournament. The Huskies fell, 80–75, against a Texas-Arlington team that earned an NIT bid. In the consolation round, NU fell to a not nearly so good Florida Southern team in overtime. In a clear case of hometown officiating, the locals assigned to the game called three times as many fouls on Northeastern as on Division II Florida Southern.[40]

Northeastern's focus might have been a little off in Florida. Earlier that week, the Huskies finally found a way to beat Boston University, inching past them, 80–78, in overtime before the home crowd at Cabot. A crowd just as loud and rabid as the one that greeted the two teams at Case the previous winter witnessed another classic up-and-down matchup. In particular, NU's football team had become a cheering section of their own, bellowing out forceful support for their fellow letterman. NU jumped out to a 13-point lead in the first half but got worn down by BU's relentless press in the second half. BU's top gun, Tony Simms, matched Pete Harris with 24 points. In overtime, NU took a quick lead and Calhoun switched to a three-guard set to keep the ball out of BU's hands. Simms clanked a potentially game-tying shot off the back of the rim with three seconds remaining, clinching the win for Northeastern and inaugurating a new era in the rivalry.

After Florida, the Huskies kickstarted another winning streak by beating UNH, 85–76. Harris and Moss combined for 52, with Harris ripping off 31 points on 12-of-18 shooting and Moss posting 21 points. Northeastern frustrated the Wildcats into submission, changing defenses every two or three times down the court. On the offensive end, NU galloped its way past the Wildcats.

"People look at all the skinny, fast kids on the team and expect us to just go wild down the court and shoot. But we don't," Calhoun said of the Huskies' simultaneously coordinated, aggressive style.[41] Building on the momentum of the UNH win, Northeastern reeled off four consecutive wins, including hard-fought victories on the road against Penn State and Siena. Against Siena, Harris and Moss went for 27 points each in a ferocious 93–92 overtime victory in Loudonville.

The now 15-3 Huskies had settled into a regular nine-man rotation featuring Rucker, Leitao, and Jefferson in the frontcourt and Harris and Moss in the backcourt. Backing them up were freshman sixth man Mark Halsel, bruising big men Charlie Heineck and Roland Braswell, with freshman Phil Robinson serving as the reserve guard.

Though less heralded than some of his teammates, Dave Leitao made substantial contributions on both ends of the floor. As a defender he was particularly fearsome. The essential role he played on the team was clear to everyone associated with Northeastern basketball. Calhoun was notably tough on Leitao, referring to him as "OD" for his tendency to over-diagnose everything going on around him on the floor. NU's coaching staff helped transform Leitao's inclination to overanalyze into a cerebral physicality that served him not only as a player, but also in his long coaching career that followed.[42]

In players like Leitao, Calhoun cultivated a sharp focus on the nuances of the game. Personally, Calhoun took the same tact toward other aspects of his life. His interests seemed narrow, but he focused intently on the things that mattered to him—namely, his family, running, and his former players.

"We talked about running a lot," Phil Lotane, who served as a team manager during the early 1980s, recalled of his boss and fellow jogger. Calhoun completed both the New York and Boston Marathons during this time period, finishing New York in an impressive three hours, twelve minutes in 1981. "His mind is always moving, always planning. Everything is always going a hundred miles an hour. He talks a hundred miles an hour." On the road, Lotane bunked with Calhoun's sons, who had a very close relationship with their father.[43]

"He's [Calhoun's] one of the best fathers of all time," Karl Fogel said.[44] The immediate and extended Calhoun family was always in attendance at NU basketball games, and Calhoun's kids were always near the program. There were often as many as three dozen Calhoun family members at Northeastern games, including his wife Pat, his sons James and Jeffrey, and his siblings. James and Jeffrey served as ball boys and often traveled with the team.

Calhoun was quick with praise for former players and maintained decades-long relationships with many of them. Years after his playing career, Bill Stanton applied for a police job in Rehoboth, Massachusetts. Stanton was a finalist for the position. It was Calhoun's reference that made the difference. "You must shit ice cream," the interviewer told Stanton when he offered him the job. The young man's college coach had sung the interviewer his praises for nearly an hour.[45]

"You wouldn't want to be on his bad side," said Phil Lotane, who remembers the coach as an inveterate yeller and screamer at practices and games. "We'd be at games where, if there were a thousand people, that would be a big crowd. He'd be yelling out instructions, and it was just kind of funny, hearing his every word in these empty gyms."[46]

"The guy [Calhoun] was a tyrant. It was always run, run, run, work, work, work. I couldn't really understand it. By my senior year, of course, I was right along with him," Pete Harris said of his always hoarse, high-strung coach.[47]

"Jim [Calhoun] was a great tactician on the court and an even better personality both on the bench and after the game. He was, as they say, a great quote but only if you were paying exact attention because he spoke so fast and barely opened his lips," the *Niagara Gazette's* Tom Koller said. Koller remembers spending more time parsing tape recordings of Calhoun to get his quotes correct than writing up accounts of games between Niagara and Northeastern.[48] "I wrote a lot about Northeastern, including a lengthy and laudatory feature on Calhoun from which he cherry-picked the one reference he didn't like to confront me with the next day," Donn Esmonde said.[49]

The Huskies had a reality check in early February when they dropped consecutive games to Long Island University and Wagner on the road, surrendering more than 90 points in a pair of back-and-forth affairs. As always, Calhoun and his coaching staff adjusted, playing more slowly and deliberately in home wins over UMass and St. Francis. The victories concluded an undefeated season at Cabot. With four regular season games remaining, NU won three more in a row on the road, including a 70–69 win at New Hampshire. Northeastern ended up 8-0 on the season in games decided by two points or fewer.

Northeastern concluded the regular season with a rematch against BU. Pitino's preoccupation that evening was clearly to stop Pete Harris and

Perry Moss. In that respect, BU succeeded, holding the duo to just 21 points. What Pitino didn't count on was the ability of Chip Rucker and Roland Braswell to completely dominate in the low post. Freshman Braswell grabbed 15 rebounds while scoring 19 points. Senior Rucker had what Calhoun called the best game of his college career, scoring 30 points. The majority of them came at the line as BU tried to shut him down in the second half by simply knocking him down each time he got the ball. Rucker went a stunning 18 for 20 from the line. Northeastern won, 83–76, at Walter Brown Arena and clinched the season series.[50] "This game was something personal for me. I had always been hurt or had a bad game when we played BU. I just calmed myself down this time," Rucker said after the win.[51] Earlier in the evening, Rucker got into it with Pitino on the way into the locker room at halftime. Whatever was said between them, Rucker channeled that energy into one of the best halves of his career.

The win also clinched 21-5 Northeastern the top seed in the ECAC North Tournament and earned them a bye through the quarterfinal round. Northeastern survived a scare in the semis at the hands of a feisty UVM team, which had upset BU in triple overtime three nights earlier. The Catamounts, too, took Northeastern to overtime, but Pete Harris sank four consecutive free throws to seal a 76–69 win at Cabot.

Northeastern would host defending champion Holy Cross in the ECAC North championship game. George Blaney's Crusaders had played in the NCAA Tournament or NIT in six of the previous seven seasons. In the seventh season, they went 20-7. There was no more storied program in the history of New England college basketball than the Jesuit school from Worcester, which played at the Boston Garden far more often than any of the Boston-area schools and almost always drew better crowds. Though Ronnie Perry was gone, pursuing a professional baseball career in the White Sox organization, Holy Cross was still a fantastic team. Point guard Eddie Thurman was a dynamic playmaker while his backcourt mate, Kevin Greaney, was a big and physical scorer. The Crusaders' all-senior frontcourt of Garry Witts, Tom Seaman, and Dave Mulguin resembled a bruising front line from the Big Ten. Holy Cross had, in essence, maintained a parallel existence in the new conference, continuing to play its traditional New England schedule while eschewing games against conference foes in both Buffalo and Boston. Holy Cross would end up leaving the conference after the 1982–1983 season for the Metro Atlantic Conference.

Long esteemed Holy Cross took the early lead on upstart Northeastern, holding serve in the game's first minutes and taking the red-and-black-clad sections of a suddenly claustrophobic Cabot out of the game. Fans in oversold Cabot were sitting on top of a block of vending machines to get a better view. The game started ten minutes late because Holy Cross got caught up in eastbound traffic on the way into the city.[52]

Then NU's press started getting to Holy Cross. The Huskies forced several turnovers, taking the lead just before the ten-minute mark. With just under nine minutes remaining, Perry Moss took an audacious 30-footer that found its way inside the rim, turning the Huntington Avenue gathering into a rip-roaring assemblage for the first time that evening. NU led by 6 at the time and held firmly to the three-basket lead for the remainder of the half, leading 41–35 after twenty minutes. Rucker (11 points) and Moss (12 points) provided NU with most of its offense.

Holy Cross got back to the basics in the second half, pounding it inside to Garry Witts, who scored a team-high 17 points. Ed Thurman, who scored 16 points himself, distributed the ball diversely through the Holy Cross lineup. Five different Crusaders ended up in double figures for the evening. But Northeastern kept finding a way to keep the lead.[53]

With 2:30 remaining, Moss drove to the hoop for a layup that gave NU a 69–66 lead. The game then came to an unexpected halt when the scoreboard went blank.

"Holy Cross championship game. Packed Cabot Gym. And I'm running the scoreboard. Someone stepped on the power chord," Scott Cohen recalls. "All of a sudden I heard Coach Fogel yelling, and if you've ever been on the receiving end of Coach Fogel's yelling, you know what I mean."[54] With everything reattached, the game continued, and Holy Cross came back to life, reeling off 6 consecutive points. Holy Cross led by 3 with eighteen seconds remaining, but an Eric Jefferson putback cut the lead to one. After failing to strip Holy Cross on the inbound pass, the Huskies fouled Eddie Thurman with four seconds remaining, sending him to the line for a one-and-one with a 74–73 lead and a chance to clinch the game. Thurman hit the first shot, extending Holy Cross's lead to 75–73.[55]

"I knew Eddie [Thurman] from AAU. He was from Lynn," Chip Rucker said. Rucker was awaiting the second shot, ready to box out Witts. "I said to him, 'Come on Eddie, you can miss one for me,' and smiled at him, and he did. I got the rebound, and I didn't panic. I dribbled a couple of times and saw Perry [Moss] up court."[56]

Moss heaved up a perfect 50-footer that sailed through the rim, through the net, and sent the game to overtime. It also sent the crowd at Cabot into bedlam—Northeastern fans. Holy Cross fans. People who'd been supporting the Huskies since the days of Dukeshire. People who'd never entered the gym before that night.[57]

"He [Thurman] made the first. The Holy Cross bench started to celebrate. Even George [Blaney] started to smile," Calhoun wrote in his memoir. "People are all over the court. I, of course, am out there, throwing people out of the way because all we won was a chance to go to overtime. Noise from Cabot and nearby Punters Pub, where the game was on the radio, was so loud that area residents thought there was an explosion."[58]

Steve Berkowitz, calling the game on WRBB along with Paul Porter, sounded like a screech owl with a Boston burr when he yelled into the microphone that this had been the "greatest shot ever in Northeastern history."[59] UPI accounts of the game lauded Moss's heroics but referred to him as "Terry."[60] The box score in the hometown *Globe* wasn't much better, referring to team captain Harris as "Keith."[61]

Now with the game tied at 75, there was still the business of overtime. Teams rarely respond well to such catharsis, but Calhoun's did. Two successful free throws by Perry Moss, who scored a team-high 24 points, and four by Pete Harris, who posted 19 points, were more than Holy Cross could muster. Dave Mulguin missed a potentially game-tying 25-footer at the buzzer. Northeastern had won, 81–79, and they were headed to their first NCAA Division I Tournament. Holy Cross accepted a bid to the NIT.[62]

Well wishes were few in number from the basketball cognoscenti. Outside of New England, Northeastern basketball was virtually unknown. Those who did have an opinion on Northeastern's NCAA bid were primarily contemptuous heavyweights who had been left out of the tournament.

Syracuse, who had finished sixth in the Big East but won the conference tournament, was on the outside looking in for the first time in a decade. "If that's the case, then why even play the tournament?" Syracuse coach Jim Boeheim said of the Big East Tournament champion's exclusion.[63]

Syracuse senior center Dan Schayes was less judicious than Boeheim in his comments. Reacting to a list of the automatic bids to the tournament, he said to the *Daily News'* Don Greenberg, "Northeastern? Pardon me while I throw up."[64]

Syracuse was far from the only club left out of the forty-eight-team field that griped over the inclusion of champions from less prominent conferences, including Northeastern from the ECAC North. Marquette's Hank Raymonds, whose team had won twenty games and appeared in ten consecutive tournaments, also made his displeasure known about his team's exclusion in favor of automatic entries like Northeastern. Legendary former Marquette coach and current CBS basketball commentator Al McGuire served as a spokesman for his former program, calling it a "farce" that Northeastern got a tournament bid while the Golden Warriors were relegated to the NIT.[65]

The unheralded Huskies headed for the West Regional in El Paso. Eleventh-seeded Northeastern drew sixth-seeded Fresno State, the champions of the Pacific Coast Athletic Association. The winner faced Utah, the number three seed. The 25-3 and eleventh-ranked Fresno State Bulldogs had actually finished the season ranked higher than fourteenth-ranked Utah. The Bulldogs played fast and physically. Their defense, the best in the country, was particularly staggering, holding opponents to just 47.1 points per game. Tiny Grant's players forced their opponents into nearly five more turnovers per game than they committed. Setting the tone for the Bulldogs was junior forward Rod Higgins, who was the team's leading scorer, rebounder, and shot blocker. He was also a lockdown defender who usually matched up against the opponent's biggest offensive threat. Higgins would go on to a twelve-year NBA playing career and serve as the general manager of the Golden State Warriors and Charlotte Bobcats. "People thought I was crazy when I said I would rather we played a UCLA or an LSU in the first round. I felt we could do something against them with our quickness. But Fresno State is quick. And we match up with them man for man," Calhoun said in El Paso.[66] By the time he made this statement, basketball writers around the country had made Fresno State into one of the most popular sleeper picks in the field.

Television commentators couldn't get out of the habit of calling Calhoun's team "Northwestern," the better-known Chicagoland school. A couple of papers even referred to Northeastern as "North Easton," the hometown of Olympic hockey hero Jim Craig—and also the way that Calhoun pronounced the name of his employer. Northeastern arrived in El Paso after a long layover in Dallas. NCAA officials cautioned all the teams in El Paso to "be careful and stay together" on any side trips to Juarez, Mexico, instructed them on where to get authentic Tex-Mex food and where to buy western-style clothing. The record remains silent on whether or not Calhoun was ever seen sporting a Stetson, bolo tie, or spurs.[67] The game would be carried live in Boston only on radio at 11:30 p.m. eastern. A tape-delayed version was shown on ESPN the next day.[68]

Several dozen Northeastern supporters joined the team in El Paso. The contingent from Boston was roughly the same size as the pep band Fresno State sent along to support their Bulldogs. The Huskies learned of the Fresno band's noise-making prowess the night before the game, as the two contingents stayed at the same truck-stop Holiday Inn. While Northeastern tried to get some sleep, the band held rowdy parties late into the evening. Several thousand Fresno State fans made the trip to El Paso, turning the twelve-thousand-seat Special Events Center at the University of Texas—El Paso into a veritable home court for the Bulldogs.[69]

Northeastern kept the crowd in check early on by hanging tough with the 8-point favorites. A 10–3 run late in the first half gave Fresno a 36–28 advantage, but an Eric Jefferson tip-in cut the lead to 6 at the break. Northeastern didn't shut down Higgins, who went for a game-high 24 points. Nor did the Bulldogs clamp down on Northeastern's backcourt as Harris netted 20 and Moss 17. But the Huskies chipped away at Fresno's lead, eventually tying the game at 53 with just over five minutes remaining. In the end, Northeastern caused Fresno State to stall out, as Calhoun adopted a tactic that his counterpart Grant used frequently late in games. After making a defensive stop, Northeastern held the ball for more than five minutes. Calhoun used a pair of timeouts to take the pressure off his guards, Moss and Harris. As the clock wound down toward zero, Perry Moss drove to the basket and suckered in Fresno's zone defense. He fed the ball to Chip Rucker in the low post who laid it in for the game-winning basket with four seconds remaining. *Northeastern 55 Fresno State 53.*[70]

"All the press reports kept calling them [Fresno State] a Cadillac team. I said after the game that today a Chevrolet beat a Cadillac, and the papers picked up on it," Rucker said.[71]

"When Calhoun walked in afterwards, we were sitting in a circle in the locker room with our legs crossed. He was holding up one finger," Charlie

Heineck remembered.[72] So much for everyone who said Northeastern didn't belong in the tournament.

"Our lack of recognition certainly gave us a chip on our shoulder when we played in the Tournament or against bigger schools," Karl Fogel said.[73] Calhoun played off that sensibility, particularly with his early NCAA Tournament teams.

"All I would ask them is, 'Did so-and-so recruit you?' No. Well, now you've got the opportunity to show them. I can't think of how many times I said that in different sorts of ways," Calhoun said.[74]

Two nights later, Northeastern's season came to an end against Utah. A thicker, longer, and more talented Utes team pummeled the Huskies, 94–69. Utah featured two lottery picks from the upcoming 1981 NBA Draft, forwards Tom Chambers and Danny Vranes. The soon-to-be top ten picks combined for 48 points in the win. Even if the outcome was well in hand by the half, Northeastern's Charlie Heineck made the game a memorable one for the future NBAers, harassing them like a wrestling heel every time he came in the game. "Tom Chambers was probably the first person to retaliate against my antics," Charlie Heineck said. Heineck poked, prodded, and pummeled opponents in a manner that would have made Bill Laimbeer proud. Chambers was in no mood to take it. "He came running through the lane on a fast break and gave me a good whack in the nuts."[75]

Northeastern finished at 24-6, the most wins in school history. Seniors Harris and Rucker both earned All-ECAC North honors. Both were selected in the NBA Draft as well. Harris went to Phoenix in the sixth round and Rucker to Milwaukee in the ninth. Neither made an NBA roster. For the season, Harris averaged 20 points per game for the third consecutive year while leading the team in assists. Moss scored nearly 17 a game, while Chip Rucker averaged better than 11 and 7. Statistically speaking, the remainder of Northeastern's rotation did not figure as prominently but collectively made up the on-floor architecture of Harris, Moss, and Rucker's success.

As a result, expectations for 1981–1982 were not as high as one might expect. Despite returning seven of their nine regulars, several New England sportswriters picked the Pete Harris– and Chip Rucker–less Huskies as low as fourth in the stacked ECAC North, behind Holy Cross, BU, and Canisius.[76]

That fall, the Northeastern athletic department installed a new, removable $50,000 basketball floor at the former Boston Arena, anticipating the team's permanent move to the larger building.[77] A widely recruited 6'3" point guard out of Providence named Walter "Skeeter" Bryant highlighted NU's recruits that fall. Bryant was in line to be heir apparent to Pete Harris but ended up behind the more rugged Phil Robinson on the depth chart.

Perry Moss and company picked up where they'd left off the previous spring, ripping off five consecutive victories to start the season before splitting a pair of in-season tournaments. The Christmas break did 7-2 Northeastern a world of good. NU kicked off the conference slate on January 6, playing host to Niagara at the Northeastern Arena. Perry Moss went for 23 points and 4 steals, while Eric Jefferson posted 18 as NU destroyed Niagara, 94–68. The Huskies continued their trek through January, amassing a 12-3 overall record and a 3-0 league mark before facing a back-to-back late January crucible of BU and BC.

Senior Perry Moss was already well on his way to earning ECAC North Player of the Year honors, averaging nearly 24 points per game while setting the school's single-season scoring record. Moss's classmates Eric Jefferson and Dave Leitao both had the best years of their collegiate careers. Jefferson averaged in double figures for the first time and led the team in assists. Leitao continued to be a defensive stalwart while increasing his production on the offensive end. Though not nearly so dynamic as Pete Harris, Robinson was a consistent performer at the other guard spot and a particularly good defender. The breakout player on the 1981–1982 Northeastern basketball team was sophomore Mark Halsel, who averaged a double-double for the season with just over 11 points and 11 rebounds per game.

Northeastern had a rough week against its Commonwealth Avenue rivals. On Tuesday night, BU came into the Northeastern Arena and embarrassed the Huskies on their home floor, 82–64. Two nights later, BC ran past them at Roberts, 87–77. Several rounds of fisticuffs marred the BU game, presaging several more donnybrooks between the clubs in the coming years. The absence of Chip Rucker in the middle was particularly pronounced that evening, as BU team captain John Teague humbled Halsel to the tune of 22 points and 9 rebounds.[78]

The losses dropped Northeastern to 12-5. For the second time that season Calhoun's team responded to back-to-back losses with fire and fury. In this instance, Northeastern responded by redoubling its efforts on the boards, always a fixation of Calhoun's, particularly the rebounding margin. Northeastern went on an eight-game winning streak down the stretch, winning the rebounding battle each time. A convincing win at home against Canisius on February 15 and an equally impressive pummeling of Holy Cross two nights later in Worcester punctuated the streak. For the season, Northeastern ended up second in the country in rebounding margin.

A deflating home loss to NIT-bound LIU ended the winning streak. Northeastern led by as much as 17 before blowing the lead in the second half to Paul Lizzo's frenetic Blackbirds. On Senior Day, NU returned to form, reaching the twenty-win plateau by posting a 74–62 win over Holy Cross. The win made Northeastern 8-1 in league play and clinched them the top seed in the ECAC North Tournament, ahead of Niagara and Canisius, who both went 7-2.

In the semifinals, NU hosted BU in a game unlike any previous contest in the shared Calhoun-Pitino era. Northeastern played more slowly and deliberately, tamping down on Pitino's press while holding its own in the low post. The Huskies had their own troubles, shooting just 35 percent from the field. Through thirty-five minutes, BU had gotten the best of them. The Terriers were in complete control of the game, leading 48–40. Once again, Perry Moss put the Huskies on his shoulders, leading Northeastern on a 9–0 run. Moss scored 7 of the points and sealed the game in the closing moments, swatting away a Jay Twyman shot as time expired to secure Northeastern the win. Without Moss's heroics, Northeastern's season would likely have come to an end. Canisius, Niagara, and BU all had excellent squads that winter. All three teams won nineteen games. And all three of them got left out of the NIT.[79]

The BU game proved to be the de facto ECAC North title game. In front of nearly four thousand fans at the Northeastern Arena, the Huskies wiped the floor with Niagara, 82–59, in the finals, earning their second straight trip to the NCAA Tournament. Perry Moss dominated play in his last home game, scoring 34 points and earning his second ECAC North Tournament MVP trophy.[80]

Once again an eleven seed, Northeastern headed to the Nassau Coliseum on Long Island for its first-round matchup in the East Region. This time, the first-round game was carried in prime time locally on Channel 56. The Huskies drew St. Joseph's, the champions of the East Coast Conference. The 25-4 Hawks were just a six seed but ranked number two in the final

Widmer Eastern College Basketball Poll, behind Georgetown. In its Big 5 meeting with Villanova, the three seed in the East Region, St. Joseph's beat Nova to a pulp, pounding their crosstown rivals, 84–64, at the Palestra.[81] Philadelphia's newspapers hyped up the possibility of a second-round St. Joe's—Nova rematch, but Hawks coach Jim Boyle dispelled such talk as premature. "I guarantee you we are not looking past Northeastern," Boyle said, citing the Huskies' upset win over Fresno State in the 1981 tournament.[82]

Boyle had a terrific team in 1982. They were a tough, talented, and basketball-savvy club that rarely turned the ball over. Many of their players contributed significantly to the 1981 St. Joseph's team, which reached the Final Eight under Jim Lynam, who had joined Dr. Jack Ramsay's coaching staff with the Portland Trail Blazers. Credit for St. Joe's elite ball handling went to its all-senior backcourt of Jeff Clark and Bryan Warrick, one of the best tandems in the country. Warrick was a long and versatile scoring threat who was selected twenty-fifth overall in the 1982 NBA Draft. Swingman Lonnie McFarlan, 6'5", contributed consistently on the offensive end while 6'10" sophomore standout Tony Costner went on to earn honorable mention All-American honors and become the leading scorer in school history.

"Coach Boyle and Coach [Brad] Greenberg described them [North-eastern] as a very physical team, but one we felt we were five to seven points better than," Tony Costner recalls. "Our focus clearly was Perry Moss. We knew he was explosive and had a lot of confidence going into the tournament, so we needed a full team effort to slow him down."[83]

Calhoun offered nothing but praise for NU's first-round opponent but ensured that his team retained its underdog edge by his public and private comments. "We've been talking to the kids a lot about the challenge. I've told them during the week that we've been overlooked in New England, we've been overlooked in the Widmer Poll. I've told people you can play. Now let's go out and prove it," Calhoun said.[84]

In the first half, Perry Moss fought through the Hawks defenses for 16 points. Matching Moss on the St. Joseph's side was Lonnie McFarlan, who led St. Joseph's with 24 of his own. At the half, St. Joseph's led, 36–35, and pounded away early in the second, slowing Moss down to just 8 second-half points. "We were up six or seven points late and thought we had made enough plays to win," Costner said. "What we did not expect was that kid [Eric] Jefferson getting a bunch of points and the other big Halsel getting loose and scoring like he did."[85]

With Moss neutralized, Halsel asserted himself down low, scoring 11 points and grabbing 13 rebounds. Eric Jefferson just kept hitting jump shots, scoring 12 of his 18 points in the second half. "We knew they'd be doubling Perry [Moss]," Calhoun said, "So we looked for the other guys to do the damage."[86]

Moss did plenty of damage himself in the game's final minutes, going on a personal 6–0 scoring run that gave NU a 61–58 lead with just over four minutes remaining. With thirty seconds to go, St. Joseph's fouled Eric Jefferson, sending him to the line with a 61–60 Huskies lead.

Boyle called two consecutive timeouts to ice Jefferson. He failed. Jefferson sank both shots to put Northeastern up, 63–60. Jefferson credited Calhoun and his teammates for keeping him loose in the huddle as he waited several agonizing minutes to take the most consequential shots of his career.[87] Northeastern found a way to make it interesting late, missing the front end of two straight one-and-ones. A Bryan Warrick basket made it 63–62, but Northeastern hung on for the win, as several hundred from the large Husky contingent stormed the court in celebration.[88] "This one was sweeter. Because it happened in the East where we play our games and because we beat the no. 2 team in the East," Calhoun said, comparing this year's opening-round upset win to the previous year's.[89] The upset victory clearly didn't impress one Nassau Coliseum security guard, who detained Calhoun on his way to the postgame presser, thinking the coach's media pass didn't look right.[90]

After the Friday night win, Northeastern advanced to Sunday afternoon and national television coverage against Villanova. On Sunday, the public address announcer at the Nassau Coliseum introduced them as "Northwestern." The sign on their locker room read "Northesten" all weekend.[91] By the end of the nationally televised game, everyone watching in person or at home knew their name. Rollie Massimino's Villanova Wildcats were unquestionably a bigger and more athletic team. The Wildcats had won the Big East's regular season championship. Eight of the nine Villanova players that appeared that afternoon were later selected in the NBA Draft. Two of them, 6'9" power forward Ed Pinckney and 6'3" guard Stewart Granger, were first-round picks. This game bore zero resemblance to Northeastern's second-round matchup the previous March against a similarly talented Utah team. For a three-hour stretch that included three overtimes, Northeastern was every bit Villanova's equal.

Two things kept Northeastern in this game: their rebounding and their otherworldly senior guard. Halsel, Braswell, Leitao, and Jefferson wasted big and brawny Villanova on the boards, winning the rebounding battle 45–30. Seniors Dave Leitao and Eric Jefferson really rose to the challenge, each grabbing a game-high 11 rebounds.

Perry Moss was just as spectacular. Playing in what proved to be his final collegiate game, Moss scored 31 points, made 4 steals, and delivered 7 assists. He played the final twenty-four minutes of the game with 4 fouls and continued to lead the Huskies on the court.

The disparity in foul shots played no small role in keeping Villanova in the game. The Wildcats got thirty cracks at it from the stripe to Northeastern's eleven. The Huskies no doubt played physically, but rough-and-tumble basketball was also Villanova's stock-in-trade, making the discrepancy even more frustrating for Calhoun and his team.[92]

Early on, Villanova led by as much as 8, but Northeastern whittled it down to 3 by the half. Villanova again opened up a big lead, 45–36, early in the second half. Northeastern again fought its way back, just hanging around, staying within a basket for most of the second half. Perry Moss's second 6–0 run in as many games knotted it at 52 with six minutes remaining before play slogged down into multi-minute possessions.

With the game tied at 56 in the waning moments of regulation, Dave Leitao forced Stewart Granger into an ugly shot that preserved the tie. Leitao nearly won it in the first overtime, getting his own rebound and tossing up a point-blank shot that rolled around the rim before falling off as time expired. In double OT, Jefferson tapped one in with one second remaining to tie the game at 65.

In triple OT, Villanova finally willed its way to victory. An Ed Pinckney dunk with 2:01 remaining gave Nova a 71–70 lead that it never relinquished. Pinckney's bucket kickstarted a 7–0 run. Villanova escaped with a 76–72 win. The Wildcats would go on to the regional final, where they lost to eventual national champion UNC.

Calhoun was unusually emotional afterward. "I'll always feel that we deserved to win this," he said. "People think we rolled in off a farm truck.

But I want everyone to know this is Northeastern University from Boston, Massachusetts, a damned good team."[93] Calhoun declared Moss the best guard in the tournament, a statement that was certainly true that afternoon.

By the time Northeastern left the court at Nassau Coliseum, the Huskies and their coach had further cemented their reputation as the team you didn't want to play in March, even if you hadn't seen them play all season. Calhoun earned ECAC North, All-New England, and District I Coach of the Year honors. He also received a nomination for the Kodak National Coach of the Year award. Less than a week after the loss to Villanova, Calhoun signed a long-term deal with Northeastern and rebuffed an offer from Duquesne for its open job, the first of many such enticing offers that welcomed Calhoun in subsequent springs.[94]

The heady winters of 1981 and 1982 gave way to a rebuilding year on Huntington Avenue. Gone from the frontcourt were four-year stalwarts Dave Leitao and Eric Jefferson. Gone too was ECAC North player of the Year and two-time Tournament MVP Perry Moss. Moss was selected by the Boston Celtics in the third round of the NBA Draft, initiating a two-decade long sojourn as a professional basketball player that included stops with the Washington Bullets, Philadelphia 76ers, and Golden State, as well as ten different teams in the Colonial Basketball Association [CBA]. The Huskies slumped to a 13-15 mark in 1982–1983, finishing sixth in the ECAC North with a 4-6 league record. Holy Cross bounced Northeastern in the quarterfinals of the conference tournament. The Huskies' frontcourt continued to dominate, as Mark Halsel averaged nearly 20 and 12 for the season and Roland Braswell put up better than 13 and 8 an evening. Halsel became Northeastern's go-to guy and came through big in the clutch on several occasions despite playing with a cracked wrist all season.[95] Unfortunately, Calhoun and company could find no one in the backcourt to replace Moss as the team's leading scorer or difference maker in the clutch. The following season would be very different. In the fall of 1983, Northeastern brought the greatest recruiting class in mid-major college basketball history to campus. Reggie Lewis, Andre LaFleur, and Wes Fuller would transform NU's pair of tournament runs into the starting point of a dynasty.

8

Like the Pacific Ocean *(Pitino)*

Year two of the Rick Pitino era began with unmitigated optimism. The Terriers joined a competitive new league that featured longtime rival Northeastern; New England powers Holy Cross and Rhode Island; and a pair of Buffalo-area schools with long traditions of basketball excellence, Canisius and Niagara. With the exception of Tom Channel, BU returned a nearly intact roster. The Terriers welcomed in a bumper freshman class, as well as 6′4″ junior college transfer Dan Harwood, who contributed meaningful minutes at forward. Pitino's team had melded further over the summer. The players had all stayed in Boston, taking classes, lifting weights, running, and playing full-court games—all unofficially but with Pitino's encouragement and a complete run of the athletic department facilities. Moreover, BU's young hotshot head coach now had a year of experience under his belt. He'd even found his team a new home court. Downstairs.

In August 1979, John Simpson announced that BU would play some of its basketball games at Walter Brown Arena. Hockey came first, Simpson asserted, but whenever possible, the basketball Terriers got a crack at the four-thousand-seat venue. Rick Pitino the salesman built on the success of Rick Pitino the basketball coach, convincing Simpson to invest $60,000 in a new floor to slap down in Walter Brown for hoops home dates. Mostly, the floor sat in storage at the ice rink.[1] The sizable investment, Pitino argued, would improve attendance by convincing better opponents to come to Babcock Street. BU would play three games at Walter Brown in 1979–1980 and planned to host eight opponents there in the 1980–1981 season. The young coach had already parlayed his connections in the coaching fraternity into several big-time road games that season. Trips to LSU, Maryland, and South Carolina punctuated BU's already stacked regional slate. Tough schedule or not, Pitino had great expectations for his Terriers.

"We weren't as good of a team as our record," Pitino said of his first BU team in the *Globe*'s 1979–1980 college basketball preview. "We did a lot of it on aggressiveness and enthusiasm and that camouflaged a lot of our deficiencies. This year we're a better team."[2] Senior tri-captains Glenn Consor, Steve Wright, and Wally West led a BU team that would regularly dig twelve-deep into its bench. The *Globe* picked BU fourth in the ECAC, behind Holy Cross, Rhode Island, and Canisius, and projected that the Terriers would have another "excellent record."[3]

BU opened the 1979–1980 season by blitzing overmatched C. W. Post and Vermont teams at Case. These lopsided contests were a prelude to the Terriers' first test, a Saturday night date with perennial New England power Fairfield. The 2,774 fans, many of them waving red-and-white pennants provided at the door, watched BU dismantle the once mighty Stags, 92–72, at Walter Brown. Wally West defended the rim with aplomb that evening, swatting away six shots while holding Fairfield star Flip Williams in check. Pitino barked orders at his charges until the final minutes of the blowout win, which improved BU's record to 3-0.

The enthusiasm BU displayed on the court was matched by the support the Terriers received that evening at Walter Brown. Clearly, promotion man Bo Ruggerio had moved the needle on attendance, helping make an event out of games that were previously gatherings of friends and family. Though by no means impressive, BU's average draw of slightly better than one thousand fans per home date in 1979–1980 was nearly three times as many as the squad had drawn in the Sigler era. At other home dates, Ruggerio and his subordinates handed out red-and-white carnations, pompoms, and T-shirts. Ruggerio hired local pep bands and sat them right behind the opponents' bench. Interns taped the words to newly minted BU cheers to every seat in the bleachers and cajoled their fellow students at the Sherman Union into joining them at the basketball games.[4]

The Terriers finished off their five-game opening home stand with blowout wins over Upsala and the College of Charleston. Five games in, opponents had yet to hold BU under 87 points in any contest. It didn't seem to matter which players took the floor. Everyone contributed on both ends. "I want to be like the Pacific Ocean, bring 'em on in waves," Pitino said of his approach to substitutions, a strategy that proved effective but required players to forgo individual achievements for the greater good of the team.[5]

"Pitino's playing like 12 people and we're all giving you like 7 points," Wally West said of his coach's approach, which was psychologically difficult for a team full of players used to being stars in their own right. Senior tri-captain West, who played the role of both team comedian and big brother, contributed profoundly to the team's sense of comradery. West was also the team's unsung hero. He was never a big scorer, but this versatile big man dominated on the defensive end. Pitino called him the squad's most improved player in 1979–1980. West was an excellent rebounder and elite shot blocker but also a deft passer, solid jump shooter, and a surprisingly strong ball handler. His contributions showed up in tangible ways in the box score and intangible ways that were known to both teammates and BU fans, who greeted his efforts with chants of "Wal-ly, Wal-ly."[6] "Wally was the one that gave us all the advice. Wally had his funny way of selling up things. Wally was the one that kept us together,'" Gene Jones said.[7] "Wally looked out for me, on court and off court. He was one of those guys who would tell me the truth about myself, the hard truth that nobody else would tell you. He'd sit me down and tell me, 'Here's what you need to do,'" John Teague recalled.[8]

The freshman "Brown Brothers" were finding ways to contribute to their respective units. Brett Brown was a firecracker off the bench, adding depth to a backcourt that featured Glenn Consor as the team's veritable quarterback, as well as the electric Johnny Ray Wall and sharpshooting Gene Jones. Arturo Brown was doing more than just finding minutes in the frontcourt alongside West, Wright, and Teague. "Artie" turned heads every time he entered the game and won over his teammates off the court immediately. "He [Arturo Brown] was probably the greatest athlete I'd ever seen in my life. When I took dunks, I jumped off of one foot. He was the first kid I'd seen go off of two feet and literally all the way from the free throw line just jump. He'd just hang in the air," John Teague said. "He could shoot it, rebound it, handle the ball. He was our LeBron James."[9] "Arturo was the most polite, sweetest, funny guy. And an unbelievable athlete. He started for us as a freshman at that small forward spot. He couldn't have been a nicer kid. He never cursed. Worked his butt off in practice. He's the kind of guy that you'd want to marry your daughter," Glenn Consor said.[10]

The only downside to the team's fast start was that leading scorer and team captain Steve Wright twisted his knee against Charleston. Despite the retinue of scorers BU could boast on the offensive end, none matched Wright, who was as versatile a scorer as any player in the country in 1979–1980. Wright would be limited in BU's next contest, its first road game. And what a road game it was.

Three days after Christmas, a crowd of more than sixteen thousand greeted Boston University in Baton Rouge. The 5-0 Terriers brought their press and fast break to LSU's Assembly Center. Pitino's squad jumped out to an 11–8 lead against the defending SEC champs. It didn't last. The Tigers' large and ferocious front line simply wasted BU for the rest of the evening. Led by big men Greg Cook, Rudy Macklin, and DeWayne Scales, LSU responded with a 28–8 run and never looked back. The Tigers led by 17 at the break and cruised to a 92–72 win. "We were intimidated early on. We're not used to playing in this kind of atmosphere, in this kind of building. Not in New England. This is why we wanted to play in it," Pitino said in defeat.[11] "When we went to LSU, we were there for a couple days," Desmond Martin recalled of his evening in LSU's "Snake Pit." "We were down there for Christmas. We get down there and we get out to practice, and I see the ninety-thousand-seat football stadium on the right-hand side and as I'm walking to the arena, I see a cage and in the cage is a live Bengal tiger. The night of the game we walk in and they were yelling 'tiger bait.' Sixteen thousand people."[12]

The crowd was the least of Martin's worries. BU's frontcourt spent the evening struggling to guard a cadre of much thicker and taller LSU big men. "Glenn [Consor] tried to take a charge [on Rudy Macklin]. Pitino was big on taking charges. Anyway, Glenn planted himself, and Macklin jumped right over him for a highlight reel dunk," Tom Masters said. "We lost this game and got punished when we got back to Boston by going straight from the airport to the gym for a midnight practice."[13]

"We got our butts whipped, but in those games we got a chance to represent Boston University," Wally West said. "And he [Pitino] was preparing those young boys for the future. We broke the ice. They took it home."[14]

BU recovered quickly in early January, gunning past a couple of non-conference cupcakes before winning a conference tussle against little heralded Colgate. An 89–69 beatdown of St. Francis of Brooklyn on January 12 was BU's fourth consecutive triumph and tenth straight home win. The victory improved BU's record to 9-1, but the Terriers left Case worse for wear. Steve Wright reinjured his groin, further depleting a roster already shorthanded by the temporary loss of freshman sensation Arturo Brown, who was sidelined with his own groin injury.

BU's depth and style of play under Pitino gave them a unique ability to bounce back from injuries. The Terriers were a team where virtually everyone played and virtually everyone contributed on both ends of the floor. For the 1979–1980 season, twelve different Terriers played at least five minutes per game. While only seniors Steve Wright (19.8 ppg) and Glenn Consor (10.6 ppg) averaged in double figures, six other players averaged at least six points per game. While no player averaged more than six rebounds per game, five different players averaged at least four. Six Terriers averaged at least one steal per game on a team that forced its opponents into nearly two hundred more turnovers than BU itself committed.

"Our press really has four parts. First, we go man-to-man, then we shift to a 2-2-1. After that, a half-court trap. Then a corner trap. Beating us man-to-man isn't enough," Pitino explained.[15] Apparently, Pitino spent many a late night at the Kenmore Square IHOP, downing entire pots of coffee and drawing up new variations of his pressing defense and fast-break offense, reviewing whatever data was available to him in the days before personal computers and point-and-click analytics.[16]

At times BU's versatile up-tempo, pressing style looked sloppy and chaotic, as it did against a dreadful, winless UMass team. The Terriers pummeled Pitino's alma mater, 78–51, at Walter Brown, despite shooting 34 percent from the field and turning the ball over on twenty-nine occasions. Thankfully, UMass proved even worse in every category. After manhandling New Hampshire, BU headed to Loudonville, New York to face always tough Siena, a member of the newly formed ECAC Metro conference. Not only were the Indians usually a solid team, but they also had a consistently boisterous crowd. "Siena was a great place to play with stands on all four sides. They'd pack the place," BU and Maine's Jeff Holmes said of Siena's Alumni Recreation Center. Holmes recalls one trip to Siena where the student body berated Maine star Jimmy Boylen with an early version of the "asshole" chant whenever he touched the ball.[17] "I can't remember a time when they [Siena] weren't sold out. It was a tough place to play," New Hampshire SID Mike Bruckner remembers.[18]

Siena matched BU bucket for bucket in the first half. The teams retreated to their locker rooms tied at 43. Albany's own Johnny Ray Wall blew the game wide open in the second half. Playing less than five miles from his childhood home, Wall scored 6 straight points out of the locker room, giving BU a lead they would never relinquish. Steve Wright's return to full-time action helped BU reassert its offensive presence in the low post. Wright led the way with 22 points in the 98–89 win.[19]

Now 12-1, BU headed south to Keaney Gymnasium for a league game with Rhode Island. The Rams weren't quite as imposing as they'd been the previous season with Sly Williams leading the way. URI was in the midst of a four-game losing streak and held an 8-6 record—hardly terrible but not the stuff of Jack Kraft's recent Rams teams. Nevertheless, creaky old Keaney Gymnasium was one of the toughest places to play in the East, thanks in large part to Rhode Island's enthusiastic fan base, which stuffed into the sweat box and rooted their hearts out every game.

Early on, the Keaney faithful had plenty to cheer. URI jumped out to a 23–8 advantage, thanks in large part to BU's dreadful shooting and Rhode Island freshman standout Horace Owens's 7 points in the first two minutes. But BU weathered the storm. Pitino's team had dealt with much larger and much louder crowds on the road already that season. Slowly but surely, BU cut into Rhode Island's lead and trailed by just 5 at the half.

The second half belonged to Steve Wright. The 6'9" forward sparked BU's attack by hitting three consecutive jumpers out of the locker room. He ended up with 25 points on the evening. The Terriers ran past Rhode Island for the remainder of the game and left Kingston with a 74–63 win, handing the Rams their first home loss in two seasons. Two nights later, BU put up 117 points at home against Marist, bringing the Terriers record to 14-1. Members of the local sports press started asking in print whether this BU team should be nationally ranked. "That's our goal right now. We're all striving to get national recognition. If we keep winning, and I think we will, the pollsters can't ignore us," Wally West said after the Marist win, when he scored a game-high 21 points, making him the eighth different Terrier to lead the club in scoring that season. *The Globe*'s Michael Madden even got in on the act, declaring Boston "the place to be in college basketball," with BU sitting at 14-1 and BC and Northeastern both at 13-4.[20]

An early February *Globe* feature on the BU coach described a business leaders' luncheon at Quincy Market, where Pitino was introduced as the coach of "the best basketball team in New England." Pitino took advantage of the opportunity to hold court. "What I'd almost rather have is that we'd be first on Babcock Street," Pitino joked, referring to the location of the Case Center, which his basketball team shared with the school's national champion hockey team.[21] The piece further mythologized the young coach, describing his hellacious practices; his reliance on a pressing, attacking style and frequent mass substitutions; the fierce loyalty he expected out of his players; and his ability to sell John Simpson on buying him a $60,000 floor, a decision that annoyed BU hockey coach Jack Parker, who hated losing ice time to a basketball team, especially since it still drew flies. "When I came here, nobody wanted to be associated with BU basketball to the point where they wouldn't even wear a BU sweatshirt in public. Now everybody's proud to be wearing a BU warmup jacket or sweatshirt or T-shirt," Pitino boasted.[22]

In a broadly syndicated AP feature, readers around the country caught a glimpse of the young coach in action, rebuilding BU's basketball program in virtual anonymity. Pitino describes his team as "12 altar boys" who worked so hard in practice and in the classroom that they didn't have time to get into trouble.[23]

The second month of the 1980s proved not nearly so kind as its first for Boston University basketball. BU dropped two of three games on a late January—early February road swing. A much-improved St. Peter's team pushed past them in a bruising 58–55 game. P. J. Carlesimo's Wagner Seahawks pulled away late for a 70–59 win, their second straight over BU. The Terriers took a huge lead against UNC-Wilmington in their next home date at Case, only to squander it by getting into early foul trouble, a near-constant problem for a team that played as aggressively as Pitino's. BU hung on for a 59–57 win, but it hardly impressed as a prelude to their annual matchup with rival Northeastern.

Pitino called the game between the rising programs at Case the "war of the century."[24] At the time, 16-3 BU held a half-game advantage in the ECAC North standings over Jim Calhoun's 16-4 Huskies. A standing-room-only crowd of 2,800 turned out at Case. More than 700 fans were turned away at the door. When BU's players were announced, Northeastern fans turned their backs and pulled out newspapers, a response to the *Globe's* assertion that the Terriers were New England's best team.[25]

The February 1980 edition of BU-Northeastern was a genuine classic, played in an atmosphere that felt like Beanpot hockey. In a game that featured sixteen lead changes, BU pulled away late when Northeastern's leading scorer, Pete Harris, who produced a game-high 30 points, received his fourth foul with just over three minutes remaining. Calhoun got a technical protesting the call. BU took advantage of all the foul shots and built a cushion that remained until the final horn: *Boston University 85 Northeastern 78*. Senior captains Steve Wright (29 points) and Glenn Consor (16 points) led the Terriers' offensive assault while BU's twelve-man press wore out Northeastern's shorter bench, forcing the Huskies into 23 turnovers.[26] "Our conditioning got to them late in the game. It's tough to go against our press for an entire game," Steve Wright said in victory.[27] "Both of these teams have been a bag of doughnuts in the past but now we have something to be proud of," Pitino said, recognizing the renewed significance of the rivalry.[28]

Wally West went for a double-double in the win despite being in rather rough shape. The day before the game, West woke up around 7 a.m. at a friend's house near the BC campus, roughly three miles west of BU. West had a few drinks and went to sleep the night before, forgetting that Pitino had scheduled a 7 a.m. practice. "I jumped out of bed, no bus, no train, middle of the winter. I just ran all the way back to Case Center. I bust into Case Center, I bust into the locker room, and the team was in there watching films, Pitino standing right by the door. I'm pouring sweat, and he looks at me. [He] turns the TV off and heads upstairs," West recalls.[29]

Pitino decided that West's punishment should fit the crime for arriving forty-five minutes late for practice. "First thing is he [Pitino] takes me to the nautilus room," West said. "He says to one of the assistants, 'Make him do forty-five reps on everything in there.' Then he says, 'Give him two basketballs. Make him dribble two basketballs for forty-five minutes.' Wally, now you've got forty-five suicides."[30]

By this point, West had deposited all the contents of his stomach onto the gymnasium floor. "I say to Pitino, 'If I could raise my arms, I would fight your little ass.' He says to me, 'All right, one more [suicide].' And I'm crying; I can't do it. I end up crawling, inch by inch. And he just turned around and walked out," West reminisced.[31] West's girlfriend (now wife) kept his knees wrapped with ice until game time. Pitino kept West on the bench throughout the first half before unleashing him in the second, when he proved a dominant force underneath.

Three nights after the Northeastern win, BU faced 11,466 screaming Terrapin fans at eighth-ranked Maryland. The trip to Cole Field House was the Terriers' second of three long-distance road games against national powers. More treacherous even than the fans in College Park were the players in Lefty Driesell's lineup, particularly the frontcourt trio of Buck Williams, Ernest Graham, and Albert King. A larger and more athletic Maryland team clobbered BU, 99–76, thanks not only to the Terrapins' low-post dominance, but also to the quick whistles that greeted the Terriers. ACC officials called BU for nearly three times as many infractions. Pitino did not hold back after the game. "It was a cheating situation out there. The fouls they called on us set college basketball back 40 years. Those guys should be robbing Wells Fargo trucks in Montana, not refereeing," Pitino said. "I wasn't that impressed with the Maryland players or coach," he continued, making no secret of his mutual enmity with Driesell.[32] "BU wasn't that bad—when I put the subs in, they cut the lead to 14," Driesell said to rub it in afterward.[33] Far closer to home BU lost another road game to a non-conference heavyweight, this time falling to UConn, 72–65.

The late-season gauntlet didn't stop for the Terriers. BU commenced a three-games-in-five-days stretch by bombing New Hampshire, 102–76, before flying down to Columbia, South Carolina, for a matchup with the Gamecocks. BU again hung tough in one of these "scheduled losses," Pitino's term for tough non-conference games.[34] South Carolina prevailed, 83–76, in an up-tempo, crowd-pleasing contest at Columbia Coliseum.

Whiplash from a trip immediately back to the Northeast clearly had an impact on the Terriers. Perennial pest Maine got past BU in a 102–91 horse race. Rufus Harris, as always, had BU's number, pumping in 36 points. It was the addition of freshman sensation Rick Carlisle, who later transferred to Virginia before embarking on a long NBA playing and coaching career, that sunk the suddenly foundering Terriers, who lost at home for the first time in sixteen games. The 6'5" gunner added 22 points of his own, hitting 10 of 11 shots from the field.

BU finished off the regular season with a 19-7 mark after beating Division II New York Tech on senior night. The late-season slide dropped long-presumed top-seed BU to second in the inaugural ECAC North Men's Basketball Tournament, behind Holy Cross. In the quarterfinals, BU hosted Niagara at Case. In a hard-fought, high-scoring, back-and-forth game, BU outlasted Niagara, 95–86, earning the Terriers' their first postseason win since the 1959 NCAA Tournament run. Senior captain Steve Wright capped off his remarkable BU home career, scoring a team-high 18 points while suffering from the flu virus that had gutted the team over the past two weeks.[35] Few on campus seemed to notice. Roughly five hundred people showed up for the game. The main event of the evening was downstairs. At Walter Brown, BU hockey was honoring the four Terriers who starred on the "Miracle on Ice" team, which had just defeated the Soviets and gone on to win the gold medal in Lake Placid.[36]

"We won the game. I go downstairs. Walter Brown Arena is filled to the rafters. I see these guys that I hung out with. With the gold medals. They had their shearling coats and cowboy hats on. We couldn't compete with that," Desmond Martin recalls.[37] Despite the disparity in support, BU athletes were a tight bunch, leading a niche existence on a campus that seemed more outward-looking toward the city than to the attractions available on their stretch of Commonwealth Avenue. "The hockey players would support us; the football players would support us. We were like a family of sportsters. All of us looked out for each other," John Teague said.[38]

Pitino and company headed to the Cumberland County Civic Center in Portland, Maine, site of the ECAC North semifinals, to play Rhode Island. BU ran past the larger, lumbering Rams in the first half, leading 53–38 at the break. From the outset, this was a physical game, filled with elbows, body blows, and the occasional fist. Officials tossed URI guard Nick Johnson for taking a swing at John Teague late in the first half.[39] Much of the starting lineup on both teams spent most of the second half in foul trouble. Rhode Island's big men, forward Jimmy Wright and center Roland Houston, took charge in the second half, piloting a 22–8 run out of the locker room. URI led for long stretches, but clutch foul shooting down the stretch helped BU seal a trip to the ECAC North finals. Senior captain Glenn Consor hit 4 free throws in the game's final minute to provide the margin of victory in an 83–79 win.[40]

Now 21-7, Boston University faced Ronnie Perry and Holy Cross in the finals. BU battered the Crusaders from the outset, leading by as much as 12 in the early going. Steve Wright exploded for 22 of his 29 points in the first half, but his counterpart in purple proved just as efficient. Perry, who became New England's all-time leading scorer that season, hit 7 of 8 shots in the first half, helping the Crusaders cut the margin to 5 at the break. The rapid-fire first half slogged down into a parade of fouls, free throws, and poor shooting in the second. The teams traded the lead on ten occasions as Holy Cross started to get the best of the exchanges. "They shot like 40 free throws. Ronnie Perry shot like 30 of them. And that boy don't miss free throws. We shot like 8," Wally West remembered.[41] It was actually 28 to 8. Perry hit 14 of the 16 he attempted, including 8 in a row in a 2:30 minute stretch. Pitino didn't complain about the disparity after the game and instead just complimented Perry on his clutch performance.[42]

Compounding the problem was BU's poor shooting down the stretch. The Terriers didn't hit a shot from the field between 7:00 and 0:28 remaining in the game. By the time BU made a field goal, the outcome was no longer in doubt. Holy Cross won, 81–75, and advanced to the NCAA Tournament. BU accepted a bid to the NIT, its first in school history.

The Terriers didn't travel far for the game—just up Commonwealth Avenue to the Roberts Center for a matchup with the same BC Eagles that had knocked them out of ECAC contention the previous February. The March 1980 version of BC-BU went about as well as the February 1979 model.[43] Tom Davis unleashed BC's press midway through the first half, and the Eagles went on a 17–3 run, forcing 7 BU turnovers. BC led by 7 at the break and by as much as 14 early in the second half before BU went on its own 12–0 run, cutting the Eagles' lead to 64–62. BC soon woke up, again blitzed BU with its press, and ran away to a 95–74 blowout win. Fans at Roberts chanted, "Davis, Davis, Davis," as the clock ticked down to zero. At the time, the BC coach was being strongly considered for the opening at Duke. Davis apparently turned Duke down. The Blue Devils went with Army's Mike Krzyzewski instead.[44] "We beat Rick [Pitino] by a lot when we played [BU] in the NIT, and, to Rick's credit, the next day he came over, knocking on the doors [at BC], saying, 'Tell me about the pressure. You guys played the whole game like you were down 20, and you beat us handily,'" BC assistant Kevin Mackey recalls.[45]

Boston University finished the 1979–1980 season with a 21-9 mark, breaking the school's single-season record for wins. The 1980–1981 season would be a quintessential rebuilding year for the Terriers, who lost three pillars of the program to graduation. Wally West, Glenn Consor, and Steve Wright had all played significant roles on the team for the past four seasons, shepherding the squad from the Roy Sigler to the Rick Pitino era. In the 1980 NBA draft, Utah selected Wally West in the fifth round, and the Celtics selected Steve Wright, three-time team MVP and leading scorer in Terriers history, in the eighth round. Neither made an NBA roster. In addition, BU lost starting forward Daryl Floyd and reserve Tom Masters, both of whom had made key contributions in Pitino's first two seasons.

The rebuild would be hastened by the surfeit of talent headed Pitino's way. Once again the "Boy Coach" drew a stellar class of recruits to Commonwealth Avenue. Headlining the class of 1984 were Detroit big man Gary Plummer and Pancho Bingham, a physical 6'3" guard from nearby Lynn Classical. Pitino compared Plummer, a 6'9" forward, to Syracuse great Lewis Orr. Plummer had averaged better than 20 points and 10 rebounds per game in high school, earning him All-Detroit honors. He received more than forty scholarship offers from around the country before selecting BU.[46]

"He [Plummer] worked his butt off. He came in looking like a beanpole and left looking pretty good," Gene Jones said.[47]

Plummer spent considerable time in the weight room building a powerful frame. Coaches watched over Plummer in the cafeteria too, making sure he was taking in enough calories to transform his ectomorphic body into one more suited for the rigors of low-post play.[48] "Everybody loved Gary. He had a terrific personality. Everybody gravitated toward him. They loved being around him," Glen Bressner said. "He was so anxious his freshman year to get his first dunk. And he went four or five games before he could dunk it. When he finally got a dunk, he got the biggest standing ovation you've ever seen from the team. His personal confidence grew dramatically."[49]

Pancho Bingham came in just as highly touted as Plummer, starring on Lynn Classical's fantastic teams of the late 1970s alongside BC basketball great Stu Primus and future BC All-American defensive back Tony Thurman. BU teammates noted his strength and physique and his ability to handle the ball as well as shoot. Bingham kept to himself but displayed supreme confidence in his abilities, a belief that, considering his skill set, was not unjustified. Stylistically, Bingham was a classic slasher in the mold of Calvin Murphy or John Lucas but clearly had the ball-handling ability to be a top-notch playmaker.

Joining Bingham in the mix for the two and three spots was transfer Jay Twyman, the son of NBA Hall of Famer Jack Twyman. Two years earlier the 6'4" Twyman had nearly signed on with Pitino at Syracuse, but when Pitino left central New York, the Orangemen lost interest. Pitino nearly convinced Twyman to follow him to BU. Instead, the deadeye shooting small forward from Cincinnati ended up at South Carolina, the most prominent program still recruiting him. Twyman's stay in Columbia was brief. "I took a visit, and I was just blown away by all the material things and by the arena and by Frank McGuire and all that kind of stuff. And then I went down there [South Carolina], and it really wasn't the right fit for me," Twyman recalls. After a year on the bench and a summer back home in Cincinnati, Twyman gave Pitino a call. "I called up the athletic department on like the first of August. I call up, get into the basketball office, and Rick picks up. And he goes, 'This is Rick Pitino. How can I help you?' All I had to say is, 'Coach.' And he said, 'Jay! I've been waiting for your call. I have a scholarship waiting for you, and I have your roommate all set up. You've got to come home here. This is where you need to be.'"[50]

"He's [Twyman] probably the most gifted shooter I've ever played against," Glen Bressner said. "The guy could just light it up. He was big, strong. I think if we'd had the three-pointer during our era, he would have been extraordinary."[51] "Very humble" is how Gene Jones described Twyman, despite Twyman's being the son of basketball royalty. "When we went to go play Cincinnati, we had dinner over at the Twymans' house after the game, and here I am, walking around Jack Twyman's house, looking at all these pictures and memorabilia," none of which seemed to affect the way Twyman presented himself to his teammates.[52] "I remember we went to their [the Twymans'] house, and I was just thinking, 'Man, this house is fantastic.' And this is how this kid grew up, but you would never know it from his personality and the way we lived in college. He was just one of the guys," John Teague said.[53] Jay's father Jack was an enthusiastic supporter of the BU program who frequently attended the team's games at home and away.

The fourth major addition to the BU basketball program had the most significant immediate impact. Jamaican-born, Toronto-raised Tony Simms was a 6′5″ shooting guard who lit up the scoreboard at Pensacola Junior College before heading to Boston. Simms was also a remarkable track athlete, later winning Canada's triple jump national championship. Before choosing to play college basketball, Simms had accepted a track scholarship to Ohio State (OSU), as well as an invitation to try out for the Buckeyes' football team, before changing his mind. Simms would soon show similar prowess in the ECAC North.[54] "Tony was a freak athlete in track as well as basketball. He could score on sheer athleticism," Jay Twyman said.[55] "Tony was very quiet at first. I think he was trying to figure out not only the culture in America, but the culture at BU and on our team. Tony was a fierce competitor, a hard worker. As he got to know us, he got more intwined," Gene Jones said.[56]

The Canadian national basketball team added Simms to its roster in 1981 as they sought to qualify for the 1984 Summer Olympics. Simms played significant minutes at small forward for Team Canada as they not only qualified for the Los Angeles games, but finished fourth overall, falling to Yugoslavia in the bronze medal game.

BU went 13-14 in 1980–1981, losing a spectacular, season-ending, triple-overtime ECAC playoff to Vermont at a packed Patrick Gymnasium in Burlington. The Terriers' record was once again weighed down by a hellacious non-conference slate that included trips to Cincinnati, Iona, and Notre Dame. Cincinnati and Notre Dame blew out BU while the Terriers scored an upset win against an Iona team that had reached the Sweet Sixteen the previous season. BU's vaunted new home schedule at Walter Brown, which featured several prominent opponents from outside the region, failed to generate more interest in the struggling team. It also threw up some awfully difficult roadblocks for the rebuilding club. The Terriers hung tough at home against Old Dominion and South Carolina, as well as BC at the Boston Garden, but eventually lost all three games.

Arch-rival Northeastern ascended to the top of ECAC North in 1980–1981, winning the league's regular and postseason championships before upsetting Fresno State in the opening round of the NCAA Tournament. The Huskies, too, won both ends of the now home-and-home series between the rival schools.

Pitino relied on a twelve-man rotation in 1980–1981 but had trouble finding a consistent starting lineup due to injuries, ineligibility, and inconsistent play. Nine different Terriers started at least five games during the 1980–1981 season. While BU had scorers up and down the lineup, nobody proved as decisive an offensive force as Steve Wright had in the two previous seasons. Freshman Tony Simms and sophomore Arturo Brown, also the team's leading rebounder, made for an excellent one-two punch. Both averaged better than 14 points per game, but neither pumped in points as consistently as veteran go-to guy Wright. Brett Brown became the team's starting point guard, excelling both as a distributor and defender, but the sophomore still lacked the scoring ability of his predecessor, Glenn Consor.

Besides BU's youth and inexperience, several other factors contributed significantly to the team's struggles in 1980–1981. Freshman guard Pancho Bingham impressed as a ball handler, defender, and scorer early in the season but missed the entire second semester after being placed on academic probation. Injuries, too, figured prominently in BU's struggles. Gene Jones, John Teague, and Dan Harwood all missed time with injuries. Senior forward Ken Fiola, who tried making a comeback after missing the two previous seasons with knee injuries, was forced to retire early in November 1980 as he faced more potentially debilitating knee problems. "At this point, Pitino and I became estranged as he threatened to take my basketball scholarship but was prevented from doing so by the university. So much for family," Fiola said. Fiola adds that Pitino later apologized to him, and the pair have reconciled.[57]

BU's attendance suffered dramatically in the difficult 1980–1981 season. Rarely did the Terriers draw more than a few hundred spectators.

"We go in there and the pregame in the old Case Gym was Patrick Ewing and Karl Hobbs of Cambridge Rindge and Latin against Malvern Prep out of Philly with Andre Hawkins, who went to Syracuse. People are hanging from the rafters. It's like four thousand people in this gym. They finish the game. It is wild. Then here comes BU and UNH, and there's about 184 people in the stands. Pitino was smoking. This is his first job. He's at podunk BU, and this is what he's got to deal with," UNH sports information director Mike Bruckner recalled.[58]

"When Pitino came in, he tried to raise the stature and profile of the program. One step was playing the games in Walter Brown Arena. Another was expanding the schedule to play in holiday tournaments and [against] teams in what we call today the Power 5 conferences," BU SID Ed McGrath recalls.[59] Reasons McGrath heard for fan apathy were an unwillingness by alumni to commute back into the city on weekends for games; a lack of engagement by alums who hadn't followed the team as undergraduates; increasing academic standards at BU that left students with less free time; and, of course, the success of the hockey team. "[Pitino's] trying to build a program, and we weren't drawing flies. He wanted me to pump up the attendance figures. I'm twenty-three years old at the time, and I say, 'Okay, whatever, Coach.' And then it got ridiculous. It was whatever the ticket manager gave me. That's what I put," McGrath said.[60]

Despite BU's struggles in 1980–1981, the season was clearly an aberration on the upward trajectory of the program. "We had young guys coming up, [and] we knew the future was bright: Gary Plummer, Tony Simms, Johnny Ray Wall, John Teague. We could tell immediately that these boys were bad. They were ballers," said Desmond Martin, the lone captain on the 1980–1981 team.[61] By the end of the 1980–1981 campaign, BU had a battle-tested corps in place. Tony Simms had asserted himself as one of the region's top scorers and was named All-New England honorable mention. Forward Arturo Brown proved himself to be one of the region's most versatile basketball talents. Joining Simms in the backcourt were Johnny Ray Wall and Brett Brown, two of the most athletically gifted players in the conference. Jay Twyman earned a reputation as one of the league's best shooters, while veteran John Teague and freshman Gary Plummer would be among the ECAC North's best returning low-post players in 1981–1982.

In recruiting, Pitino addressed BU's size and rebounding deficiencies by snagging 6'8" forward Karl Lehman from West Chester, Ohio and 6'10" center Mark Fiedor from Bowie, Maryland, both of whom the coach projected as immediate contributors.[62]

Pitino also made a pair of significant additions to his coaching staff. He hired former UNC star John Kuester to replace Bobby Warner, who left the program to pursue other career and educational opportunities. Kuester had earned All-Tournament Team honors on the Tarheels' 1977 national runners-up team, which fell in the championship game to Marquette. The twenty-six-year-old served as Dean Smith's starting point guard for two seasons before playing three years in the NBA. Kuester would be spending much of his time as Warner had, convincing recruits to sign on at Boston University. He was also a gifted teacher of the fundamentals of basketball. "He [Kuester] understood the game and had an amazing basketball IQ. He loved working with young basketball players. Having played for Dean Smith at UNC, he was a true gentleman, a great recruiter, and passionate about being a basketball coach," Steve Priscella said.[63] "John was a prolific shooter. One of the key things that he would work on would be form and position," Mike Rosen remembered.[64]

Assistant coach Bill Burke left the program to take the head coaching job at Loyola (Maryland). Pitino replaced Burke with Bob Brown, coach of Maine high school basketball power South Portland and the father of point guard Brett Brown. The elder Brown had led South Portland to state titles in both 1979 and 1980 before heading south to Boston. "When I went to recruit Brett, I don't know who I was more impressed with: Brett or his father," Pitino said. "[Bob Brown's] well organized, and a fundamentally sound coach, and he'll be a valuable addition to our program."[65]

With a strong returning team and rebuilt coaching staff in place, Pitino said he would leave the program after the 1981–1982 season if he failed to win at least sixteen games with this group.[66]

9

They Probably Achieved as Much as They Could *(Williams)*

Boston College opened the 1983–1984 season in an unusual position: ranked fifteenth nationally and picked second in the Big East coaches' poll, behind heavy favorite Georgetown. Two coaches, it is unclear who, actually picked Boston College ahead of the Hoyas. After being shut out of the previous year's preseason all-conference team, BC landed two players on the first team. Jay Murphy's and Michael Adams's names were listed alongside Georgetown's Patrick Ewing, St. John's Chris Mullin, and Villanova's Ed Pinckney. BC fans showed similarly high hopes for the season, buying up every ticket to every home game before the team even held its first official practice.[1]

It wasn't hard to understand why. Boston College had lost just two players who received any significant playing time—both from their frontcourt. New England Player of the Year John Garris was selected in the second round of the NBA Draft by the Cleveland Cavaliers, for whom he played in thirty-three games. Forward Burnett Adams, too, played professionally, embarking on a successful decade-long professional career internationally. The remainder of BC's rotation, including starting guards Dom Pressley and Michael Adams, as well as starting forwards Martin Clark and Jay Murphy, remained in place, along with a robust supporting cast that included Roger McCready, Stu Primus, Terrence Talley, Tim O'Shea, and Russ Doherty.

BC's 1983–1984 recruiting class proved a bit thin when compared to those Kevin Mackey had put together year in and year out. Second-year assistant Paul Brazeau and new assistant Stan Nance did in fact secure a pair of strong players amid the transition. They signed Rodney Rice, a highly touted guard out of Washington DC who ended up playing sparingly for the Eagles that season before transferring to Richmond. BC did much better with Troy Bowers, a 6'8" forward from northern New Jersey. The

Roselle High star was a known commodity to Williams in part because Bowers's cousin, Boo Bowers, had been one of Williams's top players at American. "BC was probably the first school in the Big East to send me a letter," Bowers recalls.[2] He was later recruited by the likes of Villanova, UConn, and Georgia Tech. Despite other offers, Bowers remained loyal to BC, appreciating the effort Williams's staff had put into recruiting him and recognizing the success his cousin had with Coach Williams.

Williams lost out at the last minute on another prized big man: Rochester, New York's Tom Sheehy, who made the awfully irritating choice to attend Virginia, the school that had just ended the Eagles' tournament run. Adding further irritation to the matter was Williams's assertion that Sheehy chose UVA in large part because it had a better building than BC. The longer Williams stayed at BC, the more his displeasure with the rustic Roberts Center seemed to grow.[3] "It didn't help you in recruiting, that's for sure," Gary Williams said about the Roberts Center. "Sixteen-, seventeen-year-old kids are impressed when they see a great place on campus, and Roberts Center wasn't that. It was old and kind of dirty looking."[4]

The same week in April 1983 that Williams announced he'd lost out on Sheehy, the school came to terms with the state of Massachusetts on four acres of wooded land near the Chestnut Hill Reservoir. BC envisioned the space as room for expansion of the then thirty-two-thousand-seat Alumni Stadium, as well as the future site of an indoor arena that could host both the basketball and hockey teams.[5]

Later that year, BC athletic director Bill Flynn announced that the school would likely have a new arena by fall 1985, but a plan for the arena had yet to be approved, let alone ground broken for the venue. Big East commissioner Dave Gavitt continued pressing BC to move more home games to the Boston Garden to bolster the league's big-time image. Member schools had made a pact to play Big East league games in venues with at least 7,500 seats. Forty-four-hundred-seat Roberts wasn't cutting it. It didn't cut it with strong non-conference opponents either. BC's biggest non-conference games in 1983–1984, Maryland and Indiana, would be played on the road. Moreover, the 1984 Georgetown home game would be once again moved out of Roberts. Credit for this goes not to John Thompson but to CBS, which planned to broadcast the late February game nationally but told the BC athletic department that the lighting in Roberts was insufficient for its production. This time, the game did not move to the Boston Garden, which was unavailable that February weekend. BC tried next to secure the Worcester Civic Center, but the building had already agreed to host motocross on that date. The Eagles' home date with Georgetown would in fact be hosted eighty-five miles away at the Springfield Civic Center, an arrangement that pleased almost nobody outside of the Berkshires.[6]

Fifteenth-ranked Boston College opened the '83–'84 season the same way it had the '82–'83 campaign. They pummeled six straight non-conference foes. Five of them were from New England. None of them stood a chance against the Eagles. "This is the same type of game that every other team schedules this time of year," Gary Williams told the *Globe*'s Jackie MacMullan after his club bloodied Stonehill, 97–63. Clearly tired of questions about BC's non-conference adversaries, Williams asserted correctly that "we have as competitive and as tough a schedule as anyone in the country," a statement that would be true if one only considered BC's Big East conference slate. Upcoming non-conference matchups against nationally ranked Maryland and Indiana clubs only made Williams's point stronger.[7]

During the early going of the 1983–1984 campaign, Williams found his frontcourt replacement for John Garris in Roger McCready, the wiry, 6'5" sophomore from Brooklyn who played little during his freshman year. It turned out that McCready gloried in playing with his back to the basket, despite being half a foot shorter than several of the men who guarded him in the Big East. "Roger was a great competitor," Gary Williams said of his undersized center, who later served as one of his assistant coaches. "He came out of New York City high school basketball, so he had no fear of playing against anybody."[8] "Having Roger in the middle is basically the same [as John Garris]," Jay Murphy said at the time of his team's new center. "John was more of a finesse player and a jumper who we lobbed the ball into. Roger has to work for his points but is still tough down low. So we'll give him the bounce pass instead."[9]

On Monday, December 12, the AP moved 6-0 Boston College up to number eight in its Top 20 poll, the highest ranking in school history. The following week, BC jumped to number six. In these heady times, Boston College finished up its non-conference New England tour with a couple of hard-fought games against genuine non-slouches in the University of Rhode Island and longtime rival Holy Cross. The Rams hung in there for forty minutes against the Eagles at Keaney Gym but fell short, 83–74. A pair of Michael Adams foul shots with eight seconds left made the difference in an 87–85 win over Holy Cross at Roberts.

Despite these close calls, sixth-ranked Boston College took to the road unscathed. The first stop was Williams's old stomping grounds at the University of Maryland. In a Christmas Eve matchup of Top 10 teams, sold-out Cole Field House took great pleasure in number eight Maryland's dismantling of BC's fast-breaking offense. Lefty Driesell deployed a triangle-and-two defense that kept Michael Adams from penetrating and distributing the ball as usual. Maryland matched BC's athleticism and clearly had it beat when it came to size and strength. Junior point guard Jeff Adkins had the hot-shooting hand, scoring a game-high 23 points. Sophomore sensation Len Bias muscled his way to 19. Maryland led by 15 at the half, and the 89–76 game was never close.

After the Christmas break, BC headed to Bloomington, Indiana, for the Hoosier Classic. BC ran past Iowa State, 88–80, in the opener before facing off with host Indiana in the finals. Bobby Knight's Indiana club was young that season. Only one senior got significant time for the Hoosiers. Indiana had struggled to a 2-3 start but had won four straight entering the contest. Sharpshooting freshmen Steve Alford and Marty Simmons had become on-court leaders for the club alongside 7′2″ Bavarian powerhouse Uwe Blab.

BC battled a spirited Indiana team as well as the officials. The Big Ten crew working the game assessed the Eagles four technicals, including two on Gary Williams. Williams got into it on several occasions with Ed Hightower, whom the BC coach openly criticized in his postgame comments. Indiana led by as many as 9 in the second half before BC tied the game up late at 66. Steve Alford knocked down 4 foul shots in the final minute to seal a 72–66 victory for the Hoosiers.

Gary Williams's team entered Big East play still in the top twenty, despite the recent blemishes. They opened with a home win over Pitt before heading south to Philadelphia to spend their first Big East Saturday at the Villanova Field House. A much younger Nova team than its predecessor had struggled in the fall semester, dropping five non-conference games and losing its Big East opener to Syracuse. Nevertheless, the Villanova Field House was one of the toughest places to play in the country. "The fans were right on top of you," Gary Williams recalled. Williams was one of many Big East players or coaches who regarded the Villanova Field

House as the most difficult place to play in the conference.[10] "It was more like a high school gym," Burnett Adams said. "I remember taking the ball out, and somebody kicked me."[11]

Amid this hostile environment, Michael Adams and Jay Murphy took charge. Adams hit 13 of 18 shots from the field and scored a career-high 34 points. In the low post, Murphy scored 22 points, while BC outrebounded a larger Villanova team, 39–38. Boston College led almost the entire way and won, 73–63.

"They [BC] gave us a hard time. They had a lot of speed up front with Mike Adams and Dominic Pressley. And then you had Jay Murphy in the back. They played a fast-paced, up-and-down, in your face kind of game," Villanova's Chuck Everson said.[12] "Michael Adams was probably the most underrated player [in the Big East]. Michael was a very good leader. The best leader is someone who brings it every day in practice, plays hard all the time, and doesn't have to be vocal. Michael led by example," Gary Williams said of his point guard, who got far more negative attention from opponents after his performance that Saturday at Villanova. For the duration of his junior and senior years, opponents were perpetually slapping, shoving, and occasionally punching Adams. On several occasions, skirmishes or outright fisticuffs broke out between Adams and his ever-more-aggressive adversaries. Nevertheless, Adams proved time and again that he was one of the best guards in the country and the on-court leader of the Eagles.[13]

After the big win at Villanova, BC stumbled against the Providence Friars. PC had opened Big East play with consecutive losses but hung tight on the road against both Seton Hall and St. John's. Friars big man Otis Thorpe dominated down low at the Providence Civic Center, scoring 18 points and grabbing 16 rebounds. Providence forward Brian Waller hit a 20-footer at the buzzer to give PC a 63–62 win.

In typical form, Boston College bounced back in a big game, knocking off tenth-ranked St. John's at the Roberts Center, 69–67. Sophomore center Roger McCready led the Eagles with 18 points and 7 boards, taking advantage of the absence of St. John's center Bill Wennington, out that evening due to a sore foot. McCready was almost always smaller than his opponent but never ceded an inch to the opposition, even when he was outplayed. On this evening, the Brooklyn native got the best of his Queens counterparts with a mix of athleticism and guile in the low post, scoring consistently with either hand.[14] "After I drove a couple of times, my confidence went up," McCready said after the game. "We were running our cutting patterns very well. I was able to beat my man on the baseline."[15]

The win over St. John's was the high point in what proved to be a very turbulent second half to the 1983–1984 season. Sixteenth-ranked BC lost on a buzzer beater at the Carrier Dome in Syracuse. With four seconds remaining, senior captain Martin Clark looked to put the finishing touches on one of the best evenings of his career. With the Eagles down, 73–71, Clark grabbed a rebound off Jay Murphy's miss, drew a foul, and scored a game-tying basket. The rebound and bucket gave Clark 21 points and 10 rebounds on the evening.

Clark, always a steady foul shooter, missed his free throw. Syracuse center Sean Kerins rebounded the ball and passed it on to the Orangemen's freshman phenom, guard Dwayne "Pearl" Washington. Pearl launched a shot from half-court that sailed through the nets, giving Syracuse a 75–73 victory. Washington continued running all the way to the locker room as some of the thirty thousand people in attendance took over the court.[16]

BC dropped another tough road game the next time out, falling to number four Georgetown, 92–83, at the similarly uninviting Capital Centre. The loss knocked BC out of the top twenty for the first time all season. The Eagles did get hot in late January, winning three straight conference games, before getting just as cold in the first half of February. They dropped back-to-back-to-back Big East games, including a pair at the Roberts Center to Villanova and Providence. As February waned, BC found itself in fourth place, now 15-8 overall and 6-6 in the league, five games behind the Georgetown Hoyas. Boston College had the look of a bubble team just weeks after being an early favorite in the Big East.

Reasons given for BC's struggles were numerous and inconclusive. BC was smaller than most of its Big East opponents but at times won the battle on the boards against larger, highly esteemed foes. For a time, Gary Williams replaced the defensive-minded Dom Pressley with the more offensive-minded Stu Primus at starting shooting guard. Despite Primus's strong play, the team's overall performance remained roughly the same. Part of it was almost certainly the result of the night-in, night-out grind of the country's best conference, especially when one considers the continuously running style that BC played. Part of it was bad luck too. Close games that BC had found a way to win in previous years were going the other way that winter. The Eagles were on the wrong end of an ungodly number of buzzer beaters in 1983–1984.

This challenging season took a bizarre and unsettling turn on Senior Night, when BC hosted Syracuse at Roberts Center. The Orangemen entered the contest just a half game back from Georgetown in the standings. The emergence of freshman guard Pearl Washington and sophomore forward Rafael Addison as two of the league's elite scorers had buoyed Syracuse's strong returning cast into competition for the regular-season conference crown. Pearl Washington's half-court buzzer beater against BC at the Carrier Dome had jumpstarted Syracuse's push toward the top of the standings.

Desperate for a win, Boston College played inspired and desperate basketball, racing up and down the court all evening against a Syracuse team that was just as suited to a fast-breaking game. This was a game of runs. BC led by 7 at the break but then fell behind early in the second half. BC took control once again, pulling ahead by as much as 11. Then Syracuse erupted once again, surmounting not only a double-digit deficit, but also taking an 84–77 lead with just over a minute remaining. Poor foul shooting by the Orangemen and a career-defining effort by Murphy, who scored 7 of his 24 points in the game's final minute, left the Eagles down by just 2 with twenty seconds remaining. Super-sub Stu Primus, who sprinted to 14 points on 7-of-8 shooting, rose to the moment, pinching an inbounds pass intended for Andre Hawkins and galloping in for a game-tying layup. Primus finished the job in overtime, cutting through the Syracuse zone with three seconds remaining to drop in the game-winning basket. BC's 90–88 win was unquestionably its biggest of the season, reviving its chances for an at-large bid to the NCAA Tournament and sending senior captain and four-year starter Jay Murphy out with a win in his Roberts finale.[17]

The evening proved a more ignominious Roberts finale for another senior captain, Martin Clark. Clark, who had seen his playing time reduced in recent weeks, was taken out of the game with nine minutes remaining and did not return to the floor. At one point, the student section started cajoling Williams with chants of "Put in Clark." In the meantime, BC was scrapping its way back into the game with a smaller and speedier lineup that featured Terrence Talley in Clark's spot on the wing. When asked about the decision after the game, Williams cited Talley's superior defensive play as the reason he stuck with the smaller lineup.[18]

Clark let his feelings on the matter be known with just over three minutes remaining and BC trailing, 74–73. After consulting with Jack McMahon, a volunteer assistant coach who had also been Clark's high school coach and legal guardian in America since he was sixteen, Clark confronted Williams. He grabbed his coach by the lapels of his jacket and demanded to be put back into the game, his final one at Roberts. The senior captain later asserted that he grabbed Williams to keep the high-strung coach from getting a technical foul at a key moment, a claim that Williams and his team roundly denied. ESPN's Bill Raftery, who was serving as color commentator that evening, exclaimed that there was a disturbance on the BC bench as cameras caught Williams pushing Clark away from him.[19]

After the game, Clark again confronted Williams. He asked to speak with Williams in the locker room. When the coach came over, Clark tried, unsuccessfully, to sucker punch him and bashed his fist into a row of lockers. Before anyone else could intervene, sixty-two-year-old Frank Power, who was standing next to Williams, took care of business. Then the coach of BC's freshman team, Power was born and raised in Mission Hill, graduated from Boston College in 1943, and served in the Navy during World War II. Power saw combat on several occasions in the Pacific on the USS *Bataan*. He came home and spent decades working in Boston public schools as a guidance counselor, teacher, basketball coach, and, eventually, headmaster at Charlestown High. Throughout his career as an educator, Power served the BC basketball program as an assistant, working for six different head coaches. He even served as BC's head coach for one season. But Power was best known for his work as a teacher of the game as BC's freshman coach, a position he held for more than twenty years until his death in June 1985.

On the occasion of Martin Clark's accosting of Williams, Power called on several decades' worth of experience in breaking up fights at tough city schools. He planted a firm fist in Clark's face, a move that brought the affair to a halt. "I heard what sounded like a smooch," Stu Primus said. "That was our assistant coach, the late great Frank Power, punching Martin Clark and knocking him out. He [Clark] tried to sucker punch Gary. Gary went down to the ground. Martin dented the locker, and Frank Power clocked him."[20] A gaggle of priests, players, and assistants then jumped in and restored order. Clark and his guardian, McMahon, soon departed, and the press had plenty of questions about what they'd heard, none of which Williams answered.

To say the least, the evening was a regrettable end to Clark's highly successful career at Roberts. He had been a key contributor to the Eagles team from the time he had stepped on campus, earning Big East All-Rookie Team honors as a freshman in 1980–1981 and proving to be a fixture in BC's attack, especially during his first two years under Tom Davis. Clark was also an incredibly hard worker and a model student-athlete, earning a reported 3.7 GPA as an economics major.

"Martin put in a lot of time on his jump shot.," Michael Adams said. "I was a gym rat as well. I'd go work on my shot, and he was always there. He was mechanical. He would get in there and work on his jump shot. He couldn't post up but he could shoot it, and he proved that in games."[21] "Early on, Martin Clark was kind of the leader," Sonny Spera said of BC's style of play under Tom Davis. "Martin Clark, I think, had a lot of influence on how things went. I think he was more comfortable in Davis's system than he was in Williams's system."[22] Certainly Clark's style of play was more suited to Davis's zone offense than to Williams's perennially fast-breaking, pressing attack. Eventually his role in the offense and time on the floor diminished. This was clearly a source of despair for Clark, who spoke openly of his desire to play in the NBA and had done no favors to his stock among pro scouts in the latter stretches of his college career. In all fairness, Clark's shrinking role in the BC rotation probably hurt his draft stock less at the time than his decision to take a swing at his college coach.[23]

Clark's evident displeasure with his diminished role and resentment of Williams served as the backdrop to the events of Senior Night, but they are not the only relevant context. For all his success, Clark was an outsider on the team. In terms of personality, he was cerebral and distant. His tightest relationship by far in the BC basketball family was with McMahon, who had discovered him as a teenager; served as a father figure, mentor, and advocate for him while he played prep basketball; and joined the Eagles program along with him in the fall of 1980. Moreover, Clark was one of the few international players not only at BC, but also in the Big East in general during the 1980s.

"Martin was a loner. He was a very smart guy, but not too many people got to know him," Michael Adams said.[24] "No one knew much about Martin," Troy Bowers said. "He stayed to himself. Jack kind of kept Martin isolated. Athletes saw each other all the time. I can't remember ever seeing Martin on campus. I'd see him at practice or lunch halls, where we're eating together as a team. I ran into every player but not Martin. The school wasn't that big. 6'8" or 6'9", how hard is it to spot somebody?"[25]

"He [Clark] was basically an asshole," in Burnett Adams's estimation. "Martin thought himself better than everyone."[26] Clark's relationship with McMahon was also a source of tension on the team. Beyond serving as Clark's handler, nobody on the team seemed exactly sure of his role. McMahon was well known in Boston basketball circles as a self-appointed cultivator of young talent, but players on the team regarded him with suspicion. "He was just a low life," Burnett Adams said. "The guy would spread rumors about suspected drug use. People not going to class. People not doing this. It was awful. And the reason they kept him around was because of Martin Clark."[27]

Williams suspended Clark indefinitely for the assault. It ended up being a one-game sanction. "The players indicated that they did not want Martin's career to end on such a tarnished note," Williams said after meeting with Clark and meeting with the team.[28]

The contest that Clark missed was the Georgetown "home" game in Springfield. Before a Saturday afternoon crowd that sounded more like the Capital Centre than the Roberts Center, Georgetown won, 83–70, pulling away late in a game that BC controlled for much of the way. The Eagles led by as much as 7 in the first half, as Michael Adams and company harassed the second-ranked Hoyas' backcourt into numerous turnovers. A combination of foul trouble and Patrick Ewing got the best of BC that afternoon. Ewing registered game highs in both points (25) and rebounds (11). The Hoyas center so dominated the lane that virtually every shot the Eagles took inside had to be adjusted to account for Ewing's presence in the middle. Adding to the trouble were all the points that Georgetown got from the line. The Hoyas hit 19 of 22 foul shots in the game's final five minutes. Two of the shots came courtesy of Gary Williams, who received a technical for zinging the basketball to an official in response to yet another call that went Georgetown's way.[29]

With 1:12 to play and the game out of reach, Ewing and Michael Adams, the tallest and smallest players on the floor, had it out. Adams had stolen the ball in the backcourt and was fouled by Georgetown's Fred Brown as he drove to the basket. Adams's momentum carried him crashing into

Ewing, who responded by picking Adams up and throwing him to the floor. Adams bounced right up and started swinging at Ewing, who by that time was duking it out with Roger McCready. Both benches cleared, but game officials restored order quickly. Referee Dick Paparo tossed Ewing and Adams for fighting. Both Williams and John Thompson later downplayed the incident. The pair embraced at game's end, and Thompson offered the BC coach words of encouragement about the Martin Clark incident.[30]

While beating Georgetown would have solidified BC's status within the NCAA Tournament field, the Eagles' next-to-last Big East game at Seton Hall was a must-win for them to remain on the bubble. Clark played little in his return, and Pirates coach P. J. Carlesimo emulated Georgetown's recent approach to Boston College, pounding it inside against the short-handed Eagles and getting their big men into foul trouble. BC lost again on a last-second shot, this time a seven-foot floater from Seton Hall's sophomore sensation Andre McCloud. The loss dropped BC to 16-10 on the season and 7-8 in the league. Boston College won its last league game convincingly over UConn but entered the Big East Tournament on the outside looking in of most projections of the NCAA Tournament bracket.

In the Big East quarterfinals, fourth-seeded BC drew fifth-seeded St. John's in the late game at the Garden. Both teams entered the game 8-8 in the league, 17-10 overall, and badly in need of a win to bolster their NCAA credentials. Playing before a full and largely pro-Johnnies house, Boston College led for most of the game, holding a 52–48 advantage with less than four minutes remaining. St. John's rallied, sparked by two clutch Chris Mullin buckets, both set up by hotshot freshman point guard Mark Jackson. Center Bill Wennington broke a 56–56 tie with five seconds remaining by sinking one of two free throws. Michael Adams hit the rim on a desperation bomb at the buzzer, sealing BC's postseason fate. St John's was headed for the NCAA Tournament. BC was relegated to the NIT for the first time since 1980.[31]

After falling on Friday night to the Johnnies, BC returned to campus and began preparing on Monday for postseason play. On Wednesday, March 14, BC held a typical afternoon practice at Roberts that included Martin Clark, who had played significant minutes in the Big East tournament game against St. John's. Immediately after practice, Clark and McMahon left the Chestnut Hill campus and headed to the studios of WBZ, Boston's CBS affiliate, in the nearby Brighton neighborhood. Shortly thereafter,

Clark went on Channel 4's six o'clock newscast with sports anchor Bob Lobel. Clark had given Lobel a two-page letter announcing that he had quit the Boston College basketball team, something he had yet to tell any of his teammates or Williams. Lobel interviewed the former BC captain on air. Clark announced that he had decided to leave the team due to what he characterized as "serious problems in the basketball program." Clark indicated that his complaints were related to academic policies in the athletics department and what he regarded as a lack of concern with players' lives outside of basketball. Refusing to delve into details, Clark stated that he had brought his complaints first to Davis, who had failed to act, and later to Williams, who also had failed to act.[32]

Williams disputed Clark's vague assertions by enumerating the academic resources available to BC basketball players, including nightly study halls, academic advisors, and tutors. Bill Flynn conceded that the graduation rate for basketball players since 1978 (roughly two-thirds) was slightly lower than for the student body as a whole. The AD further asserted that players who didn't get their degrees still got a lot out of college, a statement that was widely ridiculed in the press.[33] A rebuttal on behalf of the team written by senior guard Tim O'Shea, a highly respected reserve who was one of the team's three captains, appeared in the *Boston Globe*, as well as in *The Heights*. Clark's statements "cast an unfair and undeserved shadow of suspicion over every athlete, coach, and administrator within this department," O'Shea wrote. O'Shea defended both Williams and his predecessor, Davis, stating that both had demonstrated an "active interest in the overall development of each student-athlete." The tri-captain went so far as to demand an apology from Clark for doing damage not only to the reputation of the team, but also to Williams.[34]

Several days after Clark went on the local news, he met with Boston College president, the Rev. J. Donald Monan, to discuss his concerns about the basketball program. On the same day, the *Boston Herald* broke a story about BC superstar Jay Murphy, who, the paper alleged, had flunked out of the college of Arts and Sciences on two occasions and remained academically eligible by enrolling in BC's Evening College, a long-tenured higher-education option in the city with lower admission standards than BC's day school. Clark denied having leaked the information to the *Herald*, despite suspicions within the basketball program. BC's vice president for academic affairs, the Rev. Joseph Fahey, acknowledged the *Herald* story the next day at a contentious, hastily organized press conference but refused to comment on its particulars. Fahey announced that BC was reevaluating the policy that had kept Murphy academically eligible during his senior year.[35] An ad hoc faculty committee investigated the matter and concluded that the school should no longer allow athletes to shift over to the Evening College to stay academically eligible, a move that Monan blocked. The committee also criticized the athletic department for allowing several basketball players to fall behind on their graduation requirements and suggested that the school keep athletes' academic schedules to a steady twelve credit hours per semester.[36]

Amid all the chaos, BC basketball tried to round out its 1983–1984 season on a positive note. The Eagles faced St. Joseph's in the opening round of the NIT at the Palestra in Philadelphia. The game was a rematch of sorts from the 1981 Mideast Regional Semifinal, which St. Joe's had won, 42–41, in a grinding, slow-down game. By 1984, both teams had different coaches, and aside from seniors like Jay Murphy at Boston College and St. Joe's big man Tony Costner, few people from either team had even been at that game. Costner was the most impressive player in the 1984 edition of BC— St. Joe's, battling his way to 29 points and becoming the Hawks' all-time leading scorer in his final collegiate game. However, Boston College had a much better overall team. BC won convincingly, 76–63.

The following Monday, BC, in theory, hosted a second-round NIT matchup against Notre Dame, returning to the Springfield Civic Center for the second time that season. Digger Phelps's Fighting Irish pushed past a physically and emotionally drained BC basketball team, 66–52. BC led the game, 51–50, with just over three minutes remaining, but a combination of foul trouble, excellent free-throw shooting by the Irish, and poor shooting by BC turned the game into a runaway. The defeat ended the most trying campaign anyone could remember in Chestnut Hill, and that was really saying something, considering that the graduating seniors had played through day and night coverage of the point-shaving scandal earlier in their careers.

Not long after BC's tumultuous season ended, its conference rival, Georgetown, defeated Houston at Seattle's Kingdome to win the national championship. Georgetown was the first national champion in the five-year history of the Big East and the first team from the Northeast to win the NCAA Tournament since LaSalle in 1954. Jay Murphy received an invite to the 1984 U.S. Olympic basketball trials and was selected thirty-first overall by Golden State, who immediately traded him to the Los Angeles Clippers for Jerome Whitehead. Murphy played several years in the NBA for the Clippers and Bullets before heading overseas for a fantastic career in the French and Italian professional leagues. Martin Clark never made it to the NBA but was selected in the tenth round by the Sixers. He played professionally in the United States Basketball League and in Europe before becoming a financial advisor in the United Kingdom.

In the offseason, Gary Williams coached a team of Big East standouts that toured Yugoslavia. The roster for the seven-game junket included both Roger McCready and Dom Pressley. Williams and his staff had a more robust recruiting class coming to campus that season too. They recruited a pair of physical frontcourt players in western New York's Tyrone Scott and Trevor Gordon, a British-born 6'9" center who played his first two years of college ball at Gloucester County Community College in New Jersey. The Eagles also added sweet shooters in Skip Barry, a 6'7" forward from New Hampshire, and Jamie Benton, a 6'0" guard from Rhode Island's La Salle Academy.

That August, word came down from the athletic department that it had a plan to replace both Roberts and McHugh Forum, BC's hockey rink, which was similarly sized, similarly aged, and similarly decrepit to the Eagles' basketball home. Rather than building it on the newly acquired land, Bill Flynn announced that the new multi-purpose arena would be built alongside Alumni Stadium, the current location of McHugh Forum. Flynn assured the Big East that the new building would pass muster and seat more than 7,500 fans. McHugh would be demolished so construction could begin, but Roberts would remain in place as BC's men's and women's practice gym for basketball.[37]

BC basketball was back in its typical preseason position in 1984–1985, picked for the bottom half of the Big East. The coaches' poll slotted Boston College sixth behind the perennial four powers of Georgetown, St. John's, Syracuse, and Villanova, in that order, as well as Pittsburgh, which had landed a highly touted freshman class that included 6'11" forward Charles Smith.

The reasons for pessimism in Chestnut Hill were evident. The cluster of teams at the top of the Big East in the 1984–1985 season may have been as talented and experienced as any one conference could boast in the history of college basketball. Players like defending national champion Georgetown's Patrick Ewing, St. John's Chris Mullin, and Villanova's Ed Pinckney had been household names for most of the decade. The majority of head coaches in the conference that season ended up in the Basketball Hall of Fame, and each of the top four teams in the Big East preseason poll featured a veteran-laden roster. Compare that to BC, who lost two frontcourt starters that had played significant minutes for the Eagles since the Carter administration. While effective, BC's most experienced returning player in its frontcourt was a 6'5" center in Roger McCready. BC had one of the best backcourts in college basketball, featuring not only two-time second-team all-conference "waterbug" Michael Adams, but also defensive scrapper Dom Pressley, now a junior, as well as a pair of powerhouses off the bench in Terrence Talley and Stu Primus, both now seniors. Talley would end up starting frequently at small forward in 1984–1985 to maximize the team's speed and athleticism on the floor. For much of the non-conference schedule, though, BC would be without Primus, who was ruled academically ineligible by the school despite fulfilling NCAA standards to play. If anyone was a victim of the Martin Clark fiasco and subsequent scandal, it was Primus, whom the BC administration made an example of in the fall 1984 semester.

Primus needed to take ten courses during the 1984–1985 academic year to complete his degree. The College of Arts and Sciences decided that Primus should focus on his studies in the fall semester rather than play basketball since his course load exceeded the recommended distribution of twelve credits each semester. The senior guard appealed the decision twice but to no avail.[38] "I knew what I was doing, but they had a thorn up their ass about everything that happened with Jay [Murphy] and with Martin Clark's situation and of course the point-shaving situation. All of that has nothing to do with me. Why are you coming after me?" Stu Primus said of his suspension.[39]

Further muting enthusiasm for BC hoops that fall was the emergence of the school's football team as a national title contender and its quarterback, Doug Flutie, as the Heisman Trophy frontrunner. In 1983, BC football under Jack Bicknell went 9-3 and finished the season nationally ranked for the first time in forty-one years. Natick, Massachusetts' own Doug Flutie had finished third in Heisman voting in '83 and was a clear favorite for the award in 1984. By the time BC basketball finished non-conference play in late 1984,

Boston College's diminutive, handsome-as-hell quarterback had become the first Eagle to win the Heisman Trophy. He led the football team firmly into the top ten and had authored one of the most iconic moments in the history of college football. Flutie's game-winning "Hail Mary" pass against defending national champion Miami at the Orange Bowl offered the Friday-after-Thanksgiving national television audience an executive summary of what made the 5'10" gunslinger such a compelling player. The little guy in the mud-tattered uniform scrambling away from Miami's menacing goliaths, unleashing a bomb toward the endzone with all hope seemingly lost. Flutie and Boston College, both its football team and the idea of the small, highly selective Jesuit college competing with the big boys, became a national phenomenon. Applications to Boston College surged in the aftermath of the win, leading sports and educational analysts to coin the term "the Flutie Effect" to describe the positive impact that on-field success could have for the reputation of an institution. "Doug Flutie would show up at a basketball game and all the heads would turn, and people would be heading over to get an autograph or take a picture with him. Game's going on, and everybody just wants to take a picture with Doug Flutie," Mike Lynch recalled.[40]

Gary Williams and his Boston College basketball team put aside the bad publicity and the diminished expectations in the fall of 1984 and went to work. The Eagles won every game in the 1984 slice of their schedule, pummeling a series of overmatched opponents from New England and outlasting several more-serious foes from major conferences. What this team lacked in size, it made up for in defensive tenacity. This was a leaner and meaner Boston College club, one that could run like never before. Senior guards Michael Adams and Dom Pressley were among the nation's leaders in steals all season. Highly decorated veterans Terrence Talley and, eventually, Stu Primus added further speed, skill, and athleticism to BC's backcourt, giving the Eagles arguably America's best roster of guards that season. In the frontcourt, Roger McCready was joined by the similarly athletic Troy Bowers and Trevor Gordon, completing the transition from Davis's zone offense of previous years to a fully fast-breaking offense that was all Williams's own. "We had solid guys up and down the lineup. Hard-nosed tough guys that worked and worked to get better," Paul Brazeau said of the 1984–1985 team.[41]

Michael Adams was clearly the leader of this BC team, the fearless front man of the Eagles' relentless attack. In BC's first real test of the season, a tangle with Wake Forest at the Boston Garden on December 2, it was in fact Adams's backcourt counterpart, Dom Pressley, whose star shown most brightly. The game was the second half of a doubleheader that began with an 89–72 UNC drubbing of Boston University. Adams and Pressley went toe-to-toe with the Demon Deacons' backcourt, which featured a pair of future NBAers in Delaney Rudd and Wake's own "waterbug," 5′3″ Tyrone "Muggsy" Bogues. Pressley proved to be the standout in this frenzied affair, scoring 20 points in BC's come-from-behind 82–76 victory. Despite the presence of two marquee ACC opponents on this twin bill, ticket sales for the game were lethargic, and there were several thousand empty seats at the Garden.

"In terms of winning and losing, we'd be better off at Roberts Center. In terms of our program, we're better off at the Garden," Williams said in the leadup to the Wake Forest game.[42] Williams was never a fan of BC playing its home games at Boston Garden, which was increasingly becoming the norm the longer he stayed in Chestnut Hill. "You'd always like to do everything on campus if you could. It's easier for the students to get to the games," Williams said in retrospect. "The problem is you didn't have much access at the Garden in terms of practicing. The Bruins owned the building, and the Celtics were trying to get in there. They were practicing at Hellenic College, and they didn't get in there as much as they'd have liked. We'd get in there the day of the game, usually like 3:30–5, and that was it."[43]

The Wake Forest game was the first of four that BC played at the Garden that season—clear proof of the Big East's desire to get the Eagles into a bigger building. While playing at the Garden was a thrill for BC's players as well as their opponents, everyone involved became aware of the storied arena's shortcomings.

"To play in these bigger venues like the Boston Garden, it helped us get ready for playing bigger schools or playing in the Big East Tournament at Madison Square Garden," Michael Adams said.[44]

"There were a lot of dead spots on the floor," Syracuse forward Andre Hawkins recalled, citing a frequent complaint of visitors to the Garden.[45]

"Playing on this court that I dreamed and idolized about, the parquet floor. I go out to just shoot around and try to dribble, and the ball doesn't come back to me," Sonny Spera said. "And the locker rooms in that place were the pits. It was this old, really dilapidated room, and it was like 100 degrees in there. And then you left the locker room and you walk through this 20-degree-below-zero hallway. What a homecourt advantage. They sweat you out in the locker room, then they freeze you, then they take you on the court with all these dead spots. How can anybody win here?"[46]

Just after Christmas, a 7-0 BC club headed to San Diego for the Cabrillo Classic. The Eagles, playing with newly eligible Stu Primus, faced a serious test in their tournament opener against undefeated and seventeenth-ranked Michigan State (MSU). The Spartans were a big, physical team, potentially a mismatch for the small and speedy Eagles. The Big Ten power also featured one of the country's most heralded backcourts. Senior shooting guard Sam Vincent and junior point guard Scott Skiles both went on to long, productive NBA careers.

Boston College ran past Michigan State, 82–78, thanks in large part to the efforts of its backcourt. The Spartans led throughout the first half, but Adams, Pressley, Primus, and company kept forcing Jud Heathcote's team into turnovers. Dom Pressley tied the game at 34 just before the half after stealing a Vincent pass and hustling in for a rim-rattling dunk. In the end, BC simply outhustled the Spartans, beating them 36–26 on the boards and forcing them into 19 turnovers. "They were telling us that Sam Vincent was a first-round pick. I took that as an offense," Stu Primus recalled. "When we got on the court, I was like, 'He's soft as shit.' Scott Skiles was tough and a good ballplayer. Sam Vincent is not the one. We looked in his eyes, and he was like a deer in the headlights."[47]

"We don't let the lack of enthusiasm about what we are doing affect us. We're going to do it regardless," Dom Pressley said after the game, acknowledging that the lion's share of BC fandom was more focused on the football team, which was in Dallas, preparing to play the University of Houston in the Cotton Bowl.[48]

The next day, BC basketball did a number on Southwestern Conference (SWC) foe Texas Christian University (TCU), 92–75, in the finals. The BC press overwhelmed the Horned Frogs from the outset. Michael Adams stole the ball six times, earned seven assists, and scored 23 points in the win. The game presaged BC football's decisive 45–28 New Year's Day Cotton Bowl victory over TCU's SWC colleagues at Houston.

On January 2, 1985, the day the Boston College football team placed fifth in the final AP poll, tied for its highest finish in school history, the 9-0 basketball Eagles opened Big East play. Despite poor shooting throughout, BC defeated visiting Providence, 67–55, avenging a pair of devastating losses from the previous winter.

BC then hit the road to face off with a fellow undefeated team: the Georgetown Hoyas. While the Eagles remained outside the top 20 twenty, their opponent was the number-one ranked team in college basketball and the defending national champion. John Thompson's Hoyas had blown the doors off every opponent they'd faced thus far in the 1984–1985 campaign, including a 36-point win over nationally ranked University of Nevada–Las Vegas (UNLV) and a 20-point win over second-ranked DePaul. George-town's starting five of Patrick Ewing, David Wingate, Reggie Williams, Bill Martin, and Michael Jackson would all be selected in the first or second rounds of the NBA Draft and would go on to log significant minutes in "the Association."

Despite being a 16.5-point underdog at the Capital Centre, Boston College nearly beat the vaunted Hoyas on their own floor. BC's running style, now faster than ever, took the Hoyas out of their game. Boston College's backcourt chased and scratched at the Hoyas all afternoon, forcing the defending champions into nearly 20 turnovers. Eagles and Hoyas spent the game continually in one another's faces, reigniting the tensions that boiled over in their meeting the previous March at the Boston Garden. Georgetown ended up winning the game, 82–80, in overtime, but the loss felt an awful lot like a win for Boston College. McCready, Gordon, and Bowers more than held their own against the likes of Patrick Ewing and 6'11" Ralph Dalton. BC actually won the battle on the boards and deployed as many elbows as they received from their menacing foes.

"Ewing hated to play against him [McCready] because Roger was strong enough that Ewing couldn't push him around. The first time he'd [McCready] get the ball, he'd try to get a piece of Ewing on the way up," Gary Williams recalled.[49]

"Poor BC. Everyone feels sorry for them because they're so small and they don't have much talent. They're tougher than that," a relieved John Thompson said after the game.[50]

"From day one, we have had a great team attitude. We felt the sky was the limit in terms of what we could do. What's happening now isn't a surprise to us—just to everybody else," Dom Pressley, who scored a team-high 19 points, said after BC's surprisingly strong performance that afternoon.[51]

Despite the loss, BC entered the AP poll for the first time that season, catapulting all the way up to number twelve. In total three Big East teams (Georgetown, St. John's, and Syracuse) were ranked in the Top 10, while Villanova, then number sixteen, gave the conference five teams in the January 7, 1985, poll.

All the good press, as well as the night-in, night-out competition of the Big East, soon caught up with Boston College, at least for a while. BC traveled to the Carrier Dome and succumbed to its mass of humanity, as well as Syracuse's effective use of the trap defense. A heavily favored BC team barely hung on against Seton Hall just one week after the Eagles' close call against Georgetown.

Within two weeks of earning the number twelve spot in the polls, BC was once again unranked, in the midst of a three-game conference losing streak that included road losses to Villanova and St. John's, as well as a Big Monday stinker against Pitt. For all its success with swarming pressure defense and a relentless offensive attack, this BC team sometimes struggled against teams with elite low-post players. In the Villanova game, Ed Pinckney dominated the boards, securing 16 rebounds, including 5 offensive boards, in an 85–66 beatdown at the Villanova Field House. Against St. John's, BC's frontcourt troubles were exaggerated by the absence of Trevor Gordon. BC held him out for the game because he had yet to turn in his final paper for an incomplete class from the previous semester. The Eagles led for most of the way at the Boston Garden against the Redmen, but a combination of poor shooting, foul trouble, and Chris Mullin's 17 second-half points helped the Johnnies pull it out. Gordon returned for the Pitt game, but the Panthers' freshman phenom Charles Smith proved too much for the Eagles. BC tried to outphysical the slight 6'11" forward, but Smith responded by going 18 of 21 from the line in the 61–55 win, Pitt's first ever against the Eagles. The loss dropped Boston College to 2–5 in the league and looking up in the standings at everyone but Providence and Seton Hall.[52]

Just as quickly as BC went from nearly knocking off the number one team in the country to the bottom third of the Big East, the team ripped off five straight wins. They blew out Providence and Hartford while barely escaping Storrs with a win over UConn. An Alvin Frederick—led Huskies team whipped BC on the boards, 42–28, but Michael Adams, who led the way with 19 points and 11 assists, floated in a 14-foot baseline jumper with seven seconds remaining in OT to give the Eagles a 1-point win.

"If you saw Michael Adams shoot, you'd see he had a weird shot," Gary Williams said. "He'd shot put it. Almost shoot it straight up instead of out like you want guys to. I was smart enough not to change his shot because it went in. I asked him why he shot like that, and he said when he was in seventh or eighth grade, he was even smaller, and he had to figure out a way to get his shot off, so he started to shoot the ball straight up instead of out the way most guys shoot the ball. He just stayed with it, and it got him an eleven-year pro career and an NBA all-star team."[53]

BC's next two home games were both at the Boston Garden, against sixth-ranked Syracuse and Georgetown, who had dropped to number two after consecutive losses to St. John's and the Orangemen. Compared to their typical horse races, the BC-Syracuse game at the Garden in February '85 was a bit of a mess, a sloppy back-and-forth contest that lacked the power, speed, and finesse of their early '80s battles. Nevertheless, this Tuesday game had as dramatic a conclusion as any of their earlier contests, both down to the wire and controversial.

Syracuse led, 66–65, with seven seconds remaining when Stu Primus's 15-footer fell short. Syracuse's standout freshman center, Rony Seikaly, pulled in the rebound and drew a foul. Seikaly missed the front end of his one-and-one, which Trevor Gordon rebounded and passed awkwardly to Michael Adams, who barely stayed in bounds. In desperation, Adams heaved up a 40-footer while coming into contact with Syracuse's Andre Hawkins. From the other end of the court, referee Dick Paparo called a blocking foul on Hawkins. Adams hit both free throws, and BC left North Station with a 67–66 victory.[54] "Coach [Boeheim] lost his mind for a little bit because we should have got that call," Sonny Spera remembered.[55]

"I knew that he [Adams] would get there first and I couldn't get away from him, so I stopped, and he just threw himself into me like junior high. And then I just kept my hands vertical and let him run me over," Andre Hawkins recalled.[56] "I was surprised there was that much defense," Gary Williams said about the decisive play. "It's a tough call, I'm sure, for Syracuse but we had a couple of tough ones too."[57] With forty-five seconds remaining, Adams had been whistled for a questionable five-second violation that gave the ball back to Syracuse and helped them retake the lead.

The following Saturday, BC finished up its slate of games at the Garden against Georgetown. BC again held the Hoyas' feet to the fire, trailing by 1 with just under four minutes to play. Georgetown took advantage of several trips to the foul line late in the game to go on a 9–0 run and secure a 78–68 win. BC rebounded from the Georgetown loss by drubbing Seton Hall 101–83 in East Orange.

Villanova then traveled to the rustic and rowdy confines of Roberts for a late-season matchup. After the shellacking BC received earlier in the season at the Villanova Field House, Williams switched things up defensively, shifting from his standard full-court press to a 1-3-1 trap that enabled BC to gang up on Ed Pinckney and keep him in check, holding him to 12 points. On the offensive end, BC's low-post wizard, Roger McCready, was able to fight his way to 22 points against the much larger Wildcats frontcourt. BC took a 62–61 lead on the sixteenth-ranked visitors with just under a minute remaining off a Dominic Pressley steal and baseball-style pass up the court to Michael Adams for a layup. With four seconds left, Nova's Harold Pressley threw up a shot from more than twenty feet that McCready nabbed on the rebound to finish off the Wildcats. The win enabled 18-6 Boston College to return briefly to the national polls, sitting at number twenty with less than two weeks remaining in the regular season.

The whirlwind of the season continued as Boston College headed down to Madison Square Garden for a matchup with number-one ranked St. John's, a team that knocked Georgetown out of the top spot in late January and had lost just one game all season, a December non-conference matchup at the "Buffalo Aud" against Pete Lonergan's always dangerous Niagara team. St. John's had arguably the most talented team in the country in 1984–1985, built around the veteran leadership and prowess of Chris Mullin and Bill Wennington. The Johnnies, too, boasted a pair of the country's best sophomores in forward Walter Berry, who formed a 1–2 scoring punch with Mullin, and Mark Jackson, the latest legendary point guard bred on New York City blacktops.

Despite all of St. John's talent, BC absolutely wasted the Johnnies in the early going at MSG, leading by 12 with twelve minutes remaining in the first half. The Eagles blitzed the Johnnies with a ferocious press led that afternoon by Dom Pressley. St. John's turned the ball over to Pressley and the Eagles ten times in just ten minutes of action. "Dom [Pressley] was one of the best defensive players we had at Boston College," his roommate Michael Adams remembered. "I thought I was fast and quick. He was quicker and faster than I was. The guy could run with the best of them."[58] "You put him [Pressley] and Michael Adams in the backcourt together, and you can create mayhem. And you get someone like Terrence Talley looking for the outlet pass. We caused a lot of trouble doing that," Russ Doherty said.[59] On that particular afternoon, Pressley parlayed the mayhem he wrought at the MSG into 26 points.

The tenaciousness of BC's defense turned the game more than just physical awfully fast. Both benches cleared in the first half when Michael Adams got into it with St. John's clearly frustrated Mike Moses. For the remainder of the afternoon, the Garden crowd jeered Adams every time he touched the ball.

St. John's fought its way back into the game with timely shooting. Chris Mullin saved his best for the second half, scoring 17 of his 26 points after the break. After cutting the lead to 2 at the half, St. John's took the lead early in the second, only to trade it with BC on eight occasions in the game's final twenty minutes. BC hung around despite a leg injury to Michael Adams, which hobbled him throughout the second half. St. John's escaped with a 71–69 win but not before BC had given the nation's top team and its exhausted coach, his signature sweater stained with perspiration, all they could handle.

"You can't take prisoners with that team. You have to kill them, or they keep coming back," Lou Carnesecca said after the game.[60] Once again, an impressive outing against the number one team spelled disaster for BC in subsequent games. The Eagles traveled to Pitt's Fitzgerald Fieldhouse and again succumb to Charles Smith, who scored 23 points, including the final 4 of the 58–55 Panthers' win. In BC's home finale, the Eagles lost yet another must-win game, this time to Connecticut, 74–68.

"This team relies on emotion. We have to do a lot of things right, like not miss easy shots in the first half and get beat on the boards," an exasperated Gary Williams said after the loss to Connecticut. Making it even harder was the limited role that Adams played for the Eagles in these last two contests, still hobbled after the St. John's game.[61] Even with the expansion of the NCAA Tournament to sixty-four teams for 1985, Boston College was firmly on the bubble come conference tournament time. The Eagles had finished the regular season at 18-9—11-0 out of the league and 7-9 in the conference, slotting them sixth in the league, just as predicted by the coaches' preseason poll.

Badly in need of a resume-bolstering win in the Big East Tournament, sixth-seeded Boston College faced off with third-seeded and thirteenth-ranked Syracuse, who fell out of the Top 10 after losing three of their last four contests. With Michael Adams hobbled, the trio of Roger McCready (20 points), Stu Primus (18 points), and Terrence Talley (15 points) stepped up on the offensive end to keep BC in the game with the relentless Orangemen. After leading by 1 at the half, BC fell behind by as much as 13 before taking a lead late in the game. With twenty-two seconds remaining, Pearl Washington hit a short jumper that allowed Syracuse to retake the lead, 70–69.[62] "I got an alley-oop that Mike [Adams] threw toward me, and I tossed the ball in," Troy Bowers said, reflecting on what ESPN commentators referred to all weekend as "the shot around the world," which went in and out as time expired that evening. "And I thought we won so I turned around and I've got my fist up but then all of a sudden I saw the Syracuse fans jumping up and down and I thought, 'What the heck.' The ball rolled in; the ball rolled out."[63]

BC lost, 70–69, and its NCAA Tournament hopes at 18-10 seemed dim. After the quarterfinals game, Jim Boeheim made a point of telling reporters that he thought BC belonged in the sixty-four-team field, due not only to its competitive play in the Big East, but also to its significant non-conference wins against Wake Forest and Michigan State. Apparently, the committee agreed. BC snuck into the 1985 NCAA Tournament with an eleven seed in the Midwest Region. Awaiting the Eagles at Houston's Hofheinz Pavillion were the SWC champion Texas Tech Red Raiders. On the court Texas Tech was led by one of the country's most versatile guards in Bubba Jennings, the SWC's Player of the Year. Sixth-seeded Tech excelled at a motion offense built around Jennings, and played a stingy brand of man-to-man defense taught by head coach Gerald Myers. "I was personally looking forward to the matchup against Michael Adams. We were both the same type of player and about the same size," Jennings said.[64]

BC ran a box and 1 on Jennings for most of the game, making use of its cadre of big guards to hold Jennings to 16 points. Tech tried muscling Adams off the ball with its bigger guard, Vince Taylor. Throughout the first half, BC's pesky guards held the advantage, pillorying Tech's guards into several turnovers. The Eagles scored the game's first 7 points and held a 33–28 advantage at the half. "This kid from Texas Tech, this freshman, started talking shit on the court and I go, 'you don't know?' He says 'don't know what?' then I elbowed him in his chest and his stomach and he went down and I said 'We're in the Big East, motherfucker,'" Stu Primus said, reminiscing about the game.[65]

Texas Tech fought its way back in the second half. The Red Raiders won on the glass, 31–29, and got timely buckets from Jennings and Taylor. BC, quite uncharacteristically, struggled from the foul line. The Eagles took possession of the ball with 1:31 left and the game tied at 53. Williams instructed his team to hold for the last basket. As the clock wound down, Michael Adams scooted past Taylor and let loose one of his high-arching shots from twenty feet out. Adams's aim was true and Texas Tech was unable to get a decent look at the other end.[66]

Boston College advanced to the second round against Mike Krzyzewski's resurgent Duke Blue Devils. The third-seeded Blue Devils finished the regular season in the Top 10 for the first time since 1978. Duke's team was built around four juniors who formed one of the most heralded recruiting classes in NCAA history: big men Jay Bilas and Mark Alarie, guard Johnny Dawkins and swingman Dave Henderson. Add sophomore point guard Tommy Amaker into the equation and Duke had one of the country's most fearsome lineups—unless you spent the season playing in the Big East. "Somebody on this court is better than Georgetown or better than Syracuse or better than St. John's or better than Villanova? We just didn't see it," Stu Primus said of the confidence that BC brought to its tournament games.[67] Not to mention that BC spent its preseason scrimmaging against members of the defending world champion Boston Celtics.

Initially, the favored Duke Blue Devils looked every bit as good as BC's Big East rivals. Bilas, Alarie, and the Blue Devils' frontcourt hammered BC on the boards in the early going, helping the number three seed turn a tightly contested first ten minutes into a 31–20 lead with 4:38 remaining in the first half. For a time, Williams benched Pressley and Gordon and added little-used freshman Tyrone Scott and senior Mark Schmidt, who had not seen significant minutes since his freshman year under Tom Davis, into the lineup. Williams also shifted defenses from the 1-2-2 press to a 1-3-1 trap the team had first employed against Villanova late in the season. This change in BC's attack led to a clear change in the Eagles' attitude on the floor. Two key baskets by Scott and a pair of steals by Schmidt helped the Eagles close the gap to just 5 at the half.

"I pulled Dominic [Pressley] in and said, 'Push him [Johnny Dawkins]. Slap him,'" Stu Primus said. Pressley resisted as Dawkins had been his high school teammate and friend in Washington DC. "Dominic, you want to go home? Go fucking push him. Get in his head. Start some shit with him. Next possession down, Michael [Adams] heard it. Michael knew it was time and started a fight with Johnny Dawkins. We took his heart."[68]

A more aggressive and physical BC team took the lead in the second half, forcing Duke into bad shots and wearing out the Blue Devils' seven-man rotation with its eleven-deep bench. The absence of Dave Henderson for much of the second half exaggerated Duke's exhaustion on the floor. BC's smaller, quicker frontcourt took advantage of a winded Duke team. Center Roger McCready scored a game-high 20 points, 8 of which came from the line. He frazzled Mark Alarie and forced him into enough bad fouls to get him out of the game. Troy Bowers put in a valuable fourteen minutes in reserve, adding 8 low-post points off the bench. "We saw their tongues hanging out. We were looking at each other, saying, 'We've got these suckers.' Before the game we looked at them and said, 'Holy shit; they're so huge.' And then we just started chipping them down, chipping them down," Primus recalled.[69]

In the battle of the backcourts, Michael Adams tangled with Dawkins and Amaker all afternoon but found himself in foul trouble midway through the second half. CBS's Billy Packer commented that BC was in big trouble without Adams on the floor, but Stu Primus rose to the occasion, not only holding BC's 2-point lead, but also expanding it to 5 by the time Adams returned.

With 1:07 remaining, BC led, 73–68, after Terrence Talley hit both ends of a one-and-one. Duke had plenty of chances down the stretch to tie the game, but a sudden cold streak from the line and continued struggles from the field (36 percent shooting for the game) squelched Duke's attempt at a comeback. Boston College sewed up a 74–73 win and earned its fourth trip to the Sweet Sixteen in five years. "They [BC] are relentless in their pursuit of the basketball, which means they're always in the game. You can never relax against them," Krzyzewski said after the loss.[70]

In the regional semifinals, Boston College faced Dana Kirk's Memphis State Tigers at Dallas's Reunion Arena. The Tigers had rumbled through the Metro Conference, losing just two games all season. They had a long and large frontcourt featuring 6'10" Keith Lee and 7'0" William Bedford.

Their backcourt paired speedy point guard Andre Turner and 6'6" freshman swingman Vincent Askew. All four played in the NBA. "When we played against Memphis, it was the first time that we saw a team that was very similar to us that could run and jump. There were some athletes," Troy Bowers said.[71]

Memphis and Boston College played to a 31–31 tie through twenty minutes. The Tigers tried to outmuscle BC while the Eagles harassed Memphis's ball handlers into numerous mistakes. For the Tigers, William Bedford proved a dominant force in the middle, scoring 23 points and snatching 14 rebounds. Gary Williams delved deep into his bench once again but found a clutch performance in a familiar place, with Stu Primus scoring 14 points in reserve in twenty-seven minutes of action. Memphis keyed in on Michael Adams, as had the Eagles' previous opponents, holding him to 12 points and 4 assists.

William Bedford dominated the early part of the second half, converting several offensive rebounds into Memphis points. By the twelve-minute mark, Memphis had built up a seemingly daunting 12-point lead, but, as usual, BC fought their way back into the game, renewing its efforts in the full-court man-to-man press and forcing the Tigers into a spate of turnovers. "We trained up hill, so we got stronger later in the game. It's like the rope-a-dope almost. They think they've got you, and then we go, 'Okay. Let's put it on.' Then we began pressing, and we'd be more aggressive at the end of the game. And they'd be like, 'Where the hell did that come from?'" Stu Primus said.[72]

BC made four steals, three of them off the inbounds play, during a 12–0 run. Memphis's Bedford kept panicking in the face of BC's pressure as he tried to get the ball into his guards. Senior Terrence Talley came up remarkably big on the offensive end during this stretch, scoring 5 straight baskets. With just over four minutes remaining, Boston College and Memphis were tied at 57.[73]

And then the game slowed down. Memphis held the ball until Trevor Gordon fouled William Bedford with 2:03 remaining, sending the Memphis center to the line for a one-and-one. Bedford clanked the first shot off the front of the rim. Roger McCready snagged the rebound, and BC took its turn holding the ball.

"You could see that they were fatigued and couldn't touch us," Stu Primus said of the game's final two minutes, when he and Adams took turns toting the ball until Williams called timeout with fourteen seconds remaining. Out of the timeout, McCready inbounded the ball to freshman forward Skip Barry in the backcourt. Barry bounce passed the ball back to him immediately. McCready then dribbled the ball off his foot. Memphis's Vincent Askew scooped up the ball and drove the length of the court. Askew found himself among a cluster of BC defenders under the rim and flung the ball back out to Andre Turner. Turner drove to his left and hit a jump shot from just beyond the key as time expired.

"What just happened to us? We should have won the game," Troy Bowers said in retrospect, evoking the feelings of his teammates after the loss. "It was a mental breakdown. It wasn't just one thing. It's always a couple of things that we could have done better."[74] "We probably played as well as we could in that game," Gary Williams said of his team, which lacked any players larger than 6'9". He defended his decision to hold the ball, citing how successful that approach had been in the Eagles' first-round game against Texas Tech. "I believe if we'd won, we'd have been in a great position to get to the Final Four, but it didn't happen. That '85 team was really small. They probably achieved as much as they could have achieved given the makeup of the personnel."[75]

The Oklahoma Sooners team that Memphis State beat in the regional final had struggled against pressing and trapping teams like Boston College all season. The same weekend that Memphis punched its ticket for Lexington, Kentucky, three of BC's conference rivals—Georgetown, Villanova, and St. John's—all earned bids to the Final Four. Boston College had been part of the most dominant tournament run by any conference in NCAA history, leaving no doubt that Dave Gavitt's "Cathedral Conference" had become the best in the sport.

In a widely syndicated piece, Gary Williams broke down the teams in the Final Four, as his Eagles were the only team that had played all of them.[76] More than that, BC had defeated two of the teams (St. John's and Villanova) and lost by a bucket to the other two (Georgetown and Memphis State). Williams predicted correctly that Georgetown and Villanova would advance to the championship game. In the finals Villanova pulled off one of the most memorable upsets in the history of college basketball as the eighth-seeded Wildcats beat the Hoyas, 66–64. Villanova remains the lowest-seeded team in college basketball history to win the NCAA Tournament.

In the aftermath of another improbable BC run to the Sweet Sixteen, a number of questions surrounded the basketball program. Where would the much-in-demand Gary Williams be coaching long term? Where would Boston College be playing its home games in 1985–1986 and beyond? Who would become Boston College's on-floor leader with the departure of Adams and his battle-tested teammates?

The 1985–1986 season was unquestionably going to be a rebuilding year for the Eagles, with the loss of not only four-year starter and three-year captain Michael Adams, but also his running mates in the backcourt, Terrence Talley and Stu Primus. Collectively, this group had been the team's anchor through a turbulent but triumphant 1984–1985 season. BC would go from having the deepest, most dynamic collection of guards in college basketball to a team with only Dom Pressley as a veteran backcourt presence. As the 1980s reached their midway point, Boston College's position in the Big East pecking order would once again be challenged.

Fig 1. Gary Williams trolling the sideline with intensity during a 1985 game.
Courtesy of Boston College Athletics.

Fig 2. *(opposite top)* Dr. Tom Davis helped transform Boston College into a power in the early years of the Big East. Courtesy of Boston College Athletics.

Fig 3. *(opposite bottom)* Gary Williams fields questions from reporters. Courtesy of Boston College Athletics.

Fig 4. Future NBA All-Star Michael Adams (no. 23) providing stalwart defense against Georgetown at the Boston Garden. During his time at BC, Adams helped lead them to a Final Eight appearance and two Sweet Sixteens. Courtesy of Boston College Athletics.

Fig 5. Dana Barros was one of the deadliest shooters in the Big East and the first player in BC history to reach 2,000 career points. Courtesy of Boston College Athletics.

NCAA Regional Finalist

Fig 6. *(above)* Cartoon rendering of the 1981–1982 BC men's basketball team that reached the Final Eight of the NCAA Tournament. Courtesy of Matt Gianatassio.

Fig 7. Despite being just 6′5″, BC's Roger McCready was one of the Big East's best low-post players for several seasons during the 1980s. Courtesy of Boston College Athletics.

Fig 8. Left-handed Jay Murphy could score from anywhere. Murphy was one of the most feared offensive weapons in the early years of the Big East. Courtesy of Boston College Athletics.

Fig 9. *(above)* BC basketball great Jim O'Brien took over as the Eagles' head coach in 1986 after Gary Williams left for Ohio State. Courtesy of Boston College Athletics.

Fig 10. BC's John Bagley drives to the rim at the Roberts Center against Seton Hall. John Bagley was named Big East Player of the Year in 1981. Courtesy of Matt Gianatassio.

Fig 11. *(above)* Rick Pitino's BU Terriers team carries him off the floor after defeating Holy Cross to win the North Atlantic Conference championship in 1983. The victory earned Boston University its first trip to the NCAA men's basketball tournament in a quarter century. Courtesy of Boston University Athletics.

Fig 12. *(opposite top)* Gary Plummer was a force in the middle for BU. He played a major role in leading the Terriers to the 1983 NCAA Tournament, which he missed due to an injury he suffered in the conference tournament. Courtesy of Boston University Athletics.

Fig 13. Shawn Teague was a versatile defender, distributor, and scorer for BU under both Rick Pitino and John Kuester. Courtesy of Boston University Athletics.

Fig 14. *(opposite)* Forward Paul Hendricks was a double-double machine for several seasons at BU, playing under Rick Pitino, John Kuester, and Mike Jarvis. Courtesy of Boston University Athletics.

Fig 15. Mike Jarvis's BU Terriers team celebrates a North Atlantic Conference championship at the Hartford Civic Center in 1990. In five seasons at BU, Jarvis won 101 games and led his team to the NCAA Tournament twice. The team earned an NIT bid in his first season, 1985–1986. Courtesy of Boston University Athletics.

Fig 16. *(above)* Rick Pitino, "the Boy Coach," looks on warily.
Courtesy of Boston University Athletics.

Fig 17. *(opposite top)* Rick Pitino (seated at right) minds the clock
during an unknown game. Courtesy of Boston University Athletics.

Fig 18. Rick Pitino (center) fit in well among the coaching fraternity
of the ECAC North, a league filled with demonstrative head coaches.
Courtesy of Boston University Athletics.

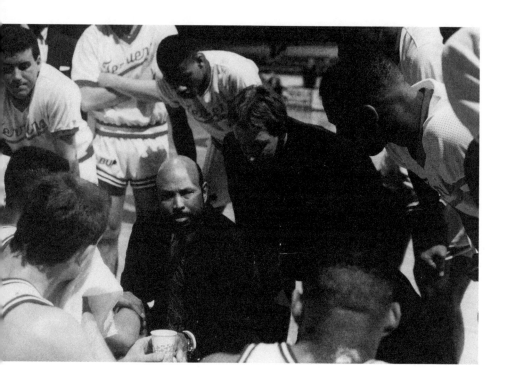

Fig 19. *(above)* Mike Jarvis addresses his BU team during a 1990 game. Courtesy of Boston University Athletics.

Fig 20. *(opposite top)* Jim Calhoun, 1972. Calhoun was hired to coach the Northeastern men's basketball team less than two weeks before the start of practice in 1972. He stayed for the next fourteen years and led the Huskies to the NCAA Tournament on five occasions. Courtesy of Northeastern University Athletics.

Fig 21. Jim Moxley (center) embodied the kind of old-school toughness that made Northeastern University a power in the NCAA College Division under Dick Dukeshire and Jim Bowman. Courtesy of Northeastern University Athletics.

Fig 22. *(above)* John Clark (left) celebrates briefly with teammates after breaking Northeastern's all-time scoring record on December 8, 1975. Clark was the first player to come out of Northeastern's "Pittsburgh Connection," a pipeline that brought more than a half dozen top-notch players to the school. Courtesy of Northeastern University Athletics.

Fig 23. Perry Moss helped lead the Huskies to a pair of NCAA Tournament births in 1981 and 1982. Moss also hit several of the most consequential shots in school history. Courtesy of Northeastern University Athletics.

Fig 24. Mark Halsel (center) was the most dominant big man in Northeastern basketball history. He played a prominent role on three Huskies teams that reached the NCAA Tournament. Courtesy of Northeastern University Athletics.

Fig 25. Reggie Lewis (no. 35) earned North Atlantic Conference Player of the Year honors on three occasions. He helped lead his team to the NCAA Tournament in all four seasons of his college career. He went on to be a first-round pick of the Boston Celtics and replaced Larry Bird as team captain. He is unquestionably the greatest player in the history of Northeastern University basketball. Courtesy of Northeastern University Athletics.

Fig 26. Jim Calhoun (center) celebrates another victory with his Northeastern University Huskies. Courtesy of Northeastern University Athletics.

Fig 27. Jim Calhoun consults with his team on the bench during a game in the 1985–1986 season. Courtesy of Northeastern University Athletics.

Fig 28. Wes Fuller, Andre LaFleur, and Reggie Lewis (left to right) celebrated North Atlantic Conference championships in all four of their seasons at Northeastern. Collectively they are one of the most successful recruiting classes in the history of college basketball. Courtesy of Northeastern University Athletics.

10

Our Best Recruiting Year Ever *(Calhoun)*

Jim Calhoun's Northeastern Huskies entered the 1983–1984 season playing in the rechristened Matthews Arena in the rechristened North Atlantic Conference (NAC), which was down to an eight-team league. After a losing 1982–1983 campaign, Northeastern looked to compete once again for a league championship. While NU would be losing hard-nosed defender Charlie Heineck, the Huskies returned most of their key contributors from the previous season.

Foremost among the veterans would be senior co-captain Mark Halsel, who averaged nearly 20 points and 12.5 rebounds a game as a junior. Halsel's classmate Roland "Baby Moses" Braswell was also a strong veteran presence in NU's frontcourt. Not only did he look like Moses Malone, Braswell was also an athletic presence in the paint cut from the same mold as his nickname-sake. Sophomore Gerry Corcoran, a highly touted 6′9″ forward from nearby BC High, gave the Huskies depth in the frontcourt. NU's backcourt now had a handful of its own veterans with returning guards Phil Robinson; Skeeter Bryant; Enndy Basquiat, who had shown flashes of brilliance as a freshman in 1982–1983; and Glen Miller, a senior who had transferred in from UConn and possessed an excellent jump shot.

Even more substantial than what Northeastern had in place was the haul of talent coming to campus in fall 1983. The Huskies brought in Junior College All-American Quinton Dale, a 6′6″ small forward who had torched the opposition at Clinton Community College in Iowa. Even more than Dale, it was the cluster of freshmen that Jim Calhoun landed that year that would transform Northeastern into a college basketball dynasty. The three outstanding newcomers were Andre LaFleur, a 6′3″ point guard from Los Angeles who had gone to high school at Governor Dummer's Academy, north of Boston; Wes Fuller, a 6′5″ forward from Camden, New Jersey; and Reggie Lewis, a 6′7″ forward from Baltimore's Dunbar

High School. "I'd say this was our best recruiting year ever. They are all very, very quick," Calhoun told the *Globe* when asked about his incoming class.[1] Certainly, they were fast. But this group arrived with a great many more attributes and intangibles that made them stand out immediately.

Andre LaFleur stood out at Governor's both for his on-court success and his prowess as an athlete. LaFleur averaged 20 points and 8 assists per game as a senior for Tom Tindall's team at Governor's. The Governors went 80-8 during LaFleur's tenure and won two state titles.[2] The guard also won the high jump, triple jump, and long jump at the state's Private School League Championships.[3] Tindall secured LaFleur a spot at Five-Star, which earned him close looks from a number of Big East schools, including Syracuse, Providence, and St. John's. The 1983 recruiting class proved remarkably deep at point guard. Syracuse landed Pearl Washington while St. John's recruited Mark Jackson. Nearby Boston College showed little interest in LaFleur while Northeastern made him a top priority. At Northeastern, LaFleur would have the opportunity to play early, something that wasn't the case at the other prospective schools. Karl Fogel started coming up to Governor's campus in Byfield to see LaFleur play. Eventually Calhoun, too, became a weeknight regular.[4]

Once they got him on campus, Northeastern's coaching staff saw ever more to like in their freshman point guard. "Andre LaFleur was like Lenny Wilkens. At 6'3", he could go by anybody," Jim Calhoun said. "He was the prototypical point guard. He came down to pass first, pass first, then layup. He really could play fast. He glided like Lenny Wilkens used to."[5] Lafleur impressed enough in the preseason to beat out Phil Robinson for the starting point guard position. The freshman's inclusion in the starting lineup put an awesome responsibility on his shoulders. LaFleur more than lived up to the billing.

At Camden High School, Wes Fuller had been a basketball and tennis star. At one point, he'd been the number-three-ranked youth tennis player in New Jersey. The skills he developed in tennis had a tremendous impact on his basketball game. "He [Fuller] had feet from tennis that you couldn't believe. Particularly defensively, he was a mismatch because he was just so quick. You couldn't go by him," Calhoun remembered.[6]

Fuller quickly developed the reputation of a player who could success-fully guard opponents of almost all sizes. "Wes was phenomenal at lateral movement. He was a great defensive player. He was a great leaper and a very good athlete," Andre LaFleur said.[7] Fuller did not start immediately, but he made immediate contributions, especially on defense.

While tennis is often regarded as a genteel sport, this particular tennis player was nothing of the sort. Coming from the gritty city of Camden, Fuller was a no-nonsense player who was more than willing to trade fists with the opposition.[8] Andre LaFleur, who later became close friends with Fuller, first met his future teammate at Five-Star. He was less than enamored with the Fuller he met at camp, who tried to intimidate him. "When I was at Five-Star, I was in some fast-break drills with Wes Fuller, and I didn't pass him the ball a couple of times. And when we got back in line, he walked over to me and said if I didn't pass him the ball next time, he was going to punch me in my face," LaFleur said.[9] The point guard briefly considered going elsewhere when he found out that Fuller was also heading to Huntington Avenue. Little did he know that Calhoun would make them roommates as freshmen and the pair would become close friends.

Reggie Lewis, the third member of Northeastern's incoming class, was a backup throughout his high school career. He did happen to play for the greatest high school basketball team of all time. Lewis was a key contributor at Baltimore's Dunbar High School, playing alongside the likes of future NBAers Muggsy Bogues, Reggie Williams, and David Wingate. Even as a senior, he came off the bench, barraging opponents with his immaculate jump shot when Williams or Timmy Dawson, who played at George Washington and Miami, needed a break. Coached by the legendary Bob Wade, the Dunbar Poets went 60-0 in Lewis's two seasons. The team was immortalized in Alejandro Danois's fantastic book, *The Boys of Dunbar* (2016), and in the similarly excellent *ESPN 30 for 30* documentary, *Baltimore Boys* (2018).

It was Karl Fogel, who had cultivated many coaching contacts in the Mid-Atlantic, that brought Reggie Lewis to Northeastern's attention, noticing him at an all-star tournament in Baltimore. While the major programs fought it out for Georgetown-bound Reggie Williams, Northeastern homed in on Lewis, whose only other major college offers came from Rutgers and Florida A&M.[10] Calhoun wanted to see for himself the stubbornly quiet, rail-thin forward with the sleek jumper that seemed to go in whether or not there was a hand in his face. The Northeastern head coach ventured through a blizzard to a basketball tournament in

Johnstown, Pennsylvania, to see Lewis play in person. That night, Lewis replaced a foul-laden Reggie Williams and bombarded the opposition for 20 points off the bench. Calhoun was sold, thinking this kid could start even as a freshman. Which he did.[11] "When he walked on the court the first day we saw him play," Keith Motley said, was the moment Northeastern's coaching staff knew that Lewis was not only a special player, but one capable of being a first round pick in the NBA Draft. "Coach Wade knew. He [Lewis] was MVP of every tourney [Dunbar] played," Motley continued. "Once I saw his wingspan. Once I saw him dunk on the first guy, I said, 'This skinny guy can do this!' Because he was a rail. But then I saw him on the wing and how he could handle. He wouldn't back down. He would just look at you."[12]

From the first time Reggie Lewis came on campus, Keith Motley played a profound role in Lewis's life as a coach, mentor, and even his boss. As an academic dean, Motley met with Lewis's family on their first visit to campus to discuss Lewis's potential future at Northeastern. It wasn't until later that Lewis learned Motley was also a coach.[13] "He [Lewis] was very quiet, but he was very observant. Nicest person in the world. Didn't even drink soda. They [his teammates] all thought he was corny because he didn't do any of that stuff," Motley said, who later employed Lewis as a work-study.[14]

Corny or not, outspoken or not, Lewis was described by many people who saw him on the court as smooth. There were plenty of other great athletes and skillful players on the Northeastern basketball team. What was unique about Lewis was the sense of finesse that accompanied his athleticism and skill set. Whether it was jumping, running, defending, or shooting, Lewis displayed a mastery over his physicality. Of all his physical attributes, Lewis's length may have been his most significant characteristic. With a 44-inch sleeve, Lewis could get to all kinds of balls that other 6'7" players couldn't come close to touching. Lewis would be starting alongside his classmate, Andre LaFleur, with whom he had developed a deep bond. "He was my best friend from day one," Andre LaFleur said. "We weren't roommates as freshmen, but we bonded together right away. We had very similar interests. Every Sunday morning we would walk from campus all the way to the Combat Zone, and we would watch Chinese karate movies all day long"—often five in a row.[15] Neither drank or was involved with the campus party scene, and both had steady girlfriends. In

Lewis's case, his girlfriend, Donna Harris, became his wife and companion for the rest of his life.[16]

As Northeastern prepared for the 1983–1984 season, the team was clearly in the midst of a youth movement. But it was the senior leadership of Mark Halsel, who had been there for the two previous tournament runs, that propelled this team back to the top. Already a two-time All-Conference performer, Halsel became the first player in NU history to be named team captain for two seasons. On and off the floor, Halsel looked out for the underclassmen, just as he had learned from the players that preceded him at Northeastern—namely, Pete Harris and Perry Moss.

"He [Reggie Lewis] didn't have to be a star immediately. The star was Mark Halsel. They protected Reg because Reg was the little skinny guy they would try to beat up," Keith Motley said. "Every game, he [Lewis] would be knocked on the floor like they were purposely trying to hurt him. But Reggie was so strong and wiry, they couldn't hurt him. He had one move: go to the baseline and shoot a jump shot in their face. Meanwhile, Mark's dunking on everybody on the other side."[17] "Mark made sure that the team's chemistry centered around what was best for the team basketball-wise. And he separated on-court stuff from off-court stuff. He was kind of our big-brother protector against the upper classmen," Andre LaFleur said.[18]

Mark Halsel was also a character. Calhoun described him as the most popular player he'd ever had. When Calhoun had the team over for Thanksgiving one year, Halsel started playing piano and singing along with the coach's seventy-year-old mother-in-law. For all his harshness on the floor, Halsel brought his teddy bear on the road with him.[19]

While a resurgence was clearly afoot at Northeastern, the *Globe* picked BU to repeat as NAC champions in 1983–1984. Despite the loss of Rick Pitino to the NBA, the Terriers had returned four of the five starters from their championship team. Picking the now John Kuester–led team first made complete sense, especially once NU lost some of its depth that season. Enddy Basquiat had been ruled academically ineligible for the first semester and ended up redshirting the remainder of the season. Big man Gerry Corcoran suffered a knee injury that forced him into a redshirt year as well.

Nor did the season start auspiciously. Northeastern got creamed by Purdue in its opener, the first round of a Thanksgiving weekend tournament hosted by Fresno State. Business picked up considerably from there. Northeastern won seven of its next eight games to finish 1983. In most instances, the Huskies blew out their opposition, winning each game by at least 10 points.

Several things were already clear. Northeastern was one of the deepest teams in the country. Nine different players made noteworthy contributions every night. As always, Northeastern got after it on the boards. Braswell, Fuller, Halsel, and Lewis all averaged more than 5 per game, and the Huskies were once again one of the country's top rebounding clubs.

"They [Northeastern] had like five or six guys that were 6'6", 6'7", and just ran like racehorses. They just kept coming at you in waves," Mike Bruckner recalls.[20] "The way Northeastern played, it obviously was a reflection of Calhoun's personality," Donn Esmonde said. "They just kept coming at you. They had that toughness, that aggressiveness. You weren't going to beat them. They were going to beat you. And you couldn't stand up to them physically or psychologically. You were going to lose. They were like the Oakland Raiders of the NAC. They had that persona, those black uniforms, and they'd come in and pound the shit out of you. They were relentless."[21] The "Oakland Raiders of the NAC" pressured opponents into frequent mistakes, transforming the nearly 16 turnovers they forced per game into clusters of fast-break points. All these high-percentage shots enabled NU to shoot better than 52 percent from the field for the season.

Mark Halsel got better every year. In 1983–1984, he would in fact become a 20-and-10 man, averaging 21 points and 10.3 rebounds a game. Halsel would win the NAC Player of the Year award and be named an honorable mention All-American. He also broke Chip Rucker's all-time NU rebounding record, crediting his former captain with helping him learn how to play in the low post at the college level.[22]

The other thing that was clear was the quality of NU's freshman class. The NAC was in for several seasons worth of hurt at the hands of Fuller, LaFleur, and Lewis. Though playing behind Braswell, Fuller had already proven himself a menace on the defensive end, capable of shutting down the opposition at either the 3, 4, or 5 position. He did this while averaging more than 7 points per game off the bench. Andre LaFleur had already asserted himself as the most productive point guard in the conference. He was averaging nearly 8 assists per game, good for fourth in the nation. Reggie Lewis was regarded as one of the best players in New England, averaging nearly 17 points per game in the first semester, a number that only went up in league play.[23] "Andre has the unusual talent of being unselfish, almost to a fault. He finds the open man better than any player I've had," Calhoun said of his freshman point guard.[24] The coach was even less reserved in his praise for Lewis. "When you look at Reggie Lewis, you never see panic on his face," Calhoun explained, comparing Lewis's game to John Havlicek's.[25]

Northeastern entered league play in January 1984 at 7-2, facing another blow to its backcourt depth. Skeeter Bryant, who had quit the team briefly on two previous occasions, left the team for good during Christmas break, never coming back from Rhode Island. Bryant was a great athlete who spent significant time in the weight room on his own and practicing martial arts. He was also an excellent player who earned significant minutes, though he never became the heir apparent to Moss and Harris, as had been expected. For whatever reason, Bryant remained aloof from his teammates and seemed disengaged throughout the fall semester. His reasons for leaving the club remain unclear.[26]

Maine gave Northeastern a scare to start 1984. The Black Bears led by as much as 14 in the second half, thanks in large part to the foul trouble that plagued Braswell and Halsel all evening. It was Reggie Lewis's 26-point effort, 18 of them in the second half, that got the Huskies back into the game. It was a buzzer-beating 27-footer by senior Phil Robinson, who played just four minutes, that kept the game from going to overtime. Northeastern escaped with an 83–81 win, the first of five consecutive wins to start the new year.

Except for a blowout win against Vermont, every other game was a nail-biter, including a road win against this same Maine club. It was veteran leadership like that shown by co-captain Phil Robinson against Maine that put Northeastern at 12-2 heading into a showdown with Boston College.

At the Roberts Center, Northeastern came as close to beating the Eagles as they had in years. Calhoun matched Gary Williams's press with his own press. Northeastern held a slight lead for much of the second half, but poor foul shooting down the stretch enabled the sixteenth-ranked Eagles to force overtime. BC prevailed, 81–78, but not before the home crowd showed its appreciation for a Northeastern newcomer. Reggie Lewis's Jerry West-like jump shot earned roaring applause from the home crowd on several occasions.[27]

Northeastern brushed itself off after the non-conference loss and just got back to pummeling the opposition. A weekend series in Buffalo loomed large on the schedule, as the Huskies had to face Canisius and Niagara over a long weekend. Mark Halsel had severely bruised his elbow in a 76–60 win over Army and was doubtful for the Buffalo series. He ended up playing limited minutes in both games.[28]

The Huskies escaped the weekend with two hard-fought wins: a 68–66 win over Canisius and a 76–70 win over Niagara. Calhoun credits Buffalo weekends in the NAC as great preparation for playing in the NCAA Tournament. "When we went to play Canisius and Niagara, we went up there and played them both in a three-day period. Much like [in] the NCAA. You'd land in Buffalo. Practice on Thursday. Play on a Friday night. Play on Saturday and come back that night. The NCAA is basically the same thing," Calhoun said.[29]

Northeastern kept on winning, including an 83–77 crosstown victory over John Kuester's struggling BU team. The game was a relatively mild affair by the rivalry's standards. Northeastern's bigs, Braswell (19 points) and Halsel (25 points), took it to the Terriers in the win. The Huskies improved to 19-3 overall and 10-0 in league play.[30]

The Huskies had little time to celebrate the win. They were headed to Raleigh, North Carolina, to face Jim Valvano's defending national champion NC State Wolfpack in their final non-conference game of the season. NC State led by 10 at the half, but Northeastern came out of the locker room and pilloried the champs with jump shots. With less than five minutes remaining, NU led by 3, but a series of mental and physical mistakes cost the Huskies the game. The defending national champions escaped with a 77–74 home win. "If you had asked me four years ago, I would have probably said it was [a moral victory], even though I don't believe there is really such a thing as a moral victory. Basketball people know about us," Calhoun said after the game at Reynolds Coliseum. Valvano told him that Northeastern belonged in the NCAA Tournament, regardless of the outcome of the NAC Tournament.[31]

Canisius and Niagara came to Boston the following weekend. Just like the matchups in Buffalo, both games were pitched battles. Against Canisius, "Sugar" Ray Hall torched the Huskies for 21 points, and the Griffins led 56–55 with just over four minutes remaining. Mark Halsel drove the length of the floor and threw down a rim-rocking dunk to retake the lead, which Northeastern never relinquished. Niagara challenged Northeastern to a track meet two nights later and nearly came out on top. The Huskies escaped with a 94–90 victory in a game that Pete Lonergan said was as well as his team could have possibly played that night.[32]

Before taking on Boston University, Calhoun implored his players to go out and become the greatest team in the history of their school, which they did. Northeastern outlasted BU, 85–83, at Matthews to finish off the first undefeated season in the NAC. Gary Plummer nearly spoiled NU's coronation, putting the Terriers on his very broad shoulders. The senior played the best game of his illustrious college career, scoring 34 points in a matchup with Mark Halsel. Plummer's counterpart had 24 points of his own in the pair's final regular-season meeting. Halsel and LaFleur sealed the deal for Northeastern, hitting 4 clutch foul shots in the final minute to secure the win. Plummer said after the game he hoped the 15-12 Terriers would get another crack at Northeastern in the conference tournament. His hopes would be dashed by 7'0" Mike Smrek, sharpshooter Sugar Ray Hall, and the rest of the Canisius Griffs in the semifinals.[33]

NU pummeled Colgate in the opening round of the NAC Tournament before getting a scare from Maine in the semifinals. It was primarily Northeastern's stars that carried them to victory in a hard-fought 83–77 game at Matthews. Mark Halsel went for 24 points and 11 rebounds, while Reggie Lewis set a career high with 30 points. In the game's final minute, though, it was Glen Miller who sealed the win, hitting 4 consecutive free throws to end the Black Bears' season.

The NAC championship game between Canisius and top-seeded Northeastern would be played at Matthews Arena. The Huskies jumped out to an 11-point halftime lead, but Canisius fought their way back in the second half. The Griffins were able to assert themselves in the paint after Roland Braswell went down with a knee injury. Led by future Los Angeles Laker Mike Smrek (17 points, 7 rebounds), Canisius won the battle on the boards, 36–33, and briefly took the lead late, 69–68. When Braswell returned to the court on crutches, his presence was an immediate emotional jolt for the Huskies. Reggie Lewis converted a steal into a thunderous dunk to retake the lead. Northeastern never looked back and pulled away for an 85–75 win.[34] After the game, tournament MVP Mark Halsel credited

Braswell with being one of the main reasons Northeastern had won another conference title. To show his appreciation for his injured teammate, Halsel gave Braswell his tournament MVP trophy.[35]

Twenty-six win Northeastern finished the season as the only team in the country with an undefeated record in their conference. Nevertheless, the tournament committee placed NU in a play-in game. In the jerry-rigged fifty-three-team format, used only in 1984, ten automatic bids from weaker conferences were forced to play for a spot among the forty-eight remaining teams in the field. The committee paired the Huskies with a familiar and contemptible foe, the LIU Blackbirds, champions of the ECAC Metro. Led by a large and long frontcourt, LIU was fourth in the country in rebounding margin and played just as up-tempo and physically as Northeastern.

In the teams' previous meeting in February 1983, Northeastern lost, 75–73, in Brooklyn. The game was marred by an ugly brawl in which mobs of LIU fans came on the floor, some of whom participated in the violence. NU guard Phil Robinson got sucker-punched during the fight and kicked in the head. The bloodied Robinson had to be helped from the floor once order was restored. Robinson spent the next two days in the NU infirmary. A passel of security guards surrounded the NU team for the rest of the game.[36] "It was very ugly. A couple of elbows were thrown, one of the Long Island guys threw a sucker punch and we had 1,000 fans on the court. I seriously considered taking my team off the court," Calhoun said.[37] After the incident, Northeastern decided against renewing its series with LIU for the 1983–1984 season.

The 4:10 p.m. Tuesday game would be broadcast on ESPN from Philadelphia's Palestra. The winner faced sixth-seeded Virginia Commonwealth (VCU) in the East Regional at the Meadowlands. NU would be severely shorthanded against LIU as Roland Braswell was unavailable. Wes Fuller would get the start in his place at center. The freshman would be matched up against 6'11" Vincent Wiggins, a player six inches taller than Fuller. Northeastern would also have virtually no fans in attendance. A blizzard would cause two busloads of NU fans who had planned to attend to turn around in Framingham.[38]

Three freshmen (Lewis, Fuller, and LaFleur); three seniors (Miller, Halsel, and Robinson); and a junior (Dale) led Northeastern to its third NCAA Tournament win in as many appearances. Wes Fuller not only held his own. He dominated Vincent Wiggins. Fuller went for 22 points and

8 rebounds. Wiggins was invisible with 2 points and 3 rebounds. The smallest center in the NCAA Tournament came up unimaginably huge—not to mention that Fuller was also a freshman making his first-ever career start. Nor to mention that he was playing across the Delaware River from his hometown, Camden, New Jersey.[39] "Nervous? Not really. This is my hometown. I've played here [the Palestra] before. I was here playing pickup games during the summers against whoever showed up," Fuller said.[40]

Despite Fuller's dominance, this game was a back-and-forth battle pitting aggressive defenses against one another. NU led by as many as 15 in the first half but LIU's disruptive press forced 22 Huskies turnovers. Paul Lizzo's trapping pressure from the sidelines wreaked havoc on Northeastern's offense.

At one point, LIU led by 1, but Northeastern reestablished an 88–85 lead with less than a minute to go. With eighteen seconds remaining, Reggie Lewis sealed the game by swatting away a shot by Robert Brown, who had been LIU's hot hand with 27 points. Glen Miller grabbed the loose ball, forwarded it to Halsel, who then passed it off to Wes Fuller for the jam to make it 90–85. LIU added a final bucket to make it a 90–87 final.[41]

Northeastern's Friday night game at the Meadowlands against VCU would not be shown in Boston until the next morning at 5:30 on ESPN. Those who avoided the score and watched the tape delay were in for another anxiety-inducing affair. The Huskies would again be without Braswell. J. D. Barnett's VCU team played chess on the basketball court, moving the ball around at a glacial pace that would have made Henry Iba proud. The Rams showed a wide range of defensive looks and proved awfully successful at stymieing the opposition. VCU finished sixth in the country in scoring defense, briefly held a spot in the Top 20 poll, and won the Sun Belt regular season title. They also had a week's worth of rest going into the game.

The Huskies proved strikingly adept at playing VCU's style of basketball. Northeastern led most of the way and displayed remarkable patience on offense, working their way into dozens of high-percentage shots. It was Reggie Lewis who turned heads that evening, putting on one of the most remarkable shooting performances in NCAA history. The freshman went 15-for-17 from the floor, scoring a game-high 31 points. Northeastern also won on the boards and stayed out of foul trouble. But they never could shake VCU. While Northeastern shot an unbelievable 75 percent from the field, VCU remained competitive with its own impressive 62 percent shooting.[42]

Foul shooting proved to be Northeastern's demise. The Huskies went just 3-for-9 from the line for the game, including three misses in the game's final three minutes. Glen Miller hit the front end of a one-and-one to give Northeastern a 69–68 lead but missed the second one, allowing VCU to regain possession and call timeout to set up a final shot.[43] Inbounding from under the hoop, Michael Brown looked first to Calvin Duncan but thought better of sending the ball his way in heavy coverage. Instead, he fired the inbound pass to Rolando Lamb, who turned toward the rim and made the shot of his life, draining a 20-foot jumper over Wes Fuller as time expired to give VCU a 70–69 win. Never had a team that shot so well lost an NCAA Tournament game.[44]

Northeastern finished the season at 27-5, the most wins in school history. The team would be losing a tremendous amount of talent and leadership going into the 1984–1985 season with the departures of starters Mark Halsel, Roland Braswell, and Glen Miller. After winning a mountain of trophies, Halsel got a shot at the pros. The Bulls selected him in the fourth round, but he failed to make Chicago's roster. Instead, Halsel played domestically in the CBA and internationally for several seasons.

In recruiting, Northeastern replenished its front- and backcourts. Returning to its Baltimore pipeline, Northeastern signed 6'7" center Kevin McDuffie, a childhood friend of Reggie Lewis who was a standout at Dunbar's rival, Lake Clifton. McDuffie would be Northeastern's next hard-nosed, athletic big man in a lineage that started with Chip Rucker. Closer to home, Calhoun signed 6'2" guard John Williams from Don Bosco in Boston's Combat Zone. Calhoun often headed over to Don Bosco games after practice. The Northeastern coach was not sold on Williams's offensive performance but was impressed with his skill as a defender and ability to make the big play in clutch situations.[45]

Once Calhoun got Williams on campus, the coach put Keith Motley to work with Williams on his form. Motley got him out of the bad habit of putting his elbow out when he shot. The close mentoring paid tremendous dividends for Williams and the Northeastern basketball program.[46]

The 1984–1985 Northeastern team may have been the youngest in the country. Most nights, Northeastern dressed thirteen freshman and sophomores, no juniors, and one senior. Despite its youth, this was an experienced team. Lewis and LaFleur started every game as freshmen. Fuller and Dale posted significant minutes and moments all season. Gerry Corcoran would be returning from injury and competing with freshman Kevin McDuffie for the center spot. Erratic but often excellent guard Enndy Basquiat would also be returning to the club. John Williams, too, looked ready to compete for minutes as a freshman. Calhoun brought in recent graduate and NU great Dave Leitao as an assistant that season, giving the younger players a near-peer to work with on the coaching staff. Leitao would also be hitting the recruiting trail like a madman.[47] "With the kind of athletes that Northeastern recruits, they are head and shoulders above the rest of the league," Canisius coach Nick Macarchuk said before the season.[48]

There were many occasions during the 1984–1985 season when the Huskies did not appear head and shoulders above the competition. It was a season of streaks and perseverance by this extraordinarily young team. Northeastern started out 3-0 before running into trouble in non-conference tournament season. The Huskies lost in Missoula to the home-town Montana Grizzlies in the Champions Holiday Classic. Northeastern dropped two straight in the Fleet Classic at the Providence Civic Center. Despite Reggie Lewis's 32-point, 18-rebound effort, NU fell, 92–84, to a very good Illinois State team. In the consolation game, unheralded West Texas State upset Northeastern, 81–74. In defeat, the Huskies were not nearly as dominant as usual on the boards and got into the bad habit of turning the ball over, particularly when facing a press like West Texas State's.[49] In mid-December, Northeastern blew an 11-point second half lead at the Springfield Civic Center and lost to a seemingly down-and-out UMass team.[50] All told, Northeastern ended 1984 on a four-game losing streak and with a 3-4 overall mark entering league play.

Just as quickly as Northeastern got cold in December, they got hot in January, ripping off seven consecutive wins. Highlights of the streak included a come-from-behind win at home against Niagara. Reggie Lewis blocked two shots, snagged a key rebound, and made an open-court steal in the game's closing minutes to seal a 73–70 win in front of a suddenly small crowd at Matthews. The gate had been down all season for uncertain reasons. Basketball fans were certainly willing to come to Matthews for the right attraction. Earlier that day, a Celtics Old Timers Game had drawn five times as many fans to Matthews.[51]

Another cold front moved through Northeastern basketball in late January. On the 24th, a 2-14 New Hampshire team ended NU's 23-game NAC winning streak. Gerry Friel's Wildcats took advantage of Northeastern's turnovers and poor foul shooting to sneak out of Matthews with a 57–55 win. "I got home that night and my wife goes, 'What happened, how bad?'" New Hampshire's Mike Bruckner recalled. "I said, 'We won.' She said, 'You did not' and rolled over and went back to bed. And the phones kept ringing. AP kept calling to see that they got the score right."[52]

A weekend in Buffalo compounded the hurt. Canisius and Niagara both beat Northeastern. Northeastern concluded January 1985 with a track meet against nemesis Boston College. As usual, Northeastern hung tough against the Eagles before a nearly full house at Matthews, but BC prevailed in the end, 82–75. The win was BC's twenty-first consecutive win in the series. The recent BC-NU contests had apparently been too close for comfort on Chestnut Hill. The schools would not play again until 2003.

Now 10-8 and three games back in the NAC, Northeastern had one of its most consequential regular-season matchups in recent memory as they played host to Canisius, who was 10-0 in the league, in early February. Though often irascible and given to pessimism in his comments, Jim Calhoun was not one for overstatement. He referred to the Canisius game as a must win for the Huskies.[53]

"My freshman year, I viewed Niagara as our rivals, but after my freshman year, it wasn't really Niagara. It was actually Northeastern with Reggie Lewis and Perry Moss and Boston University with Gary Plummer. Those were the teams we were going to have to bump heads with if we wanted to try to get to the tournament or do anything special," Sugar Ray Hall said.[54] Then a senior, Hall became the leading scorer in Canisius history and averaged close to 21 points per game. Canisius was right around twenty wins every season, and its 1984–1985 team may have been the best of Nick Macarchuk's career.

As Northeastern fought its way back into the race, Lewis and Lafleur led the way. Against Canisius, Reggie Lewis kept a pregame promise to Coach Motley. He broke the NAC's single game scoring record, going for 38 points and leading the Huskies to a 99–91 victory.[55] Northeastern would not lose another regular-season game. The Huskies cruised past Colgate and BU before heading back to the Meadowlands for a non-conference showcase game against Big Ten power Ohio State. Now it was Andre LaFleur's chance to put the team on his shoulders.

"I was trying to do more than I normally do because I figured we'd need that help with all the guys that graduated," LaFleur said of his play during the losing streak. After the loss to BC, LaFleur met with Calhoun for more than two hours. The coach encouraged him to focus on being a point guard, leading the team on the floor and making plays, rather than trying to do everyone else's job. It clearly worked.[56] LaFleur broke a 74–74 tie against Ohio State, knocking down a 17-footer with two seconds remaining to seal the victory.

The Huskies cruised through their next four contests before concluding the regular season against BU. A measles outbreak on the Commonwealth Avenue campus led to a ban on spectators at the Case Center. Calhoun expressed reticence about playing amid an outbreak, but after consulting with his AD, decided that BU had put adequate measures in place to keep both teams safe.[57] Maine's upset win over first-place Canisius helped too, opening the door for NU to secure a tie for the league's regular season title. All players, coaches, and staff on both teams were inoculated for measles in advance of the game.

The Terriers came out swinging and led 41–39 early in the second half, thanks in large part to Mike Alexander's 21 points and the BU press. John Kuester, inexplicably, turned down the pressure on defense, allowing Andre LaFleur to pick the Terriers apart to the tune of a 22–8 run. Northeastern won going away, 80–69.[58]

Canisius and Northeastern ended the regular season tied in first place. The conference came up with a solution that pleased no one, deciding to award Canisius the top seed but to play the championship game at Siena if the one and two seeds met in the final. This meet-me-halfway approach annoyed Calhoun, who argued that Northeastern was the hotter team down the stretch. Canisius's Nick Macarchuk was even more annoyed. He argued that Canisius had been number one all season and that a game played at the Aud in Buffalo would mean much more revenue for the conference. "They've [The NAC] tried having the finals in Boston and no one goes. If we had it at our school [Canisius], there would be 10 or 11 thousand people," Macarchuk said. It proved to be a moot point.[59]

Northeastern pounded Maine in the NAC quarterfinals. Reggie Lewis and Quinton Dale both went for 32 points as Northeastern got into triple digits. The semis against Siena were a very different affair. New to the NAC, Siena impressed in year one, playing tough, deliberate basketball. Their center, 6'6" Doug Poetzsch, was a banger in the paint who had finished third in the league in scoring. John Griffin's Indians played physical defense and kept turnovers to a minimum. "Our [Siena] style of play was grinding, physical, blue-collar workman-like. You had a bunch of guys who were not gifted athletically but had good basketball intelligence and a desire to improve and worked hard. I think Coach Griffin brought that Philly attitude to the program," Siena point guard Art Tooles said of his coach, who had starred at St. Joseph's in the 1970s.[60]

After losing twice to Northeastern during the regular season, Griffin, who was not yet thirty years old, took a different approach to the Huskies. Instead of trying to slow the Huskies down, he tried to make the semifinal a two-man game: pump the ball into Poetzsch and knock Lewis around with as many bodies as necessary. For thirty-four minutes, it proved remarkably effective. Poetzsch fought his way to 26 points, and the Indians held Lewis to 5 of 16 shooting. Siena led 60–53 with less than six minutes remaining. The downside to Griffin's strategy was that Northeastern spent the afternoon at the line and virtually everyone in Siena's rotation was in foul trouble. The Huskies ended up taking 47 foul shots and hitting 39 of them. Reggie Lewis scored 13 of his 23 points from the stripe as Northeastern hung on for a 73–69 win.[61]

The finals would be played at Matthews Arena. Despite a 13-14 regular season, Boston University fought its way to the conference finals. Veterans Shawn Teague, Mike Alexander, and Paul Hendricks shepherded the Terriers to upset road wins over Niagara and Canisius. The remnants of the Rick Pitino era brought that fighting spirit with them to the NAC championship.

It took a special night by Reggie Lewis, even by his lofty standards, to secure another NAC title. Less than five minutes into the game, Lewis crashed to the floor after a collision with BU big man Tom Ivey. Lewis landed on his wrist and tried unsuccessfully to make a go of it for the rest of the half. The sophomore sharpshooter threw up three consecutive airballs. At the half, he couldn't grip a basketball. BU led by 3 midway through the second half, 54–51. Everyone contributed to the BU effort as five different Terriers reached double figures. It was then that Reggie Lewis entered into a duel with his rivals. Matching them shot for shot, Lewis hit 6 consecutive jumpers, battered wrist and all. On the night, Lewis scored 29 points on 14-for-22 shooting, earning him tournament MVP honors. Center Kevin McDuffie, who had quietly put together a competitive freshman campaign, provided the margin of victory by hitting the front end of a one-and-one with twenty-one seconds remaining. Nearly five thousand fans saw Northeastern defeat its rival, 68–67, to earn its fourth trip to the NCAA Tournament in five years. Calhoun called Lewis's performance the gutsiest he'd ever seen.[62]

Northeastern, 22-8, was again slighted with its seed in the NCAA Tournament, the first sixty-four-team field in tourney history. The Huskies got a 14 and were scheduled to face off Friday at noon against number three Illinois. Swollen wrist and all, Reggie Lewis planned to play against the Illini in Atlanta. The Huskies would certainly need him. Illinois was a quintessentially corn-fed, slow-down Big Ten team that relied on its big men. The Illini's front line was all at least 6'8", all taller than Northeastern's center, Kevin McDuffie.

Vegas made twelfth-ranked Illinois a 10.5-point favorite for the East Regional matchup. As usual, Vegas knew its stuff. Illinois blew out Northeastern, 76–57. Lou Henson's team led by a dozen at the half and never looked back. The board-crashing Huskies got knocked around by the likes of Ken Norman and Efrem Winters, winning the rebounding battle 32–25. Lewis went just 11-for-28 on the evening. Besides a 10-point effort by senior Quinton Dale, the Huskies couldn't get much going offensively.

Later that spring, Northeastern University inducted Calhoun into its Athletic Hall of Fame. The forty-three-year-old coach rejected an offer from George Washington to become their new head basketball coach, completing what had become one of his rites of spring. The Colonials shifted their attention across town and hired BU coach John Kuester. A few weeks earlier, there had been talk of Providence hiring Calhoun, but the Friars instead went with another former BU coach, Rick Pitino.

While talk of Calhoun's heading to Providence swirled in the print and broadcast media, the idea that Reggie Lewis might turn pro also began to germinate. The NAC Player of the Year had averaged 24.1 points per game as a sophomore, good for seventh in the country. Capable of playing either shooting guard or small forward, Lewis also led the team in steals and rebounding. In the end, Calhoun decided to stay at Northeastern, a result that tamped down talk of Lewis's leaving for the pros.[63] Moreover, Calhoun had another great team coming back. With the exception of Quinton Dale, every major contributor would still be around for the 1985–1986 season.

"What North Carolina is to the Atlantic Coast Conference, Northeastern is to the ECAC North. The Huskies are the standard of excellence," Bob Ryan wrote as Northeastern approached its 1985–1986 season, coming off its fourth trip to the NCAAs in five seasons. *Sports Illustrated* ranked Northeastern thirty-seventh in its preseason poll—one better than BC and one worse than defending champ Villanova.[64]

The Huskies spent much of the preseason rather beaten up. Andre LaFleur, John Williams, and Enndy Basquiat all battled nagging injuries. At one point, Calhoun canceled practice because he didn't have enough healthy guards to play.[65]

Northeastern upgraded the experience for upscale fans at Matthews in fall 1985, investing more than $750,000 in the Varsity Club. The club featured a modern kitchen, dining room, and bar—not bad for a building that had been on its last legs five years earlier. Nor was it too shabby for fans to be able to buy cocktails while watching a team that, until recently, had shared its locker room at Cabot with faculty members who were in various states of undress while players prepared for practices or games.[66]

Injuries won out over great expectations early in the 1985–1986 season. Eleven thousand seething Terps fans greeted Northeastern at Cole Field House for the Huskies' regular season opener at Maryland. Calhoun conceded afterward that his team seemed intimidated by the atmosphere. The Huskies provided ample evidence for the aphorism "Shooting doesn't travel," hitting less than 40 percent of their shots. Still Northeastern found a way to hang in the game. Down low, Kevin McDuffie and Wes Fuller banged their way to a draw with Maryland's big men. In the second half, Lewis tore up the Terrapins, scoring 20 of his 30 points and driving Northeastern to a 64–62 lead with 6:27 remaining. Lefty Driesell's Maryland team counterpunched with fury, going on a 22–8 run to finish the game and win, 84–72. Maryland's All-American power forward Len Bias led the charge, scoring a team-high 23 points. In the game's closing minutes, Lewis cooled down and point guard Andre LaFleur could not find another scorer to pick up the slack.[67]

Nevertheless, the *Baltimore Sun*'s Bill Tanton, who witnessed the Lewis-Bias duel, declared a decisive winner. "For my money, the best player on the floor was Northeastern's Reggie Lewis, the 6'7 junior out of Dunbar,"

Tanton wrote, highlighting the four Baltimore-area players on the Huskies' roster. "Reggie showed that he can score inside or outside. He can rebound and play defense. And he is a better passer than Bias."[68] Little did anyone know that night that the triumphs and tragic ends of both young men would be tethered together through their relationships to the Boston Celtics.

In game two, the Pitino-Calhoun rivalry resumed as Northeastern played Providence at the Providence Civic Center. Pitino's newest band of full-court press antagonists obliterated Northeastern, forcing the Huskies into 25 turnovers and a pitiful night of shooting. The Friars led by 12 at the half and continued pounding away, winning 83–68. Calhoun gave himself an "F" on his coaching job that afternoon but would soon return to his mean.[69]

Northeastern coasted past its next four opponents, heading for the Christmas break with a 4-2 record. Floor general Andre LaFleur created opportunities for other weapons to emerge on offense alongside Lewis. In the low post, Wes Fuller and Kevin McDuffie both increased their production, averaging just under 10 and just over 9 points respectively that season. LaFleur himself got better as a scorer every year. As a junior, he averaged 10.8 points per game. The breakout offensive contributor was shooting guard John Williams, who kept fine-tuning his offensive game. Williams came to Huntington Avenue shooting the ball with his arms akimbo. As a sophomore, he shot better than 50 percent from the field, finished second on the team in scoring, and was regarded as the team's best defensive guard.

Williams torched Duquesne for 25 points in the opener of the Connecticut Mutual Classic, held at the Hartford Civic Center just after Christmas. After dispatching with Duquesne, 5-2 Northeastern tangled with Dom Perno's 8-0 Connecticut team. In the finals, nearly twelve thousand fans watched Northeastern embarrass the hometown UConn Huskies, 90–73. Northeastern led by 17 at the half and by as much as 25 in the second half before emptying the bench. Things got a lot worse in the coming weeks for Dom Perno's Huskies.

The same could not be said for Jim Calhoun's team, which swept its seven January games to improve to 13-2. Junior Reggie Lewis lived up to his status as the league's best player. With all the lights focused on him, Lewis continued to thrive, averaging 23.8 points per game, grabbing more than 9 rebounds and 2 steals and blocking nearly three shots per night. Lewis's success was even more remarkable considering the amount of pressure that opponents placed on him each game. He was forever double-teamed, punched, pushed, and knocked down. He went head-to-head with the fastest and most physical players on every opposing team. Lewis was always recovering from bruises, sprains, and abrasions that opponents planted on him each game. Lewis never complained, sometimes to the chagrin of a coaching staff that wanted to know when he was playing hurt or when to pick their spots in giving him a breather.[70]

Losses at Canisius and Siena, two of the toughest places to play in the league, were the only blemishes in the remaining weeks of the regular season. The Huskies issued harsh receipts in their rematches with Canisius and Siena, beating them by 33 and 23 respectively. Against Siena, Lewis went for 41 points as the crowd chanted "REG-GIE" throughout the second half.[71] Northeastern clinched its third consecutive NAC regular-season title by bombing BU, 90–70, at Matthews. Andre LaFleur had the offense running in particularly high gear that night, scoring 13 points and dishing out 9 assists. Despite defenders clinging to him all evening, Reggie Lewis managed 28 points while the frequently open John Williams added 24.

As the season came toward an end, talk of Reggie Lewis leaving early as a hardship case resurfaced. NBA scouts were comparing his size and game to that of George Gervin and talking him up as a number one pick. But Reggie Lewis was having none of it, making his intention to stay in school known.[72] "I'll be here next year. I knew I was going to be here for four years to get an education. I know I won't be able to play basketball forever," Lewis said in February 1986. He conceded that he considered entering the draft after winning Conference Player of the Year as a sophomore, but Coach Calhoun had encouraged him to stay to do more weight training and work on his ball handling. Even if he was now ready for the NBA, Lewis wanted to finish his degree before pursuing his professional aspirations.[73]

Northeastern downed Vermont, 82–61, in the quarterfinals before a crowd of just 1,364 at Matthews. The game was most noteworthy for a scare with Reggie Lewis, who landed awkwardly on his left leg after throwing down a formidable dunk. Trainers determined it to be a strained patella tendon, and Lewis spent the game's last six minutes on the bench with ice wrapped around his knee.[74] Lewis played against Siena in the semifinals but started slowly. Eventually he warmed up into a 21-point, 15-rebound afternoon as Northeastern advanced to the conference finals against BU, who upset Canisius in the other semifinal.

The BU team Northeastern would face in the finals was young, focused, and hungry. Just as the Huskies reflected Calhoun, the 1985–1986 Terriers reflected their new coach, Northeastern alum Mike Jarvis. Northeastern had won convincingly in their two previous matchups that season, but there was something different about Mike Jarvis's Terriers. They were a disciplined team with a back-to-basics approach. Everything they did, they did well, especially play defense. Jarvis had been a defensive specialist in college and cultivated a sense of intensity on that side of the ball at every coaching stop. BU also had some very good players with veterans Tom Ivey, Paul Hendricks, and Dwayne Vinson; sophomore scoring machine Drederick Irving; and freshmen point guards Tony DaCosta and Jeff Timberlake. Coming into the league championship game at Matthews, BU had won eleven of its last thirteen games. Their only losses came to the Huskies. "Part of the problem [against Northeastern] is our kids get too emotionally high for that game. That's what happened the last time. But there's such a pride factor involved. It's almost like [they're] playing for their manhood," Jarvis said after BU's second loss to Northeastern that season.[75]

Though Calhoun and Jarvis hadn't been close in recent years, there was clearly a mutual respect between the coaches. From Calhoun's perspective things were certainly very different coaching against a master tactician and motivator like Jarvis than they'd been the two previous years against Kuester. "John [Kuester] was very low key. They had good talent but they just didn't play as hard. Once John came, boom! It just let all the air out of the balloon," Calhoun said at the time.[76]

The Huskies would find out how different things were that Saturday afternoon in front of a full house at Matthews and a regional television audience on NESN. Led by defensive specialist Peter Gabriele, BU held a still sore Reggie Lewis in check for most of the first half, trailing by just 1 at the break. The rest of the Huskies picked up the slack. Wes Fuller, who always shone brightest in the biggest games, pulled down 16 rebounds and scored 11 while contributing to the defensive effort against Drederick Irving, who was held to 12 points. Andre LaFleur (14 points) and John Williams (16 points) both had strong offensive performances as the Huskies chipped away at BU's defensive foundations. Northeastern won, 63–54, in a game that was much closer than its final tally.[77]

The victory sent Northeastern to its fifth NCAA Tournament in six seasons. Despite losing just four games. Despite featuring one of the country's most exciting players. Despite Northeastern's track record in March, the tournament committee slapped NU with a thirteen seed. The Huskies were headed to the Greensboro Coliseum for a matchup with the fourth-seeded Oklahoma University (OU) Sooners.

Oklahoma won twenty-five games in the 1985–1986 season, averaged nearly 89 points per game and had appeared in the Elite Eight the previous season. Much like Northeastern, Oklahoma played fast and physical basketball, but you wouldn't have known that about the Huskies from talking to OU's head coach, Billy Tubbs, who described the hard-charging Northeastern Huskies as a "slow down team." His players shared his lack of familiarity with their first-round adversary. OU guard Anthony Bowie thought they were playing Northeastern Louisiana, a Sooners opponent in previous seasons. The Sooners seemed less focused on their opponent and more concerned that shooting guard Tim McCallister, an 18-points-per-night man, had been suspended for the first round after throwing ice at an official during the Big 8 Tournament.[78]

Northeastern shot the ball atrociously against Oklahoma, hitting just 37 percent of their shots that afternoon. Tubbs blanketed Reggie Lewis with defenders and hammered him on numerous occasions. Lewis went 11 for 13 from the line but just 12 of 34 shooting on the night, missing many of those shots late in the second half. Wes Fuller got into double figures with 11 points, but Calhoun could find few other reliable targets for Andre LaFleur's passes. Six different Huskies had at least four fouls and spent significant time on the bench. John Williams fouled out with close to eight minutes remaining in the game. Kevin McDuffie and Gerry Corcoran would also be banished. Nevertheless, Northeastern hung tight with the Sooners.[79]

"Shooting doesn't always travel. But speed does. Rebounding does. And our style of play was built upon something. The things that we did were tangible things that you could grab a hold of. Rebounding. We were one of the better rebounding teams in the country. Shot blocking. We had great athletes who could get up there. Fast breaks. Possessions were important to us. I think our team was built to be good any place, not just at home," Calhoun said.[80]

Against the Sooners, Northeastern did all those tangible things well. The Huskies beat a much bigger Oklahoma team on the boards, 43–39. Reggie Lewis grabbed several of his own shots on a 15-rebound day. Andre LaFleur (3 steals) and Wes Fuller (2 steals) harassed Bowie and company all game, while Gerry Corcoran played a gutsy twenty-two minutes off the bench, scoring 6 points and snagging 6 rebounds. The Huskies led for much of the first half, but foul trouble forced Calhoun to wade deep into his bench. Oklahoma ended the half on an 11–2 run and took a 32–31 lead on a 35-foot buzzer-beater by Bowie. Northeastern made enough timely baskets and timely stops in the second half to find themselves within 2, 74–72, with less than two minutes remaining. A controversial fifth foul call on Corcoran sent Sooners center David Johnson to the line, where he gave Oklahoma 2 more points' worth of breathing room. Northeastern never got any closer, falling in the end, 80–74.[81]

In defeat, Calhoun was dejected, focusing on the tough spot the tournament selection committee put his team in every March despite their hard-earned reputation on the court. "I was talking with the chairman of the selection committee and he said we would have been better off with three or four more losses but against the real strong teams," Calhoun said.[82] He planned to spend the next week seeking out such opponents for the Huskies next season, which would be Lewis's, LaFleur's, and Fuller's last one on Huntington Avenue.[83] As it turned out, Calhoun had just coached his last game at Northeastern.

Truly a Team of Character *(Pitino)*

"BU was my first visit," Karl Lehman said. Lehman had been a Five-Star kid, a heavily recruited 6'8" power forward from just north of Cincinnati. Tennessee, Virginia Tech, and Dayton all came calling, but Lehman felt immediately at home at Boston University.[1] "Coach [Pitino] was pretty straightforward," Lehman recalled. "He said, 'I'll be honest with you. I'm a pretty hardball coach. There's going to be days when you want to hug my neck and days when you want to punch my mouth. If you can live with that, I'd like you to come.'"[2]

"What I saw was a team that was really a team," Lehman said. "All those guys really hung out together. When I came in, they were like, 'Hey, we're glad to have you here. We need you. We're trying to build a winning reputation.' I really saw the camaraderie and a team that really liked hanging out."[3] BU's team was also a genuinely integrated team where white players and Black players formed close bonds of affection. Conversely, Lehman found on other campus visits that his suitors placed him with white, suburban players for the weekend. It seemed like white and Black players on some teams led parallel lives while inhabiting the same roster.[4] To this day, the young men who played for Pitino at Boston University remain an incredibly tight group, a cadre of men in their late fifties and sixties with a shared set of intense experiences that have bound them together for life.

Karl Lehman became a Terrier in the fall of 1981 as BU basketball looked to bounce back from a down season. The *Globe*'s Lesley Visser, the only writer who, according to Pitino, gave his BU program the time of day, picked the Terriers third in the ECAC North, behind Holy Cross and Northeastern. She described BU as "deceptively bad" in 1980–1981. Visser expected Gary Plummer to emerge as a force in the middle, alongside BU frontcourt veterans Arturo Brown and John Teague. BU's deep backcourt of Tony

Simms, Brett Brown, Johnny Ray Wall, and Gene Jones would be aided further in the second semester by the return of Pancho Bingham, who would, hopefully, regain his eligibility.[5]

The 1981–1982 team picked senior John Teague and junior Brett Brown as their co-captains. The selection of Teague was no surprise. Despite being undersized in the low post, John Teague competed with an intensity and physicality few could match. He asserted his presence on the floor with every ounce of his chiseled physique. Teammates admired his work ethic, his intelligence on and off the court, and the way he led by example, even from his earliest days at BU. Teague's selection as team captain was the culmination of a substantial college basketball career. It was an honor and a responsibility befitting this building block of Rick Pitino's program.

Teague's senior year was also a special one for him in another way. His brother, Shawn, a highly recruited 6'2" guard who spent his freshman year at Missouri, transferred to BU. While Shawn took classes at BU in 1981–1982 and sat out the transfer year, the brothers competed with a uniquely fraternal intensity in practice. When teamed up in intersquad scrimmages, the Teague brothers were an unstoppable force. "In practice, the coach would literally have to separate us because between the two of us we would literally eat everybody up," John Teague said.[6]

On first glance, junior Brett Brown's selection as co-captain may have been surprising. Brown's role on the floor was not well established until his sophomore year, when he took over point guard duties on the team. Despite BU's struggles during Brown's sophomore season of 1980–1981, the Maine native grew rapidly into one of the team's on-court and off-court leaders. A quintessential coach's son, Brown excelled at the game's fundamentals, especially his footwork, dribbling, and foul shooting. He developed an emotional intelligence about the game, too, learning how to tempo an offense, respond to the hot and cold streaks that make up a game, and restrain his impulse to shoot-shoot-shoot from the top of the key, a lesson he had learned from a head coach who'd come to understand the same thing over the course of his college career. "He [Brett Brown] knew the game better than anybody did. He took charges. He just knew how to play. And he was incredibly quick," Glenn Consor said.[7] "We used to call [Brett] 'White Lightning' because for a Caucasian kid, this dude was awful quick," said John Teague, who also remembers Brown as one of the team's funniest guys.[8]

While the likes of Tony Simms and Arturo Brown were no longer secrets in New England basketball circles, sophomore center Gary Plummer seemed like the Terrier poised to have a breakout season. Plummer had a surprisingly muted freshman campaign but, by all indications, appeared on the verge of something special. Pitino made a point of boosting Plummer in his preseason comments to reporters. "If he keeps on improving the way he has, Gary's going to make himself some money playing this game," Pitino said two days before the Terriers' home opener.[9] Ever the psychologist, Pitino built Plummer's confidence up with encouragement, having seen how the reassurances of teammates helped Plummer work through early struggles as a freshman. This tactic differed considerably from Pitino's approach to his first great scorer, Steve Wright. Pitino had essentially frightened Wright into reaching his potential as a player.

In the opener against St. Francis, Plummer put in a workmanlike 12 points while grabbing 8 rebounds in an 87–76 win. The 6'9" sophomore was one of five Terriers to reach double figures on the evening, foreshadowing the depth of BU's offensive output in 1981–1982. Jay Twyman, who came off the bench for a game-high 21 points, was one of five Terriers (along with Plummer, Simms, Teague, and Arturo Brown) who averaged more than 10 points per game on the season.

Plummer broke out in game two, throwing down 23 points in a blowout win over Delaware State. Two nights later Twyman again led the way with 21 points in a 91–65 annihilation of UMass. Now 3-0, BU traveled to Storrs shorthanded. Tony Simms suffered a hamstring injury against Delaware State that nagged him for the rest of the season. It cost him three straight games, including the trip to UConn. The Terriers hung tight with the Huskies in the early going, trailing by just 5 at the break, but the hometown team took control in the second half. UConn forced BU into cluster after cluster of bad shots and cruised to a 73–54 win.

The Terriers got past Drexel at home before heading out to the West Coast for a date with college basketball's most prestigious program. Ten-time national champion UCLA was several years removed from its title runs under John Wooden but remained a formidable program. The Bruins had been national runners-up in 1980 and were ranked in the top twenty early in the 1981–1982 season under new head coach Larry Farmer. A hobbled Tony Simms returned for the matchup at Pauley Pavilion, but the Terriers were no match for UCLA. The Bruins buried Pitino's team in a "scheduled loss," 77–43.

"I'm a kid who grew up loving John Wooden. My heroes were Kareem Abdul-Jabbar and Bill Walton, and we're playing in Pauley Pavilion," Karl Lehman recalled. Several years into his tenure at BU, Pitino still got his players to buy into the significance of these non-conference games against national powers. "We were excited about it and we knew we'd probably get our butts handed to us, but we knew it was going to help us be better in the long run," Lehman said.[10]

It didn't take the Terriers long to recover. In the days of Auld Lange Syne, they won three out of four, improving their record to 7-3 by the start of the second semester. With Simms still worse for wear, BU relied on the leadership of captains John Teague and Brett Brown, the emerging offensive prowess of Gary Plummer, and the versatility of Arturo Brown, who made obvious contributions as a scorer and rebounder while disrupting opposing offenses with his speed and length. "He [Arturo Brown] was just a freak as far as jumping ability. The game was in slow motion for him," Jay Twyman said.[11] Brown's vertical was measured at 36 inches. He could also run a mile in under five minutes. Now a junior, Arturo Brown, the team's leading rebounder as a sophomore, led the team in both scoring and rebounding in the 1981–1982 season.

"Artie was a close friend. He was humble, and he was an awesome player," Gene Jones said.[12] Arturo Brown had every reason not to be humble. He was the embodiment of everything that's great about college sports—a serious student who took advantage of the educational and personal opportunities his athletic skills opened to him. Brown was born into poverty in Panama. He migrated with his family to the United States at age thirteen with his mother, two sisters, a younger brother, and, later, his father. They settled into a hardscrabble existence in one of Brooklyn's toughest neighborhoods.

Arturo saw basketball for the first time not long before his family moved to America. He soon became infatuated with the sport. Brown grew to 6'6" and became a star at Brooklyn basketball powerhouse Nazareth High School. Though less highly recruited than his teammate Stewart Granger, Brown earned plenty of attention from scouts during his All-City senior season. He chose Boston University because of the school's excellent academic record and his connection to former Nazareth coach and current BU assistant Bill Burke. Brown never regretted the choice of BU over big-time programs like Syracuse and Virginia. He found a home in Boston. "Since I've started playing basketball, there's been no other team closer than BU's. They're like my brothers," Brown told the BU *Daily Free Press*.[13]

Brown neither drank nor smoked. He studied with the same diligence he played basketball, making himself a regular on the dean's list in the School of Management. Despite studying for a career in finance, Brown dreamed of a career in the NBA so that he could afford to move his mother out of their two-room Brooklyn apartment and into a home of her own. In the off-season, Brown worked at Faneuil Hall so he could send money back to his mother in New York.[14] In 1979, Brown had played for the Panamanian basketball team in the Pan-Am Games and had been selected to play on Team Panama as they competed for a spot in the 1984 Summer Olympics. In March 1982, he was one of ten players named to the ECAC District I All-Star team, literally an all-star team of all-star teams from conferences across the Northeast.

Even if BU's basketball stars remained relatively anonymous on campus, the Case and Walter Brown faithful reserved some of their loudest cheers for Brown, who wowed with fierce slam dunks that showed off his natural athleticism, as well as the power he'd developed in BU's weight room, which was top-notch, thanks to the investments John Simpson had been able to secure for Terrier athletics.[15] BU basketball also had its own locker room and training room. The team benefitted further from the presence of BU's esteemed Sergeant School for Physical Therapy on campus.[16]

Once fall semester grades came out, Pancho Bingham, too, returned to the fold. Bingham made notable contributions for BU down the stretch. He played in twenty-one games, starting four while averaging roughly sixteen minutes, six 6 points, and a steal per contest. Nevertheless, the fit between Bingham and the BU program proved less than ideal. Bingham was notably self-assured and something of a loner, an untenable combination on a team where togetherness and self-sacrifice were cardinal virtues.

"He [Bingham] had problems with Pitino because he wanted to do things his way, and Coach Pitino had his way. There was a clash of personalities," John Teague said.[17] "One day in practice, he [Bingham] just didn't want it anymore," Glen Bressner recalls. "Late in practice, we were sent outside to run a mile in freezing weather. When we got back, Pancho just said,

'I'm done.' He took a basketball, threw it from one end of the court to the other, and just left."[18] Eventually Bingham made a triumphant comeback at the college level, becoming one of the country's best guards in the National Association of Intercollegiate Athletics (NAIA) and a genuine team leader at Lander College in South Carolina. A knee injury late in Bingham's senior year derailed his shot at a professional career.

On January 12, 1982, 7-3 BU traveled to Worcester and beat Holy Cross for the first time in eight years. Arturo Brown and Tony Simms both pumped in 22 points as a healthy BU team topped the Crusaders, 96–82, in a game the Terriers controlled throughout. As was often the case, the Terriers' suffocating defense prompted their lightning-fast offensive attack. Pitino had taken to calling his team the "Kamikaze Kids," an homage to Dick Harter's Oregon teams that adopted the same nickname during the 1970s. The label was rarely more fitting than on that night in Worcester when BU forced the Crusaders into 27 turnovers.

The momentum from the Holy Cross win proved short-lived as Iona came into Walter Brown and put on a shooting clinic the following Saturday night, hitting nearly 60 percent of their shots from the field in a 77–68 win. The defeat snapped a seven-game home winning streak for BU, which had developed quite a home-court advantage despite meagre attendance. This proved particularly to be the case at Walter Brown, which was a consistently miserable place to play for both home and away teams.

"I preferred playing in Case. It was a more intimate setting. It was where we practiced, so there was a lot of familiarity with the rims," Jay Twyman said.[19]

"I preferred Case because it was closer to the fans. It was warmer. Sometimes if you go down to Walter Brown and nobody's down there, it's freezing," Desmond Martin said.[20]

"At Walter Brown, they put a portable floor on top of a hockey rink. They'd crank up the heat, but the temperature in there was probably in the fifties. It was not a shooter's gym either. You had the big, dark background," Jay Twyman remembered.[21]

"Playing on an artificial floor, you're going to have dead spots. You're going to have condensation. It [Walter Brown] didn't have the lift like Case Center did. You're playing on ice," Desmond Martin said.[22]

"When you were down on the ice rink, the floor was cold and there were slippery spots. And it exposed the fact that there weren't a whole lot of fans at times. You'd see these gaps in the floor. It [Walter Brown] wasn't really hospitable as far as basketball because everybody was so far away," John Teague said.[23]

Wednesday, January 20, 1982 was not a good day for BU basketball. The school ruled Gary Plummer academically ineligible for the rest of the term. Plummer apologized in tears to his teammates and spent the remainder of the season sitting dutifully at the end of the bench in a blazer. The evening of the 20th was even worse. A crowd of just four hundred at Walter Brown watched BU fall, 69–67, to conference rival Niagara. Without Plummer's presence, Pitino exaggerated his full-court press even further but failed to shut down the Purple Eagles' outstanding tandem of Mike Phillips and James Speaks, who combined for 40 points. In a game laden with lead changes, Niagara came up with several clutch rebounds and hit clutch foul shots down the stretch to secure the win.[24] "Against Pitino you had to handle his full-court press. Then you'd have a chance," Niagara coach Pete Lonergan recalled.[25] Lonergan's teams were uniformly tough, disciplined, and well prepared, creating a perennial matchup problem for Pitino's clubs, which convinced less-disciplined opponents to match BU's freewheeling style of play.

Pitino was in no mood in defeat. He blamed the loss on the "devastating blow" of Gary Plummer's absence. Niagara asserted its will in the low post all evening. Despite his angst about Plummer's ineligibility, Pitino offered no criticism of the decision. Pitino's supervisor, John Simpson, also refused to weigh in, saying the decision was an academic one beyond the jurisdiction of the athletic department. Pitino weighed in instead on another subject: the lack of fan support his team received from the BU community.[26]

"I've had it. I'm sick of working 18 hours a day to coach in front of a CYO crowd. We beat Holy Cross last week in one of the biggest wins in school history and I have to go around stuffing student mailboxes with coupons for the game," Pitino said. "I know what it's like to play in front of crowds. BU isn't ready for basketball and its tragic. Everyone just blames campus apathy. Well look at BC and look at Northeastern. This isn't the 1950s. This is 1982 and kids in college care about basketball."[27] His comments did not go unnoticed. "Petulant Rick Pitino's complaint about BU's basketball apathy is puzzling to one who remembers the packed gyms there during the coaching regimes of Matt Zunic and John Burke," veteran *Globe* sportswriter Ernie Roberts opined.[28]

Unsubstantiated talk of Pitino's impending resignation made it onto the sports report of multiple local evening newscasts. BU president John Silber mocked Pitino's comments, stating, "I guess we're not Texas Aggies." Silber, a native Texan, knew full well that the Aggies were at Texas A&M and his former employers at the University of Texas were the Longhorns. But the dismissive remark indicated where basketball attendance stood in Silber's mind as an issue of concern on his campus. Rah Rah and Ballyhoo were the stuff of cow colleges, populated by "Aggies."[29]

For the remainder of the season, commentary on Pitino's comments became the frame of reference for any coverage BU basketball received in the local press. Litigating the merits of Pitino's offhand assertion got more attention than the fine season the young Terriers team enjoyed on the basketball court. On campus, the *Daily Free Press* interrogated the subject from every possible angle. One such article featured man-on-the-street interviews with students who purported not to even know the name of the school's mascot. "No one on campus is familiar with the competition. They don't know the difference between playing Vermont and North Carolina. So when BU plays a nationally known team, no one cares," Paul Rachman, a senior from New York City, said, quite astutely.[30]

If nothing else, Pitino's outburst got the Terriers some much needed attention. On Saturday night, BU drew over one thousand fans as the Terriers pummeled Vermont, 85–67. Arturo Brown led the way with 22 points, while Tony Simms pumped in 20 and dished out 10 assists. A second-half alley-oop from Brett Brown to John Teague brought down the larger-than-usual house at Case.[31]

Now 9-5, BU's next contest was their annual confrontation with Northeastern, an event whose profile grew every year. At the time, 12-3 Northeastern sat atop the ECAC North, with Canisius second and BU third. The Terriers would be traveling over to Northeastern Arena this time, facing a Huskies team led by senior Perry Moss, who was averaging better than 22 points per game. Northeastern's board-crashing frontcourt was the architecture around which Moss generated his diverse offensive output. While BU could throw a cadre of "Kamikaze Kids" at Moss to try to slow him down, the Gary Plummer-less Terriers came in clearly shorthanded in their efforts on the glass.[32]

The 3,340 fans in attendance got more than the classic breakneck, back-and-forth, claustrophobic contest that had become the signature of the series. The January 27, 1982 edition of BU-Northeastern was much rougher than its predecessors in the shared Pitino-Calhoun era, setting the tone for the frequent fisticuffs that punctuated the rivalry for the rest of the decade. Just five minutes into the game, Pancho Bingham traded punches with Northeastern's Eric Jefferson. Huskies captain Dave Leitao intervened with a fist to Bingham's jaw. Only Bingham and Jefferson were ejected in what turned out to be the first of two bench-clearing brawls. Leitao returned a few minutes later with a taped-up hand. In all, officials handed out five technicals that evening. There were several other breaks in the action to extinguish skirmishes between opposing players. "After the second or third scuffle broke out," BU's Ed McGrath recalls, "I'm sitting like ten seats down from [Northeastern SID] Jack Grinold, and I throw back my chair, take off my coat, and I'm like, 'Come on, Jack,'" McGrath said, raising his fists and laughing.[33]

At the time of the first skirmish BU held a 10-9 advantage. From that moment onward Brett Brown and John Teague shepherded the Terrier attack. Brown scored a career-high 21 points and commandeered the BU press and fast break into an all-out assault on the Huskies. John Teague had a career night against Northeastern, outbattling All-ECAC center Halsel and company on the way to a 22-point, 9 rebound game. On the offensive end, Northeastern got little going besides Perry Moss, who was unbelievable as always, scoring a game-high 34 points. Boston University left Huntington Avenue with an 82–64 blowout win over their archrival.[34]

"John Teague just morphed into being 6'9" or 6'10". He had a lot of dunks that night," Jay Twyman remembers.[35] At one point, Brett Brown lobbed an in-bounds pass toward the rim that John Teague threw down for a vicious dunk. "I dunked it, and the fans ran onto the court," John Teague recalls. "Somebody ran onto the court from our bench. When they saw who it was, it was my brother [Shawn Teague]. They were issuing technicals, and Pitino turns to the ref and says, 'He's not with us,' so they escorted my brother out of the gym, leaving him out in the snow because the bus driver was inside. When we came out afterward, my brother is standing outside with all this snow in his hair, and I had just had one of the games of my life."[36]

BU built on the momentum of the Northeastern game and pounded nemesis Wagner, 89–70, on its Staten Island home floor before losing the last game on their road trip, a return visit to Old Dominion. The absence of Gary Plummer shown through at the Norfolk Scope, as Mark West dominated BU on the inside in a 71–61 win.

Back at Walter Brown, attendance returned to the mean. Only 502 people watched Arturo Brown pour in 30 points as BU blazed past Farleigh Dickinson, 99–82, in a game that the *Globe* described as "playground ball." When asked about the attendance, Pitino said he expected the home date against Metro Conference power Cincinnati to draw an excellent crowd.[37]

The excellent crowd Pitino hoped BU would draw for the University of Cincinnati (UC) turned out to be 1,525 fans. The game was broadcast on Cincinnati-area television on WXIX for the Bearcats' rabid fanbase. Cincinnati was a young, rebuilding team but was also much larger than BU, boasting a physical front line that was all at least 6'8". The February 1982 BU-UC matchup was the return date from the 102–82 beatdown Boston University had taken at Riverfront Coliseum the previous January. The game in Cincinnati had been particularly memorable for hometown kid Jay Twyman, who was not only returning to his old stomping grounds but also playing against the school where his NBA Hall of Famer father, Jack, had been a legend. The Twymans hosted the team at their home the night before the game. While the game had not gone especially well for BU, it had been a fantastic evening for Twyman, who scored a career-high 29 points. The evening was equally memorable for a couple of his teammates, though not in so pleasant a manner.

"When we played at Cincinnati, we were waiting for the bus in the hotel lobby at 5 o'clock," Twyman recalled. "At 5:01, here comes Brett Brown and Dan Harwood, running through the lobby to meet the bus. Rick [Pitino] looks at them like, 'What the hell?' We go to the game, play the game, lose the game. It was a blizzard. We're showering after the game. Everybody gets on the bus. Brett and Dan start to get on the bus. 'No,' Pitino says, 'you guys are running behind the bus on the way back to the hotel.' There we are, everybody on the bus except Brett and Danny. It was about a mile and a half they had to run through the snowstorm back to the hotel."[38]

The BU-UC rematch was different from its predecessor in every respect. The first game had been a high-scoring track-meet-turned-blowout played in front of a jam-packed arena. The second game was a grinding, low-scoring, back-and-forth contest played in front of a half-empty hockey rink. Cincinnati muddled to an early second-half lead before Johnny Ray

Wall broke out, scoring three straight baskets to give BU a 38–33 advantage. Cincinnati hung tough, thanks in large part to point guard Bobby Austin, who scored 16 points, including a pair of free throws late in regulation that sent the game to overtime, tied at 48. After a slow-down, slog of a pre-shot-clock overtime, BU and Cincinnati were tied at 50 when the Terriers took possession with nine seconds remaining. John Teague got the ball to Jay Twyman near the top of the key. Finding no one open, Twyman dribbled to the baseline and popped in a game-winning 10-footer with longtime friend Bobby Austin practically hanging from him.[39] "He [Pitino] called a play off the pick, I got it, ball-faked him [Austin], took one dribble, and made the shot," Twyman remembered.[40]

Twyman's teammates mobbed him as the final buzzer sounded. Pitino described the win as more "nationally significant" than their earlier victory over Holy Cross, which he regarded as having a lower national profile than the multi-time national champion Bearcats.[41] "Everybody back home [in Cincinnati] thinks I go to Boston College. Now maybe they won't make the mistake of calling us Boston College now that we've beaten them," Twyman said after the game.[42]

BU's erratic side showed up the next time out in an 88–83 loss to little-heralded U.S. International University, a virtually anonymous San Diego—based college that played almost all its games on the road. Tony Simms suffered a brand-new calf injury that night, which cost him the remainder of the regular season. Four other BU players fouled out of the game, providing the Gulls with plenty of free throws and significantly narrowing Pitino's rotation. After the loss, Pitino could be heard berating his team on the sideline. The phrase "You disgust me" stood out to the assembled reporters.[43]

Pitino could hardly be disgusted by BU's performance in their next string of games. BU ripped off consecutive wins over George Mason, UNH, and Maine to improve their record to 16-7 and take first place heading into a crucial league contest against Canisius. During this stretch of February games, reports surfaced in the New York sports press that Big East doormat Seton Hall was considering Pitino for its head coaching vacancy. Pitino quelled these rumors by signing a three-year extension. Instead, Wagner's P. J. Carlesimo, a frequent BU nemesis, accepted the job in East Orange.[44]

Second-place Canisius entered the contest with an impressive 16-6 record but was coming off a blowout loss to Northeastern the previous night. The Griffins were led by arguably the conference's most explosive backcourt, which featured senior Phil Seymore, one of the league's most accurate shooters, and freshman sensation "Sugar" Ray Hall, an explosive 6'4" guard who had turned down offers from more prominent programs to stay home in Buffalo.

"You had to be prepared for the trip to BU and Northeastern or else you were going to lose two," Canisius coach Nick Macarchuk recalled. "Not only did you have to be ready for the basketball. You [also] had to be ready to go to Boston because you were going to be there for three nights with all of the distractions there."[45] For both Canisius and Niagara, the annual trip to Boston was a major event on the athletic department's calendar. Canisius held large alumni gatherings at the swank Hotel Lenox in Boston's Back Bay that were not only a major social gathering, but also integral to the school's fundraising and networking efforts.[46]

Rather than the anticipated shootout, the game turned into a plodding affair as BU went to a 2–3 zone and Canisius stayed with a purposeful man-to-man which kept either club from breaking out. Neither team led by more than 5 in the second half. Every time BU looked ready to take control, Sugar Ray Hall answered with a clutch jumper of his own. Canisius's Seymore knocked down a jump shot from the foul line to give the Griffins a 48–46 lead with five seconds remaining. Pitino called timeout and designed a play to get Gene Jones an open look from the corner. Jones's attempt to tie the game bounced in and out, giving Canisius a huge 48–46 road win at Walter Brown. The loss dropped BU to third in the conference standings, shoving it out of the driver's seat for home-court advantage in the tournament.[47] "Not having Gary Plummer and Tony Simms definitely hurt BU. Pitino has done a fantastic job with all the injuries he's had," Macarchuk said after the win.[48]

BU closed out the 1982 regular season at home by pounding C. W. Post, 85–57, and a now feeble Fairfield club, 76–56, improving the Terriers' record to 18-8 as they entered ECAC North tournament play. Ralph Groce, the 5'8" senior guard, a favorite of both teammates and the home crowd, put in the final basket in his home finale. Despite the wins, BU ended up falling to fourth in the ECAC North standings, behind Niagara, due to the quirky, uneven league scheduling in the fledgling conference. While BU was 6-2 in the ECAC North, Niagara was 7-2. The one bright spot was that Tony Simms had been cleared to play for the first time in nearly a month.

Fourth-seeded BU hosted fifth-seeded Holy Cross in the quarterfinals, fulfilling Pitino's long-stated wish to have the Crusaders visit Comm Ave for a game. This one had a much different feel than the 96–82 January track meet BU won in Worcester. In another grinding slow-down game, BU outlasted the Crusaders, 50–49, at Case. Arturo Brown led the Terriers to victory, playing all forty minutes and battling for 19 points and 9 rebounds in the come-from-behind win. A twelve-foot bank shot by Tony Simms gave BU the lead with six seconds remaining, and it proved to be just enough. Holy Cross, which had kept BU out of the NCAAs two years earlier, would not receive an NCAA or NIT bid for the first time since 1974. BU would be moving onto the semifinals against Northeastern.

More than three thousand fans, including a large BU contingent, greeted the Terriers across town at Northeastern Arena. The pace and performance of both teams in this ECAC semifinal looked a lot more like BU's recent games against Canisius and Holy Cross than the typical BU-Northeastern horse race. BU focused in on Perry Moss, putting the clamp down on NU's top scorer. The Terriers' backcourt harassed Moss, the ECAC Player of the Year, into his worst shooting night of the season. The senior guard's offensive woes were reflective of the difficulties both teams faced putting the ball in the basket. Neither club sniffed at 40 percent shooting. For the first thirty minutes of action, the game remained low scoring. Neither team ever led by more than 4.[49]

BU looked to be in charge with six minutes remaining when Arturo Brown heaved a baseball pass down court to Jay Twyman, who laid it in to give the Terriers a 48–40 lead. Then Perry Moss proved why he'd been named ECAC North Player of the Year. The senior captain posted 7 points in a 9–0 Huskies run to give Northeastern a 49–48 lead. BU held the ball in the game's closing minute, using two timeouts as Pitino tried to manufacture the best possible shot to win the game. With one second remaining, Tony Simms inbounded the ball from under the Northeastern net to Jay Twyman, BU's best shooter, who stood twenty feet from the rim. Moss vaulted over to Twyman and slapped his shot out of the air, giving Northeastern a 49–48 win. The Huskies would beat Niagara in the finals and return to the NCAA Tournament.[50]

"We outplayed them for 39 minutes and however many seconds. It's almost tragic that it had to end this way," Pitino said after the game.[51] Many in New England basketball circles were surprised that a 19-9 BU team was left out of the 1982 NIT. The committee instead went with 17-10 UConn, out of the more prestigious Big East, to represent the region. Connecticut was also a much better potential live draw. Often, the Huskies drew more than ten thousand fans to their games at either the Hartford Civic Center or New Haven Coliseum. Either way, Dom Perno's club didn't last long. They bowed out in the first round to Dayton.

Nevertheless, BU's 1981–1982 season had been a strikingly successful one. Considering the significant absences of both Gary Plummer and Tony Simms from the BU lineup, a 19-9 mark was awfully impressive. In Plummer's absence, BU posted an 11-5 record. Without Tony Simms, it still managed to stay above .500 at 6-5.

After a modest haul the previous year, Pitino brought in a larger recruiting class for fall 1982, one that boasted the most impressive credentials of any he'd yet brought to campus. In addition to sophomore transfer Shawn Teague, BU signed 6'9" Tom Ivey, who followed in Wally West's footsteps as the Terriers' next great big man from Chicagoland; Dwayne Vinson, a running and gunning 6'2" guard from Long Island's Malverne High, the alma mater of Rick Pitino's similarly talented college teammate, Al Skinner; and Mike Alexander, a sweet shooting 6'5" swingman from Washington DC basketball power DeMatha. BU also recruited a highly athletic 6'5" forward originally from the Virgin Islands named Paul Hendricks, who redshirted the 1982–1983 season after breaking his wrist.

"BU was coming to my practices in my senior year," Tom Ivey recalled. "The students knew the recruiters. They knew John Kuester. I'd see John Kuester sitting in the cafeteria, sitting in the hallway, hanging out with students. At that time, you could do that. I thought, 'Wow, this guy really wants me to come to Boston.'"[52] Ivey brought size, strength, and a high basketball IQ to the court. He'd learned about rebounding from Connie Hawkins at Five-Star and put that court knowledge to use from day one at Boston University.

"Dwayne [Vinson] was a 6'2" guy that played like [he was] 6'6". He was a great jumper with long arms. He had great hands and was a funny guy too," Jeff Holmes remembered.[53] Vinson proved almost immediately to be one of the best defenders on the team.

Pitino later said that the slightly built Mike Alexander would have been hotly recruited by the nation's top programs if he were twenty pounds heavier, a statement with which Alexander's high school coach, the legendary Morgan Wooten, agreed. Wooten described the 175-pounder as a "late bloomer." Despite leading a city champion DeMatha team in scoring, Alexander had never been a starter and was lightly recruited by everyone but Boston University. In many respects, Alexander's path to BU paralleled that of Reggie Lewis to Northeastern. Lewis also came off the bench throughout his high school career and led his team in scoring as a senior, playing for the equally heralded Dunbar High, just up I-95 in Baltimore.[54]

Adding this collection of talent to a BU roster that returned Arturo Brown, Tony Simms, Brett Brown, and Gary Plummer made the Terriers the prohibitive favorite in the league. Two-time defending ECAC North champs Northeastern would be in rebuild mode with the departures of Perry Moss, Eric Jefferson, and Dave Leitao in the now North Atlantic Conference. Pitino contributed to the renaming of the league in a fruitful bull session in the U.S. Air lounge at the Pittsburgh airport. Those present included Pitino, Canisius coach Nick Macarchuk, and Niagara's Pete Lonergan, who was also Niagara's athletic director and president of the ECAC North Conference. "We [Lonergan, Pitino, and Macarchuk] started saying, 'We've got to change that. We can't be the ECAC North. Who knows what that is?' So we fooled around with some names and we said, 'Why don't we call it the North Atlantic Conference? Because there's the Atlantic 10, and there's the Metro Atlantic, and there's the Atlantic Coast Conference. Maybe some of our recruits will think that we're one of them instead of what we really are,'" Lonergan recalls.[55] The name change soon won approval for the 1982–1983 season.

As the BU basketball team prepared for the inaugural season of NAC basketball, an unspeakable tragedy hit the Terriers program. In September 1982, the members of the BU basketball team held their typical "captain's practices," which amounted to intersquad scrimmages organized by the players rather than the coaches. On Friday, September 17, co-captains Arturo Brown and Brett Brown called for an afternoon practice and broke the players up into teams. In the midst of competition, Arturo Brown collapsed and stopped breathing. Brett Brown ran to the office to get trainers and assistant coach John Kuester, who performed mouth-to-mouth resuscitation while players summoned an ambulance and prayed. Brown arrived at the emergency room of Brigham and Women's Hospital at just after 6 p.m. He was pronounced dead at 6:40. The medical examiner later confirmed that he had died of a heart attack.[56] "No matter where I go, I have his picture on my wall in my office," Gene Jones said. Jones, who has gone on to a long and distinguished career as an educator and high school principal, was just starting his first teaching job in Norfolk, Virginia, when he got a call out of the blue from Brett Brown letting him know that Artie had died.[57]

Recently, Tom Ivey returned to Case for the first time in years as part of a college tour with his daughter. The visit brought up bittersweet memories when he ran into the building's longtime manager. "I told him who I was and when I played, and the first thing he said was, 'You were here when Arturo was here.' I said, 'Yeah, I was on the court.' And he took us upstairs to the court. We walked up the stairs, and you could just feel that same feeling. You could see the elevator they tried to put him in. It was tough," Ivey recalled.[58]

At Brown's memorial service at BU's Marsh Chapel, an inconsolable Pitino eulogized his twenty-one-year-old captain, describing him as a "perfect ten," a sentiment shared by everyone who knew him. More than 350 people attended the hour-long service, including university president John Silber and athletic director John Simpson.[59] Brown's body was flown home to Brooklyn for the funeral. More than forty current and former BU basketball players traveled to New York to honor him at the service.[60] "To be there [at the funeral], to see his family, to see his little brother, and know that he [Arturo Brown] was going to be an NBA player. It was heartbreaking," Karl Lehman said.[61] "If he hadn't passed away, I guarantee you he would have been a first-round pick," John Teague said.[62]

The BU Student Union set up a scholarship fund in Brown's memory.[63] Joe Rastellini, owner of T. Anthony's Pizzeria, the site of many pregame and postgame meals for BU basketball players, coaches, and fans, set up a fund to help support Brown's mother and siblings.[64] Rick Pitino, too, with no fanfare or public mention provided support for Arturo Brown's family in subsequent years, as he did for several people in the BU basketball family long after he left Commonwealth Avenue.

Following Arturo Brown's funeral, BU returned to their dogged preparation for the upcoming season. Despite the loss of their best and most beloved player (who was almost certainly the best returning college player in New England), BU was still picked to win the North Atlantic Conference by the *Globe*. The combination of BU's veteran cast of Brett

Brown, Tony Simms, and Gary Plummer with highly touted newcomers like Mike Alexander and Shawn Teague gave the Terriers a leg up on rebuilding Holy Cross and Northeastern teams as well as youthful rivals at Canisius and Niagara.[65] "It wasn't 'Let's do it for Arturo' because we knew we could play. We knew we had this unique talent. It was the hand of Arturo bonding us closer together," Tom Ivey said.[66]

A heavy-hearted BU basketball team began the 1982–1983 season just two months after Arturo Brown's death, still hopeful that they could have a spectacular season. It didn't start well. A bigger, stronger Purdue team manhandled BU at Walter Brown in the regular-season opener. The Terriers then traveled to Syracuse for the Carrier Classic and lost both games, falling by 1 to Princeton and by 2 to Alcorn State. Both of their opponents at the Carrier Dome ended up making the NCAA Tournament. BU beat Siena at home before falling, 51–50, in a 41-turnover trudge of a game against Connecticut. Just 966 people made it out to see BU take on a regional rival who had made it to the NCAAs or NIT in each of the four previous seasons. After the game, the *Globe*'s Barry Cardigan asked Pitino if he thought the poor attendance that evening was the result of going head-to-head with the much anticipated, nationally televised Virginia-Georgetown matchup featuring Ralph Sampson and Patrick Ewing. "It wouldn't be any different if the President was getting elected," Pitino said. "This is our crowd."[67]

Attendance remained a headache for BU in 1982–1983, despite all the attention and success the program had achieved over the four previous seasons under Pitino. On several occasions BU drew fewer than five hundred fans that season, including a home date against Vermont with a published attendance of three hundred. Senior captain Brett Brown even penned a late January editorial in the campus newspaper, simply encouraging his fellow students to give a basketball game a try.[68]

One of the three hundred souls in attendance at the Vermont game was the Reverend Robert Thornburg, dean of BU's Marsh Chapel and an ordained Methodist minister. Standing 6'5" but never a basketball player, Thornburg had come to the now largely secular campus in 1978 to play the most prominent spiritual role at an institution that had, in the nineteenth century, been the castle keep of Methodism in the northern United States. Thornburg had little association with the BU basketball program until the afternoon Arturo Brown collapsed at Case. Police summoned Thornburg, who soon joined the basketball team at the hospital. For hours Thornburg remained, praying, keeping vigil, learning about Arturo Brown, and finally mourning his loss alongside the team. For the entire season, Thornburg maintained close contact with Pitino and the basketball team, attending every BU home game, while Pitino and many players attended his Sunday sermons. Thornburg always sat at midcourt, as close as he could get to the floor. He was the loudest person at every Terriers game, a reputation he maintained for the next thirty years. Thornburg attended virtually every BU basketball game between 1982 and his death in 2013.[69]

Suddenly 1-4, Boston University responded by tearing through its next five opponents, ending 1982 and beginning 1983 with a string of mostly blowout victories. By the time BU started league play at Northeastern on January 25, the Terriers were back above .500. On defense Pitino developed an unpredictable streak, playing far more zone than he had in previous seasons to make use of the newfound size in his lineup. A different offensive dynamic emerged as well. Throughout Pitino's tenure at BU, the Terriers relied on a lot of different players making solid contributions on the offensive end. Oftentimes, seven, eight, or even nine players averaged at least 5 points a game for BU teams that averaged 80 or more points per game. BU's offensive output had not diminished. For the 1982–1983 season, BU again averaged nearly 80 points per game and finished twenty-first in the country in scoring.

This time, though, it was a trio of scorers who produced the majority of the team's points. For the season, Tony Simms, Gary Plummer, and Mike Alexander all averaged better than 16 points per game. Alexander's emergence was particularly striking as he replaced Arturo Brown in the starting lineup and unquestionably rose to the challenge. The freshman played away from the basket far more often than Brown and became a gunner who lurked on the wing, always on the lookout for a chance to score.

At point guard, Shawn Teague became the primary starter, offering more length and athleticism than Brett Brown while still displaying top-notch play-making ability. Brett Brown continued to be a major contributor on both ends of the floor, playing close to twenty minutes per game while typically coming off the bench. Another lineup shift that paid notable dividends was the replacement of Mark Fiedor at center with freshman Tom Ivey, who was a superior rebounder. The combination of Ivey and Plummer in the low post made BU a more competitive team defensively down in the blocks.[70]

The trip to Northeastern's St. Botolph Street arena, now renamed Matthews, went exceedingly well for BU. The Terriers ran Northeastern out of the gym in a 104–86 victory. In a game punctuated by a Gary Plummer—Roland Braswell scuffle, as well as a Jim Calhoun technical, BU blew things wide open late in the first half. Northeastern trailed by 17 at the break and never again got it closer than 13. Tony Simms (30), Mike Alexander (27), and Gary Plummer (23) combined for 80 points in BU's first 100-point outing in three seasons.[71] BU hammered Cleveland State and Colgate to finish January 1983 at 9-5 overall and 2-0 in the league. Next on the agenda was the first of many BU long weekends in Buffalo.

And a long one it was. It began on Thursday night at Niagara's Gallagher Center, a 2,400-seat gymnasium where the distinction between court and stands was virtually nonexistent. While Pete Lonergan's Purple Eagles had struggled in the early stretches of the 1982–1983 season, Niagara was a fearsome force in front of its always bellowing partisans. In this chaotically intimate setting, a Niagara team that featured only one senior rose to the occasion, forcing BU into foul after foul around the rim. Niagara led by 10 with less than eight minutes remaining, but BU battled back and eventually tied the game.[72] "We score and go up one with about eight seconds to go," Niagara coach Pete Lonergan recalls. "Brett [Brown] gets the ball and goes straight to the basket. People go to jail for less than we did to Brett Brown. But there's no whistle. Pitino runs by me, gives me like a slap instead of shaking my hand 'cause he's chasing the officials to their dressing room at the Gallagher Center. He's pounding on the door, 'Get out here! I'll kick your ass!' All I could do was laugh and think, 'Oh Ricky, you'll learn.'"[73]

BU had little time to lick its wounds from its 76–75 loss in Niagara Falls. On Saturday night, the Terriers faced Canisius at "The Aud," Buffalo's Works Progress Administration—built Memorial Auditorium, an eighteen-thousand-seat venue that was way too large for the roughly 2,800 fans in attendance that evening. Canisius, who remained a strong program throughout the 1980s, had the perennial problem of not knowing whether to schedule games in the Koessler Center, its tiny on-campus gym, or the massive "Aud." In this instance, fans in attendance at the massive venue got to see Sugar Ray Hall put on a show, ripping BU's defense for 30 points in a 74–64 Griffins victory. Canisius's defense also forced BU into 18 first-half turnovers in a game whose outcome was clear for most of the second half.[74]

In the aftermath of the lost weekend in Buffalo, BU basketball created a brief hubbub by declaring its intentions to leave the NAC. Holy Cross had already announced its plans to leave for the New York—centric Metro Atlantic Conference, which consisted entirely of Catholic institutions except for West Point. John Simpson stated that BU would be playing as an independent in 1983–1984, having already scheduled a slate of games that included St. Bonaventure, Connecticut, North Carolina, and Penn State. He said the reason for the move amounted to geography. "Most of our alumni are in the corridor from Boston to Washington and the schools currently in our league are not covered in that area," Simpson said.[75] Speculation centered on BU's eventually joining Holy Cross in the Metro Atlantic or replacing the moribund Massachusetts program in the Atlantic 10.[76] For the time being, this all proved to be much ado about nothing. BU later walked back its statement about going independent, remaining in the NAC, in large part because of its automatic bid to the NCAA Tournament. Only Holy Cross ended up leaving the league after the 1982–1983 season, but all this going independent clamor presaged a radical remaking of the conference over the next few seasons.

Amid all the talk about BU basketball's future, the team responded by simply taking care of business, winning six of its next seven games in February, improving their record to 14-8. In particular, Gary Plummer played like a man possessed in the season's final weeks. Against Vermont and Penn State, he scored 30 and 27 respectively in road wins. Plummer went for a double-double while Mike Alexander missed just one shot in an 82–70 win over Maine to kick off a season-ending five-game homestand.[77]

BU fell by 1 at home to St. Joseph's and pummeled Merrimack in advance of the two games that would cement the Terriers' postseason fortunes— home dates against Northeastern and Holy Cross.

A mere 884 people showed up to Case for the BU-Northeastern game, indicative not only of BU's lack of support while playing for first place, but also the fragility of Northeastern's support, despite having earned two consecutive NCAA Tournament bids. The Huskies were 13-12 at the time, playing out the final regular-season games in a rebuilding year.[78] Despite the lack of fan support, the game was as intense as always. This time it was a rugged, sloppy affair that Pitino described as the most physical game he'd seen between the rivals. Turnovers and fouls piled up by the dozens in the 76–70 BU win. Despite all the rough play, the two coaches were highly complimentary of one another's teams. Pitino called Northeastern's Mark Halsel, who almost single-handedly kept his team in the game with 21 points and 17 rebounds, the "premier forward in the East." Calhoun countered by congratulating his rivals, who would be in a de facto playoff for the number one seed in their regular-season finale against Holy Cross. "No one plays with more heart [than BU]," Calhoun said.[79]

Holy Cross, as always, could play at a high level in a variety of tempos and against a variety of attacks. In their 1983 regular-season finale at Case, the Crusaders went toe-to-toe with the Terrier fast break and press in a game that brought out the best in both clubs. The teams were tied at 39 at the half and continued to redline for the next twenty minutes. Holy Cross's 1–2 tandem of 6'9" forward Chris Logan and 6'2" guard Jim Runcie pilloried BU all evening. Logan scored a game-high 28, while Runcie commanded the offense and scored 27.

Conversely, it was BU's depth that kept them in the back-and-forth game. Six different BU players reached double figures. None came up bigger than freshman Dwayne Vinson, who came off the bench to lead his team with 21 points on 8-for-11 shooting while grabbing 4 steals and dishing out 4 assists.[80] BU took control midway through the second half, leading by as many as 13, but a furious Holy Cross comeback gave the Crusaders a 97–95 lead with less than ten seconds remaining. It was then that point guard Shawn Teague took charge, taking an inbound pass, driving up the left side of the court, before abruptly shifting to the right for a reverse layup over Logan, whom officials whistled for his fifth foul. Teague completed the three-point play, and BU earned a 98–97 win and an outright ECAC North regular season title.[81] "I was going up strong on the left side but he [Logan] came over to block it, so I angled it to the right," Teague said of the decisive basket.[82] "The official was the MVP for that call. It was a clear-cut chop, and I respect him for having the guts to call it when he did," Pitino said of the foul, which made Holy Cross coach George Blaney go apoplectic. Blaney had been on edge all evening after receiving a technical in the first half protesting a goaltending call.[83]

The postseason began the following Tuesday as top-seeded BU hosted eighth-seeded Vermont in the quarterfinals of the NAC Tournament. Bill

Whitmore's Catamounts hung tough all night, even making a late-game run that gave them a 70–68 lead with less than five minutes remaining. Another clutch performance by Shawn Teague, who hit 4 consecutive foul shots in the game's final ninety seconds, sealed an 80–75 Terriers victory. The hard-fought win over a surprisingly game Vermont team was overshadowed by a season-ending injury to one of BU's top performers. Gary Plummer went down in the second half with a twisted knee. Plummer's knee sprain proved so severe that team trainers soon realized he would be unavailable for the remainder of the postseason.[84]

"Without him [Plummer], we are in trouble. Our freshmen couldn't defend a trolley train," Pitino said after the game.[85] In the short term, things did not prove nearly as dire as Pitino anticipated. Freshman Tom Ivey and sophomore Mark Fiedor did a fantastic job in the low post in Plummer's stead. Tony Simms moved into the frontcourt while Dwayne Vinson took over at Simms's starting position.

In the semifinals, BU got revenge on Niagara, blowing past them with an attack led by Tony Simms. The senior earned career highs in points (34) and rebounds (14) in the 95–82 win. The victory was BU's twentieth of the season and set up a rematch of the 1980 ECAC title game with Holy Cross. On the morning of the championship game, the *Globe*'s Neil Singelais encapsulated BU basketball's accomplishment amid campus indifference. "Only a handful of BU followers apparently care," Singelais wrote about the team's opportunity to reach the NCAA Tournament. "That fact became a way of life for the Terriers at the Case Gymnasium, where home games were often played to empty stands disguised as fans. And they're not showing up for playoff games either. It's a real shame too. For if ever there was a team that deserved the respect of friend and foe alike, it is this BU bunch. It is truly a team of character."[86]

BU jumped out to a 9–0 lead over the Crusaders before Holy Cross started finding seams in the Terrier defense. All-ECAC performers Logan (17 points) and Runcie (14 points) helped Holy Cross eradicate BU's lead. By the half, Holy Cross led, 27–25. The Crusaders led by as much as 8 early in the second half before BU's freshmen made their presence felt. In the absence of Gary Plummer, Dwayne Vinson, Tom Ivey, and Tony Simms put up a hellacious fight on the boards, more than hanging tough with Holy Cross's big men. Freshman Mike Alexander paced BU's offensive attack in the stomach-churning affair, scoring 16 of his game-high 20 points in the second half. BU took the lead with 6:35 remaining and never relinquished it. With less than ten seconds remaining, Shawn Teague intercepted a Jim Runcie pass to seal the 63–62 victory for Boston University. Pitino's players carried him off the court on their shoulders to celebrate the school's first tournament bid since the Eisenhower administration.[87] "I don't like freshmen. I don't like to play them. But these guys, they showed outstanding character," Pitino said in victory.[88]

Pitino told reporters he wasn't sure that his team could make it past the semifinals after Plummer went down. Privately he told his team differently. "'Gary's out; the rest of you guys are going to have to step up,'" is how Karl Lehman recalls that Pitino addressed the injury to their star player. Pitino's matter-of-fact response to the situation was reflective of his broader coaching philosophy. "He [Pitino] told us how we were going to win, how people were going to fill the gaps. He said it doesn't matter who starts; it matters who finishes. And so everybody on the bench was ready to play at anytime," Lehman said. And it was that approach that made BU a championship team.[89]

The Terriers drew East Coast Conference champ LaSalle in the opening-round game in the East Region. Lefty Ervin's Explorers had posted just a 17-13 record, despite winning both the East Coast Conference's regular season and tournament championships. A series of early-season injuries and a tough non-conference slate contributed to LaSalle's relatively modest record. Pitino knew full well that this was a big, rugged, and, finally, healthy opponent that a Gary Plummer-less BU team would find difficult to surmount. "We're happy to be in the NCAAs with such a young team," Pitino conceded while expressing pride in his team's overcoming "extreme adversity" to earn a tournament bid.[90]

The location of the game didn't help either. The Terriers would be playing in LaSalle's hometown of Philadelphia at the Palestra, the University of Pennsylvania's home court and one of the most storied venues in college basketball. LaSalle made multiple trips annually from their North Philly campus down to University City's "Cathedral of College Basketball" to play in the local Big 5 rivalry games. The winner of the play-in game would earn the number twelve seed and face off with fifth-seeded VCU. Stalwart Boston UHF station WLVI, Channel 56, secured the local rights to show the Tuesday night BU-La Salle game live at 9:40 p.m. ESPN planned to show a taped version of the game on Wednesday at 3 a.m. and at 5 p.m.[91]

BU hung tight in the first half but failed to consistently penetrate the Explorers' zone defense. By not scoring consistently, BU could not wield its press as a counterpunch when LaSalle inbounded the ball. The Explorers presented a balanced attack, busting the ball inside with center Tom Piotrowski and forwards Albert Butts and Ralph Lewis, while sophomore guard Steve Black banged in a series of jump shots. LaSalle led 33–28 at the break and dominated early in the second half. Straight from the locker room, LaSalle went on a 14–4 run. BU simply could not get anything going in the low post. The Terriers' frontcourt scored just 8 points all evening. The outcome was not in doubt after LaSalle's dominant start to the second half. In the end the Explorers won, 70–58, and BU ended the season at 21-10, overcoming a uniquely heart-wrenching set of adversities on route to the NCAA Tournament.[92]

"Some high school teams are bigger than we are," Pitino said afterward. "We wanted to press them but we didn't score enough points to press. We couldn't get the ball inside. [Tony] Simms was running into mountains." He expressed pride in his team's performance, particularly the three freshman (Ivey, Vinson, and Alexander), who had played so hard and so well in the tournament game.[93] Pitino made particular note of the versatility that Dwayne Vinson had shown filling in at shooting guard.[94]

Despite the team's success, BU landed relatively few postseason honors. Mike Alexander was named NAC Rookie of the Year, as well as Most Outstanding Player in the conference tournament. Tony Simms was named to the All-Conference team. And that was it. The depth of BU's roster no doubt contributed to the dearth of individual honors. When ten different players make consistent contributions, it is much tougher for any specific performer to stand out. As Rick Pitino and BU looked to the 1983–1984 season, there was no reason to doubt that this team could return to the NCAA Tournament. Certainly the losses of seniors Tony Simms and Brett Brown would put a huge dent in BU's backcourt. Yet the returning guard tandem of Shawn Teague and Dwayne Vinson would be one of the league's best. The Terrier frontcourt would certainly be the NAC's best with Gary Plummer, Tom Ivey, Mark Fiedor, and Karl Lehman in the blocks, returning Rookie of the Year Mike Alexander at the three, and highly touted swingman Paul Hendricks coming back from injury. Whether or not BU remained in the NAC, the Terriers were on the verge of becoming a perennial eastern power.

12

I Was Happy at BC *(Williams)*

A non-canonical list of schools that offered Gary Williams their head coaching job between March 1982 and March 1985:

Seton Hall
Duquesne
Boston College
The University of Miami (Florida)
Clemson
Arizona State
Providence

During the spring and summer of 1985, the SWC's Arkansas and the ACC's Wake Forest joined the list, making serious runs at Williams that offered him more money, better facilities, larger arenas, and larger fan bases than he had at Boston College. In Fayetteville, Arkansas and Winston-Salem, North Carolina, Williams's prospective teams would have been the only games in town all winter. He turned them both down. "It just wasn't the right time to make a move. I talked to the Arkansas people three times over the weekend and decided the only reason I would have taken the job would have been for the money and I didn't want to base my decision on that," Williams said after spurning the Razorbacks' offer.[1] The Boston College head man concluded that rival coaches started most rumors of his imminent departure from Chestnut Hill as a tactic on the recruiting trail.[2]

Williams came much closer to accepting Wake Forest's offer to replace longtime coach Carl Tacy. "I'm very happy at BC but it's an ACC job and I would have to listen," said Williams, a product of ACC power Maryland, when the *Globe* reported that Wake Forest AD Greg Hooks received permission to interview him.[3] After heading south for an elaborate dog-and-pony show in Winston-Salem that incorporated almost the entirety of the city's civic establishment, Williams decided to stay at Boston College, citing his family's happiness in Boston and his commitment to his corps of returning and incoming players.

Williams showed his hand more than a little in the process, calling the ACC "probably the best conference in the country," despite his own Big East's dominance of the most recent NCAA Tournament. The Boston College coach went on to note the temptation of coaching where "it's the only show in town. And even if you go .500 at Wake Forest, they still support you."[4]

Several BC players expressed surprise and relief that Williams wasn't leaving, the veterans having been through the departure of a head coach earlier in their college career. "I've been through this before with Tom Davis," senior Roger McCready said. "He recruited me and then packed up and left. It's discouraging. But I can understand why coach Williams was tempted. It's big stuff down there. They get 10,000 people on a bad night."[5]

Big East commissioner Dave Gavitt joined Williams on stage at the impromptu Chestnut Hill presser announcing that the coach was staying put. Behind the scenes, Gavitt and several of the conference's leading coaches lobbied Williams to remain in Boston. Gavitt's short-term success in keeping Williams piggybacked on his achievement of a longer-term goal at Boston College. The Big East commissioner had finally cajoled the Jesuit school into building a big on-campus arena. In April 1985, BC announced plans for a multi-sport complex that would incorporate Alumni Stadium, the school's thirty-two-thousand-seat football field, and an arena that would house the university's basketball and hockey programs. Ground-breaking was slated for spring 1986, following the completion of BC's upcoming hockey season. For the 1985–1986 season, BC basketball would continue to practice and play the majority of its home dates at Roberts. The number of BC basketball "home games" at the Boston Garden crept up to five for the 1985–1986 season and would grow to eight in the 1986–1987 and 1987–1988 seasons during construction of what came to be known as the Silvio O. Conte Forum. Despite the prestige of playing at the Garden, BC's lack of access to the court and the proximity of many of its Big East rivals to Boston made these games often feel like neutral-site affairs.

The Eagles brought in a large recruiting class in the fall of 1985 that was highlighted by the touted tandem of Steven Benton and Dana Barros. 6'5" Steven Benton was one of Philadelphia's best high school players of the

1980s, a versatile scorer, rebounder, and distributor for city champion St. John Neumann. Capable of playing the two or the three, Benton was well suited for the style of play that Gary Williams cultivated at Boston College. More than two hundred schools recruited Benton. He received significant interest from Big East powers Syracuse and Villanova before deciding on Boston College, selecting the school both for its strong academics and its recent on-court success. He'd been impressed by BC assistant coach Stan Nance's pitch on the school and had a great experience with his host, Eagles superstar Michael Adams, during his campus visit.[6]

Drawing even more attention than Benton was his soon-to-be backcourt running mate, Dana Barros. A native of Boston's Mattapan neighborhood, Barros was as esteemed as a wide receiver at Xaverian Brothers High School in Westwood, Mass., as he was as a shooting guard. Despite his 5'10" frame, Barros set fistfuls of records on the gridiron and on the basketball court. Barros was a legitimate scoring machine, both when driving to the basket and hoisting up shots from the outside before Massachusetts added the three-pointer. As a sophomore and junior, he led the state's most competitive prep basketball conference in scoring. As a senior, he averaged more than 30 points per game in the regular season and nearly 50 a game in the state tournament.[7] "Dana's as good a pure shooter as has ever been around BC. He's just a great athlete with speed and shooting ability. He could handle the ball. He's a heck of a competitor and a tough guy," Paul Brazeau said of Barros, whom the BC assistant doggedly pursued and convinced to sign on with the Eagles.[8] The most rigorous competition for Barros came not from other Big East basketball schools but from Jack Bicknell and the BC football program. In January 1985, Barros made his intentions to play basketball for Boston College known, drawing many huzzahs from the Roberts faithful.[9]

The preseason coaches' poll projected BC tied for fourth in the Big East. This was a surprisingly high pick, considering the tendency of the league's cognoscenti to underestimate the Eagles and the significant losses BC had suffered from its 1985 Sweet Sixteen roster. Michael Adams had been selected in the third round of the NBA Draft by Sacramento and fought his way onto the Kings' roster, kicking off a fantastic eleven-year career in which he twice finished in the top ten in assists and steals and twice led the league in three-pointers. Adams earned his sole NBA All-Star bid in 1992 for the Washington Bullets. Stu Primus, who was selected in the sixth round by the Pacers, and Terrence Talley were also significant contributors who would no longer be donning the maroon and gold.

The Eagles were far from the only Big East team in transition entering the 1985–1986 season. In the afterglow of the conference's ascension at the '85 Final Four, the league lost many of its marquee names to the NBA, including Patrick Ewing, Chris Mullin, Ed Pinckney, and, of course, Michael Adams. BC was particularly bereft of star power, landing exactly zero players on the league's preseason first or second team. In spite of this snub, BC had a solid returning nucleus on paper. Newcomers Barros and Benton would be joining a battle-tested corps on BC's roster that included senior co-captains Roger McCready and Dom Pressley, as well as big men Troy Bowers, Russ Doherty, and Trevor Gordon. Strong shooters Skip Barry and Jamie Benton also looked to make larger contributions in 1985–1986.

Despite BC's strong cluster of veterans, the Eagles, as usual, lacked size in the brawny and bruising Big East. Williams dreaded the impact of Michael Adams's departure on the team. "The one thing that worries me is that he [Adams] had the ball so much. He controlled our offense to the point that he took the responsibility off everyone else," Williams told the *Globe*.[10]

Boston College began the 1985–1986 season in typical fashion, playing several smaller programs from around New England but not looking quite as dominant as usual. The Eagles were short-handed in the low post during these fall semester non-conference games. For the second straight year, BC judged a player to be ineligible whose grades met NCAA requirements but failed to meet the school's beefed-up standards for student-athletes. Senior center Trevor Gordon would be unable to play until fall grades came out in mid-December. The School of Management deemed his marks and course load insufficient to graduate on time given the progress he had made by the beginning of the 1985–1986 school year.[11]

Senior Roger McCready put on a show in BC's opener, scoring 30 points against Maine in a workmanlike 82–69 win in Bangor. The Eagles proceeded to tear through the early part of their non-conference slate. After getting a scare at the hands of New Hampshire, BC outlasted Williams's tempters from Wake Forest in Winston-Salem, 62–60. Closer to home, BC blew out overmatched URI and Utica clubs in weeknight contests. Freshman Dana Barros asserted himself as BC's heir apparent to Michael Adams during the road trip, averaging nearly 15 points per game while leading the team in assists and steals. The performances on the road earned the 5'10" guard Big East Rookie of the Week honors. BC returned to Roberts and improved to 6-0 by drubbing Holy Cross, 84–57, thanks in large part to the athletic play in the post by Roger McCready, who netted 26 points, and Troy Bowers, who went 8-for-9 from the field and finished with 18 points. "Troy was a nice guy and a hard worker," Gary Williams said of Bowers, who contributed more every season during his career at BC. "He could rebound, score at times, and he worked very hard on defense."[12]

The 1985 portion of BC's schedule concluded with two warm-weather holiday tournaments. Trevor Gordon returned to action in the Red Lobster Classic in Orlando, Florida, on December 22 and 23. In the opener, BC pummeled Valdosta State but suffered its first loss of the season in the finals against Auburn. The Tigers could not only run with Boston College, which they did for forty minutes, but could clearly outmuscle them. Auburn's brawny forwards, Chris Morris and future NBA Rookie of the Year Chuck Person, combined for nearly 50 points, and each grabbed 8 rebounds in the 89–85 win. Though the loss to Auburn was BC's first of the season, it proved to be a bellwether for the rest of the 1985–1986 season, particularly when BC faced larger, more physical opponents in the Big East. The Eagles always fought, scratched, and clawed like a Gary Williams team, but when this roster faced off with the elite talent in the country's best conference, it often fell short during the spring semester. While BC's backcourt got better as the 1985–1986 season went on, it lacked the reach and grip of its 1984–1985 predecessor, which often made the difference against beefier opponents.

At the Fiesta Classic in Tucson, BC faced a similar set of problems to the ones that had shown up against Auburn. After beating Wisconsin in the tournament opener, BC was overwhelmed in the championship game by host Arizona. The Eagles' guards proved consistently unable to penetrate the Wildcats' 2–3 zone or sink enough jump shots to make their hosts pay for it. On the offensive end, Arizona's slick shooting tandem of Sean Elliott and Steve Kerr rained in more than 30 points collectively. Unexpectedly, this turned into one of BC's roughest affairs of the season. Williams earned three technical fouls and an ejection, while Arizona reserve guard Kenny Lofton punched Barros in the ribs with less than five minutes remaining. Teammate Skip Barry restrained Barros during the game, but the freshman guard lunged at Lofton during postgame handshakes and had to again be restrained.[13]

Now 8-2, Boston College opened conference play at the Carrier Dome, where the fourth-ranked Syracuse Orangemen hammered BC, 68–52, before a deafening assemblage of more than thirty thousand. Two nights later, Troy Bowers swatted away a last-second shot by Phil Gamble to preserve a 61–60 home win over Connecticut.

After barely escaping against UConn, Roger McCready strapped BC to his shoulders against tenth-ranked St. John's. Playing before a nearly full house at the Boston Garden, McCready outhustled and outwitted St. John's heralded frontcourt, putting in 29 points and grabbing 7 offensive rebounds in the contest.[14] "If I could get a player to emulate some of the things that Roger McCready did on the basketball court, those guys would be pros today," Michael Adams said. "Roger was only 6'5", but he could pump fake with the best of them. He'd get a defender off the ground so he could get a foul and the bucket. He had the best pump fake of any player I've ever seen."[15]

From day one as Boston College coach, Williams preached to his teams the importance of playing with emotion on the floor. BC's performance against St. John's that evening exemplified the Gary Williams ethos. Senior Dom Pressley and freshman Dana Barros harassed Johnnies superstar point guard Mark Jackson, while St. John's big man Walter Berry never got comfortable with the Georgetown-style box-and-one defense with which Gary Williams plied him all evening. St. John's shot below 50 percent for the first time all season. After forty minutes, the teams, which were never separated by more than 6 points, were tied at 69. In overtime, Pressley sank 3 of 4 free throws in the final minute as BC posted its most impressive win of the season. *Boston College 79 St. John's 77.*[16]

After a rough patch in December, Boston College looked like a team that was coming together at just the right time. Events proved otherwise. Five days after upsetting St. John's, BC put up a stinker before a raucous Storrs Field House crowd, falling 80–69 to Connecticut. The Huskies' backcourt of junior Earl Kelley and freshman Phil Gamble, who played all forty minutes, combined for 45 points in the win. The Eagles appeared to have learned little from their previous matchup with UConn, turning the ball over with impunity and committing a cornucopia of fouls.

BC returned to the Roberts Center to face Big East newcomer Rick Pitino's plucky but lightly regarded Providence team. The Friars were 0-4 in the conference but had hung tough against St. John's, Villanova, and Pitt, losing the latter two games by 1 point each. For anyone who had seen Pitino's BU teams, this Providence club looked awfully familiar: a scrappy, pressing, trapping team that went about eleven deep on the bench. It also looked like a Gary Williams—coached Boston College team. Leading the way for Pitino's Friars was an unheralded junior guard named Billy Donovan, who'd spent the first two years of his college career on the bench. Pitino had transformed Donovan into his on-court alter ago, a tenacious defender and sly distributor who, it turned out, could shoot as well as anyone in the Big East.

Two similarly minded teams took to the floor before a standing-room-only crowd at Roberts and put on a show, an unwavering assault of pressure defenses that BC led at the half, 39–36. Providence took the lead midway through the second half and held it for almost the remainder of regulation. Billy Donovan, who led the Friars with 22 points, had a chance to put the Eagles away but missed his second free throw on a one-and-one with four seconds remaining. Donovan made up for it in overtime, sinking a 14-foot jumper as time expired to give Providence a 76–75 win, Pitino's first in the Big East.[17]

Two days after falling to Providence, Boston College took a break from Big East play for a nationally televised contest with the Ohio State Buckeyes at the Boston Garden. Eldon Miller's Ohio State team had been ranked earlier in the season but had dropped some surprising games near the end of its non-conference schedule. The Buckeyes boasted two players who averaged 20 points per game: 7-footer Brad Sellers, who was leading the country in rebounding and near the top of the list in blocked shots, and 6'5" guard Dennis Hopson, who, like Sellers, went on to spend many years in the NBA.[18]

Playing some of its best basketball of the season, BC spanked Ohio State, 87–74, in a game that never seemed as close as the final tally. The 8,312 in attendance at the Garden saw BC's senior captains Dom Pressley and Roger McCready take charge against the Buckeyes: Pressley led the Eagles' no-holds-barred defensive stand while McCready wiped the floor with Sellers, manufacturing a game-high 29 points.

Steven Benton started his first game against Ohio State, taking over the small forward position from Skip Barry. Benton proved an immediate spark, scoring 10 of his 14 points in the game's first six minutes. He soon found himself a regular in the BC lineup. "[Gary Williams] had an old school approach," Steven Benton recalled. "He was an honest guy. I asked him how I could start, and he said, 'If you work hard, I'll play you.' And he started me eight games. He was a man of his word."[19] The lone downside to the afternoon was that freshman standout Dana Barros sustained a sprained wrist, which limited him in the team's upcoming slate of Big East games.[20]

The season took a turn for the worse in the aftermath of the Ohio State game. BC's already familiar low-post nemesis Charles Smith engineered Pitt's third straight win over the Eagles, scoring 20 points in a 64–62 Panthers win at Fitzgerald Fieldhouse, another one of the league's jalopy gymnasiums. BC returned to Boston for "home dates" at the Garden against Georgetown and Syracuse. BC led by 12 at the half against the Hoyas but fell apart in the game's final twenty minutes and dropped a 73–66 decision. The Syracuse game was not nearly as competitive. Pearl Washington, Rony Seikaly, and the Orangemen put together a 25–2 run to close out the first half and won, 80–55, in a game whose outcome was only briefly in question.

After winning decisively at home on January 30 against Seton Hall, BC began another losing streak, dropping four consecutive league games as the once 10-3 Eagles descended to 12-12 overall and the bottom rung of the Big East standings. The Eagles were small, inexperienced at several positions, and not nearly as deep as they'd been in previous seasons. The lack of depth on BC's roster demonstrated the continuing impact that the departure of master recruiter Kevin Mackey had on the program. The most evident flaw with this BC team, though, was its shooting, which had been dreadful throughout the losing streak, falling below 40 percent in each of its four consecutive losses. Plus injuries to Dom Pressley and Dana Barros left Boston College even more short-handed in several contests.

Amid BC's rough patch in the Big East regular season, the rumors started anew. Not long after the Eagles hammered Ohio State at the Boston Garden, the Big Ten school announced that Eldon Miller would not be returning for 1986–1987. Media outlets in both Boston and Columbus soon tagged Gary Williams's name to the opening. In early February, Bob Lobel on Boston's Channel 4 and Mike Lynch on Boston's Channel 5 reported separately that Williams would be heading to Columbus to interview for the Ohio State job. The reports incensed Williams, who was headed to Washington DC for a recruiting trip at the time he was said to be headed to Columbus. Ohio State AD Rick Bay also denied reports that Williams had interviewed for the job but did not deny his interest in the BC coach. Williams denied other reports in February that he was headed for FSU.[21]

On Senior Night, Boston College got revenge against Pitt, beating them for the first time in two seasons. In his Roberts finale, Roger McCready outplayed Charles Smith in the post and scored a game-high 23 points. After the 71–68 win, BC closed out its 1985–1986 regular season with back-to-back road games against Georgetown and Villanova. BC never led in a 90–76 loss to the Hoyas but hung in the game until the closing minutes thanks to substantial offensive efforts by Bowers (22 points) and McCready (24 points). Against Villanova, BC led for almost the entire contest before collapsing in the game's final minutes. A combination of foul trouble and the same poor shooting bug that had bothered BC all season turned a 56–56 game with 4:17 remaining into a 74–63 Villanova victory. The loss dropped BC to 4-12 in the league and 13-14 overall—the worst mark Boston College had ever posted in the Big East and the first time the Eagles had finished the regular season below .500 since 1976–1977.

The Eagles' visit to New York for the Big East Tournament proved predictably short. Seventh-seeded Boston College faced second-seeded Syracuse, a team that had lost just four games all season. The Orangemen pummeled Boston College for the third time that winter, reaching triple digits in a 102–79 rout. In the paint, it was too much Rony Seikaly and Wendell Alexis, who combined for 39 points. On the rest of the floor, it was too much Pearl Washington, who scored 27, dished out 7 assists, and went on to win Tournament MVP honors despite the fact that Syracuse lost in the finals to St. John's. In the end, BC's down year turned out to be a symptom of a down year for an entire conference. Not one of the Big East's four NCAA Tournament entries in 1986 made it past the first weekend just one year after three of its teams made it to the Final Four.

Soon after the Big East Tournament, reports of Gary Williams's imminent departure for Ohio State resurfaced. Williams conceded that he'd interviewed for the job but denied reports of various cloak-and-dagger meetings between himself and Rick Bay in such locations as LaGuardia Airport and the Meadowlands. The imminence expressed in such reports grew as several other high-profile candidates turned down the perennial Big Ten power. Apparently, Bay offered the job to Syracuse's Jim Boeheim, Tennessee's Don DeVoe, and Purdue's Gene Keady, but all had said no. Boeheim encouraged Bay to look closely at Williams, whom Boeheim regarded as one of the best coaches in the country.[22]

After a week of caginess on all sides, Ohio State named Gary Williams its new head basketball coach on March 15, 1986. Bay had interviewed Williams twice, including once on campus, before deciding on him as the Buckeyes' new head coach. Williams's total package would pay $145,000 per season for five years—a guaranteed contract that replaced his much smaller year-to-year deals at Boston College. In his introductory press conference, Williams, now forty years old, cited the job security he now had at Ohio State as one of his primary reasons for leaving Chestnut Hill.[23]

"I was happy at BC," Williams said in his introductory press conference at Ohio State. "It wasn't like there were big problems there but I reached a point where I wasn't sure there would ever be great attention put on our program."[24] In Columbus, his Buckeyes would be the main attraction and would have access to the resources of one of the biggest and most well-heeled athletic departments in the country. The challenge he faced keeping players eligible at a Boston College now hyper-vigilant about student-athlete academic performance would not be nearly so daunting in Columbus. His Buckeye teams would play in 13,276 seat St. John Arena, which was hardly the newest venue on the block but a veritable coliseum when compared to the Roberts Center. In addition, Williams would be inheriting a strong roster that returned four of its top five scorers in 1986–1987. While Ohio State struggled to a 14-14 regular season mark in 1985–1986, the team he was taking over was in the process of winning five straight games for Eldon Miller to take home its first NIT championship. Seventy-six wins, a regular season Big East title, and two Sweet Sixteens later, Williams had come a long way from the coach that came back to Chestnut Hill after trolling the sidelines at an armory in Arlington, Virginia, four years earlier.

"There was this underground speculation that Gary might be leaving," Troy Bowers said. "You hear the whispers, but you don't really pay attention till the hammer comes down."[25] "As it got toward the end of the season, a couple of guys started saying stuff that coach might be gone, and I started to think about it, and it made sense. He'd been here four years. It happened to the previous coach. It seemed to be a theme," Russ Doherty said. Doherty, who would have been a redshirt senior in 1986–1987, earned his degree in 1986 and chose not to stay on for a final season.[26] "When [Gary Williams] went to Ohio State, I almost left. I contacted their office and I was going to transfer, but I let things go kinda long and just ended up staying," said Steven Benton, whose style of play was perfectly suited to Williams's system.[27]

Though brief in duration, Gary Williams's tenure in Chestnut Hill was a tremendous success. He built on the legacy his predecessor and mentor Tom Davis had developed at Boston College, cementing BC's status as a force to be reckoned with inside the Big East and in the NCAA Tournament. He tweaked Tom Davis's potent basketball formula, transforming BC into the home of a uniquely breakneck style of play that nobody on their schedule looked forward to playing. Though often characterized as "underachievers," this confrontational team that so resembled its passionate coach formed a much-feared constellation in the physical, brawny, blacktop universe that was the nation's best basketball conference. And every player that Gary Williams brought to Boston College left with their degree. "Gary was the kind of guy who looked your parents in the face and said, 'I'm going to do everything I can to make sure your kid leaves with his degree.' And they did. Gary was accountable for his players," Troy Bowers said.[28] Boston College would have a colossal and immediate task in replacing Williams, but they knew just where to look.

13

Where Did You Get That Guy? *(Calhoun)*

Every year the offers got more enticing. In late March 1986, Jim Calhoun interviewed for another Big East job, this time with his nemesis, Boston College. Eagles athletic director Bill Flynn went instead with native son Jim O'Brien, who took a rough road to renaissance before eventually getting BC back to basketball prominence. Calhoun turned down Wichita State before taking much more seriously an offer from Northwestern, the school where much of the sports media seemed to think he coached already. He went to Dallas for the Final Four and interviewed for two days with the Chicagoland Big Ten school. Northwestern reportedly offered him a salary three times higher than the $70,000 he was making annually at Northeastern. Calhoun announced on the last day of March that he was turning down Northwestern's offer. He cited the comforts of home and stability that life in Boston afforded his immediate and extended family, which lived almost exclusively inside Massachusetts Route 128.[1]

Moreover, what Calhoun had in Boston was special. He had created a dynasty at Northeastern with no end in sight. He had one more year of Wes Fuller, Andre LaFleur, and Reggie Lewis and a bushel of excellent younger players to keep it all going. And his Huskies couldn't be beat at Matthews. They'd lost just two games at home in the last three seasons. Plus, a conversation he had in Dallas with Bobby Knight gave him a new perspective on which jobs to consider and which ones to avoid. Knight advised him that nobody could win at Northwestern. He convinced Calhoun that the elite institution would not provide him with the resources to compete against the Big Ten's big state universities. Northwestern also had a marginal fan base and little basketball tradition. Moreover, Northwestern's stringent admissions standards would make it even more difficult for Calhoun to build up a talented team. Knight encouraged him to wait for an offer from a state school that would have more resources and a built-in fan base.[2]

Just such a New England school soon had an opening. Longtime UConn coach Dom Perno was forced out after four consecutive losing seasons. Once a New England power, UConn had struggled in the Big East, failing to finish higher than seventh place since 1981. Calhoun had recent and distant memories of Connecticut. While at AIC, his Aces had been overwhelmed on several occasions by the Yankee Conference front runner. The previous season at Northeastern, his Huskies of the NAC had annihilated the Huskies of the Big East, who had become a conference bottom feeder. Calhoun conceded his interest in the position, stating that he would only consider jumping for a job like this one because it was so close to home.[3]

As the Big East came calling, small gripes with the Northeastern job became more noticeable to Calhoun. He'd just lost out on a prized recruit named Cedric Ball, who'd chosen UNC-Charlotte over Northeastern. If Calhoun was recruiting from a Big East school, there was no way he'd have lost that recruit to a Sun Belt school.[4] In addition, the ceiling on Northeastern's success seemed more constricting than it had in the past. "The downside at Northeastern was that the program probably never would be much more than it was," Calhoun wrote. "There never was going to be a big arena, big crowds. Plucky Northeastern always would be plucky Northeastern."[5]

The idea of Calhoun's coaching at Connecticut was not a new one to John Toner, the school's athletic director. He'd invited Northeastern to play in the Christmastime Connecticut Mutual Classic to get a closer look at the coach. The decline of Connecticut's most prestigious sports program did not portend well for Toner's own future at the school. Already laying the groundwork for Perno's departure, Toner watched in awe from the scorer's table as Northeastern dismantled Connecticut. "I could see that Northeastern was bigger, stronger, faster, and in much better condition than the other teams we brought in. I was very impressed with that," Toner said.[6] Apparently, Calhoun was his first call after Perno's resignation. Toner was in search of a program builder, and Calhoun fit the bill as well as anyone in the country.

After just one phone conversation with Calhoun, John Toner was sold. Calhoun preached defense-defense-defense on the call, a stance that appealed greatly to the former football coach. Toner's instincts told him that Calhoun was a dedicated New Englander who would not go hopping off to the next job the minute he got the UConn program in decent order. He'd found himself a generational head coach.[7]

The next person to convince was UConn President John T. Casteen, who had recently arrived in Storrs after serving as dean of admissions at the University of Virginia and as the state of Virginia's secretary of education. In the aftermath of Perno's departure, Casteen put together a task force to audit the school's athletic department. The task force found an organization adrift, unmoored from the rest of the university and failing to make good choices when it spent money.[8] More broadly, Casteen found a similarly aloof relationship between the university and the surrounding state. He wanted to build closer bonds between the university and the state's residents. Working in concert with the Board of Trustees, Casteen tried to do this by centralizing the diffuse state university campus all in Storrs. A major part of this effort was a significant investment in new facilities on the main campus, something that hadn't happened in a generation. A major plank in this platform was the construction of Gampel Pavilion, a large, on-campus arena to replace the school's aging fieldhouse. For years, Connecticut had played its marquee matchups at either the New Haven Coliseum or the Hartford Civic Center. To make that new on-campus arena a genuine campuswide and statewide unifier, Toner, Casteen, and company needed to pick the right man to lead the basketball program and serve as the face of UConn athletics. Toner told Casteen that he thought Calhoun could win at UConn. The athletic director was also convinced that they could win over Calhoun. The construction of Gampel Pavilion demonstrated that UConn was committed to competing in the Big East.[9]

"I asked for an evening with Jim [Calhoun]. We went to a steakhouse in East Hartford and spent the evening there," Casteen said.[10] The pair traded stories about their backgrounds and families before talking UConn basketball. Casteen told the Northeastern coach that he wanted to hire someone who could build a program capable of competing for a national championship. In his public pronouncements, Casteen made it clear that he viewed the progress of the basketball program as essential to increasing the profile of a university that was improving across the board. When he asked Calhoun how he intended to win a national title at UConn, the coach thought a great while before answering. Calhoun described a national approach to recruiting that would lure players from outside the Big East's traditional pipelines. Calhoun, someone who knew all about fighting for media attention, described the importance of winning over the local print and broadcast media to their cause. He also talked about taking a first step by competing for an NIT championship, treating it not as a consolation prize but instead as a source of momentum for the program.

"I left the meeting believing he [Calhoun] could do it. I left understanding that he was a quiet, thoughtful guy. I left the meeting thinking he was tough—particularly tough in terms of the way his brain works when he attacks an issue. And I believed that he had the ability to be a major public figure in Connecticut and succeed," Casteen said.[11] Calhoun was soon offered a seven-year contract worth more than $100,000 per year when including a local television deal and a summer basketball camp.[12]

On May 15, 1986, Jim Calhoun accepted the UConn job. Calhoun and his family were late that day for a lunch with Casteen because the coach wanted to tell his players in person that he was leaving. It was a painful morning for all involved.[13]

"I wanted to give myself a chance to see what I could do at a different place. I can tell you right now I almost didn't go from Northeastern because I loved the place so much. I loved my kids so much," Calhoun said in retrospect.[14] "It did surprise me a little when he [Calhoun] left. He had created a great situation for himself at NU. But the call of the Big East and a high major job won out. It was the best move he ever made," Karl Fogel said.[15]

Less than a week after Calhoun left for Connecticut, Northeastern hired Fogel to replace him. Senior captains LaFleur, Fuller, and Lewis expressed their strong support for him. Athletic Director Irwin Cohen said Fogel had been the choice from the moment the job opened, a source of continuity in a program that had become a force in college basketball. Fogel himself had been a hot commodity on the coaching market. Jim O'Brien had offered him an assistant's job at Boston College, and the University of Vermont had strongly considered him for its coaching vacancy. "We didn't want some outsider coming in and messing up what we had already built over all those years with Coach Calhoun and his staff," Andre LaFleur said. "So Reggie, myself, and Wes Fuller, we stepped up and went to the administration, and we lobbied for Karl Fogel to get the coaching job. Because he knew us. He was a really good coach, and it was our senior year."[16]

While Calhoun found himself on ground zero of a rebuild, Northeastern was once again dominating the NAC, cruising to another league championship while Reggie Lewis set the school's career scoring mark and Andre LaFleur set the assist record. The most meaningful of the team's twenty-seven wins that season came in the season opener. At the Great Alaska Shootout, Northeastern outran, outrebounded, and outscored second-ranked Louisville, the defending national champion. The 88–84 win was arguably the most impressive in school history. "At the Great Alaska Shootout dinner, Louisville laughed when we walked by. When Reggie and [the others] finished whooping their behind, there was nothing they could say. We pressed them, and they couldn't get the ball over half court," Keith Motley recalls.[17]

Lewis, LaFleur, and Fuller won three more games that season against BU, including another victory in the NAC title game. The trio never lost a game to BU in their careers, going 10-0 against their crosstown rivals. Despite Northeastern's remarkable season, the committee again treated them with disrespect, giving them a fourteen seed and a first-round date with seventh-ranked Purdue. Northeastern battled valiantly with the Boilermakers, running and gunning against them for 40 minutes. But they came up short at the Carrier Dome, falling 104–95 to a Gene Keady—coached team that included four future NBA players.

After the season, Northeastern's own NBA prospect, Reggie Lewis, found that he would be staying in a familiar place. After two years' worth of commentary by the basketball cognoscenti on Lewis's status as a first rounder, the kid from Northeastern fell all the way to twenty-two, the next to last pick in the first round. The Boston Celtics gladly selected the forward from the other end of the Orange Line.[18] "For Reggie [Lewis] to be drafted twenty-second by the Celtics gives you a sense of where we [Northeastern] fit in in the grand scheme of things," Calhoun said.[19]

The Celtics did incredibly well by the pick. In year two Lewis went from role player to regular, replacing Danny Ainge in the starting lineup after his February 1989 trade to Sacramento. Lewis helped extend the excellence of the Boston Celtics as the likes of Bird, McHale, Parish, and Dennis Johnson began to show their age. That same year, Northeastern retired Lewis's number 35, hanging it from the rafters at Matthews in a ceremony attended by many of his former Huskies and current Celtics teammates.[20] In essence, Lewis replaced the Celtics' 1986 first-round pick, Len Bias, who had died tragically of a cocaine overdose just days after his selection in the plans of an organization in transition. Lewis evolved from merely a good NBA player into an All-Star. In 1992, he represented the Eastern Conference at the forty-second edition of the game, held that year in Orlando, Florida. In October 1992, the Celtics named him team captain, replacing Larry Bird after twelve seasons.

Profound tragedy struck the Boston basketball community again on July 27, 1993, when Reggie Lewis collapsed at the Celtics practice facility at Brandeis University in Waltham, Massachusetts. During the 1993 NBA playoffs, Lewis had collapsed in a game against the Charlotte Hornets. Doctors determined that a serious heart condition had caused him to collapse. A team of doctors from New England Baptist Hospital told him the condition was career-ending. A second opinion convinced Lewis that the condition wasn't quite as serious as originally thought. The twenty-seven-year-old began working out on his own toward a comeback that ended that terrible afternoon in Waltham. Attempts to revive Lewis proved unsuccessful, and he was pronounced dead at Weston Hospital in Waltham. His death was attributed to hypertrophic cardiomyopathy, a rare heart condition. An autopsy revealed significant scarring on his enlarged heart. Several members of his family also suffered from serious cardiac ailments, including his mother and his younger brother.[21]

"The speculation was that he [Reggie] hid his family's history along with his own heart murmur as a child because he did not want to be forced to retire from the game he loved," Alejandro Danois wrote in *The Boys of Dunbar*.[22] Flags flew at half-mast at Northeastern University on the late July day the school honored its greatest athletic hero. Mourners filled Matthews Arena to pay tribute to the player and the man whose impact on their lives was indescribable.[23] The Celtics, too, later retired their captain's number 35, hanging it in the Garden rafters alongside the names and numbers of Russell, Cousy, Havlicek, Bird, and every other legend that trolled the parquet floor for the green and white.

Sadly, the death of Reggie Lewis has been seen by many through the prism of Len Bias's death, a view that is both understandable and unfair. The impact of Len Bias's cocaine-related death less than forty-eight hours after being selected by the Celtics in the 1986 NBA Draft is hard to encapsulate.

It had a profound impact on the University of Maryland's basketball program, leading to Lefty Driesell's departure. More significantly, it had a massive impact on federal drug policy, clearing the way for a draconian new regime of penalties for drug-related offenses. In Boston, the death of Len Bias cast a pall over the future of the Celtics organization as fans and commentators alike spent years conjuring his presence on the parquet floor, projecting the Maryland star as the motor that would have kept the franchise's 1980s dynasty running. Bias' death also cast a pall over Lewis, the next designated savior of the Celtics' dynasty. Lewis's life ended tragically as well, though resolutely not due to drugs. In death, Lewis became an extension of the what-might-have-been that began with Bias, but, more cruelly, the narrative surrounding Bias's drug-related death informed coverage of Lewis's. Cynical reporters relying on unfounded rumors pushed the idea that Lewis's death may too have been related to cocaine. It wasn't. But, sadly, that half-remembered lie continues to inform fuzzy memories of Lewis's death almost thirty years later.

While Northeastern basketball reached its apex in the late 1980s, Calhoun set forth on a rapid rebuild at Connecticut. In his first season, the Huskies won just nine games. In year two, Calhoun hit his self-ascribed benchmark, leading UConn to an NIT championship, the first national championship of any kind at the school. In these early years at Connecticut, Calhoun and his staff figured out quickly who among the incumbent roster wanted to play big-time college basketball while adding talent from around the country and around the globe.

UConn found recruits far outside the traditional turf of the Big East, including Israeli forward Nadav Henefeld, who was the Big East Rookie of the Year in 1989–1990. Calhoun, too, cut down on all the poaching from the Nutmeg State, securing elite local recruits like Scott Burrell and Chris Smith, who a few years earlier might have ended up at a different Big East school. Taking the same tack he had at Northeastern, Calhoun instilled a chip on his players' shoulders as early as their recruitment, cultivating the sense among his prospective players that the big-time programs were overlooking them and UConn was giving them a chance to prove the powers-that-be incorrect.[24]

Calhoun's UConn teams played tough, physically, and fast, closely resembling the teams he had coached on Huntington Avenue. "When I watched

UConn, I saw a lot of guys like Eric Jefferson, Mark Halsel, and myself out there—big, athletic threes and fours, plus talented guards that played like Pete [Harris] and Perry [Moss]," Chip Rucker said.[25]

Calhoun soon won over the fans in Connecticut with his demonstrative sideline demeanor and acerbic Boston sense of humor. His coach's TV show, broadcast on Channel 8 across Connecticut, won a loyal following just as his Huskies were doing the same thing statewide. "I'm on the 6 o'clock news every week," Calhoun said in 1989. Some difference from the anonymity of Boston. "Our games are on the ABC affiliate. We'd bump *Moonlighting*. We're the state's athletic team."[26] "People took pride in what was happening [at UConn]. I can remember meeting with some faculty colleagues after one of the early games we had won, and as the group got settled, a guy from the School of Education said, 'Where did you get that guy?'" John Casteen remembers.[27]

The 1989–1990 season was the breakout year for UConn basketball. The Huskies moved into their new on-campus arena in January 1990. Jim Calhoun built a team capable of filling it. The Huskies won twenty-eight games and their first Big East title in school history. UConn finished the season fourth in the AP poll and earned a number-one seed in the NCAA Tournament, making it the first Connecticut team since 1981 to even make it to the Big Dance. Once again Calhoun's postseason hopes were dashed at the Meadowlands as Christian Laettner hit his first tournament buzzer-beater to push Duke past UConn in the East Regional Final. After Calhoun led the Huskies to the Elite Eight and earned National Coach of the Year honors, Toner rewarded him with a four-year extension worth twice his original salary.

For much of the 1990s, there UConn remained, a perennial power in the Big East that just couldn't finish in March. That changed on the back end of the decade, as UConn became a destination for big-time talent rather than an alternative. The university itself grew in prestige as its basketball teams, both men's and women's, became standard-bearers in college basketball. In 1998, Calhoun's team reached its first Final Four. In 1999, the Huskies got their revenge on Duke on an even bigger stage, upsetting the Blue Devils in the national title game to earn UConn the national championship that Casteen and Calhoun had started talking about thirteen years earlier at an East Hartford steakhouse. From there, UConn became the gold standard in March, winning national championships in 2004 and 2011. Calhoun retired before the start of the 2012–2013 season, citing a series of recent health problems. In 2014, Calhoun protégé Kevin Ollie, coaching many players Calhoun had recruited to Connecticut, added a fourth national title to UConn's trophy case. If one looks at the durable success that Jim Calhoun fostered at both Northeastern and Connecticut, one can easily argue that he is the best program builder in the history of college basketball. Behind John Wooden, of course. One could also argue that he belongs in the conversation for the second-best coach in NCAA history. No team dominated the best league in the history of college basketball for nearly as long as the Huskies ran roughshod over the Big East.

Through it all, Calhoun had a good memory, and he didn't take kindly to slights. The same Boston College that overlooked Calhoun in 1986 had a twenty-four-game losing streak against UConn that began in 1988 and ended in the year 2000. The same Jim Boeheim whose Orangemen had run the score up on Northeastern back at Manley Field House was on the losing end of UConn's first Big East tournament title in 1990. Boeheim may lead their all-time head-to-head series, but UConn certainly surpassed Syracuse when it came to national prestige, racing past the Orangemen in conference titles and national championships.

While Jim Calhoun remade UConn into a national power, Northeastern was starting to lose its grip on the NAC. In 1988, Mike Jarvis and BU finally beat the Huskies and advanced to the NCAA Tournament. In 1989, it was Siena's turn. In 1990, Northeastern shared the regular season title with BU but lost to the Terriers in the league title game. Northeastern returned to the NCAAs in 1991, but, from there, things went south quickly as newcomers Delaware and Drexel became the league's new powers. On the heels of a 5-22 season, Northeastern relieved Karl Fogel of his duties in 1994.

Northeastern's decline had several causes, not the least of which was the strength of the league itself. A dropoff in recruiting is probably the most significant reason for Northeastern's waning fortunes. There is a correlation between the rise of UMass basketball under John Calipari, a Pittsburgh native, and the decline of Northeastern during the early 1990s. Calipari's UMass became the mid-major of choice for players just below the radar of the Big East programs in the mid-Atlantic states and southern New England. Players like Jim McCoy, Lou Roe, and Marcus Camby, who ended up Minutemen, may have found themselves in red and black a few years earlier.

In 1994, thirty-three-year-old Dave Leitao, who had spent the previous eight seasons with Calhoun at UConn, took over as head coach at Northeastern, promising to build a strong local recruiting base to reignite the program. Leitao failed to right the ship immediately and returned to Connecticut after just two seasons. He went on to a highly successful head coaching career that included two stints at DePaul and a stint at Virginia.

The 2000s have been much kinder to Northeastern basketball, as Ron Everhart (2001–2006) and Bill Coen (2006–present) have had highly successful runs as head basketball coaches. Neither has reached the heights of the Huskies during the 1980s, but Northeastern has clearly been reestablished as a highly respected program in eastern college basketball. Under Everhart, the Huskies returned to the NIT in 2005, the year before Northeastern moved to the Colonial Athletic Association. Bill Coen has been even more successful, bringing the Huskies to two NCAA Tournaments and two NITs, posting five twenty-win seasons, and eventually surpassing Calhoun as the winningest coach in school history.

Jim Calhoun won 920 games as a college basketball coach—248 at Northeastern, 625 at Connecticut, and most recently 47 at the University of St. Joseph, the Division III school in West Hartford he revitalized before retiring abruptly early in the 2021–2022 season. At Northeastern, Calhoun won the North Atlantic Conference regular season championship six times and the conference tournament five times. At UConn, his teams won ten Big East regular-season titles and seven Big East tournament titles. He won an NIT championship and three NCAA Tournament championships. His Connecticut Huskies made eighteen appearances in the NCAA Tournament. At St. Joseph, his Blue Jays won a Great Northeast Athletic Conference championship and earned a bid to the Division III Tournament. Thirty-five of Calhoun's former players made it to the NBA, thirty-three from UConn and two from Northeastern. An all-time Calhoun team would include NBA All-Stars like Reggie Lewis, Caron Butler, Kemba Walker, and Cliff Robinson; standouts like Rudy Gay, Emeka Okafor, and Rip Hamilton; as well as future Hall of Famer Ray Allen. Just as impressive is the coaching tree that springs forth from Calhoun, which includes dozens of former players and assistants who went on to successful careers in the college and high school ranks. Karl Fogel, Dave Leitao, Kevin Ollie, Karl Hobbs, Glen Miller, Steve Pikiell, and Mike Jarvis all served as Calhoun assistants before going on to successful careers at the Division I level.

In 2005, Calhoun was inducted into the Naismith Memorial Basketball Hall of Fame, followed a year later by his induction into the College Basketball Hall of Fame. On the evening of his induction in Springfield, Calhoun spoke briefly, thanking his family, his colleagues, the administrators who took a chance on him, and the unremembered New England basketball coaches that came before him. He concluded his speech by asking the more than fifty former players in attendance from his time at Dedham, Northeastern, and Connecticut to stand for an ovation. "As I receive this honor tonight, I want you to know that I take a piece of each and every one of you into the Hall with me," Calhoun said shortly before returning to his seat.[28]

Through it all, the frame of reference for Calhoun's success was rooted in Boston—lessons from his father and from Fred Herget, ideas he had picked up in Braintree summer leagues or at the Tech Tournament, memories of AIC or coaching high school kids in Dedham. But the firmest foundation for everything Calhoun built in Connecticut had its roots in Cabot Gymnasium. His coaching metaphors were steeped in the young men who made Northeastern into a basketball juggernaut. The likes of Emeka Okafor and Donyell Marshall heard about how Mark Halsel boxed out his opponents. Kemba Walker and Ray Allen heard about Reggie Lewis's ability to create his own shot. Every point guard that ever came through Storrs learned the names of John Clark, Pete Harris, Perry Moss, and especially Andre LaFleur, who coached many of them personally in his tenure as a Calhoun assistant. The men who donned the red and black for Jim Calhoun were never in his past. They were always there on the floor with him as part of his present, central to his every success.

14

Proper Perspective *(Pitino)*

"I'm at the scorer's table with the timer, the clock operator, the scoreboard operator, and the official scorer. It's an hour before the game. There's like eight people in the stands. The kids are just coming out to warm up. Pitino comes out and just roasts these guys at the table. He says, 'You guys weren't on last game. You've got to be better. We've gotta be more intense' and stuff like that. I'm talking to these guys afterward, and I ask, 'Do you guys get paid?' And they say, 'No.' 'You let him yell at you like that?'" UNH SID Mike Bruckner asked the BU basketball managers at Case, the first time he ever encountered a Rick Pitino—coached basketball team. "He [Pitino] was just so wound up an hour before a game. He just had to get somebody excited. I honestly knew the first two games I saw Pitino coach at BU that he was going to be good because he was concerned with every single detail. He was worried about everything. He was either going to die of a heart attack or be a really good coach."[1]

By the spring of 1983, everyone else in eastern college basketball knew what Mike Bruckner had known several years earlier, including Penn State athletic director Jim Tarman, who suddenly had a head coaching vacancy. Dick Harter resigned abruptly as Penn State's basketball coach in March 1983. Formerly the head man at Oregon, Harter enjoyed five largely successful seasons in Happy Valley. Tarman regarded Pitino as an obvious candidate for the post. Pitino favored the swarming defensive approach Harter adopted both at Oregon and Penn State to the point of commandeering Harter's self-affixed nickname for his Ducks teams, the "Kamikaze Kids," at BU.[2] Moving to Penn State would have increased Pitino's salary, placed him in a more high-profile program, and secured him a job in a more esteemed conference. He interviewed for the snug-fitting job, but Penn State instead hired William and Mary's Bruce Parkhill.

After the Penn State intrigue, the off-season seemed to be proceeding smoothly for BU basketball. Pitino's team prepared for the next fall with the same confidence and work ethic that had become the program's trademarks over the past five years. Despite losing Brett Brown and Tony Simms, BU entered the summer of 1983 with the best returning team in the NAC. In recruiting, the Terriers added significant depth to their roster. They signed Jim Christian, a hotshot point guard out of St. Dominic's on Long Island, Rick Pitino's alma mater, whose game bore more than a passing resemblance to his soon-to-be head coach's. Jeff Holmes, a 6'4" guard, one of the top scorers in New Hampshire basketball history, joined Christian in BU's backcourt of the future. The third prong in BU's 1983–1984 recruiting class was 6'8" Peter Gabriele, a tough, athletic big man from Hamilton, Ontario.

Jeff Holmes met Pitino at a basketball camp in New Hampshire after his junior year in high school. "He [Pitino] pulled me and Skip Barry, who played at BC, and he put us through some drills, and after that he recruited me," Holmes said. "He came to my house and was one of those guys that could talk bark off a tree." Holmes signed on to play at BU early that fall.[3]

"Back then very few people came up to Canada. Leo Rautins went to Syracuse, but that was about it," Peter Gabriele recalled.[4] Gabriele was one of Ontario's top prep players, averaging better than 20 points and 20 rebounds per game. Nevertheless, he received scant notice from American colleges and had to grab for the brass ring on his own. Gabriele drove to Syracuse with some friends to watch the Orangemen and ran into Rautins after the game. Rautins told him to contact Syracuse assistant Bernie Fine. Syracuse didn't have any openings, but Fine made some phone calls. BU's John Kuester was soon boarding a flight for Hamilton. After seeing Gabriele in action, Pitino invited him to Boston for a visit. "Coach Pitino asked me if I could dunk the ball, and I said, 'Which way?'" Gabriele said, proceeding to put on a show of one-handed, two-handed, backward, and 360 dunks that impressed Pitino enough to offer him a scholarship. His only D-I offer.[5]

Jim Christian, the third member of BU's incoming class, displayed his elite passing and shooting skills with showmanship. "[Christian] had that whole Pistol Pete flair to his game. Back in the day, that ball would come whipping and hit you in the head," Jeff Holmes said.[6]

The three newcomers to the BU program spent the summer in Boston, getting ahead on their classes, getting to know their teammates, and getting themselves into playing shape. Through the Fourth of July weekend, the entirety of BU's basketball program appeared to be ramping up for another run to the NCAA Tournament. Then came the announcement.

On July 6, 1983, Rick Pitino announced that he was leaving Boston University to become Hubie Brown's assistant coach with the New York Knicks. Brown, whose personality and coaching style closely resembled his new assistant's, had been a mentor to Pitino since the Boston University coach was a camper at Five-Star. Brown approached Pitino a week earlier at the annual gathering at Robert Morris College, asking him to replace another member of the camp's family, Mike Fratello, who had been hired to coach the Atlanta Hawks. After announcing his decision, Pitino met briefly with his players and returned to his home in Needham just long enough to put it up for sale. On July 7, Rick Pitino headed for New York.[7]

"I never even thought about pro basketball before but when it came up I pursued it with the Knicks because of the tremendous amount of respect I have for Hubie Brown," Pitino said, not to mention that the move was a return home.[8] Despite never having considered pro basketball before, Pitino's friendship with Brown was well known to his players. When the Knicks played in New York, Hubie Brown's team would practice at Case. When the Terriers traveled to New York for Arturo Brown's funeral, they had attended a Knicks game during the trip.[9]

In all, Pitino went 91-51 at BU, winning nearly two-thirds of his games at a school that had suffered through five straight losing seasons before his arrival. Despite all the success, Pitino had barely moved the needle on campus interest in basketball. In his final year at BU, the Terriers' average attendance per game was just 648.[10]

To say Pitino's departure was tough on his players would be an understatement. It unmoored many of them from everything they'd worked to build up in the first years of their adulthood. "It was a surprise. I struggled my sophomore year a little bit, and I wasn't happy with my play," Karl Lehman said. "But after the loss to LaSalle, I'd had a really good game. It was probably my best game of the whole year, and coach said, 'You really stepped up. We need to work on this and this. I hope you look forward to having a great junior year.' Then he decides to leave and go to the Knicks, so it was a big blow. I didn't have any pre-knowledge of it. I don't think anybody did till he announced it. He just pulled us into the locker room and told us what was going on. It was emotional because he'd had such an impact on all of us."[11]

Lehman transferred to St. Anslem in Manchester, New Hampshire, to play for Pitino assistant Bob Brown. Two of the three incoming freshman would also end up transferring. Jim Christian eventually left for Rhode Island for basketball reasons, while New Hampshire native Jeff Holmes transferred to the more laid-back University of Maine. Mike Alexander, too, left the program for a time.[12]

"We were in summer school, we were coming down to campus to work out, and we got to the Case Center. One of the maintenance gentleman said, 'Hey man, did you hear Pitino is leaving?' We went up to the office, and Kuester was there. We asked, 'What's the word? Coach is leaving?' 'Yeah, he's going to the Knicks. But then Kuester's like, 'But I'm going to be around.' And I'm like, 'Yeah, that's great, big brother,'" Tom Ivey recalled.[13]

Pitino's quick exit from BU proved surprisingly sticky. A clause in the coach's contract required him to pay back the remaining years if he left early. Dave Hollowell, BU's associate vice president of administrative services, announced that Pitino would be expected to pay $90,000 for the two remaining years on his contract. This assertion shocked Pitino, who had been told by John Simpson that the clause would not apply since he was leaving for a pro job. Simpson remained aloof, branding it as a dispute between the university and his former basketball coach. This wasn't the first time that BU administrators jousted with a coach in search of greener pastures. In 1980, BU's highly successful football coach, Rick Taylor, had nearly left for Penn but balked at the idea of having to pay for a buyout. Pitino and Hollowell later released a joint statement saying they had come to an undisclosed settlement. As part of the statement, BU conceded that Pitino's job with the Knicks did not constitute a conflict of interest under the terms of his existing contract.[14]

Ten different D-1 coaches applied immediately for the BU opening. From the time of Pitino's announcement, John Kuester, the BU assistant with the Dean Smith pedigree, was the favorite for the job. Less than a week after initiating a search, John Simpson hired Kuester, who promised to keep Pitino's attacking style of play in place while steeping it in the training he'd received in Chapel Hill. "I like Rick's style, having a pressing defense and I like to move the ball quickly on offense. Basically, we have the same style of play," Kuester asserted while making it clear that he was not a sideline screamer like his boss for the two previous seasons. "Basically, I'm low-key like Dean Smith," Kuester said.[15]

Despite Kuester's distinguished coat of arms, evident ability to explain the game's fundamentals, and success as a recruiter, his hiring proved to be a tremendous misstep by John Simpson. Despite the treasure chest of talent on BU's roster, the Terriers went just 16-13 and 15-15 in Kuester's two years at the helm. BU finished third in the NAC in 1983–1984 and fifth in 1984–1985. Kuester's teams lost every game they played against Northeastern. BU would not, in fact, defeat Northeastern again until February 1988.

Part of the issue was the difficultly of the NAC, which was a genuine mid-major in its day that featured several high-quality opponents. The addition of a consistently competitive Siena club to the league in 1984–1985 was a worthy replacement for one-time power Holy Cross, which spent the late 1980s in a downward spiral. BU's always difficult non-conference schedule certainly played into its woes under John Kuester as well. Trips to Southern Cal, Iowa, Purdue, and North Carolina all ended up in the loss column.

And then there was John Kuester's inexperience as a game manager and tactician. Kuester expended a significant amount of time putting in place the kind of sets that North Carolina used in its motion, shuffle, and four corners offenses. This more deliberate, structured offensive approach cut significantly into BU's counterpunching, defensive-driven attack. Pitino's final BU team raced to just under 80 points per game, while Kuester's BU teams galloped to an average of just over and just under 70 per game. "It's like having a tenured professor hand the class over to the grad assistant. You're not handing it over to your colleague who'd been in the trenches with you teaching these large classes," Tom Ivey said.[16]

"It was a challenging year with the change of coach and the high expectations. We still had Shawn Teague and Gary Plummer and Mike Alexander. But that league was really good," Jeff Holmes said of Kuester's first year. "[Kuester's] obviously a tremendous basketball mind. My take on it is that every coach has to have his own personality, but he may have tried to emulate Rick too much, and that wasn't his style."[17]

"Pitino could just pull the ultimate out of the underdog. He had a knack for getting underdogs to play harder and better," said Mike Rosen, who served as team manager under both Pitino and Kuester. "John Kuester was used to coaching bluebloods. He was a North Carolina boy. He knew the system and the methodology."[18]

"I thought [Kuester] was a nice, very personable guy. Knowledge-wise, I thought he was great until he started coaching. He could not coach basketball. Shawn [Teague] got so mad at the way he was coaching. Kuester would say, 'We're going to fall back into a zone defense,' and Shawn was like, 'Are you crazy?' Shawn would come out and huddle everyone together on the court and overrule Kuester. And he managed to get us to the finals. Shawn drove us almost to a conference championship," Peter Gabriele recalled.[19] Teague and the team's tournament-tested core nearly fought bu back into the ncaa Tournament in March 1985, upsetting Niagara and Canisius on consecutive nights in Buffalo before nearly knocking off Northeastern in the nac title game at Matthews Arena. bu led for much of the second half, but Reggie Lewis, who led all scorers with 29 points, willed Northeastern to a 68–67 win.

Regardless of bu's on-court struggles, Kuester continued to land excellent recruits. He brought a trio of guards to Commonwealth Avenue that would have a profound impact on the future of the program: Tony DaCosta, Jeff Timberlake, and Drederick Irving.

"They were like thunder and lightning," Tom Ivey said of DaCosta and Timberlake, who shared point guard duties. "They were complimentary bookends. If you want a player that mirrors Russell Westbrook or a James Harden that fills every line of the stats, that's both of them combined. They put on a show." DaCosta became one of the best outside shooters in bu history, while Timberlake remains bu's all-time assist leader. Both players scored more than 1,000 points in their collegiate careers.

"Drederick [Irving] could have transferred after he played one basketball game. As soon as people saw what skills that kid had, he literally could have gone and played anywhere he wanted," Mike Rosen said.[20] Early in his freshman year, Irving outplayed unc great Kenny Smith in a blowout loss at Boston Garden. Raised in the Bronx, the rail-thin Irving earned All-City honors as a guard at Adlai Stevenson High School. Initially, bu was one of the few programs to show interest in the slightly built guard. Mike Rosen, who often went on recruiting trips for Kuester, remembers sitting alongside big-time Division I coaches in the stands at New York City high school basketball tournaments and seeing how impressed they were with Irving.[21]

Apparently, few probed much further, fearing that Irving's frame would not stand up to a winter's worth of physical play. By the time Big East powers St. John's and Villanova inquired, Irving had signed on with Boston University. Blessed with track star athleticism and a soft shooter's touch, Irving made up for his size with skill and work ethic. He built up his body too. Irving took advantage of BU's excellent strength and conditioning program, increasing his bench press from 90 to 230 pounds over the course of his time on Commonwealth Avenue. Irving would go on to be one of the finest players in BU history.[22]

As a freshman, Irving showed enough flashes of brilliance to earn significant time as a reserve but never cracked the starting lineup. The speed and athleticism that drove Irving's game were not well suited to the more mannered style of play favored by John Kuester. "I was sort of upset with how things were going. Coach Kuester and I had a different opinion on how the game is played. We just didn't get along," Irving told the *Globe*'s Jackie MacMullan in retrospect.[23] Nevertheless, Irving earned NAC All-Rookie Team honors. He too considered transferring, but events worked themselves out in his favor.

The John Kuester era at Boston University ended as quickly as it started. In early May 1985, George Washington announced Kuester as its new head basketball coach. A Richmond, Virginia native, Kuester noted his excitement to coach in Washington DC, compete in the Atlantic-10, and be much closer to his family.[24]

"I was in the locker room, sitting in my chair, and I had my hat on cockeyed because I knew what was coming, and I had a huge smile on my face. I congratulated [Kuester]. I said, 'Good luck, and I told you so,'" Peter Gabriele remembered. Kuester had threatened to pull Gabriele's scholarship when he suffered a hamstring injury as a freshman. Gabriele told Kuester he would outlast him in the program, which in fact he did. The Canadian center enjoyed a productive four-year career with the Terriers.[25]

Like Kuester, Pitino spent just two years in his new position. In retrospect, Pitino's experience in New York looks like an early-career sabbatical, an opportunity for the coach to work with his longtime mentor in an exclusively basketball environment.[26] Pitino credits Brown with teaching him about the primordial analytics of basketball and showing him how to get a team prepared for a game. "Spending two years with Hubie Brown was like spending ten years in a basketball library," Pitino wrote in his memoir.[27] Pitino worked in concert with Knicks advance scout Richie Adubato, breaking down the opposition and getting the Knickerbockers prepared for each contest. He spent the games charting nearly thirty different factors, from ball deflections to the particulars of every offensive and defensive possession, feeding Brown data during breaks in the action.[28]

Pitino spent two very different seasons with the Knicks. In his first year, the Knicks reached their apex under Brown, led on the court by powerhouse center Bill Cartwright, erratic but brilliant point guard Ray Williams, and, especially, Bernard King, who was arguably the league's most electrifying offensive player of the 1980s before the emergence of Michael Jordan. The 1983–1984 Knicks won forty-seven games and defeated Chuck Daly's first Pistons team in the opening round before losing in seven games to the eventual world champion Boston Celtics in one of the decade's most memorable playoff series. Things could not have gone much differently for the Knicks in 1984–1985. Bill Cartwright missed the season with a foot injury, and Hubie Brown convinced team management not to re-sign Ray Williams, whom Brown regarded as an insubordinate on the floor. Bernard King put on a one-man show for the Knicks, averaging a league-leading 32.9 points per game, but his season too came to an early end. In March, King tore his ACL, an injury from which he never fully recovered. Without any of their key pieces in place by season's end, the Knicks finished sixteen games behind the next worst team in the Atlantic Division.

Amid the Knicks' atrocious 1984–1985 campaign, Pitino got a call from Providence AD Lou Lamoriello. In February 1985, Joe Mullaney resigned as Providence's men's basketball coach. The once proud program won eleven games under Mullaney in 1984–1985, a figure that was not out of line with its recent performances. The Friars had just one winning season since Dave Gavitt left in 1979 to serve as the Big East's first commissioner.

Lamoriello was tasked with finding the man to return Providence basketball to the standard it set under Gavitt. He looked into more high-profile candidates, including Gary Williams and Willis Reed but soon got stuck on a New York Knicks assistant who came recommended by Gavitt himself. Pitino initially brushed off Lamoriello, preferring to stay in New York with his friend Brown to taking on a seemingly hopeless rebuild. Providence's chances of ever competing in a league that later that season became the first in NCAA history to land three teams in the Final Four seemed remote.

Eventually, Lamoriello persuaded Pitino to meet him at an Irish pub in Manhattan's Kips Bay neighborhood. The Abbey Tavern was just up the street from Pitino's first childhood home, a three-story brownstone on Twenty-Sixth Street, where his grandparents and aunt and uncle also resided. More significant, it was far enough away from Madison Square Garden to avoid the sightlines of anyone in the basketball community. Earlier that evening, Pitino and Lamoriello had separately watched St. John's annihilate Providence in the quarterfinals of the Big East Tournament, 90–62.[29]

After one conversation, Lamoriello said he knew Pitino was the man for the job. Pitino too said the opportunity to become a head coach in college basketball's best conference was just too enticing an offer to turn down. They agreed that the best way to proceed was to keep a lid on the story for as long as possible. The next night, Pitino drove up to Rhode Island and took a 2:30 a.m. tour of the campus with Lamoriello. Soon thereafter, the pair started negotiating terms for a contract. Hubie Brown gave Pitino his immediate blessing and the thirty-two-year-old left the last-place Knicks in late March for a shot at the Big East.[30]

Several weeks after Providence hired Rick Pitino, BU embarked on its second coaching search in three years. Already well into the off-season, new athletic director Rick Taylor found himself at a significant disadvantage as most programs already had their coaching staffs in place by May. At the time of John Kuester's sudden departure, the *Globe*'s Jackie MacMullan suggested that current BU assistants Tom McCorry and Rodney Johnson, both Kuester hires, and St. Anslem's Bob Brown, a Pitino assistant at BU, were the leading candidates for the position. Taylor also inquired about Northeastern's Karl Fogel, Siena's John Griffin, and Duke assistant Pete Gaudet, who had been a finalist for the BU job back in 1978.[31]

Rick Taylor instead went in a radically different direction, reaching across the Charles River to hire Cambridge Rindge and Latin coach Mike Jarvis, already a local coaching legend at age forty. Jarvis had served as an assistant at his alma mater, Northeastern, and for Satch Sanders at Harvard during the 1970s but had earned his reputation over the past seven seasons at Rindge, guiding the Falcons to three state championships, winning nearly 90 percent of his games, and mentoring the likes of Patrick Ewing, Karl Hobbs, and Rumeal Robinson.

Taylor said he was looking for a good basketball coach with strong ties to Boston. The BU athletic director fixated on Jarvis, whose reputation as one of the game's best teachers preceded him.[32] The Rindge coach was a community pillar in Cambridge whose esteem locally had grown beyond the basketball court in part because of his conscientious handling of Patrick Ewing's recruitment. Coach Jarvis kept a lid on the surrounding hoopla by ensuring that Ewing's interests as a student and a person, as well as the comfort of his family, were central to the process. Jarvis himself said he was only interested in the BU job because it did not require the lifelong Cambridge resident to move his family. In a none-too-light parting shot at Kuester, Taylor also said he was seeking out an experienced coach. "We wanted someone with maturity, not a Young Turk who'd be coming in here for two years and leaving."[33]

Mike Jarvis came in and instilled an old-fashioned toughness in his BU teams, not dissimilar to the style of play he had learned at Northeastern under Duke Dukeshire. "We didn't have a lot of players. We had seven or eight scholarship players," Jarvis recalls. "They were good, tough players, but they needed a little bit different structure and system. The coach before me, John [Kuester], was really young. I had more coaching experience than John. John had come from North Carolina, and I think what John tried to do was basically incorporate the North Carolina system, which was a little bit confusing. So when I came in, I brought a much more simplified system."[34]

Players appreciated the clarity and confidence Jarvis brought to the position. Jarvis is a deeply religious man and a genuine family man who displayed a keen emotional intelligence. When the time and place called for him to be a gentleman, he was a gentleman. When it came time to stand up, Jarvis would stand his ground against anyone. "It was night and day. He [Jarvis] would get on you when he needed to get on you. But he had a way of talking with us that made sense. He didn't talk to you like a small child. He talked to you like a man, which we all appreciated," Peter Gabriele said.[35]

Jarvis displayed a painstaking attention to the details of the BU basketball operation, both on and off the court. On the road Jarvis would be the first one at breakfast, sitting there with a cup of coffee and making sure the bill was accounted for correctly per NCAA regulations.[36]

"Our main emphasis was defense, something I knew better than anything else because that's what I played most of the time when I was in college, so that's what we built our team around," Jarvis said. "I always tried to build my teams and model my teams to play like the Celtics played—in other words, you play an up-tempo game, but you play a team game and you play with the whole Red Auerbach philosophy of defense wins," Jarvis continued, describing the approach he'd used previously at Rindge to mold championship teams. He moved away from the complex offensive schemes Kuester installed and instead focused on pillorying opponents with a range of defensive looks.[37] "It was controlled chaos," Peter Gabriele said. "Full court presses or we'd press and fall back or we'd come out in a zone and end up trapping. Or we'd go into a zone and end up in a man and one."[38] "They [BU] played very physically, and there was a lot of talking. They did not respect the new kids on the block and felt like we didn't even belong," Siena's Art Tooles remembered of the conference newcomer's early games against BU.[39]

Year one of the Mike Jarvis era at BU had a strikingly similar feel to the first year of the Rick Pitino era. Jarvis, like Pitino, invigorated the talent put in place by the previous regime. BU won twenty-one games and earned a bid to the NIT. The Terriers won thirteen conference games in what proved to be the peak year for the NAC. In addition to BU, Northeastern, Canisius, and Siena also posted twenty-win seasons. BU's rugged, physical veterans included senior center Tom Ivey, who earned second-team All-Conference honors, and Peter Gabriele, who harassed any opponent that dared enter the key. Despite not having one player in the top seven in rebounding, BU's collective efforts on the boards made them one of the league's best rebounding teams. Junior forward Paul Hendricks and sophomore Larry Jones, a 6'6" forward who transferred from C. W. Post, made notable contributions as rebounders while producing consistently on the offensive end.

The centerpiece to the attack, though, were freshmen Tony DaCosta and Jeff Timberlake, both of whom Jarvis convinced to keep their commitment to BU after Kuester left. Jarvis regards his success at persuading both players to stay as the biggest recruiting win of his tenure at BU.[40] DaCosta and Timberlake directed BU's multi-pronged offensive attack, getting the ball into the hands of the team's many significant offensive contributors, including Hendricks, Ivey, Jones, and senior small forward

Dwayne Vinson. "Our team was built on togetherness, toughness, and tenacity. The two freshman point guards [DaCosta and Timberlake] really were the guys that ran the team and were the heart and soul of the team, along with Drederick [Irving]," Jarvis said of his first BU team.[41]

More than any of the contributors on Jarvis's first BU squad, it was the offensive juggernaut of sophomore Drederick Irving that rebuilt BU into a championship contender. Named to the league's All-Rookie Team as a freshman, Irving earned All-Conference honors as a sophomore, averaging 18 points per game and finishing second to Northeastern's Reggie Lewis in scoring. Like Lewis, Irving became the focus of virtually every opponent's defensive strategy. Irving could best opponents by using his agility and cunning to traverse his way to the rim. His jump shot was just as effective a weapon in his offensive arsenal. For an offensive force of his magnitude, Irving was strikingly unselfish with the ball. Never a volume shooter, Irving averaged just 12.5 attempts per game during his college career.

Northeastern remained BU's nemesis and the measuring stick not only for the Terriers, but also for the entire conference. In 1985–1986, Northeastern defeated BU in all three of their meetings, including a 63–54 Huskies win in the NAC title game. The following year, Karl Fogel's first at the helm and the senior year for NU's championship triumvirate of Reggie Lewis, Andre LaFleur, and Wes Fuller, Northeastern again beat BU three straight times, including a victory in the NAC finals, which earned Northeastern its sixth NCAA Tournament bid in seven years. But all three of the 1986–1987 games were competitive, unlike several contests during the mid-1980s. Whether competitive or not, the BU-Northeastern games had become increasingly physical affairs where hard fouls and fights were the norm to an even greater extent than during the Calhoun-Pitino era of the rivalry. "It was all-out war. It was like the Pistons and the Bulls back in the 90s," Peter Gabriele recalled. Gabriele and Jeff Timberlake were frequently tasked with guarding Reggie Lewis, trying to jar him with continuous physicality. On the other side, Northeastern played just as physically against Irving.[42]

"Back in those days in a lot of college games at our level and beyond, there were brawls that would take place, whether it be between the players or the coaches. Guys did not get penalized as much when they were in a fight. The fight was broken up, and the game continued. The games [against Northeastern] were very intense and oftentimes ended up in fisticuffs," said Jarvis, who once got into it with Calhoun during a game in his first season at BU. "When you had a city rivalry like Boston University and Northeastern, where you had a coach that had played at Northeastern and coached at Northeastern but was now the head coach at the rival school, I think that just intensified the rivalry, and the schools were competing for what little ink they could get in the local newspapers."[43]

In the winter of 1988, BU finally got past Northeastern, pummeling the Huskies in both regular-season meetings. BU won twenty-three games, including three consecutive convincing wins at the Hartford Civic Center to capture the NAC title. Junior point guard Jeff Timberlake engineered the Terriers attack and earned tournament MVP honors. By the time of the 1987–1988 season, the youthful core of Jarvis's first BU team was now a cadre of veterans. While the thunder and lightning of Timberlake and DaCosta paced the Terrier attack, seniors Drederick Irving and Larry Jones capped off their collegiate careers by achieving significant milestones. Irving led the conference in scoring and became the all-time leading scorer in BU basketball history. Larry Jones led the conference in rebounding while averaging more than 17 points per game, earning him NAC Player of the Year honors. The Terriers lost to a Duke team in the first round of the NCAA Tournament that eventually represented the East Region in the Final Four.

After a twenty-one-win season and a heartbreaking loss to Siena in the NAC Finals in 1988–1989, BU again returned to the NCAA Tournament in 1990 after ripping past three straight conference rivals at the Hartford Civic Center. Jarvis earned NAC Coach of the Year honors for his rebuilding efforts. In the NCAA Tournament, Jarvis's team made a quick exit from March Madness at the hands of old rival Jim Calhoun's number-one-seeded Connecticut Huskies. This proved to be Jarvis's last game at Boston University. In May 1990, Jarvis took advantage of a familiar opportunity in the Atlantic-10. He signed a five-year deal with George Washington University to replace the man he had replaced at BU five years earlier, John Kuester. The Colonials had posted five consecutive losing seasons under Kuester, bottoming out in 1988–1989 as a 1-27 team before improving to 14-17 in Kuester's last season.[44] The winning basketball culture that Mike Jarvis had reinvigorated at BU he made from scratch at George Washington, a program that had just one winning season during the 1980s. In year three, Jarvis had the Colonials in the Sweet Sixteen and had transformed them into a national program.

Rick Pitino's reclamation project in Rhode Island closely resembled the one he enacted on Babcock Street. He started by whipping his charges into shape and realized that he had a hungry, loyal, and surprisingly talented corps of players already on campus. Pitino required several of his returning players to drop excess pounds before the 1985–1986 season if they had any hope of playing on his team. This group included Billy Donovan, a fellow Long Islander who spent his first two seasons near the end of Joe Mullaney's bench. Donovan embraced the conditioning program and regimen of drills aimed at improving specific basketball skills as thoroughly as anyone Pitino ever coached. As Glenn Consor, Shawn Teague, and Brett Brown had before him, Donovan became an extension of Pitino on the floor. Veterans and newcomers, starters and reserves alike bought in to Pitino's aggressive style of play and the costs of preparing to play the game this way. The pressing, clawing, attacking 1985–1986 PC team fought its way to a 17-14 record and a respectable 7-9 mark in the Big East. Providence went on to win two games in the NIT before falling in the quarterfinals to Louisiana Tech.

The Providence team Pitino rebuilt in his image in his first season would look quite different in year two. He'd lost half of his regular rotation to graduation but had an excellent incoming guard with junior transfer Delray Brooks. Brooks had been Indiana's Mr. Basketball in 1984 and was a prize recruit for his home-state Hoosiers. Bobby Knight, though, had relegated Brooks to the bench. Brooks decided to finish his college career and education elsewhere. Brooks, Donovan, and Pop Lewis, a 6'4" small forward from Philadelphia, became the focal points of Pitino's reworked attack. While Pitino is often characterized as a defensive-minded coach focused largely on his full-court press, he has proven throughout his career a willingness to adjust to changing circumstances, as he did with the NCAA-wide adoption of the three-point shot for the 1986–1987 season.

Pitino drilled Donovan, Brooks, and Lewis continually in the three-point shot as they prepared for its installation. In preseason practices, Pitino prohibited all three players from taking any shots inside of the arc. When league play commenced in January 1987, the Big East was in for a tremendous surprise. Providence's "bomb squad" turned the Friars into not only the Big East's best outside shooting team, but the best one in major college basketball.[45] The Friars hit nearly twice as many three-point field goals as the next closest team in their league. Donovan and Pop Lewis were the number one and two outside shooters in the Big East respectively, while Delray Brooks finished seventh. Adding this tool to Providence's press and freewheeling offense transformed a team that had never won more than five Big East regular-season games into an overnight power. PC finished ninth in the country in scoring, averaging more than 86 points per game. The Friars went 10-6 in the Big East, won twenty-five games overall that season, and reached the Final Four for the first time since 1973, pummeling Georgetown in the Southeast Regional Final. And Pitino did it largely with the talent he had on his roster when he arrived in Providence. Four of the team's five regular starters were Providence Friars on the day that Pitino became head coach. Pitino convinced some fine players to come to Providence, including future NBAers Eric Murdock and Marty Conlon, but there is no better evidence of his ability to remake a seemingly pedestrian team into winners than his Final Four team at Providence.

Pitino's Cinderella team at Providence remade the once "Boy Coach" into a national figure. Only in his early thirties, Pitino had earned the reputation as one of the game's great teachers, motivators, and minds. The heartbreak surrounding the team's success—the death of Pitino's six-month-old son Daniel from congestive heart failure on the day Providence received its NCAA Tournament bid—served not only to further bind the Providence basketball family, but transformed millions of empathetic viewers around the country into overnight Providence fans.

Pitino soon moved on again, heading back to New York to become head coach of the Knicks. Wherever he went, he brought his unrelenting press; his unique ability to rebuild players from the ground up; and an outspoken, matter-of-fact sense of self-confidence that won him more than his share of detractors. Pitino has certainly been a controversial figure, particularly in the latter half of his career, for his alleged actions or inactions on and off the court. In spite of this, it is hard to argue with the sum total of his life's work.

Pitino rebuilt the Knicks just as he had BU and Providence, bringing his unrelenting pressing style to the NBA. He also brought his newfound commitment to the three-point shot, creating his own Madison Square Garden "bomb squad" of Mark Jackson, Rod Strickland, and Johnny Newman, among others.

Pitino's 1987–1988 club got better as the season wore on, winning twenty-two of its last thirty-seven games and securing the Knicks' first playoff appearance in four seasons. The next year, they won the NBA's Atlantic Division. Pitino left New York just as quickly as he got there, bolting from the contentious relationship he'd developed with Knicks GM Al Bianchi for a shot to coach Kentucky.

The return to college basketball set Pitino back on the course that earned him a spot in the Naismith Memorial Basketball Hall of Fame in 2013. By leading Kentucky, Louisville, and, most recently, Iona to the NCAA Tournament, Pitino became the only coach in college basketball history to bring five different schools to the tourney.

He has won more than eight hundred games as a college coach and nearly 75 percent of his games. Pitino won national championships at Kentucky in 1996 and Louisville in 2013. Pitino's teams reached the NCAA Tournament on twenty-two occasions and made it to the Final Four seven times. For all of the great players that Pitino has coached over his nearly fifty-year career, there is a distinct possibility that not one of them will be inducted into the Basketball Hall of Fame as a player (though Billy Donovan will almost certainly be inducted as a coach, and Tubby Smith, who served as Pitino's assistant at Kentucky, ought to be). There may be no better testimony to Pitino's greatness as a molder of teams than this footnote to his curriculum vitae.

As far as the on-court performance of Pitino's teams goes, the one hiccup in his career was his return to Boston and return to the NBA in 1997 to lead the Celtics. Pitino resigned thirty-four games into his fourth season at the helm in Boston, having failed to make the playoffs even once as the team's coach and president of basketball operations. Pitino's confidence came off as foolhardy smugness as several of his personnel moves backfired and the new generation of professional players seemed immune to his brand of persuasion and pedagogy. Nevertheless, Pitino said in his Hall of Fame induction speech how grateful he was for his time with the Celtics: "I learned more than I gave," Pitino said of his return to Boston. He said he learned patience and humility from his time with the Celtics, not only because of the losing, but also the way that the franchise's legends—including Bill Russell, Bob Cousy, and John Havlicek—carried themselves as Celtics alumni.[46] During his return to Boston, Pitino put these skills to work in his efforts on behalf of Boston University.

Upon his return to Boston, Pitino was the keynote speaker at a $100-per-plate athletic department fundraising dinner at BU. His triumphant return to the campus, where his teams once played in anonymity, drew nearly as many people as most Terrier basketball games in the early 1980s. Pitino regaled the crowd with stories of his salad days at the school—how he stayed up all night shining his shoes the night before his job interview; how he put his players through the ropes in practice; and how he courted prospects in his company car: a subcompact Renault LeCar. Pitino often received $50,000 for such speaking engagements. In this instance, he did it for free. The fundraiser was far from Pitino's first act of post-BU generosity toward the school's athletic department. Two years earlier, he'd bought the basketball program a state-of-the-art video recording system.[47]

In the decades since Rick Pitino, Mike Jarvis, and all of their fine players left Commonwealth Avenue, BU basketball has remained a consistently competitive program. Former Pitino assistant Bob Brown's Terrier teams struggled in the early 1990s before Dennis Wolff turned things around later in the decade. Wolff led BU to NCAA Tournament births in 1997 and 2002, as well as a trio of appearances in the NIT. BU's current coach, Joe Jones, has piloted the program to steady success in its new conference, the Patriot League, which the school joined in 2013. Jones's teams have reached the postseason on four occasions and would have earned a fifth postseason bid in 2020 had March Madness not been scrapped because of the pandemic. Nevertheless, BU continues to play for modest crowds at Case Gym, rarely crossing the one-thousand-fan threshold even before the onset of COVID-19.

BU's footprint on the basketball landscape in Boston remains small. Nationally, it is virtually invisible. Even so, Terrier basketball is in the unique situation of having a grip that exceeds its reach. Case and Walter Brown were the spaces where two of the most impressive college coaching careers of the last half century took shape.

15

Homecoming *(Williams)*

"I was very fortunate to be at Ohio State. I thought I had a lifetime job and that was going to be it," Gary Williams said in his Basketball Hall of Fame induction speech in 2014.[1]

The late 1980s proved to be a time of transition for the coaching milieu from which Gary Williams emerged. Williams's stay at Ohio State was a relatively short one, even shorter than his stint in Chestnut Hill. During that time, he would rebuild the Buckeyes' program while crossing paths with his mentor, Tom Davis, in the Big Ten and sharing a state with his former assistant, Kevin Mackey, whose star shone brightly in the coaching fraternity ever so shortly. The Boston College program Williams left would spend several seasons in transition—both adjusting to its new home, the Silvio O. Conte Forum, and to new leadership under Jim O'Brien. By decade's end, Gary Williams would be headed home, taking on the job that would become his life's work and professional legacy. That tangled path began in March 1986, not long after he left Boston for the Midwest.

Within days of Gary Williams's leaving for Columbus, Boston College athletic director Bill Flynn brought candidates to campus to fill the sudden opening in the basketball program. Many were familiar names from the 1982 coaching search, including Mitch Buonaguro, Bob Dukiet, and Jim Satalin. Quickly emerging from the cluster of familiar candidates was St. Bonaventure's Jim O'Brien, who had interviewed for the job four Marchs earlier and boasted as robust a BC basketball pedigree as anyone alive.

Jim O'Brien. Class of '71. New England Player of the Year, 1971. Point guard for Bob Cousy's 1968–1969 NIT runners-up. Veteran of the already legendary ABA. Right-hand man to UConn's Dom Perno when the Huskies were still an eastern power. In 1982, O'Brien moved his young family to the small town of Olean in western New York and his first head coaching job at St. Bonaventure University. He took over Jim Satalin's 14-14 Bonnies team of 1981–1982 and coached them up into a twenty-win club that earned a 1983 NIT bid, earning him Atlantic-10 Coach of the Year honors. In subsequent years under O'Brien, St. Bonaventure hovered around the middle of the pack in the highly competitive Atlantic-10, a league that garnered multiple NCAA and NIT bids most seasons.

"When Gary [Williams] left and the job opened, I talked to Bill Flynn again," Jim O'Brien said. "He [Flynn] said, 'We definitely want you to come up and interview again.'"[2] Until Flynn called, O'Brien was in the uncomfortable position of sitting around waiting to hear from his alma mater. In the meantime, everyone in the basketball press checked in on O'Brien to see if he thought he was the front runner for the job, had been told he was the front runner for the job, or had already gone from front runner to new BC head basketball coach. As he waited for the word to come down from Chestnut Hill, O'Brien told the *Globe*'s Jackie MacMullan that he didn't really want to say anything because he "[didn't] want to do anything to alienate BC."[3]

While O'Brien clearly wanted the Boston College job and it appeared that Flynn and company wanted him to take the job, a couple of other names popped up amid the search: Kevin Mackey and Jim Calhoun. Since Mackey left Chestnut Hill in 1983, he had remade the Cleveland State basketball program in his image. He recruited a dozen tough, generally overlooked city kids to CSU's downtown commuter school campus. Entering the 1985–1986 season, his team was built around a point guard from Cleveland's east side named Clinton Smith, who left Ohio State after a season of sitting on Eldon Miller's bench; Eric Mudd, an offensively minded center out of Cleveland's Benedictine High; an undersized forward from Toledo named Clinton Ramsey; a 5'10" guard from Boston's Dorchester neighborhood named Ed Bryant; and a playground legend out of New York City's Lower East Side named Ken "Mouse" McFadden. Mackey brought the East Coast "city game" with him to Cleveland. His CSU Vikings pursued the ball with reckless abandon. They flew up and down the court like few teams in the country. Cleveland State's opponents faced forty minutes of trapping, pressing, fast breaking, and alley-ooping by a ten-deep bench every time out.[4]

In 1984–1985, the Vikings won twenty-one games and the Mid-Continent Conference's regular season title. In 1985–1986, CSU improved from seventh in the country in scoring to second, averaging just under 90 points per game. The Vikings won their conference's regular and postseason championships, entering the NCAA Tournament with twenty-seven wins. Little heralded Cleveland State drew a fourteen seed in the East Region and a March 14 date at the Carrier Dome with Bobby Knight's Indiana Hoosiers. "Mackey's Misfits" wrote the final chapter of John Feinstein's *Season on the Brink* that afternoon, laying waste to an Indiana team full of players who would never have considered an offer from Cleveland State. Twelve months later, nearly the exact same Hoosiers roster won a national championship. In the second round, Cleveland State wreaked havoc on sixth-seeded St. Joseph's, blowing past the Hawks with the same run-and-gun attack that took out Indiana. The Vikings finally bowed out in the Sweet Sixteen, falling by one to David Robinson and Navy—mostly to David Robinson.

While BC was interviewing a series of candidates who were on the outside looking in at March Madness, Mackey's availability to travel back to Boston was limited. His Cleveland State team was busy writing one of the first Cinderella stories of the sixty-four-team tournament era. When asked about the BC opening, Mackey said he wouldn't even consider it until after his season at Cleveland State ended. Bill Flynn said he wasn't even sure if Mackey would be interested in the job if asked, as Mackey could continue to build up his program at a school with open enrollment—free of the academic constraints he would face getting student-athletes accepted at the Jesuit school. By the time Navy knocked CSU out of the tournament, the BC athletic department was well on its way to hiring a new coach.

In March 1986, Jim Calhoun brought his Northeastern Huskies to the NCAA Tournament for the fifth time in six years. Reggie Lewis, Andre LaFleur, and the rest of Calhoun's wrecking crew put a serious scare into Billy Tubbs's fourth-seeded Oklahoma team in the first round, falling 80–74. Following Northeastern's departure from the NCAA Tournament, Calhoun interviewed with Bill Flynn for the BC job. Several other schools, including Northwestern, Wichita State, and Connecticut were hotly pursuing Calhoun as well.

BC decided instead to stick with one of its own. Eleven days after Gary Williams left for Columbus, Boston College named Jim O'Brien its new head basketball coach. After a fortnight of waiting, the decision was a momentary relief to O'Brien and his family, whose lives had been on hold in a strikingly public manner.

"He's [O'Brien] young and he's hungry. I'm also pleased because he's someone that won't use this job as a steppingstone, which the last 4 or 5 coaches have to some degree," O'Brien's former coach Bob Cousy said of the hire.[5] The idea that BC's new hire was rooted in Boston and committed to staying at the school was particularly important to Bill Flynn, whose two previous hires had both left for greener pastures.[6] "I knew about the past at BC and I knew all about the accolades that Jim O'Brien had, being a star player at BC, playing in the ABA. I knew he was a terrific player coming in to coach us at his alma mater," Ted Kelley said of the hire.[7]

Unlike BC's previous coaching search, the team's veteran players played no role in selecting the coach. They learned about the hire when everyone else did. "I didn't hear anything. New coach. Boom! You read about it in the *Boston Globe*," Troy Bowers recalled.[8]

O'Brien's relief was quickly replaced by the realization that he needed to get to work. BC had signed exactly zero new players for the upcoming season and needed to find replacements for a pair of four-year program pillars in Roger McCready and Dom Pressley. As O'Brien's predecessors could attest, bringing Big East caliber players to Chestnut Hill was a significant challenge for several oft-repeated reasons.

"We needed to do some recruiting, and it was a little bit of a struggle. It has been well documented that there are a lot of academic constraints recruiting at BC. We had some issues that a lot of other schools didn't have," O'Brien said.[9] Recruiting challenges were nothing new for O'Brien. At St. Bonaventure, he had to navigate recruits to the small town of Olean, New York, ninety miles south of Buffalo along largely back roads. By comparison, pitching kids on playing in Boston was a lot easier, though the kind of players O'Brien would need to compete in the Big East were a different caliber than those he needed to compete in the Atlantic-10.

O'Brien faced another hurdle as he tried to adjust BC's style of play to his own preferences. As an assistant at UConn and head coach at St. Bonaventure, O'Brien had coached teams built around big, physical, low-post players like the Huskies' Corny Thompson and Chuck Aleksinas or the Bonnies' All-Atlantic-10 power forward Barry Mungar. At BC, his best returning big man was the versatile Troy Bowers, whose game and size were not those of a classic center. Moreover, O'Brien favored a much more deliberate, conventional offensive tempo than Williams or Davis. His approach on the defensive end was also much more conservative than the continuous pressure defense BC's opponents had grown used to under Williams.[10]

"My style of play was better adapted to Gary Williams's approach. In high school, I was a slasher, and we had a pretty fast-paced, pressure style. I liked Gary's style. Go after it. Be the aggressor. Jim was a little bit more conservative," Steven Benton said.[11] "Jim [O'Brien] was just as intense as Gary [Williams]," Ted Kelley said. "It was very much a transition year, and I'm very thankful for the opportunity he gave me to start, play, and have some big moments." The fifth-year senior Kelley had been a reserve throughout his tenure at Chestnut Hill but provided veteran leadership on O'Brien's first BC team. He served as a team captain and started in BC's backcourt alongside Dana Barros, displaying both basketball smarts and tough-minded play, especially on the defensive end.[12]

O'Brien relied on a smaller rotation than either Davis or Williams, playing mostly an eight-deep bench with Barros, Kelley, and Jamie Benton in the backcourt, Steven Benton and Skip Barry on the wing, and Troy Bowers, Tyrone Scott, and freshman Bob Francis in the low post. The absence of Bowers, who missed much of the non-conference schedule with a knee injury, proved a further obstacle for O'Brien's team.

BC struggled again in 1986–1987, winning just eleven games all season. They went a meagre 3-13 in Big East play. Unfortunately for the Eagles, the program's second straight losing season came at a time of unprecedented local exposure. In addition to regular appearances on ESPN, USA Network, and CBS, BC's games were also appearing more frequently on local television outlets such as WSBK, NESN, and Sports Channel New England. Radio coverage of BC basketball appeared on a major local station for the first time in decades in 1986–1987, as WBZ signed on for coverage of both Eagles football and basketball. Moreover, the shifting of an unprecedented eight home games that season to the Garden made BC a regular at the region's most revered arena.[13]

The emergence of sophomore Dana Barros as one of the Big East's top players was among the few highlights for the Eagles in 1986–1987. Barros averaged nearly 19 points per game and proved himself to be one of the league's best outside shooters in the first year of the three-point shot. BC's best win of the season came at the Garden against Rick Pitino's upstart Providence team, which earned a trip to the Final Four just two years removed from the Big East basement. Senior leadership took charge for

BC in the 67–66 victory. Troy Bowers pumped in 20 points, while Ted Kelley dropped in the game winner after snagging an offensive rebound with four seconds remaining.

Despite the Eagles' struggles in 1986–1987, O'Brien developed a strong rapport with veterans and underclassmen alike. "I was very fortunate to play for two great coaches [Williams and O'Brien]. Jim O'Brien takes a back seat to no one as a coach. I was a grad assistant for a year after, and he's as knowledgeable as anyone around about the game," Ted Kelley said.[14]

While BC struggled under Jim O'Brien in 1986–1987, Gary Williams was beginning a rebuild of his own at Ohio State. The Buckeyes had hardly struggled under Williams's low-key predecessor in Columbus, Eldon Miller. OSU had earned four NCAA and one NIT bid during Miller's ten seasons, but Ohio State boosters expected more out of the well-heeled program than the longtime coach produced. The Buckeyes had not won the Big Ten or advanced beyond the Sweet Sixteen since 1971, several seasons before Miller took over as head coach.

Williams brought a decidedly different demeanor to practice and the coach's box than Miller's. His practices were the gauntlets that BC players came to know well. The new coach remade a brawny Big Ten team, built around cramming the ball into the low post, into a unit capable of playing up-tempo basketball. He installed his fast-breaking variant of Tom Davis's "zone offense," which later came to be known as the "Maryland flex offense," replete with backdoor cuts, screens, and bounce passes from the wing. Ohio State also adopted the pressure defense that became Boston College's signature during Williams's four years in Chestnut Hill. Williams's famed intensity also showed up in the preparations for the 1986–1987 season—they'd never seen Eldon Miller punt a basketball into the stands or stomp around on the sidelines in practice, let alone during a game.[15]

The cultural shift in Columbus under Gary Williams paid immediate dividends for the Ohio State program. The 1986–1987 Buckeyes held their own in, arguably, the strongest field in Big Ten history. Ohio State went 9-9 in a league that included four of the top eleven teams in the final AP poll. While Ohio State's roster included just one future NBA player, Dennis Hopson, the other five Big Ten teams that earned bids to the NCAA Tournament all had at least three future NBA alumni on their rosters. Hopson, a 6′5″ shooting guard/small forward, was tailor-made for Gary Williams's offense. Blessed with elite athleticism and possessing a comparably elite jump shot, Hopson was the dynamo behind Ohio State's success in 1986–1987. Already one of the Big Ten's top scorers (he averaged 20.9 points per game as a junior), Hopson averaged 29 per game in Gary Williams's stampeding offense. He earned Big Ten Player of the Year honors, ahead of the likes of Indiana's Steve Alford and Michigan's Gary Grant. In June 1987, the New Jersey Nets selected Hopson third overall in the NBA Draft.

The 19-13 Buckeyes were slotted ninth in the East region and knocked off Eddie Sutton's Kentucky Wildcats in the first round. Williams's team put a genuine scare into a familiar foe in the second round, John Thompson's Georgetown Hoyas. Ohio State blitzed the Hoyas in the first half, as so many of Williams's BC teams had in previous years. The Buckeyes took a 10-point lead into the locker room and led by as many as 15 in the second half. The Hoyas' size and depth, as well as 20 second-half points by Georgetown senior forward Reggie Williams, were too much for Ohio State. Georgetown squeezed out an 82–79 victory.

Part of the logjam that Gary Williams faced at the top of the Big Ten came from the sudden presence of his mentor in the league. Less than a month after Williams signed on at Ohio State, his former boss at Boston College joined him in the Big Ten. After four seasons, Tom Davis left Stanford to take over from George Raveling at Iowa. Raveling himself was swapping conferences with Davis and heading to Southern Cal. The experience at Stanford had been a frustrating one for Davis. He led the Cardinal to just one winning season in four and faced many of the same recruiting hurdles in Palo Alto as he had in Chestnut Hill. The return to his native Midwest did Davis a world of good. Iowa had won twenty games and earned an at-large bid to the NCAA Tournament under Raveling in 1985–1986. The Hawkeyes' returning roster featured an incredible seven future NBA players, including center Brad Lohaus, swingman Kevin Gamble, and point guard B. J. Armstrong.

The Hawkeyes' roster in 1986–1987 was simultaneously big, athletic, and cerebral, a perfect vessel for Davis's zone offense. Iowa finished sixth in the country in scoring in 1986–1987, averaging 87.3 points per game. The Hawkeyes spent the entire season in the top ten, including a week at number one. Iowa finished the season number six in the AP poll but just third in a stacked Big Ten that included four of the country's top eleven teams. Davis's thirty-win Hawkeyes made it all the way to the Elite Eight, losing the West Regional Final to UNLV in one of the most breakneck games in tournament history. Iowa's toe-to-toe battle with Jerry Tarkanian's Runnin' Rebels was a near replica of BC's showdown five years earlier in the Final Eight against Houston's Phi Slamma Jamma.

As a consolation prize, Davis earned Big Ten Coach of the Year honors and was named AP College Basketball Coach of the Year in 1987. Never again did Davis's Iowa squad reach the Elite Eight, let alone the Final Four. But Davis established the Hawkeyes as one of the country's most consistently successful programs, leading them to nine NCAA Tournaments and two NITs in his thirteen years at Iowa. Davis is the winningest coach in Hawkeye history, and his Iowa teams never lost a first-round game in the NCAA Tournament.

Iowa and Ohio State met for a pair of extraordinary clashes during Davis's and Williams's first year together in the Big Ten. On January 24, 1987, Ohio State traveled to Iowa City for a nationally televised Saturday afternoon contest with the number-one-ranked and undefeated Hawkeyes. Iowa was coming off three consecutive wins over top ten teams from Illinois, Purdue, and Indiana. Rather than try to outrun or outrebound Iowa's bigger, more talented, and more athletic team, Williams adopted a tactic he employed frequently in his Big East days. He threw a variety of defensive looks at Davis's Hawkeyes but settled on a zone that forced Iowa to take an unusually high number of perimeter shots—one of Iowa's few weaknesses. On the offensive end, Dennis Hopson took charge, pouring in 36 points and rising to every challenge in the back-and-forth game. After six lead changes early in the second half, Ohio State took a 53–48 lead with just under fifteen minutes remaining in the game. The Buckeyes hung on to that slim advantage for the rest of the afternoon, defeating the number-one-ranked Hawkeyes, 80–76.[16] Three weeks later, the teams met for another nailbiter, this time at St. John Arena in Columbus. Iowa prevailed, 82–80, in a similarly fraught affair. In the three seasons that Gary Williams and Tom Davis coached against each other in the Big Ten, Iowa and Ohio State split the season series each time.

While Williams faced off with his close friend Davis in conference, his former colleague Kevin Mackey had turned a commuter college two hours north of Columbus into, arguably, Ohio's top college basketball program. Mackey's Cleveland State Vikings continued to prosper in the aftermath of their 1986 NCAA Tournament run, winning twenty-five games in 1986–1987 and twenty-two games in 1987–1988. The Vikings reached the second round of the NIT in both seasons. The success of CSU basketball spurred construction of a fifteen-thousand-seat arena that came to be known as the Wolstein Center. The school broke ground on the $55 million venue in August 1989, and it opened for the 1991–1992 season. For a time, it was both the largest arena in the city of Cleveland and the largest university-owned arena in the state, nearly two thousand seats larger than Ohio State's St. John Arena. Unfortunately, by the time the Vikings started playing at the Wolstein Center, Kevin Mackey was no longer the school's basketball coach. Mackey's substance abuse problems came to light after an arrest in July 1990, just days after he signed a new two-year deal to continue as CSU head coach. Rather than allowing him to go to rehab and return to work, Cleveland State fired the most successful coach in its history.

Mackey never returned to college coaching. Following a successful stint in rehab, he took over the Miami Tropics of the U.S. Basketball League in 1991, beginning a decade of great achievement in minor professional leagues. For much of the last twenty years Mackey served as a scout for the Indiana Pacers, working for an old friend from Boston: Larry Bird.

Cleveland State basketball wasn't quite so lucky. Without Mackey guiding the ship, the program has failed for thirty years to recapture the on-court success or interest of the late 1980s. The Wolstein Center has been something of a white elephant in downtown Cleveland. The program has never averaged more than 4,500 fans per game at the building and frequently has drawn far less. The 2020–2021 Cleveland State team was the first to reach the NCAA Tournament since the Sweet Sixteen run of 1986.

Back in Boston, Jim O'Brien was rebuilding the basketball program that Davis, Williams, and Mackey had built into a Big East power. After consecutive losing seasons, the Eagles bounced back in the winter of 1987–1988—not to the heights of the Tom Davis and Gary Williams years but well enough to be a feared foe in the Big East. The trio of Jamie Benton, Steven Benton, and, especially, Dana Barros developed into one of the best perimeter shooting units in the country. Barros nailed better than 40 percent of his outside shots in 1986–1987, a rate he improved to nearly 45 percent in 1987–1988, while averaging nearly 22 points per game (Barros later became BC's all-time leading scorer.) At the same time, Jamie and Steven Benton both became credible threats from beyond the arc. BC played well enough to earn a bid to the NIT, where the Eagles won three consecutive games to reach the semifinals at Madison Square Garden. BC fell to conference rival and eventual NIT champ UConn, 73–67.

UConn's victory in the 1988 NIT finals came at the expense of Gary Williams's Ohio State team, which had struggled all season to replace the offensive firepower of Dennis Hopson. The Buckeyes averaged 10 points fewer per game in 1987–1988 than they had the previous season. Despite a .500 finish in the Big Ten, a string of non-conference losses likely kept Ohio State out of the 1988 NCAA Tournament. The Buckeyes made the most of it in March, winning three straight games in the NIT to earn one of the four spots at Madison Square Garden. The most memorable of these early-round games was an 86–80 second-round win over Cleveland State at St. John Arena. The sold-out crowd was as shambolic as the action on the court that evening, as the Buckeyes' and Vikings' dueling presses and fast breaks made for a unique show on the floor. Ohio State overcame a 42–38 halftime deficit to pull past Cleveland State and win some in-state bragging rights.

After beating Colorado State in the semis, Ohio State fell to Jim Calhoun's upstart UConn team in an exciting 72–67 championship game that bore a strong resemblance to the battles Williams experienced in the Big East Tournament. Coming out of the 1988 NIT, Calhoun's UConn program clearly had a sense of momentum, as the recent doormat of the Big East earned some national recognition after three weeks' worth of postseason heroics. Ohio State, too, built up a head of steam coming out of the 1988 NIT. Entering the 1988–1989 season, the Buckeyes returned six of their top seven scorers from the previous season and placed seventeenth in the preseason AP poll. Through mid-February, Ohio State remained nationally ranked, but a terrible neck injury suffered by senior guard Jay Burson, the team's leading scorer, derailed both the young star's career and Ohio State's push for an NCAA Tournament bid. Without Burson, who spent three months in traction after fracturing his fifth cervical vertebra, the Buckeyes fell apart, losing their last eight conference games in a row. Ohio State returned to the NIT, where it won two games before bowing out to St. John's in the quarterfinals.[17]

Despite the bleak conclusion to the 1988–1989 season, Ohio State's future looked incredibly bright. Williams and assistant Randy Ayers had convinced a pair of McDonald's All-Americans, both from Ohio, to play their college ball in Columbus. Toledo's Jim Jackson, a near clone of Dennis

Hopson, and Mark Baker, a point guard out of Dayton's Dunbar High, would be the Buckeyes' backcourt of the future.

The 1988 run to the NIT semis also served as momentum for a BC program that moved into Conte Forum that fall. Performance-wise, the momentum was tough to see in the subsequent seasons. BC struggled to compete in the Big East at the end of the 1980s and the beginning of the 1990s, but recruiting-wise, the new, multi-purpose venue proved an asset in luring talented players to Chestnut Hill. "We were able to showcase that we had a legitimate arena, and that was good for the league," O'Brien said, "but again with that came a little bit of a disadvantage of never practicing on the main area. We had to share that with the women, we had to share it with hockey, and hockey was the main attraction in that arena, so the ice was always down. When we had games, they would put the floor down, and as soon as the games were over, the floor came up. It was a hockey arena that turned into basketball."[18]

In addition to sharing the space with women's basketball and men's hockey, Conte lacked the home-court advantage of the rustic Roberts. "Anytime you practice in a facility that you don't play in, you're going to be put at a disadvantage," Al Skinner, O'Brien's successor at BC, said of Conte. "Playing in a hockey facility, it puts your fans a little further away. If it is a true basketball facility, you can bring those fans closer. And it's those fans that are closer that make it so loud. It didn't allow for the kind of intensity you want in a building."[19]

Despite BC basketball's continued struggles, Bill Flynn and his successor as AD, Chet Gladchuk, remained patient with O'Brien, who more than just righted the ship when he was able to recruit a cluster of big-time players in the early 1990s. "We got lucky with Bill Curley, but getting to that point was not easy," O'Brien said.[20] BC was in the second of three consecutive seasons stuck at the bottom of the Big East when O'Brien signed a bumper class of 1994. Headlining the class was the aforementioned Curley, an athletic, sweet-shooting 6'9" forward from Duxbury, Massachusetts, who was named a McDonald's All-American. Curley chose to stay home over a slew of offers from the blue bloods of the Big East and ACC. Joining Curley in Chestnut Hill were a trio of talented guards: Malcolm Huckaby from Bristol, Connecticut, as well as Howard Eisley and Gerrod Abram, both of whom hailed from Detroit.

After finishing last in the Big East for three consecutive seasons, BC turned it around thanks in large part to this quartet. The Eagles posted a winning record in 1991–1992, made it to the final eight of the NIT in 1992–1993, and had a breakout 1993–1994 campaign. In 1994, BC earned its first trip to the NCAA Tournament in nine seasons, where it scored three consecutive upset wins en route to the Elite Eight. Most memorably, BC knocked off the number-one-ranked and defending national champions from the University of North Carolina in the second round. The victory put BC basketball back on the national map and earned Bill Curley a spot on the cover of *Sports Illustrated*. In three of the next four seasons, O'Brien's BC teams earned bids to the NCAA Tournament.

While Jim O'Brien and Boston College were finding the players that made the school a force once again in March, a new opportunity opened up for Gary Williams. In May 1989, the University of Maryland forced out head coach Bob Wade after a brief and difficult tenure. Wade, the first African American coach in the history of the ACC, took over from the legendary Lefty Driesell just weeks before the start of the 1986–1987 basketball season. Driesell had been fired four months after the death of Len Bias. Bias, the finest player Driesell ever coached at Maryland and arguably the finest player in the history of the ACC aside from Michael Jordan, died from cocaine intoxication just two days after being selected second overall in the NBA Draft by the Boston Celtics.

The tragedy of Bias's death brought unprecedented media scrutiny to Driesell's basketball program. It soon came to light that five Maryland players, including Bias, had failed out of school right after the previous basketball season. The inattention to academics under Driesell led university chancellor John B. Slaughter to relieve the wildly popular and successful coach of his duties.[21] Slaughter replaced Driesell, the most famous name in Maryland college basketball coaching, with Bob Wade, the most famous name in Maryland high school basketball coaching. Wade, a former NFL defensive back, had turned Baltimore's Dunbar High into one of the country's best high school basketball programs, training future college and NBA stars such as Reggie Lewis, Muggsy Bogues, David Wingate, and Reggie Williams. Wade did this all while maintaining a firm grip on his program and the academic performance of his players, earning him the reputation of a by-the-book taskmaster.

Wade walked into a bad situation that only got worse. Several of Maryland's best players were deemed academically ineligible for the upcoming season. The Terrapins went winless in the ACC for the first time in their history in 1986–1987. Buoyed by a strong recruiting class and the return of two key players, Maryland bounced back in 1987–1988, fighting its way to the second round of the NCAA Tournament. Wade also excelled at replenishing Maryland's cupboard, bringing in the likes of Jerrod Mustaf, Walt Williams, and Tony Massenberg, all of whom went on to significant NBA careers. The good times for Wade proved short-lived. Two of Maryland's top returning players transferred before the 1988–1989 season, and another was ruled academically ineligible. A spate of alleged recruiting violations and a 1-13 record in the ACC brought Bob Wade's tenure as the University of Maryland's head basketball coach to an end.

After Wade's resignation, Maryland athletic director Lew Perkins got in contact with Williams and ended up offering him the chance to come home. On June 13, 1989, the University of Maryland announced Gary Williams as its new head basketball coach. Williams, in his memoir, said he made an "emotional decision" when he took the job at his alma mater.[22] He soon realized the predicament he faced in College Park. This predicament had nothing to do with a conference schedule filled with national powers like Duke, North Carolina, and Georgia Tech either. Unbeknownst to Williams, the ongoing NCAA investigation into the Maryland basketball program led to a series of significant sanctions. He would be hamstrung by three years of rigid recruiting restrictions, making it even more difficult for the Terrapins to compete in the ACC. In addition, Maryland received a two-year ban from playing in the NCAA Tournament and would not be allowed to play on television for two seasons.

"If I would have known what things would be like at Maryland, I would never have left Ohio State," Williams wrote.[23] The Ohio State program he took over in 1986 was in more than fine fettle by the time he departed in 1989. His former assistant, Randy Ayers, took over a now loaded Buckeyes roster and brought them to three consecutive NCAA Tournaments. With a backcourt of Jim Jackson and Mark Baker leading the way, Ohio State finished in the top five in consecutive seasons, earning number one seeds in the NCAA Tournament both years. Conversely, Maryland was at the bottom looking up at one of the best conferences in college basketball, struggling to compete after receiving a demi-death penalty from the NCAA.

In Williams's first year at Maryland, the combination of his dynamic, 94–50 approach to the game and the significant amount of talent Wade had brought into the program enabled Maryland to rebound to a nineteen-win season and an NIT birth. After that initial shot in the arm, attrition from Maryland's severe NCAA penalties whittled away at the reserve of talent built up during the Bob Wade years. Maryland got worse for three straight seasons, bottoming out at twelve wins and a 2-14 ACC mark in the 1992–1993 campaign.

"During those three years of sanctions, I made up my mind that I was going to stay and see it through," Williams wrote.[24] During this time, Williams built up relationships on a campus that had turned on basketball in the aftermath of Len Bias's death. Just as important, Williams and his staff (which included future Siena coach Jimmy Patsos and future LaSalle coach Billy Hahn) built up their relationships with respected high school coaches in Maryland, Virginia, and Washington DC, enabling Maryland to develop a mid-Atlantic recruiting base strong enough to compete with the heavyweights in the ACC. Right in Maryland's DMV backyard, Williams signed a versatile 6'5" guard from Washington's Dunbar High named Johnny Rhodes; a long and lean leaper from Harker Prep in Potomac, Maryland named Exree Hipp; and 6'0" point guard Duane Simpkins, a born play-maker hailing from Washington basketball power DeMatha. Williams broke through an informal recruiting boycott of the University of Maryland by Baltimore city high school coaches following Bob Wade's departure. He signed future All-American small forward Keith Booth from the same Dunbar High that Wade had turned into a national power. Maryland ventured as far as Norfolk, Virginia, to recruit standout power forward Joe Smith, who went on to become the number one pick in the 1995 NBA Draft.

This homegrown fivesome became the architecture for Maryland's transformation into a perennial contender for the ACC and NCAA championships. This bunch of freshmen and sophomores made it to the Sweet Sixteen in 1994. In 1995, they finished in the top ten nationally and were part of a four-way tie for the ACC regular-season title. The flourishing of this young Maryland club into a championship-caliber team was the starting point for a run of eleven consecutive tournament appearances for the Terrapins.

"He [Gary Williams] recruited that whole team from twenty minutes away from Maryland. He wouldn't deal with the AAU guys. He wouldn't cheat," Williams's friend Tom Brennan said.[25] Indeed, Williams gave no quarter to the shady characters that became par for the course in college basketball recruiting. He built Maryland into a national power by building relationships close to home. At times, Williams took flak in the basketball press for not landing as high-profile recruits as many of his peers. Instead, Williams committed himself to building a program and a basketball culture the right way—with the tools at his doorstep in College Park. Following his retirement from coaching in 2011, Williams has been a vocal critic of the influence that sneaker companies, proxy agents, and AAU coaches have had on the college game, particularly in the current "one-and-done" era.

As Gary Williams's Terrapins became fixtures of March Madness, the "Maryland flex offense" they ran became as feared as the players who executed it. Like Williams's teams at American, Boston College, and Ohio State, Maryland employed the "flex" with consistency and excellence. The offense created open shots, wore down opponents, and emboldened point guards to drive the tempo in this fast-breaking system. With the proliferation of talent now wearing red, black, and gold, opponents were hard pressed to stop all of the able targets perpetually cutting and screening, disrupting the defensive fundamentals of their opponents.[26]

The success of Terrapin basketball under Williams played no small role in helping the University of Maryland further establish its reputation as a major national university. The on-court success of Maryland in the 1990s and 2000s contributed to the momentum of a university that was becoming a destination for fine minds from around the world. While Cole Field House was regaining its reputation as one of college basketball's most raucous venues, the University of Maryland was taking advantage of its increasing profile and proximity to the nation's capital to become the home of several major federal institutions. During the 1990s and 2000s, the university welcomed an extension of the National Archives, branches of the Department of Defense and the Food and Drug Administration, as well as the National Oceanic and Atmospheric Administration's National Center for Weather and Climate Prediction. Maryland also built a new $125 million basketball arena, the eighteen-thousand-seat Comcast (later Xfinity) Center, in 2002 to replace Cole Field House. Williams played a direct role in helping Maryland raise the capital commensurate to its aspirations, co-chairing the $1 billion Great Expectations fundraising campaign between 2004 and 2012.[27]

By the early 2000s, Gary Williams was the first name on two simultaneously dubious and flattering lists. He was the best active coach not to have been to a Final Four and the best active coach not to have won a national championship. Maryland's 2000–2001 team erased his name from the first list, upsetting top-seeded Stanford in the West Regional Final before falling to perennial ACC nemesis Duke in the national semifinal. The Terrapins' 2001 trip to the Final Four was the first in school history. Williams's 2001–2002 team removed his name from the second list, as Maryland earned the right to cut down the nets at Atlanta's Georgia Dome by beating Kansas on Saturday night and Indiana on Monday night. In true Gary Williams fashion, not one player on his national championship team was a McDonald's All-American.

By the time Gary Williams retired from coaching in 2011, he was the winningest coach in Maryland history and the third winningest coach in ACC history, behind Dean Smith and Mike Krzyzewski. He'd won a national championship and an ACC championship and had been to two Final Fours. In his thirty-three years as a college head coach, Williams's teams had competed in seventeen NCAA Tournaments and nine NITs. Williams enjoyed great success at all four of his head coaching stops and sprouted a coaching tree that included the likes of Fran Fraschilla, Rick Barnes, Fran Dunphy, Mike Lonergan, Jimmy Patsos, Randy Ayers, Paul Brazeau, and Frank Haith. In 2014, Williams was inducted into the Naismith Memorial Basketball Hall of Fame and the College Basketball Hall of Fame. In the years since his twin Hall of Fame inductions, Williams has continued to contribute to the University of Maryland, taking on a senior role in alumni outreach and development for the athletic department.

Epilogue

March 31, 1988

On March 31, 1988, the University of Connecticut defeated Ohio State, 72–67, at Madison Square Garden to secure their first NIT championship. Ten years and 363 days later, UCONN would win its first NCAA Men's Basketball Tournament at Tropicana Field in St. Petersburg, Florida. The reaction from UCONN's fan base was pure ecstasy in each instance. For UCONN fans specifically and Connecticut residents generally, the championship game victory over Gary Williams's Buckeyes team was a moment of unspeakable communal pride. Thousands of Connecticut fans who caravanned down to New York from all corners of the state stormed the court to celebrate with Calhoun, tournament MVP Phil Gamble, and future NBAers Tate George and Cliff Robinson. Back in Storrs, a crowd of thousands of undergraduates celebrated until dawn around a roaring bonfire kept burning by enough dorm furniture to equip a small liberal arts college.

Jim Calhoun, John Toner, and John T. Casteen had not thought of the NIT as a second-rate tournament but instead as tangible proof of the program's progression. Casteen figured it might be five years before the Huskies reached this point. Calhoun got there in two. UCONN's fan base didn't treat the NIT like a consolation prize either. The basketball program did a great job communicating this "trust the process" sensibility long before such language became a coach-speak cliché. Moreover, sports fans in Connecticut were clearly on the hunt for something that was all their own. The city of Hartford honored their NHL Whalers, the state's only professional sports franchise, with a parade two years earlier after getting knocked out in the second round of the playoffs. Rather than a single day's parade, Connecticut residents from then on honored the Huskies year in and year out with one of the country's most passionate college basketball fan bases. Calhoun's teams rewarded them in similarly consistent fashion.

The 1988 NIT played out like a dramatis personae for this book. The cast of coaches that hustled throughout the previous decade to make meaningful careers for themselves in major college basketball virtually all made appearances. Calhoun and Williams, two of the three subjects of this book, battled it out at MSG for the NIT title. Ohio State and UConn were playing on the home floor of the third subject, Rick Pitino, who was in the process of remaking the Knicks into an Eastern Conference contender. In the semifinals, Gary Williams's team survived a 73–67 scare from Jim O'Brien's Boston College team, which had won seven more games than it had the previous season and included four Williams recruits in its starting lineup. In the second round, Ohio State had knocked off Kevin Mackey's Cleveland State team, 86–80. That same March, Mike Jarvis brought BU back to the NCAA Tournament for the first time since Pitino's departure.

What each of these coaches accomplished in subsequent years is a credit not only to their own efforts, but to what their teams in Boston achieved as a collective enterprise. While the number of people who remember what Northeastern's or BU's or BC's basketball teams accomplished during this era gets smaller every year, the subsequent successes of the men who coached them are themselves silent repositories of everything these teams achieved. The high-profile careers that Pitino, Calhoun, and Williams enjoyed at other schools are living, breathing extensions of "Boston Ball." The Huskies, Terriers, and Eagles discussed in this book are the frame of reference and foundation upon which three Hall of Fame careers were built. By immortalizing each coach, the Naismith Memorial Basketball Hall of Fame made the story of college basketball in Boston during the 1970s and 1980s essential to the telling of the story of the game in full.

Notes

INTRODUCTION

1. Axthelm, *The City Game*; Goodman, *The City Game*.
2. Pitino with Kaufman, *Pitino*.
3. Williams and Vise, *Sweet Redemption*.
4. Calhoun and Montville, *Dare to Dream*.

1. PAY CUT

1. "Dukeshire Doubts He'll Stay with NU," *Boston Globe*, September 22, 1972, 32.
2. "NU Eyes Dedham Coach," *Boston Globe*, September 29, 1972, 54.
3. Jim Bowman, interview with the author, May 14, 2021.
4. Peter Gammons, "Who Plays the Best? New NU Coach Wonders," *Boston Globe*, October 3, 1972, 59.
5. Calhoun and Montville, *Dare to Dream*, 62.
6. Jim Connors, interview with the author, June 11, 2021.
7. Paul Solberg, interview with the author, June 3, 2021.
8. Calhoun and Montville, *Dare to Dream*, 45–47.
9. Jim Calhoun, interview with the author, April 9, 2021.
10. Jim Calhoun, interview with the author, April 9, 2021.
11. Calhoun and Montville, *Dare to Dream*, 50.
12. Calhoun and Montville, *Dare to Dream*, 45–49.
13. Jim Calhoun, interview with the author, April 9, 2021.
14. Glenn Feldman, "Newest Husky Coach, Also Most Successful," *Northeastern News*, January 26, 1973, 10.
15. Marvin Pace, "State Basketball Tourney Ready to Roll," *Boston Globe*, February 27, 1972, 80.
16. Calhoun and Montville, *Dare to Dream*, 59.
17. Jim Calhoun, interview with the author, April 9, 2021.
18. "Lecy Quits Basketball for Marriage, Studies," *Northeastern News*, December 1, 1972, 16.

19. Gammons, "Who Plays the Best? New NU Coach Wonders."
20. Glen Field, interview with the author, May 29, 2021.
21. Mike Jarvis, interview with the author, May 21, 2021.
22. Glen Field, interview with the author, May 29, 2021.
23. Jim Bowman, interview with the author, May 14, 2021.
24. Bill Stanton, interview with the author, June 7, 2021.
25. Paul Solberg, interview with the author, June 3, 2021.
26. Glen Field, interview with the author, May 29, 2021.
27. Glen Field, interview with the author, May 29, 2021.
28. Paul Solberg, interview with the author, June 3, 2021.
29. Paul McDonough, interview with the author, June 4, 2021.
30. Ed Minishak, interview with the author, June 28, 2021.
31. Bill Stanton, interview with the author, June 7, 2021.
32. Glen Field, interview with the author, May 29, 2021.
33. Joe Delgardo, interview with the author, June 11, 2021.
34. John Boutin, interview with the author, June 2, 2021.
35. Paul McDonough, interview with the author, June 4, 2021.
36. Cited in Peter Gammons, "Who Plays the Best? New NU Coach Wonders," *Boston Globe*, October 3, 1972, 59.
37. John Clark, interview with the author, June 4, 2021.
38. Joe Delgardo, interview with the author, June 11, 2021.
39. Jim Calhoun, interview with the author, April 9, 2021.
40. John Boutin, interview with the author, June 2, 2021.
41. John Boutin, interview with the author, June 2, 2021.
42. John Boutin, interview with the author, June 2, 2021.
43. Ed Minishak, interview with the author, June 28, 2021.
44. Bill Stanton, interview with the author, June 7, 2021.
45. John Boutin, interview with the author, June 2, 2021.
46. Cited in "Hoopsters Rely on New Coach, Youth, Jellison," *Northeastern News*, December 1, 1972, 16.
47. "Hoopmen Stopped by BU in Opener," *Northeastern News*, December 6, 1972, 11.
48. Ed Minishak, interview with the author, June 28, 2021.
49. Bill Stanton, interview with the author, June 7, 2021.
50. Jim Connors, interview with the author, June 11, 2021.
51. John Clark, interview with the author, June 4, 2021.
52. Cited in Peter Gammons, "Clark Slick Husky," *Boston Globe*, January 9, 1973, 25.
53. Bill Stanton, interview with the author, June 7, 2021.

54. Cited in Peter Gammons, "Surprise! NU Five Just Rolling Along," *Boston Globe*, January 29, 1973, 43.

55. "B-Ball No. 5 and Rising," *Northeastern News*, February 9, 1973, 18.

56. Gammons, "Surprise!"

57. "Huskies Fretting in Limbo of Sorts," *Boston Globe*, February 27, 1973, 29.

58. John Boutin, interview with the author, June 2, 2021.

59. "Huskies Fretting in Limbo of Sorts."

60. John Boutin, interview with the author, June 2, 2021.

61. "Huskies Fretting in Limbo of Sorts."

62. "Huskies Win at Gun," *Boston Globe*, March 4, 1973, 97.

63. Cited in Bob Monahan, "NU's Chances for NIT Bid Could Hinge on Final Game," *Boston Globe*, February 22, 1973, 69.

2. YOU COME HIGHLY RECOMMENDED

1. Ed McGrath, interview with the author, April 14, 2021.

2. Ed McGrath, interview with the author, April 14, 2021.

3. Glenn Consor, interview with the author, May 4, 2021.

4. Ed Leibowitz, interview with the author, September 21, 2021.

5. Ed Leibowitz, interview with the author, September 21, 2021.

6. Ed Leibowitz, interview with the author, September 21, 2021.

7. Glenn Consor, interview with the author, May 4, 2021.

8. Ed Leibowitz, interview with the author, September 21, 2021.

9. Glenn Consor, interview with the author, May 4, 2021.

10. Ed Leibowitz, interview with the author, September 21, 2021.

11. Ed Leibowitz, interview with the author, September 21, 2021.

12. Wally West, interview with the author, August 10, 2021.

13. Desmond Martin, interview with the author, August 10, 2021.

14. Glenn Consor, interview with the author, May 4, 2021.

15. Gary Curtis, "Terriers Win Finale," BU *Daily Free Press*, March 1, 1978, 8.

16. "Pitino to Be Basketball Coach at BU," *Boston Globe*, March 31, 1978, 43.

17. Nack, "Full Court Pressure," 80–84.

18. "How Howard Garfinkel Became the Godfather of Grassroots Basketball," SB *Nation*, April 27, 2016; https://www.sbnation.com/college-basketball/2016/4/27/11501618/five-star-basketball-camp-howard-garfinkel-recruiting-john-calipari. Accessed January 8, 2022.

19. "Rick Pitino's Basketball Hall of Fame Induction Speech," *Official Hoop Hall*, September 9, 2013; https://www.youtube.com/watch?v=QTMUKbuSePE. Accessed January 8, 2022.

20. Scott Cacciola, "His Basketball Camp Made Hall of Famers, Now He's One Too," *New York Times*, September 11, 2021, 85.

21. Al Skinner, interview with the author, May 12, 2021.

22. Nack, "Full Court Pressure," 83–84.

23. Al Skinner, interview with the author, May 12, 2021.

24. Matt Bonesteel, "Rick Pitino Began His Career under Suspicion. It'll End There Too," *Washington Post*, September 28, 2017, 48.

25. Frank Litsky, "Pitino Goes One Up on Orr, Who Played under Him," *New York Times*, December 15, 2002, 86.

26. "Jim Boeheim: Crashing Rick Pitino's Wedding," *In Depth with Graham Bensinger*, March 29, 2017; https://www.youtube.com/watch?v=P2EzPoUGol8. Accessed January 8, 2022.

27. Cited in "Basketball Jells under 'Boy Coach' Pitino," *Boston Globe*, January 21, 1979, 42.

28. Cited in Pitino with Kaufman, *Pitino*, 18.

29. Gary Curtis, "BU's Cager Coach to Be Syracuse's Rick Pitino," BU *Daily Free Press*, March 31, 1978, 12.

30. Ed McGrath, interview with the author, April 14, 2021.

31. Pitino with Kaufman, *Pitino*, 18–19.

32. "Pitino to Be Basketball Coach at BU."

33. Jack Craig, "Pitino Hopes to Rival BU Hockey," *Boston Globe*, April 1, 1978, 23.

34. Cited in Jack, "Pitino Hopes to Rival BU Hockey."

35. Mike Lynch, interview with the author, February 20, 2021.

36. "Assistant Basketball Coach Packs It In," BU *Daily Free Press*, April 26, 1978, 11.

37. Ed Leibowitz, interview with the author, September 21, 2021.

38. Cited in Jack, "Pitino Hopes to Rival BU Hockey."

39. John Teague, interview with the author, August 8, 2021.

40. Glen Bressner, interview with the author, May 10, 2021.

41. John Teague, interview with the author, August 8, 2021.

42. John Teague, interview with the author, August 8, 2021.

43. John Teague, interview with the author, August 8, 2021.

44. Gene Jones, interview with the author, September 6, 2021.

45. Gene Jones, interview with the author, September 6, 2021.

3. NOT THAT MUCH IS EXPECTED

1. Mike Lynch, interview with the author, February 20, 2021.

2. Williams and Vise, *Sweet Redemption*, 17.

3. Michael Rolfes, "Williams Named Basketball Coach," *The Heights*, April 19, 1982, 23.

4. Michael Madden, "BC Names Williams as Coach," *Boston Globe*, April 6, 1982, 33.

5. Gary Williams, interview with the author, February 6, 2021.

6. Gary Williams, interview with the author, February 6, 2021.

7. Gary Williams, interview with the author, February 6, 2021.

8. Tom Brennan, interview with the author, March 20, 2021.

9. Jim O'Brien, interview with the author, February 17, 2021.

10. Mike Lynch, interview with the author, February 20, 2021.

11. Kevin Mackey, interview with the author, June 21, 2021.

12. Kevin Mackey, interview with the author, June 21, 2021.

13. Stu Primus, interview with the author, July 23, 2021.

14. Paul Brazeau, interview with the author, February 23, 2021.

15. Jay Murphy, interview with the author, April 26, 2021.

16. Kevin Mackey, interview with the author, June 21, 2021.

17. Michael Adams, interview with the author, May 1, 2021.

18. Gary Williams, interview with the author, February 6, 2021.

19. Paul Brazeau, interview with the author, February 23, 2021.

20. Paul Brazeau, interview with the author, February 23, 2021.

21. Gary Williams, interview with the author, February 6, 2021.

22. Burnett Adams, interview with the author, July 16, 2021.

23. Burnett Adams, interview with the author, July 16, 2021.

24. Stu Primus, interview with the author, July 23, 2021.

25. Mike Rolfes, interview with the author, April 26, 2021.

26. Matt Gianatassio, interview with the author, May 2, 2021.

27. Jay Murphy, interview with the author, April 26, 2021.

28. Rolfes, "Williams Named Basketball Coach."

29. Madden, "BC Names Williams as Coach."

30. Burnett Adams, interview with the author, July 16, 2021.

31. Burnett Adams, interview with the author, July 16, 2021.

32. Stu Primus, interview with the author, July 23, 2021.

33. Stu Primus, interview with the author, July 23, 2021.

34. Lesley Visser, "Davis Eyes Stanford," *Boston Globe*, March 29, 1982, 35.

35. "Coaches," *Austin American Statesman*, March 21, 1982, D.

36. Cited in "Why Did Dr. Tom Leave BC?" *The Heights*, April 5, 1982.

37. Michael Adams, interview with the author, May 1, 2021.

38. "Boston College Five Finally Has to Say 'Wait Til Next Year,'" *Hartford Courant*, March 22, 1982, 32.

39. Michael Madden, "BC Finishes Interviews," *Boston Globe*, April 5, 1982, 33.

40. Rolfes, "Williams Named Basketball Coach."

41. Stu Primus, interview with the author, July 23, 2021.

42. Jim O'Brien, interview with the author, February 17, 2021.

43. Jim O'Brien, interview with the author, February 17, 2021.

44. Madden, "BC Names Williams as Coach."

45. Lesley Visser, "The Davis Wake," *Boston Globe*, March 31, 1982, S1.

46. Paul Brazeau, interview with the author, February 23, 2021.

47. Paul Brazeau, interview with the author, February 23, 2021.

48. Jay Murphy, interview with the author, April 26, 2021.

49. Kevin Mackey, interview with the author, June 21, 2021.

50. "Big East Conference Preview," *Boston Globe*, November 28, 1982, 102.

4. GETTING OVER A HUMP

1. Paul Porter, interview with the author, June 1, 2021.

2. Glenn Feldman, "Husky 'Appealing' Bait for Syracuse Orangemen," *Northeastern News*, January 29, 1976, 12.

3. Paul Porter, interview with the author, June 1, 2021.

4. Jim Connors, interview with the author, June 11, 2021.

5. Dave Caligaris, interview with the author, July 28, 2021.

6. Dave Caligaris, interview with the author, July 28, 2021.

7. Mike Jarvis, interview with the author, May 21, 2021.

8. Mike Jarvis, interview with the author, May 21, 2021.

9. Jim Connors, interview with the author, June 11, 2021.

10. Bill Stanton, interview with the author, June 7, 2021.

11. Joe Delgardo, interview with the author, June 11, 2021.

12. Joe Delgardo, interview with the author, June 11, 2021.

13. Joe Delgardo, interview with the author, June 11, 2021.

14. John Clark, interview with the author, June 4, 2021.

15. John Boutin, interview with the author, June 2, 2021.

16. Cited in Joe Concannon, "Friars Stay Up There," *Boston Globe*, January 22, 1974, 21.

17. Cited in Barry Cadigan, "NU's Clark Shuns Spotlight of Two Basketball Marks," *Boston Globe*, December 14, 1975, 84.

18. Bill Stanton, interview with the author, June 7, 2021.

19. Hank Anthony, "Huskies Send Fairfield Away Disappointed," *Northeastern News*, December 5, 1974, 11.

20. Dave Caligaris, interview with the author, July 28, 2021.

21. Dave Caligaris, interview with the author, July 28, 2021.

22. John Clark, interview with the author, June 4, 2021.

23. Jim Calhoun, interview with the author, April 9, 2021.

24. Jim Connors, interview with the author, June 11, 2021.

25. "Former Hoopster Italy Bound," *Northeastern News*, May 20, 1976, 11.

26. John Clark, interview with the author, June 4, 2021.

27. Paul Porter, interview with the author, June 1, 2021.

28. Keith Motley, interview with the author, October 8, 2021.

29. Keith Motley, interview with the author, October 8, 2021.

30. Dave Caligaris, interview with the author, July 28, 2021.

31. Calhoun and Montville, *Dare to Dream*, 63.

32. Keith Motley, interview with the author, October 8, 2021.

33. Keith Motley, interview with the author, October 8, 2021.

34. Keith Motley, interview with the author, October 8, 2021.

35. Cited in Jackie MacMullan, "Coming Together," *Boston Globe*, March 9, 1984, 25.

36. MacMullan, "Coming Together."

37. Cited in MacMullan, "Coming Together."

38. Dave Caligaris, interview with the author, July 28, 2021.

39. Paul Porter, interview with the author, June 1, 2021.

40. Steve Feldman, "Caligaris Comes of Age," *Northeastern News*, March 13, 1975, 11.

41. Dave Caligaris, interview with the author, July 28, 2021.

42. Dave Caligaris, interview with the author, July 28, 2021.

43. Jim Calhoun, interview with the author, April 9, 2021.

44. Bill Loughnane, interview with the author, August 6, 2021.

45. Dave Caligaris, interview with the author, July 28, 2021.

46. Bill Loughnane, interview with the author, August 6, 2021.

47. Scott Cohen, interview with the author, June 4, 2021.

48. Keith Motley, interview with the author, October 8, 2021.

49. Phil Lotane, interview with the author, March 5, 2021.

50. Dave Caligaris, interview with the author, July 28, 2021.

51. Chip Rucker, interview with the author, June 17, 2021.

52. "Men's Basketball Preview," *Northeastern News*, November 16, 1977, 15.

53. Bill Loughnane, interview with the author, August 6, 2021.

54. Jim Calhoun, interview with the author, April 9, 2021.

55. "Hoop Whiz Harris Stresses Academics," *Northeastern News*, December 1, 1978, 11.

56. MacMullan, "Coming Together."

57. Dave Caligaris, interview with the author, July 28, 2021.

58. Rich McSweeney, "Calhoun Lauds Young, Quick Team," *Northeastern News*, November 29, 1978, 11.

5. GREAT KIDS

1. Desmond Martin, interview with the author, August 10, 2021.

2. Glen Bressner, interview with the author, May 10, 2021.

3. Wally West, interview with the author, August 10, 2021.

4. John Teague, interview with the author, August 8, 2021.

5. Glen Bressner, interview with the author, May 10, 2021.

6. John Teague, interview with the author, August 8, 2021.

7. Jay Twyman, interview with the author, May 12, 2021.

8. Glenn Consor, interview with the author, May 4, 2021.

9. Wally West, interview with the author, August 10, 2021.

10. Glenn Consor, interview with the author, May 4, 2021.

11. Pitino with Kaufman, *Pitino*, 22.

12. "Hoop Season Begins with Midnight Practice," BU *Daily Free Press*, October 16, 1978, 8.

13. Tom Masters, interview with the author, June 14, 2021.

14. Wally West, interview with the author, August 10, 2021.

15. Pitino with Kaufman, *Pitino*, 1.

16. Desmond Martin, interview with the author, August 10, 2021.

17. Steve Priscella, interview with the author, May 13, 2021.

18. Cited in Gary Cohen, "Nothing Wrong with Steve Wright," BU *Daily Free Press*, January 26, 1979, 3.

19. John Teague, interview with the author, August 8, 2021.

20. "College Basketball," *Burlington Free Press*, November 26, 1978, 40.

21. Cited in "NE College Basketball," *Boston Globe*, November 26, 1978, 102.

22. Cited in "Sports Teams Promise Exciting Years," BU *Daily Free Press*, September 5, 1978, 18.

23. Gary Cohen, "Apathy a Foe for BU Teams," BU *Daily Free Press*, January 30, 1979, 4.

24. Cited in "Terrier Hoopsters Welcome Pitino," BU *Daily Free Press*, November 15, 1978, 7.

25. Cited in "Terrier Hoopsters Welcome Pitino."

26. "Terrier Hoopsters Welcome Pitino."

27. "College Basketball," *Boston Globe*, February 23, 1979, 72.

28. Wally West, interview with the author, August 10, 2021.

29. John Teague, interview with the author, August 8, 2021.

30. "Terriers Top St. Peter's 75–71," BU *Daily Free Press*, November 28, 1978, 8.

31. Desmond Martin, interview with the author, August 10, 2021.

32. "Terriers Top St. Peter's 75–71."

33. Desmond Martin, interview with the author, August 10, 2021.

34. Jeff Holmes, interview with the author, August 5, 2021.

35. Casey Eisner, "Maine Beats Terriers," BU *Daily Free Press*, December 4, 1978, 7.

36. Cited in Lesley Visser, "BU Bid at Holy Cross Falls Short," *Boston Globe*, December 8, 1978, 34.

37. Cited in Lesley Visser, "HC Fights Off BU," *Boston Globe*, December 8, 1978, 40.

38. Gary Cohen, "Nothing Wrong with Steve Wright," BU *Daily Free Press*, January 26, 1979, 3.

39. Desmond Martin, interview with the author, August 10, 2021.

40. Gene Jones, interview with the author, September 6, 2021.

41. Pitino with Kaufman, *Pitino*, 20.

42. "College Basketball," *Boston Globe*, January 10, 1979, 25.

43. "Apathy a Foe for BU Team," BU *Daily Free Press*, January 30, 1979, 4.

44. "College Roundup," *Boston Globe*, January 12, 1979, 61.

45. Carey Eisner, "BU Tops Huskies," BU *Daily Free Press*, January 18, 1979, 8.

46. Michael Madden, "Turnaround at BU," *Boston Globe*, January, 21, 1979, 42.

47. Cited in Madden, "Turnaround at BU."

48. "BU Surge Tops Siena," BU *Daily Free Press*, February 7, 1979, 8.

49. Carey Eisner, "Terriers Upset Rhody," BU *Daily Free Press*, February 9, 1979, 1.

50. John Teague, interview with the author, August 8, 2021.

51. Cited in Gail Ciampa, "Rick Pitino, Will You Be My Valentine?" BU *Daily Free Press*, February 14, 1979, 8.

52. Red Levinsohn, "BU Upends Richmond," BU *Daily Free Press*, February 13, 1979, 8.

53. Lesley Visser, "Cobb Fires BC over BU," *Boston Globe*, February 22, 1979, 39.

54. Cited in Visser, "Cobb Fires BC over BU."

55. Cited in "BU Rips Assumption," BU *Daily Free Press*, February 26, 1979, 8.

56. "College Basketball," *Boston Globe*, February 23, 1979, 72.

57. "College Basketball," *Boston Globe*, March 2, 1979, 66.

58. Bob Monahan, "Pitino Signs for Four," *Boston Globe*, March 14, 1979, 76.

59. Cited in Don Markus, "Recruiting Means Lots of Hotels, Hot Dogs," *Newsday*, April 7, 1979, 21.

60. Andrew McLeod, "New England Basketball Recruiting," *Hartford Courant*, July 15, 1979, 71.

61. Larry Mahoney, "Boston University Signs Cougars' Mike Bouchard," *Bangor Daily News*, March 7, 1979, 20.
62. Pitino with Kaufman, *Pitino*, 20.

6. WE'RE OFF TO ALBUQUERQUE

1. Jay Murphy, interview with the author, April 26, 2021.
2. Jay Murphy, interview with the author, April 26, 2021.
3. Russ Doherty, interview with the author, April 21, 2021.
4. Jay Murphy, interview with the author, April 26, 2021.
5. Steven Benton, interview with the author, July 9, 2021.
6. Mike Rosen, interview with the author, August 24, 2021.
7. Stu Primus, interview with the author, July 23, 2021.
8. Gary Williams, interview with the author, February 6, 2021.
9. Gary Williams, interview with the author, February 6, 2021.
10. Troy Bowers, interview with the author, August 16, 2021.
11. "Big East Conference Preview," *Boston Globe*, November 28, 1982, 102.
12. Cited in "Big East Preview," *Hartford Courant*, November 28, 1982, C13.
13. Cited in Michael Madden, "Williams Points the Way for BC," *Boston Globe*, November 28, 1982, 89.
14. Russ Doherty, interview with the author, April 21, 2021.
15. Stu Primus, interview with the author, July 23, 2021.
16. Jay Murphy, interview with the author, April 26, 2021.
17. Gary Williams, interview with the author, February 6, 2021.
18. Stu Primus, interview with the author, July 23, 2021.
19. Jay Murphy, interview with the author, April 26, 2021.
20. Stu Primus, interview with the author, July 23, 2021.
21. Bob Monahan, "Unbeaten BC (7-0) Rolls over Fairfield, 99–79," *Boston Globe*, December 22, 1982, 55.
22. Williams and Vise, *Sweet Redemption*, 25.
23. Chuck Everson, interview with the author, June 18, 2021.
24. Lesley Visser, "Beastly Opener for BC," *Boston Globe*, January 5, 1983, 25.
25. "Villanova Recovers from BC Knockdown," *Newsday*, January 5, 1983, 89.
26. Ron Stewart, interview with the author, June 16, 2021.
27. "Eagles Thwart Redmen, 68–64," *Boston Globe*, January 16, 1983, 73.
28. Ron Stewart, interview with the author, June 16, 2021.
29. Ron Stewart, interview with the author, June 16, 2021.
30. "BC Rocks Redmen, Rolled by Orangemen," *The Heights*, January 24, 1983, 13.
31. Cited in "Eagles Thwart Redmen, 68–64."
32. Gene Waldron, interview with the author, April 26, 2021.

33. Sonny Spera, interview with the author, May 11, 2021.
34. Gene Waldron, interview with the author, April 26, 2021.
35. "BC Rocks Redmen, Rolled by Orangemen."
36. Cited in Lesley Visser, "Syracuse Shreds BC," *Boston Globe*, January 18, 1983, 57.
37. Kevin Mackey, interview with the author, June 21, 2021.
38. Mike Jarvis, interview with the author, May 21, 2021.
39. Mike Jarvis, interview with the author, May 21, 2021.
40. Mike Jarvis, interview with the author, May 21, 2021.
41. Kevin Mackey, interview with the author, June 21, 2021.
42. Sonny Spera, interview with the author, May 11, 2021.
43. Ted Kelley, interview with the author, April 20, 2021.
44. Matt Gianatassio, interview with the author, May 2, 2021.
45. Cited in Mike Madden, "The Ewing Letter," *Boston Globe*, February 20, 1981, 33.
46. Kevin Mackey, interview with the author, June 21, 2021.
47. Vin Sylvia, "Hoyas Tip BC at Finish," *The Heights*, January 31, 1983, 13.
48. Lesley Visser, "BC's Williams May Have Some Hints on Beating Hoyas," *Boston Globe*, January 28, 1983, 29.
49. Sylvia, "Hoyas Tip BC at Finish."
50. "Revenge! BC Knocks Off 'Nova," *The Heights*, February 7, 1983, 1.
51. Chuck Everson, interview with the author, June 18, 2021.
52. Peter Gammons, "BC Still Running on Outside in National Polls," *Boston Globe*, February 14, 1983, 25.
53. "Boston College Knocks Off St. John's A Second Time," *Pittsburgh Press*, February 16, 1983, D2.
54. Russ Doherty, interview with the author, April 21, 2021.
55. Chuck Everson, interview with the author, June 18, 2021.
56. Kevin Mackey, interview with the author, June 21, 2021.
57. Matt Gianatassio, interview with the author, May 2, 2021.
58. Cited in John Gill, "BC's Showstopping Act," *The Heights*, March 7, 1983, 1.
59. Lesley Visser, "Garris Holds Off Hoyas," *Boston Globe*, March 3, 1983, 57.
60. Cited in Lesley Visser, "BC Passes First Test in Big East," *Boston Globe*, March 11, 1983, 21.
61. Leigh Montville, "Extra! BC Back in Closet," *Boston Globe*, March 12, 1983, 25.
62. Cited in "Syracuse Edited Out of Big East Tournament," *Boston Globe*, March 12, 1983, 25.
63. John Gill, "On the Third Day," *The Heights*, March 14, 1983, 1.
64. Ted Kelley, interview with the author, April 20, 2021.

65. Matt Gianatassio, interview with the author, May 2, 2021.

66. Gary Williams, interview with the author, February 6, 2021.

67. Cited in Lesley Visser, "St. John's Too Strong for Eagles," *Boston Globe*, March 13, 1983, 71.

68. Lesley Visser, "BC's Press Didn't Impress," *Boston Globe*, March 22, 1983, 59.

69. "Eagles Anxious to Challenge Cavaliers," *Salt Lake Tribune*, March 24, 1983, 45.

70. Cited in "The Men in the Middle," *Boston Globe*, March 24, 1983, 50.

71. "Sampsonian Psychology," *The Heights*, March 28, 1983, 11.

72. Cited in Michael Madden, "If Only He Hadn't Left," *Boston Globe*, March 26, 1983, 25.

73. Lesley Visser, "BC Eliminated by Virginia, 95–92," *Boston Globe*, March 25, 1983, 49.

74. Kevin Mackey, interview with the author, June 21, 2021.

75. Kevin Mackey, interview with the author, June 21, 2021.

7. NORTHWESTERN

1. "A Season of Change," *Rochester Democrat and Chronicle*, December 5, 1979, 55.

2. Ken Gordon, "New Conference; Same Problems," *Northeastern News*, November 7, 1979, 11.

3. Nick Macarchuk, interview with the author, March 2, 2021.

4. Donn Esmonde, interview with the author, March 2, 2021.

5. "NU Purchases Boston Arena," *Boston Globe*, October 4, 1979, 44.

6. "Matthews Arena," *NUHuskies.com*, 2022; https://nuhuskies.com/sports/2010/1/28/matthewsarena.aspx. Accessed May 1, 2022.

7. John Ahern, "Matthews Arena Opens Tomorrow," *Boston Globe*, November 13, 1982, 31.

8. Jim Calhoun, interview with the author, April 9, 2021.

9. Keith Motley, interview with the author, October 8, 2021.

10. "A Season of Change"; "ECAC North," *Boston Globe*, November 25, 1979, 103.

11. "HC the Class of ECAC North," *Boston Globe*, November 25, 1979, 103.

12. Cited in Michael Madden, "Northeastern-BU: A Big Game at Last," *Boston Globe*, February 5, 1980, 27.

13. Bill Loughnane, interview with the author, August 6, 2021.

14. Chip Rucker, interview with the author, June 17, 2021.

15. "Harris Lifts Hoopsters to Fifth Straight," *Northeastern News*, February 9, 1980, 10.

16. Chip Rucker, interview with the author, June 17, 2021.

17. "Harris, Moss Sparkle as NU Breezes," *Boston Globe*, February 7, 1980, 40.

18. "Northeastern-BU: A Big Game at Last."

19. Lesley Visser, "BU Wins, 85–78," *Boston Globe*, February 9, 1980, 23.

20. Bill Loughnane, interview with the author, August 6, 2021.

21. Glenn Consor, interview with the author, May 4, 2021.

22. "Cagers Gear Up for Playoff Debut," *Northeastern News*, February 20, 1980, 16.

23. Cited in Michael Madden, "BC Pins NU," *Boston Globe*, February 21, 1980, 43.

24. Cited in "Great Year Ends in Disappointment," *Northeastern News*, February 27, 1980, 12.

25. Keith Motley, interview with the author, October 8, 2021.

26. Karl Fogel, interview with the author, June 17, 2021.

27. Ernie Roberts, "NU's Harris Courts His 2000th," *Boston Globe*, February 11, 1981, 61.

28. Scott Cohen, interview with the author, June 4, 2021.

29. Cited in Lesley Visser, "Perry Moss," *Boston Globe*, March 2, 1982, 49.

30. Visser, "Perry Moss."

31. Paul Porter, interview with the author, June 1, 2021.

32. Jim Calhoun, interview with the author, April 9, 2021.

33. Lesley Visser, "He's a Secret in Name Only," *Boston Globe*, January 13, 1984, 41.

34. Karl Fogel, interview with the author, June 17, 2021.

35. Jim Calhoun, interview with the author, April 9, 2021.

36. Lesley Visser, "For Coach Calhoun, Secret Is Work," *Boston Globe*, December 17, 1980, 71.

37. Cited in Visser, "For Coach Calhoun, Secret Is Work."

38. "Northeastern, UNC-Charlotte Open with Best Wins," *Bangor Daily News*, December 27, 1980, 8.

39. "College Basketball," *Rutland Herald*, December 28, 1980, 10.

40. "N.E. College Basketball," *Boston Globe*, January 11, 1981, 74.

41. Lesley Visser, "Harris (31) Paces NU Past UNH," *Boston Globe*, January 16, 1981, 47.

42. Jim Calhoun, interview with the author, April 9, 2021.

43. Phil Lotane, interview with the author, March 5, 2021.

44. Karl Fogel, interview with the author, June 17, 2021.

45. Bill Stanton, interview with the author, June 7, 2021.

46. Phil Lotane, interview with the author, March 5, 2021.

47. Cited in Jackie MacMullan, "Coming Together," *Boston Globe*, March 9, 1984, 25.

48. Tom Koller, interview with the author, March 5, 2021.

49. Donn Esmonde, interview with the author, March 2, 2021.

50. "Northeastern Muscles Past BU, 83–76," *Boston Globe*, February 25, 1981, 28.

51. Cited in "Northeastern Muscles Past BU, 83–76."

52. Calhoun and Montville, *Dare to Dream*, 64–65.

53. Walter Haynes, "NU Goes to the NCAAs," *Boston Globe*, March 8, 1981, 57.

54. Scott Cohen, interview with the author, June 4, 2021.

55. "Northeastern Wins, Gains NCAA Birth," *Hartford Courant*, March 8, 1981, D8.

56. Chip Rucker, interview with the author, June 17, 2021.

57. Cited in Haynes, "NU Goes to the NCAAs," 57.

58. Calhoun with Montville, *Dare to Dream*, 64–65.

59. "WRBB Calls 1981 Northeastern Championship Game," YouTube.com. April 1, 2012; https://www.youtube.com/watch?v=ta0YS8l_7H4. Accessed May 13, 2022.

60. "Northeastern Wins, Gains NCAA Birth."

61. Haynes, "NU Goes to the NCAAs," 57.

62. Haynes, "NU Goes to the NCAAs," 57.

63. Cited in Don Greenberg, "NCAA's Tourney Snub Angers Orangemen," *Daily News*, March 10, 1981, 1.

64. Cited in Greenberg, "NCAA's Tourney Snub Angers Orangemen."

65. "Raymonds: Conference Tournaments Unfair," *Rochester Democrat and Chronicle*, March 12, 1981, 35.

66. Cited in "NU's Ready for Stingy Fresno State," *Boston Globe*, March 13, 1981, 34.

67. Leigh Montville, "They're North Who . . . ," *Boston Globe*, March 12, 1981, 57.

68. Walter Haynes, "NU: The Dogs Have Their Day," *Boston Globe*, March 15, 1981, 56.

69. Calhoun and Montville, *Dare to Dream*, 65–66.

70. "NCAA West," *New York Daily News*, March 14, 1981, 30.

71. Chip Rucker, interview with the author, June 17, 2021.

72. Charlie Heineck, interview with the author, July 1, 2021.

73. Karl Fogel, interview with the author, June 17, 2021.

74. Jim Calhoun, interview with the author, April 9, 2021.

75. Charlie Heineck, interview with the author, July 1, 2021.

76. Andy Gardiner, "Holy Cross the Favorite to Win," *Burlington Free Press*, November 24, 1981, 24.

77. Ernie Roberts, "NELTA," *Boston Globe*, June 13, 1981, 26.

78. "It's a Blowout—BU Drubs Northeastern, 82–64," *Boston Globe*, January 27, 1982, 25.

79. "Terriers' Hopes End in Heartache," BU *Daily Free Press*, March 5, 1982, 1.

80. Dan Shaughnessy, "NU on Way to NCAA," *Boston Globe*, March 7, 1982, 61.

81. Michael Madden, "BC Joins NU in NCAAs," *Boston Globe*, March 8, 1982, 30.

82. Cited in "High Flying Hawks Severe Test for Huskies," *Boston Globe*, March 11, 1982, 40.

83. Tony Costner, interview with the author, June 1, 2021.

84. Cited in "Underdog Huskies Take on St. Joe's," *Boston Globe*, March 12, 1982, 45.

85. Tony Costner, interview with the author, June 1, 2021.

86. Cited in Michael Madden, "Huskies Upset St. Joseph's, 63–62," *Boston Globe*, March 13, 1982, 25.

87. Madden, "Huskies Upset St. Joseph's, 63–62."

88. Madden, "Huskies Upset St. Joseph's, 63–62."

89. Cited in Madden, "Huskies Upset St. Joseph's, 63–62."

90. "Pain Lingers for St. John's," *New York Daily News*, March 16, 1982, 75.

91. "Pain Lingers for St. John's."

92. Michael Madden, "Not Even Respect Consoles Huskies," *Boston Globe*, March 15, 1982, 30.

93. Cited in "Huskies Bow Out in Triple OT, 76–72," *Boston Globe*, March 15, 1982, 29.

94. "Dukes to Interview Williams," *Pittsburgh Post-Gazette*, March 17, 1982, 16.

95. "NU's Halsel Sheds Cast and Defenders," *Boston Globe*, January 8, 1983, 37.

8. LIKE THE PACIFIC OCEAN

1. Michael Madden, "The New Kids on the Block," *Boston Globe*, February 8, 1980, 52.

2. Cited in "HC the Class of ECAC-North," *Boston Globe*, November 25, 1979, 103.

3. "HC the Class of ECAC-North."

4. Madden, "The New Kids on the Block."

5. Cited in Madden, "The New Kids on the Block."

6. Cited in "Wally West Gives BU Cagers a Big Lift," BU *Daily Free Press*, March 13, 1980, 8.

7. Gene Jones, interview with the author, September 6, 2021.

8. John Teague, interview with the author, August 8, 2021.

9. John Teague, interview with the author, August 8, 2021.

10. Glenn Consor, interview with the author, May 4, 2021.

11. "BU Gets Bombarded by Louisiana State," *Boston Globe*, December 29, 1979, 23.
12. Desmond Martin, interview with the author, August 10, 2021.
13. Tom Masters, interview with the author, June 14, 2021.
14. Wally West, interview with the author, August 10, 2021.
15. Cited in Lesley Visser, "BU Blasts St. Francis," *Boston Globe*, January 13, 1980, 74.
16. "Students at BU Just Don't Court Basketball," *Boston Globe*, January 26, 1982, 30.
17. Jeff Holmes, interview with the author, August 5, 2021.
18. Mike Bruckner, interview with the author, March 2, 2021.
19. "BU Beats Siena," BU *Daily Free Press*, January 23, 1980, 12.
20. Mike Madden, "Boston's Getting to Be the Place," *Boston Globe*, January 30, 1980, 57.
21. Cited in Madden, "The New Kids on the Block."
22. Cited in Madden, "The New Kids on the Block."
23. Cited in "Blessed Are the Altar Boys," *Binghamton Press*, February 5, 1980, 23.
24. "Terriers Take on NU Tonight," BU *Daily Free Press*, February 8, 1980, 11.
25. Lesley Visser, "BU Wins, 85–78," *Boston Globe*, February 9, 1980, 23.
26. Visser, "BU Wins, 85–78."
27. Cited in "Cagers Remain on Top," BU *Daily Free Press*, February 11, 1980, 8.
28. Cited in Visser, "BU Wins, 85–78."
29. Wally West, interview with the author, August 10, 2021.
30. Wally West, interview with the author, August 10, 2021.
31. Wally West, interview with the author, August 10, 2021.
32. Cited in Lesley Visser, "Maryland Trounces BU, 99–76," *Boston Globe*, February 12, 1980, 33.
33. Cited in Visser, "Maryland Trounces BU, 99–76."
34. "Bring Back Beanpot?" *Boston Globe*, January 20, 1982, 64.
35. "BU Cruises Along, 95–86," *Boston Globe*, February 27, 1980, 28.
36. "Cagers Best Niagara," BU *Daily Free Press*, February 27, 1980, 11.
37. Desmond Martin, interview with the author, August 10, 2021.
38. John Teague, interview with the author, August 8, 2021.
39. Walter Hayes, "BU Almost Gives It Away," *Boston Globe*, February 29, 1980, 39.
40. "BU Edges URI," BU *Daily Free Press*, February 29, 1980, 8.
41. Wally West, interview with the author, August 10, 2021.

42. Steve Marantz, "Perry (30) Puts HC in NCAAs," *Boston Globe*, March 2, 1980, 64.

43. "Terriers Dumped in NIT," BU *Daily Free Press*, March 10, 1980, 8.

44. Michael Madden, "BC Rolls over BU, 95–74," *Boston Globe*, March 7, 1980, 54.

45. Kevin Mackey, interview with the author, June 21, 2021.

46. "Pitino Lands Blue Chipper," *Boston Globe*, April 8, 1980, 35.

47. Gene Jones, interview with the author, September 6, 2021.

48. Jay Twyman, interview with the author, May 12, 2021.

49. Glen Bressner, interview with the author, May 10, 2021.

50. Jay Twyman, interview with the author, May 12, 2021.

51. Glen Bressner, interview with the author, May 10, 2021.

52. Gene Jones, interview with the author, September 6, 2021.

53. John Teague, interview with the author, August 8, 2021.

54. "Athletic Abilities Help Simms Lead," BU *Daily Free Press*, January 12, 1981, 12.

55. Jay Twyman, interview with the author, May 12, 2021.

56. Gene Jones, interview with the author, September 6, 2021.

57. Ken Fiola, interview with the author, May 11, 2021.

58. Mike Bruckner, interview with the author, March 2, 2021.

59. Ed McGrath, interview with the author, April 14, 2021.

60. Ed McGrath, interview with the author, April 14, 2021.

61. Wally West, interview with the author, August 10, 2021.

62. "The New Recruits," *Boston Globe*, May 10, 1981, 86.

63. Steve Priscella, interview with the author, May 13, 2021.

64. Mike Rosen, interview with the author, August 24, 2021.

65. Cited in "BU Lands Crop of Recruits," BU *Daily Free Press*, April 24, 1981, 37.

66. "BU Lands Crop of Recruits."

9. ACHIEVED AS MUCH AS THEY COULD

1. Michael Rolfes, "No Hoop Tix Left," *The Heights*, September 19, 1983, 14.

2. Troy Bowers, interview with the author, August 16, 2021.

3. "Sheehy Snubs BC," *Boston Globe*, April 12, 1983, 36.

4. Gary Williams, interview with the author, February 6, 2021.

5. "Why Does BC Want Four More Acres of Land?" *The Heights*, April 18, 1983, 1.

6. "Letter to the Editor: Flynn Defends Move of Georgetown Game," *The Heights*, November 1, 1983, 1.

7. Cited in "BC Belabors Stonehill, 97–63," *Boston Globe*, November 29, 1983, 39.

8. Gary Williams, interview with the author, February 6, 2021.

9. Cited in Jackie MacMullan, "McCready: BC's Little Big Man," *Boston Globe*, December 10, 1983, 27.

10. Gary Williams, interview with the author, February 6, 2021.

11. Burnett Adams, interview with the author, July 16, 2021.

12. Chuck Everson, interview with the author, June 18, 2021.

13. Gary Williams, interview with the author, February 6, 2021.

14. Ted Kelley, interview with the author, April 20, 2021.

15. Cited in "Boston College Foul Shots Hold Off St. John's 69–67," *New York Daily News*, January 15, 1984, 64.

16. Vin Sylvia, "Eagles Split Thrillers," *The Heights*, January 23, 1984, 9.

17. Lesley Visser, "Primus Keys BC in OT, 90–88," *Boston Globe*, February 23, 1984, 41.

18. Visser, "Primus Keys BC in OT, 90–88."

19. Vin Sylvia, "Roberts Finale Soured," *The Heights*, February 27, 1984, 13.

20. Stu Primus, interview with the author, July 23, 2021.

21. Michael Adams, interview with the author, May 1, 2021.

22. Sonny Spera, interview with the author, May 11, 2021.

23. Michael Rolfes, "BC's Twin Towers," *The Heights*, January 30, 1984, 15.

24. Michael Adams, interview with the author, May 1, 2021.

25. Troy Bowers, interview with the author, August 16, 2021.

26. Burnett Adams, interview with the author, July 16, 2021.

27. Burnett Adams, interview with the author, July 16, 2021.

28. Cited in Lesley Visser, "Clark Returns to Eagles," *Boston Globe*, February 28, 1984, 37.

29. "Ewing Mars His Flawless Game with an Ugly Mark," *Boston Globe*, February 26, 1984, 39.

30. John Feinstein, "Ewing Gets 25 in Hoyas' Victory, Is Ejected," *Washington Post*, February 26, 1984, 26.

31. Michael Rolfes, "BC Basketball's Winter of Discontent," *The Heights*, March 13, 1984, 15.

32. Jeff Wagenheim, "Clark Bids Eagles Adieu with Much Televised Ado," *Boston Globe*, March 15, 1984, 51; Vin Sylvia, "Clark Quits, Alleges Poor Academic Policies," *The Heights*, March 19, 1984, 1.

33. Ian Thomson, "Clark Puts BC on Defensive," *Boston Globe*, March 16, 1984, 69.

34. Cited in "Fan's View," *Boston Globe*, March 25, 1984, 62.

35. Michael Madden, "Blurred Vision," *Boston Globe*, March 23, 1984, 31; John Gill, "Clark Details Hoop Conflict," *The Heights*, March 26, 1984, 17.

36. "'82 Faculty Report Criticized BC Policy," *Boston Globe*, March 27, 1984, 40.

37. Bob Monahan, "Dual BC Facility Planned," *Boston Globe*, August 10, 1984, 69.

38. "Neenan Refuses to Address Primus' Claims," *The Heights*, December 3, 1984, 6.

39. Stu Primus, interview with the author, July 23, 2021.

40. Mike Lynch, interview with the author, February 20, 2021.

41. Paul Brazeau, interview with the author, February 23, 2021.

42. Cited in Bob Ryan, "Hoop Junkies' Garden Party," *Boston Globe*, December 2, 1984, 70.

43. Gary Williams, interview with the author, February 6, 2021.

44. Michael Adams, interview with the author, May 1, 2021.

45. Andre Hawkins, interview with the author, June 21, 2021.

46. Sonny Spera, interview with the author, May 11, 2021.

47. Stu Primus, interview with the author, July 23, 2021.

48. Cited in Dan Shaughnessy, "'Other' Eagles Prevail," *Boston Globe*, December 29, 1984, 33.

49. Gary Williams, interview with the author, February 6, 2021.

50. Cited in Jackie MacMullan, "Georgetown Dodges BC," Boston Globe, January 6, 1985, 77.

51. Cited in Bob Ryan, "A Small Force in Big East," *Boston Globe*, March 12, 1985, 67.

52. Jackie MacMullan, "A First for Pitt," *Boston Globe*, January 22, 1985, 62.

53. Gary Williams, interview with the author, February 6, 2021.

54. "BC Fouls Up Syracuse, 67–66," *Boston Globe*, February 6, 1985, 36.

55. Sonny Spera, interview with the author, May 11, 2021.

56. Andre Hawkins, interview with the author, June 21, 2021.

57. Cited in "Boston College Upsets Syracuse 67–66 after Disputed Call," *Atlanta Constitution*, February 6, 1985.

58. Michael Adams, interview with the author, May 1, 2021.

59. Russ Doherty, interview with the author, April 21, 2021.

60. Cited in Jackie MacMullan, "BC's No. 1 Shot Falls Short," *Boston Globe*, February 21, 1985, 45.

61. Cited in Jackie MacMullan, "BC Still in Shock," *Boston Globe*, February 26, 1985, 53.

62. "Miss at Finish Leaves Eagles on Rim, 70–69," March 8, 1985, *Boston Globe* 43.

63. Troy Bowers, interview with the author, August 16, 2021.
64. Bubba Jennings, interview with the author, May 26, 2021.
65. Stu Primus, interview with the author, July 23, 2021.
66. Jackie MacMullan, "Adams Lifts BC, 55–53," *Boston Globe*, March 16, 1985, 29.
67. Stu Primus, interview with the author, July 23, 2021.
68. Stu Primus, interview with the author, July 23, 2021.
69. Stu Primus, interview with the author, July 23, 2021.
70. Cited in Jackie MacMullan, "BC's Trap Lures Duke," *Boston Globe*, March 18, 1985, 37.
71. Troy Bowers, interview with the author, August 16, 2021.
72. Stu Primus, interview with the author, July 23, 2021.
73. "Eagles Fall at Finish," *Boston Globe*, March 22, 1985, 34.
74. Troy Bowers, interview with the author, August 16, 2021.
75. Gary Williams, interview with the author, February 6, 2021.
76. "Boston College Coach Gary Williams' View of the Final Four," *Fort Worth Star-Telegram*, March 29, 1985, 7D.

10. OUR BEST RECRUITING YEAR EVER

1. Cited in Jackie MacMullan, "Northeastern, BU Wait for Mail," *Boston Globe*, April 14, 1983, 52.
2. Jackie MacMullan, "Fresh Start for NU," *Boston Globe*, March 13, 1984, 29.
3. MacMullan, "Northeastern, BU Wait for Mail."
4. Andre LaFleur, interview with the author, August 4, 2021.
5. Jim Calhoun, interview with the author, April 9, 2021.
6. Jim Calhoun, interview with the author, April 9, 2021.
7. Andre LaFleur, interview with the author, August 4, 2021.
8. Quinton Dale, interview with the author, June 20, 2021.
9. Andre LaFleur, interview with the author, August 4, 2021.
10. MacMullan, "Northeastern, BU Wait for Mail."
11. Jackie MacMullan, "He's Made the Jump," *Boston Globe*, February 19, 1984, 66.
12. Keith Motley, interview with the author, October 8, 2021.
13. Keith Motley, interview with the author, October 8, 2021.
14. Keith Motley, interview with the author, October 8, 2021.
15. Andre LaFleur, interview with the author, August 4, 2021.
16. "A Partner in Every Way," *Boston Globe*, July 29, 1993, 64.
17. Keith Motley, interview with the author, October 8, 2021.
18. Andre LaFleur, interview with the author, August 4, 2021.

19. Lesley Visser, "He's a Secret in Name Only," *Boston Globe*, January 13, 1984, 41.

20. Mike Bruckner, interview with the author, March 2, 2021.

21. Donn Esmonde, interview with the author, March 2, 2021.

22. Visser, "He's a Secret in Name Only."

23. Jackie MacMullan, "He's Made the Jump," *Boston Globe*, February 19, 1984, 66.

24. Cited in Jackie MacMullan, "Fresh Start for NU," *Boston Globe*, March 13, 1984, 29.

25. Cited in MacMullan, "He's Made the Jump."

26. "College Basketball Notebook," *Boston Globe*, December 6, 1984, 92.

27. MacMullan, "He's Made the Jump."

28. David Camiel, "Halsel Injured, but Huskies March On," *Northeastern News*, February 8, 1984, 22.

29. Jim Calhoun, interview with the author, April 9, 2021.

30. Lesley Visser, "Pressure Point for NU, BU," February 11, 1984, 33.

31. Cited in Michael Madden, "Huskies Standing on Their Own," *Boston Globe*, February 18, 1984, 33.

32. "Niagara Falls to NU, 94–90," *Boston Globe*, February 28, 1984, 37.

33. Jackie MacMullan, "NU Gets the Edge," *Boston Globe*, March 2, 1984, 21.

34. Jackie MacMullan, "Northeastern Hangs Tough, Gains NCAAS," *Boston Globe*, March 11, 1984, 48.

35. Leigh Montville, "In Deed, There Are Two MVPS," *Boston Globe*, March 11, 1984, 52.

36. "College Basketball Notebook," *Boston Globe*, March 1, 1983, 36.

37. Cited in "College Basketball Notebook," *Boston Globe*, March 1, 1983, 36.

38. Jackie MacMullan, "NU Outruns LIU 90–87 in NCAAS," *Boston Globe*, March 14, 1984, 29.

39. Leigh Montville, "Huskies Stood Short but Came Up Tall," *Boston Globe*, March 14, 1984, 29.

40. Cited in Jackie MacMullan, "NU Outruns LIU 90–87 in NCAAS," *Boston Globe*, March 14, 1984, 29.

41. Montville, "Huskies Stood Short but Came Up Tall."

42. "VCU's Buzzer Beater Shocks Huskies," *Northeastern News*, March 21, 1984, 1.

43. Jackie MacMullan, "VCU Beats Buzzer, NU," *Boston Globe*, March 17, 1984, 27.

44. "NCAA Regionals," *Fort Worth Star-Telegram*, March 17, 1984, 68.

45. Ian Thomsen, "Williams Doing His Think at NU," *Boston Globe*, March 11, 1986, 75.

46. Jackie MacMullan, "NU in the Bonus Situation," *Boston Globe*, January 1, 1985, 79.

47. "Leitao Completes Husky Career in Style," *Northeastern News*, November 28, 1984, 21.

48. Cited in Bob Ryan, "NU Target of Praise in ECAC North," *Boston Globe*, November 25, 1984, 63.

49. "Providence, NU Both Go Sour," *Boston Globe*, December 30, 1984, 81.

50. Jerry Higgins, "UMass Shoots Past NU," *Boston Globe*, December 16, 1984, 72.

51. Barry Cadigan, "Lewis Lifts NU," *Boston Globe*, January 6, 1985, 91.

52. Mike Bruckner, interview with the author, March 2, 2021.

53. "Basketball Notes," *Northeastern News*, February 6, 1985, 21.

54. Ray Hall, interview with the author, June 15, 2021.

55. "NU's Lewis Already Pro Rated," *Boston Globe*, March 3, 1985, 61.

56. "College Basketball Notebook," *Boston Globe*, February 20, 1985, 48.

57. Jackie MacMullan, "Spot Checks," *Boston Globe*, February 27, 1985, 26.

58. Ron Borges, "Huskies Rise to the Top," *Boston Globe*, March 1, 1985, 65.

59. Cited in "NU No. 2," *Boston Globe*, March 2, 1985, 28.

60. Art Tooles, interview with the author, June 3, 2021.

61. Ron Borges, "The Eyes Have It for the Huskies," *Boston Globe*, March 8, 1985, 52.

62. Ian Thomsen, "NU Tops BU for Title, 68–67," *Boston Globe*, March 10, 1985, 39.

63. "NU's Lewis Already Pro Rated," *Boston Globe*, March 3, 1985, 61.

64. Bob Ryan, "NU Is the Dean of ECAC North," *Boston Globe*, December 1, 1985, 70.

65. Ryan, "NU Is the Dean of ECAC North."

66. "College Notebook," *Boston Globe*, December 27, 1985, 77.

67. Larry Whiteside, "Maryland Denies Huskies, 84–72," *Boston Globe*, November 24, 1985, 78.

68. Bill Tanton, "Terps Fail to Impress in Opener," *Baltimore Evening Sun*, November 25, 1985, 47.

69. "Pitino's Friars Put Huskies on Grill, 83–68," *Boston Globe*, December 3, 1985, 84.

70. Barry Cadigan, "Bang Up Job by NU, 71–68," *Boston Globe*, December 15, 1985, 70.

71. Bob Ryan, "Lewis (41) Sets Record Straight," *Boston Globe*, February 20, 1986, 51.

72. Owen Canfield, "College Basketball," *Hartford Courant*, December 28, 1985, 42.

73. Cited in Ian Thomsen, "Lewis Will Go the Distance at NU," *Boston Globe*, February 6, 1986, 38.

74. "NU Rolls Ahead," *Boston Globe*, March 5, 1986, 81.

75. Cited in "BU Still Hot on NU Trail," *Boston Globe*, February 25, 1986, 69.

76. Cited in Ian Thomsen, "Dual Duels: NU-BU and Calhoun-Jarvis," *Boston Globe*, February 8, 1986, 34.

77. Michael Madden, "Sold on the Game," *Boston Globe*, March 15, 1986, 89.

78. Ian Thomsen, "Sooners Will Study NU Later," *Boston Globe*, March 13, 1986, 39.

79. "NU Will Count on Senior-ity System," *Boston Globe*, March 15, 1986, 23.

80. Jim Calhoun, interview with the author, April 9, 2021.

81. "NU Will Count on Senior-ity System," *Boston Globe*, March 15, 1986, 23.

82. Cited in "NU Will Count on Senior-ity System."

83. Cited in "NU Will Count on Senior-ity System."

11. TRULY A TEAM OF CHARACTER

1. Karl Lehman, interview with the author, August 10, 2021.

2. Karl Lehman, interview with the author, August 10, 2021.

3. Karl Lehman, interview with the author, August 10, 2021.

4. Karl Lehman, interview with the author, August 10, 2021.

5. Lesley Visser, "The Race Heats Up in ECAC North," *Boston Globe*, November 29, 1981, 90; Despite Pitino's protestations, the *Globe's* Michael Madden also gave BU basketball excellent coverage during the coach's tenure on Commonwealth Avenue.

6. John Teague, interview with the author, August 8, 2021.

7. Glenn Consor, interview with the author, May 4, 2021.

8. John Teague, interview with the author, August 8, 2021.

9. Cited in "Gary Plummer Ready to Break Loose?" BU *Daily Free Press*, November 9, 1981, 11.

10. Karl Lehman, interview with the author, August 10, 2021.

11. Jay Twyman, interview with the author, May 12, 2021.

12. Gene Jones, interview with the author, September 6, 2021.

13. Cited in Angel Hernandez, "Arturo Brown," BU *Daily Free Press*, February 5, 1981, 8.

14. Gene Jones, interview with the author, September 6, 2021.

15. Hernandez, "Arturo Brown."

16. Gene Jones, interview with the author, September 6, 2021.

17. John Teague, interview with the author, August 8, 2021.

18. Glen Bressner, interview with the author, May 10, 2021.

19. Jay Twyman, interview with the author, May 12, 2021.

20. Desmond Martin, interview with the author, August 10, 2021.

21. Jay Twyman, interview with the author, May 12, 2021.

22. Desmond Martin, interview with the author, August 10, 2021.

23. John Teague, interview with the author, August 8, 2021.

24. "Niagara Drowns Out BU," *Boston Globe*, January 21, 1982, 53.

25. Pete Lonergan, interview with the author, March 2, 2021.

26. "Niagara Drowns Out BU."

27. Cited in Lesley Visser, "'I've Had It,' Pitino of BU Says," *Boston Globe*, January 21, 1982, 49.

28. Ernie Roberts, "Meyer Rooting for Gregg and Co.," *Boston Globe*, January 23, 1982, 33.

29. Cited in "Athletic Support," BU *Daily Free Press*, January 22, 1982, 4.

30. Cited in Lesley Visser, "Students at BU Just Don't Court Basketball," *Boston Globe*, January 26, 1982, 30.

31. "Hoopsters Skin Catamounts," BU *Daily Free Press*, January 25, 1982, 8.

32. Mark Hurlman, "Rivals to Do Battle," BU *Daily Free Press*, January 27, 1982, 7.

33. Ed McGrath, interview with the author, April 14, 2021.

34. Lesley Visser, "It's a Blowout—BU Drubs Northeastern, 82–64," *Boston Globe*, January 27, 1982, 25.

35. Jay Twyman, interview with the author, May 12, 2021.

36. John Teague, interview with the author, August 8, 2021.

37. Dan Shaughnessy, "BU Guns, Runs Away from FDU, 99–82," *Boston Globe*, February 4, 1982, 56.

38. Jay Twyman, interview with the author, May 12, 2021.

39. "Twyman's 'Prayer' at the Buzzer," BU *Daily Free Press*, February 8, 1982, 8.

40. Jay Twyman, interview with the author, May 12, 2021.

41. "Twyman's 'Prayer' at the Buzzer."

42. Cited in Dan Shaughnessy, "Twyman, BU Tip Cincy," *Boston Globe*, February 7, 1982, 72.

43. Lesley Visser, "BU Suffers Letdown," *Boston Globe*, February 10, 1982, 75.

44. Mike Moretti, "SHU Candidate List Keeps Growing," *Newsday*, February 16, 1982, 22.

45. Nick Macarchuk, interview with the author, March 2, 2021.

46. Dan Starr, interview with the author, February 15, 2021.

47. Michael Madden, "Canisius Takes Big One from BU," *Boston Globe*, February 18, 1982, 64.

48. "Canisius Upsets Terrier Title Hopes," BU *Daily Free Press*, February 18, 1982, 8.

49. Dan Shaughnessy, "Huskies Tip BU," *Boston Globe*, March 5, 1982, 35.

50. "Terriers' Hopes End in Heartache," BU *Daily Free Press*, March 5, 1982, 1.

51. Cited in "Terriers' Hopes End in Heartache."

52. Tom Ivey, interview with the author, September 18, 2021.

53. Jeff Holmes, interview with the author, August 5, 2021.

54. Jackie MacMullan, "Alexander Finds a Home," *Boston Globe*, March 8, 1983, 62.

55. Pete Lonergan, interview with the author, March 2, 2021.

56. Barbara Barr, "Basketball Star Dies of Heart Attack," BU *Daily Free Press*, September 20, 1982, 1, 8.

57. Gene Jones, interview with the author, September 6, 2021.

58. Tom Ivey, interview with the author, September 18, 2021.

59. Barr, "Basketball Star Dies of Heart Attack."

60. "Arturo Brown," *Boston Globe*, September 20, 1982, 17.

61. Karl Lehman, interview with the author, August 10, 2021.

62. John Teague, interview with the author, August 8, 2021.

63. Matthew Horowitz, "Memorial Fund to Honor Brown," BU *Daily Free Press*, September 21, 1982, 1.

64. Maria Kovach, "Fund to Aid Family of BU Star," BU *Daily Free Press*, September 24, 1982, 5.

65. "The No. American," *Boston Globe*, November 28, 1982, 103.

66. Tom Ivey, interview with the author, September 18, 2021.

67. Cited in "Giscombe, UConn Steal One from BU," *Boston Globe*, December 12, 1982, 100.

68. "Basketball Star Asks for Fan Support," BU *Daily Free Press*, January 22, 1983, 7.

69. Dan Fost, "A Faithful Supporter," BU *Daily Free Press*, March 15, 1983, 8.

70. "Basketball," BU *Daily Free Press*, January 25, 1983, 8.

71. "A Heat on Huntington," BU *Daily Free Press*, January 26, 1983, 12.

72. "Hoopsters Drop 2 of 3," BU *Daily Free Press*, February 10, 1983, 10.

73. Pete Lonergan, interview with the author, March 2, 2021.

74. "Hoopsters Drop 2 of 3."

75. Cited in Lesley Visser, "BU Going Independent," *Boston Globe*, February 9, 1983, 71.

76. Bob Haskell, "BU Quits NAC," *Bangor Daily News*, February 10, 1983, 18.

77. "Forward Leads Hoopsters Streak," BU *Daily Free Press*, February 25, 1983, 10.

78. Jon Diamond, "Huskies Leashed," BU *Daily Free Press*, March 4, 1983, 8.

79. Cited in "BU Slogs Past NU, 76–70," *Boston Globe*, March 4, 1983, 47.

80. "College Basketball," *Newsday*, March 6, 1983, 229.

81. Jackie MacMullan, "Terriers Throw HC," *Boston Globe*, March 6, 1983, 52.

82. Cited in MacMullan, "Terriers Throw HC."

83. Cited in MacMullan, "Terriers Throw HC."

84. "Vermont Loses in ECAC Tourney Play," *Bennington Banner*, March 9, 1983, 11.

85. "Costly Victory for BU," *Boston Globe*, March 9, 1983, 41.

86. Neil Singelais, "BU Earns Respect in Bid for NCAAs," *Boston Globe*, March 12, 1983, 30.

87. Jackie MacMullan, "BU Gets Past HC for Title," *Boston Globe*, March 13, 1983, 70.

88. Cited in MacMullan, "BU Gets Past HC for Title."

89. Karl Lehman, interview with the author, August 10, 2021.

90. Cited in "BC, BU Earn NCAA Berths," *North Adams Transcript*, March 14, 1983, 10.

91. "BC Gets Bye, BU Starts Early in NCAA Tourney," *Boston Globe*, March 14, 1983, 23.

92. Jackie MacMullan, "LaSalle Knocks Out BU," *Boston Globe*, March 16, 1983, 45.

93. Cited in "LaSalle Advances in NCAA Prelims," *Lancaster New Era*, March 16, 1983, 34.

94. "Coaches Lead Terriers to Post-Season Tourneys," BU *Daily Free Press*, March 24, 1983, 11.

12. I WAS HAPPY AT BC

1. Cited in "Williams Nixes Ark. Job," *Boston Globe*, April 9, 1985, 36.

2. "Williams Satisfied with Season," *The Heights*, April 1, 1985, 12.

3. Cited in Bob Ryan, "Williams Listening," *Boston Globe*, July 18, 1985, 31.

4. Cited in "BC's Williams Delays Wake Forest Decision," *Boston Globe*, July 24, 1985, 61.

5. Cited in Jackie MacMullan, "Williams Keeps Commitment at BC," *Boston Globe*, July 24, 1985, 49.

6. Steven Benton, interview with the author, July 9, 2021.

7. Bob Ryan, "Barros Picks Twice: BC and Basketball," *Boston Globe*, January 31, 1985, 44.

8. Paul Brazeau, interview with the author, February 23, 2021.

9. Bob Ryan, "BC's Bargain Recruit," *Boston Globe*, March 5, 1985, 53.

10. Cited in "No Respect for Eagles til NCAAs," *Boston Globe*, December 1, 1985, 69.

11. "Gordon Can't Start for BC," *Boston Globe*, November 26, 1985, 66.

12. Gary Williams, interview with the author, February 6, 2021.

13. Jackie MacMullan, "Barros Loses His Cool," *Boston Globe*, December 30, 1985, 35.
14. Jackie MacMullan, "BC Stuns St. John's in OT," *Boston Globe*, January 8, 1986, 73.
15. Michael Adams, interview with the author, May 1, 2021.
16. "This Time, Redmen Bow in OT," *New York Daily News*, January 8, 1986, 52.
17. Barry Cadigan, "Providence Burns BC," *Boston Globe*, January 17, 1986, 76.
18. Barry Cadigan, "BC Regroups for Ohio State," *Boston Globe*, January 18, 1986, 35.
19. Steven Benton, interview with the author, July 9, 2021.
20. Barry Cadigan, "Eagles Trounce Ohio St.," *Boston Globe*, January 19, 1986.
21. Bob Ryan, "Williams Fuming," *Boston Globe*, February 7, 1986, 51.
22. Jackie MacMullan, "Ohio State Low-Keys Reports on Williams," *Boston Globe*, March 13, 1986, 30.
23. "Williams Signs with Ohio State," *Boston Globe*, March 16, 1986, 51.
24. Cited in "Williams Signs with Ohio State."
25. Troy Bowers, interview with the author, August 16, 2021.
26. Russ Doherty, interview with the author, April 21, 2021.
27. Steven Benton, interview with the author, July 9, 2021.
28. Troy Bowers, interview with the author, August 16, 2021.

13. WHERE DID YOU GET THAT GUY?

1. "Calhoun Moves Deadline to Today," *Boston Globe*, April 1, 1986, 71.
2. Calhoun and Montville, *Dare to Dream*, 28.
3. Jackie MacMullan, "Perno Quits as UConn Coach," *Boston Globe*, April 15, 1986, 29.
4. "Slim Pickings on Letter Day," *Boston Globe*, April 9, 1986, 38.
5. Calhoun and Montville, *Dare to Dream*, 28.
6. Cited in Bob Ryan, "Calhoun's Huskies Are the Alpha Dogs," *Boston Globe*, April 7, 2004, 54.
7. Ryan, "Calhoun's Huskies Are the Alpha Dogs."
8. O'Neil, *The Big East*, 168.
9. John T. Casteen III, interview with the author, August 6, 2021.
10. John T. Casteen III, interview with the author, August 6, 2021.
11. John T. Casteen III, interview with the author, August 6, 2021.
12. "Big East Deal Satisfies Calhoun," *Hartford Courant*, June 10, 1986, C5.
13. Jackie MacMullan, "Calhoun to UConn," *Boston Globe*, May 15, 1986, 49.
14. Jim Calhoun, interview with the author, April 9, 2021.
15. Karl Fogel, interview with the author, June 17, 2021.

16. Andre LaFleur, interview with the author, August 4, 2021.
17. Keith Motley, interview with the author, October 8, 2021.
18. "First Came Robinson, Then Came Some Surprises," *Boston Globe*, June 23, 1987, 76.
19. Jim Calhoun, interview with the author, April 9, 2021.
20. "His Number's Up at Northeastern," *Boston Globe*, January 22, 1989, 50.
21. Danois, *The Boys of Dunbar*, 226–227.
22. Danois, *The Boys of Dunbar*, 226–227.
23. "Reggie Lewis, 1965–1993," *Boston Globe*, July 29, 1993, 66.
24. O'Neil, *The Big East*, 169–171.
25. Chip Rucker, interview with the author, June 17, 2021.
26. Cited in "Home Edge Is Rare around Here," *Boston Globe*, November 26, 1989, 64.
27. John T. Casteen III, interview with the author, August 6, 2021.
28. Cited in "Jim Calhoun's Hall of Fame Enshrinement Speech," *Basketball Hall of Fame*, February 17, 2012; https://www.youtube.com/watch?v=fDGoF2KcOxI. Accessed May 1, 2022.

14. PROPER PERSPECTIVE

1. Mike Bruckner, interview with the author, March 2, 2021.
2. "Penn State Screening Applicants," *Pittsburgh Post-Gazette*, April 1, 1983, 33.
3. Jeff Holmes, interview with the author, August 5, 2021.
4. Peter Gabriele, interview with the author, August 13, 2021.
5. Peter Gabriele, interview with the author, August 13, 2021.
6. Jeff Holmes, interview with the author, August 5, 2021.
7. Jackie MacMullan, "Pitino Named Knicks Assistant," *Boston Globe*, July 7, 1983, 39.
8. Cited in MacMullan, "Pitino Named Knicks Assistant."
9. Tom Ivey, interview with the author, September 18, 2021.
10. MacMullan, "Pitino Named Knicks Assistant."
11. Karl Lehman, interview with the author, August 10, 2021.
12. Jeff Holmes, interview with the author, August 5, 2021.
13. Tom Ivey, interview with the author, September 18, 2021.
14. "BU Settles with Pitino," *Boston Globe*, July 20, 1983, 53.
15. Cited in "BU Won't Be Changing Its Style, Says Kuester," *Boston Globe*, July 21, 1983, 62.
16. Tom Ivey, interview with the author, September 18, 2021.
17. Jeff Holmes, interview with the author, August 5, 2021.
18. Mike Rosen, interview with the author, August 24, 2021.

19. Peter Gabriele, interview with the author, August 13, 2021.
20. Mike Rosen, interview with the author, August 24, 2021.
21. Mike Rosen, interview with the author, August 24, 2021.
22. Jackie MacMullan, "Irving Accomplished," *Boston Globe*, January 26, 1988, 76.
23. Cited in MacMullan, "Irving Accomplished."
24. "Kuester's New Job in 'Hotbed,'" *Durham Sun*, May 4, 1985, 10A.
25. Peter Gabriele, interview with the author, August 13, 2021.
26. Lesley Visser, "Relishing the Change," *Boston Globe*, November 1, 1983, 37.
27. Pitino with Kaufman, *Pitino*, 27.
28. Pitino with Kaufman, *Pitino*, 28–29.
29. Pitino with Kaufman, *Pitino*, 29–33.
30. "Friars Name Pitino," *Boston Globe*, March 23, 1985, 33.
31. Jackie MacMullan, "G. Washington Picks Kuester," *Boston Globe*, May 3, 1985, 72.
32. Bob Duffy, "BU Names Jarvis Coach," *Boston Globe*, May 25, 1985, 29.
33. Cited in Duffy, "BU Names Jarvis Coach."
34. Mike Jarvis, interview with the author, May 21, 2021.
35. Peter Gabriele, interview with the author, August 13, 2021.
36. Ed McGrath, interview with the author, April 14, 2021.
37. Mike Jarvis, interview with the author, May 21, 2021.
38. Peter Gabriele, interview with the author, August 13, 2021.
39. Art Tooles, interview with the author, June 3, 2021.
40. Mike Jarvis, interview with the author, May 21, 2021.
41. Mike Jarvis, interview with the author, May 21, 2021.
42. Peter Gabriele, interview with the author, August 13, 2021.
43. Mike Jarvis, interview with the author, May 21, 2021.
44. "Jarvis Makes No Promises," *Washington Post*, May 11, 1990, 37.
45. O'Neil, *The Big East*, 136–140.
46. "Rick Pitino's Basketball Hall of Fame Induction Speech," *Official Hoop Hall*, September 9, 2013; https://www.youtube.com/watch?v=QTMUKbuSePE. Accessed January 8, 2022.
47. Dan Shaughnessy, "Pitino Restores BU's Appetite," *Boston Globe*, November 12, 1997, 41.

15. HOMECOMING

1. "Gary Williams' Basketball Hall of Fame Induction Speech," *Official Hoop Hall*, August 10, 2014; http:// https://www.youtube.com/watch?v=MI-Yzpngk48. Accessed April 10, 2021.
2. Jim O'Brien, interview with the author, February 17, 2021.

3. Cited in Jackie MacMullan, "bc's Search Is On," *Boston Globe*, March 18, 1986, 67.

4. "The Mouse That Scored," *Newsday*, March 18, 1986, 104.

5. Cited in Jackie MacMullan, "bc Will Name O'Brien Today," *Boston Globe*, March 26, 1986, 73.

6. "Who Is the Actual Opponent of the Eagle Basketball Program?" *The Heights*, April 7, 1986, 16.

7. Ted Kelley, interview with the author, April 20, 2021.

8. Troy Bowers, interview with the author, August 16, 2021.

9. Jim O'Brien, interview with the author, February 17, 2021.

10. "Up Close with Jim O'Brien," *The Heights*, April 22, 1986, 20.

11. Steven Benton, interview with the author, July 9, 2021.

12. Ted Kelley, interview with the author, April 20, 2021.

13. Jack Craig, "weei Lands a Double Bill at bc," *Boston Globe*, January 31, 1986, 42.

14. Ted Kelley, interview with the author, April 20, 2021.

15. Williams and Vise, *Sweet Redemption*, 36–37.

16. "Ohio State Snaps Iowa's String at 18," *Des Moines Register*, January 25, 1987, D1.

17. Hank Hersch, "By the Skin of His Neck."

18. Jim O'Brien, interview with the author, February 17, 2021.

19. Al Skinner, interview with the author, May 12, 2021.

20. Jim O'Brien, interview with the author, February 17, 2021.

21. "Lefty Takes Fall Alone," *Los Angeles Times*, October 31, 1986, 21.

22. Williams and Vise, *Sweet Redemption*, 3.

23. Williams and Vise, *Sweet Redemption*, 2.

24. Williams and. Vise, *Sweet Redemption*, 2.

25. Tom Brennan, interview with the author, March 20, 2021.

26. Don Markus, "Terps Muscle Puts 'Flex' Back in Style," *Baltimore Sun*, March 20, 2003, E1.

27. "Maryland's Basketball Coach Williams Retires after 33 Years," *Charlotte Observer*, May 6, 2011, C4.

Bibliography

INTERVIEWS

Adams, Burnett. Phone interview with the author. July 16, 2021.

Adams, Michael. Phone interview with the author. May 1, 2021.

Benton, Steven. Phone interview with the author. July 9, 2021.

Boutin, John. Phone interview with the author. June 2, 2021.

Bowman, Jim. Phone interviews with the author. May 14 and June 3, 2021.

Bowers, Troy. Phone interview with the author. August 16, 2021.

Brazeau, Paul. Phone interview with the author. February 23, 2021.

Breen, Paul. Email interview with the author. April 20, 2021.

Brennan, Tom. Phone interview with the author. March 20, 2021.

Bressner, Glen. Phone interview with the author. May 10, 2021.

Bruckner, Mike. Phone interview with the author. March 2, 2021.

Caesar, Herb. Email interview with the author. June 2, 2021.

Calhoun, Jim. Phone interview with the author. April 9, 2021.

Caligaris, Dave. Phone interview with the author. July 28, 2021.

Casteen, John T., III. Phone interview with the author. August 6, 2021.

Clark, John. Phone interview with the author. June 4, 2021.

Cohen, Scott. Phone interview with the author. June 4, 2021.

Connors, Jim. Phone interviews with the author. June 11, 2021.

Consor, Glenn. Phone interview with the author. May 4, 2021.

Costner, Tony. Email interview with the author. June 1, 2021.

Dale, Quinton. Email interview with the author. June 20, 2021.

DeCaro, Angelo. Email interview with the author. June 17, 2021.

Delgardo, Joe. Phone interview with the author. June 11, 2021.

Demos, Michael. Email interview with the author. February 22, 2022.

Doherty, Russ. Phone interview with the author. April 21, 2021.

Esmonde, Donn. Phone interview with the author. March 2, 2021.

Everson, Chuck. Phone interview with the author. June 18, 2021.

Field. Glen. Email interview with the author. May 29, 2021.

Fiola, Ken. Email interview with the author. May 11, 2021.

Fitzgerald, Ray. Email interview with the author. June 26, 2021.

Fogel, Karl. Email interview with the author. June 17, 2021.

Gabriele, Peter. Phone interview with the author. August 13, 2021.

Gianatassio, Matt. Phone interview with the author. April 28, 2021.

Hall, Ray. Phone interview with the author. June 15, 2021.

Hawkins, Andre. Phone interview with the author. June 21, 2021.

Heineck, Charlie. Email interview with the author. July 1, 2021.

Henry, Rich. Email interview with the author. May 31, 2021.

Holmes, Jeff. Phone interview with the author. August 5, 2021.

Ivey, Tom. Phone interview with the author. September 18, 2021.

Jarvis, Mike. Phone interview with the author. May 21, 2021.

Jennings, Bubba. Email interview with the author. May 26, 2021.

Jones, Gene. Phone interview with the author. September 6, 2021.

Kelley, Ted. Phone interview with the author. April 20, 2021.

Koller, Tom. Email interview with the author. March 5, 2021.

LaFleur, Andre. Phone interview with the author. August 4, 2021.

Lehman, Karl. Phone interview with the author. August 10, 2021.

Leibowitz, Ed. Phone interview with the author. September 21, 2021.

Lobel, Bob. Email interview with the author. June 16, 2021.

Lonergan, Pete. Phone interview with the author. March 2, 2021.

Lotane, Phil. Phone interview with the author. March 5, 2021.

Loughnane, Bill. Phone interview with the author. August 6, 2021.

Lynch, Mike. Phone interview with the author. February 20, 2021.

Macarchuk, Nick. Phone interview with the author. March 2, 2021.

Mackey, Kevin. Phone interview with the author. June 21, 2021.

Maddock, John. Phone interview with the author. March 2, 2021.

Martin, Desmond. Phone interview with the author. August 10, 2021.

Masters, Tom. Phone interview with the author. June 14, 2021.

McDonough, Paul. Phone interview with the author. June 4, 2021.

McGrath, Ed. Phone interview with the author. March 2 and April 14, 2021.

Minishak, Ed. Phone interview with the author. June 28, 2021.

Motley, Keith. Phone interview with the author. October 8, 2021.

Murphy, Jay. Phone interview with the author. April 26, 2021.

O'Brien, Jim. Phone interview with the author. February 17, 2021.

Pinone, John. Email interview with the author. April 27, 2021.

Porter, Paul. Phone interview with the author. June 1, 2021.

Primus, Stu. Phone interview with the author. July 23, 2021.

Priscella, Steve. Email interview with the author. May 13, 2021.

Rolfes, Mike. Phone interview with the author. April 26, 2021.

Rosen, Mike. Phone interview with the author. August 24, 2021.

Rucker, Chip. Phone interview with the author. June 17, 2021.

Santifer, Erich. Email interview with the author. April 26, 2021.

Skinner, Al. Phone interview with the author. May 12, 2021.

Solberg, Paul. Phone interview with the author. June 3, 2021.

Spera, Sonny. Phone interview with the author. May 11, 2021.

Stanton, Bill. Phone interview with the author. June 7, 2021.

Starr, Dan. Phone interview with the author. February 15, 2021.

Stewart, Ron. Email interview with the author. June 16, 2021.

Teague, John. Phone interview with the author. August 8, 2021.

Tooles, Art. Email interview with the author. June 3, 2021.

Twyman, Jay. Phone interview with the author. May 12, 2021.

Waldron, Gene. Phone interview with the author. April 26, 2021.

West, Wally. Phone interview with the author. August 10, 2021.

Williams, Gary. Phone interview with the author. February 6, 2021.

SECONDARY SOURCES

Axthelm, Pete. *The City Game.* New York: Buccaneer Books, 1970.

Calhoun, Jim, and Leigh Montville. *Dare to Dream: Connecticut Basketball's Remarkable March to the National Championship.* New York: Broadway Books, 2000.

Danois, Alejandro. *The Boys of Dunbar: A Story of Love, Hope, and Basketball.* New York: Simon & Schuster, 2016.

Goodman, Matthew. *The City Game: Triumph, Scandal, and a Legendary Basketball Team. New York*: Ballantine Books, 2019.

Hersch, Hank. "By the Skin of His Neck." *Sports Illustrated*, March 6, 1989, 46–49.

Nack, William. "Full Court Pressure." *Sports Illustrated*, February 26, 1996, 80–84.

O'Neil, Dana. *The Big East: Inside the Most Entertaining and Influential Conference in College Basketball History.* New York: Ballantine Books, 2021.

Pitino, Rick, with Seth Kaufman. *Pitino: My Story.* New York: Diversion Books, 2018.

Williams, Gary, and David Vise. *Sweet Redemption: How Gary Williams and Maryland Beat Death and Despair to Win the NCAA Basketball Championship.* New York: Sport Publishing, 2002.

Index

325